Spectacle and the City

Cities and Cultures

Cities and Cultures is an interdisciplinary humanities book series addressing the interrelations between contemporary cities and the cultures they produce. The series takes a special interest in the impact of globalization on urban space and cultural production, but remains concerned with all forms of cultural expression and transformation associated with contemporary cities.

Series editor: Christoph Lindner, University of Amsterdam

Advisory Board:

Ackbar Abbas, University of California, Irvine
Nezar AlSayyad, University of California, Berkeley
Derek Gregory, University of British Columbia
Stephanie Hemelryk Donald, University of New South Wales
Shirley Jordan, Queen Mary, University of London
Geoffrey Kantaris, University of Cambridge
Bill Marshall, University of London
Ginette Verstraete, VU University Amsterdam
Richard J. Williams, University of Edinburgh

Spectacle and the City

Chinese Urbanities in Art and Popular Culture

Edited by Jeroen de Kloet and Lena Scheen

AMSTERDAM UNIVERSITY PRESS

This book is published in print and online through the online OAPEN library (www.oapen.org)

OAPEN (Open Access Publishing in European Networks) is a collaborative initiative to develop and implement a sustainable Open Access publication model for academic books in the Humanities and Social Sciences. The OAPEN Library aims to improve the visibility and usability of high quality academic research by aggregating peer reviewed Open Access publications from across Europe.

Cover illustration: Jeroen de Kloet

Cover design: Kok Korpershoek, Amsterdam
Lay-out: Heymans & Vanhove, Goes

Amsterdam University press English-language titles are distributed in the US and Canada by the University of Chicago Press.

ISBN   978 90 8964 445 9
e-ISBN   978 90 4851 702 2 (pdf)
e-ISBN   978 90 4851 703 9 (ePub)
NUR   646

© J. de Kloet, L. Scheen / Amsterdam University Press, Amsterdam 2013

All rights reserved. Without limiting the rights under copyright reserved above, no part of this book may be reproduced, stored in or introduced into a retrieval system, or transmitted, in any form or by any means (electronic, mechanical, photocopying, recording or otherwise) without the written permission of both the copyright owner and the author of the book.

Every effort has been made to obtain permission to use all copyrighted illustrations reproduced in this book. Nonetheless, whosoever believes to have rights to this material is advised to contact the publisher.

We are living in the time of urban spectacle. Contemporary art projects, booming across the globe, are an integrate part of the rapid expansion of this spectacle. In the last decade, Asian Cities are "catching up" with this wave with even more intense and tsunami-like enthusiasm, along with the unprecedented urban growth, marked by the latest Beijing Olympics spectacles and urban explosion.

Hou Hanru

Table of Contents

	Acknowledgements	9
	Introduction: Imagining Chinese Cities *Jeroen de Kloet and Lena Scheen*	11
1.	Speed and Spectacle in Chinese Cities *Ackbar Abbas*	21
2.	Planned Demi-monde and its Aestheticisation in Singapore *Chua Beng Huat*	27
3.	Coming of Age in RMB City *Robin Visser*	43
4.	The Architecture of Utopia: From Rem Koolhaas' Scale Models to RMB City *Yomi Braester*	61
5.	Imagining a Disappearing and Reappearing Chinese City *Jeroen de Kloet*	77
6.	Tuning Urban China *Jeroen Groenewegen-Lau*	97
7.	The City's (Dis)appearance in Propaganda *Stefan Landsberger*	121
8.	Claiming the Past, Presenting the Present, Selling the Future: Imagining a New Beijing, Great Olympics *Gladys Pak Lei Chong*	135
9.	Shanghai in Film and Literature: The Danger of Nostalgia *Gregory Bracken*	157
10.	Nostalgia, Place, and Making Peace with Modernity in East Asia *Margaret Hillenbrand*	171
11.	Femme Fatales and Male Narcissists: Shanghai Spectacle Narrated, Packaged and Sold *Lena Scheen*	191
12.	City Regeneration and Its Opposition *Ou Ning*	211
13.	Law, Embodiment, and the Case of 'Harbourcide' *John Nguyet Erni*	227
	Contributors	243
	Index	247

Acknowledgements

This book is the outcome of a workshop hosted by the Amsterdam School for Cultural Analysis (ASCA) and the International Institute for Asian Studies (IIAS). We are indebted to Martina van den Haak who made us believe the workshop was organized by itself. Manon Osseweijer and Max Sparreboom invented an ingenious way to support this project. We are grateful for The Netherlands Organisation for Scientific Research (NWO), as this workshop is part of a project that is supported by them. During the workshop, numerous people gave invaluable input, for this we like to thank Maghiel van Crevel, Dina Heshmat, Mark Hobart, Christoph Lindner, Luo Jialing, Pal Nyiri, Leonie Schmidt, and Peter van der Veer.

Special thanks are due to Christoph Lindner for his continuous support and encouragement over the past years, and for having our book in his series. We thank the peer reviewers for their insightful comments and constructive suggestions. The support of Amsterdam University Press (AUP), in particular Chantal Nicolaes and Jeroen Sondervan, has been indispensable for completing this project. We thank Penn Ip and Chris Scheen for their great help in making the index. Miyan Cheung helped us from afar with the editing of all chapters. Different people have supported us over the past years, we like to thank in particular Cyrus Amani, Yiu Fai Chow, Michel Hockx, Giselinde Kuipers, Helen Hok-sze Leung, Song Hwee Lim, and Benjamin van Rooij. Finally, we would like to thank the contributors for all their work and patience. Without both, this book would not have been here.

Introduction
Imagining Chinese Cities

Jeroen de Kloet and Lena Scheen

The arts only ever lend to projects of domination or emancipation what they are able to lend to them, that is to say, quite simply, what they have in common with them: bodily positions and movements, functions of speech, the parcelling out of the visible and the invisible.
– Jacques Rancière (2004: 19)

When a newly independent art paints its world in brilliant colours, then a moment of life has grown old. By art's brilliant colours it cannot be rejuvenated but only recalled to mind. The greatness of art makes its appearance only as dusk begins to fall over life.
– Guy Debord (1995 [1967]: 133)

An old man dressed in a Mao suit walks slowly into The Village, a new shopping area in the diplomatic and rich part of Beijing. He enters an Apple Store and anxiously looks around with bewildered eyes: the man remembers the old neighbourhood that has now vanished completely to be replaced by these icons of global capitalism. Utterly puzzled, he continues wandering, feeling forever lost in the city that used to be so familiar to him.

In his fictional documentary *Beijing is Coming* (2008), the Hong Kong filmmaker Bono Lee tells the story of an old man who returns to Beijing after 30 years. Like so many Asian cities, Beijing has grown dramatically over the past two decades. The unprecedented scale, scope and speed of these changes makes a returning visitor easily lose his or her way – as parks have been replaced by buildings, neighbourhoods have morphed into parks. In Lee's documentary, the Asian city serves as a trope for probing into the alienation that comes with China's speedy march into modernity. But the story steers away from being a one-dimensional critique on the transformation of the city. Instead, it also speaks of the emergence of *new* intimacies that are rendered possible by the changing city. In the story, a love relationship unfolds between record shop owner Jun and a girl named Ling, who are both part of a new generation born after 1980. The girl had planned to study abroad, but she stayed to experience the summer of 2008, to be with Jun; or, as she wonders, maybe she stayed because of the city of Beijing itself. But in the course of the summer, the girl wonders if she really is in Beijing, and says: 'At the end you can't even tell this is Beijing […] You never know, maybe the fine weather was artificial too. As everything could be artificial nowadays'.

Which and whose Chinese city, then, are we experiencing in this movie? What is real and what is fake, especially in a place where even the weather is claimed to be manufactured by the authorities? Indeed, at the end of the movie the voiceover articulates the impossibility of representing the city; it claims, while the camera freezes on an old wall of the Forbidden City filled with graffiti, that…

> In Beijing, it's quite impossible to search for the past anymore. Everyone's memory about Beijing is so different. I remember one day when I was shooting in Tiananmen Square, what came to my mind was, when Antonioni was shooting here in 1972, there is only one single camera in the square possible. But everyone seems to be shooting by his own phone nowadays. But nobody can claim that his Beijing represents the real Beijing. But then what is the real Beijing? Beijing is only the product of a particular moment.

By the end of the quote, the camera has moved to Tiananmen Square, zooming in on young Chinese tourists who are having their picture taken with the large portrait of Mao Zedong featuring prominently in the background. With the advancement of technology, the possible ways to represent the city have multiplied, the voiceover rightly claims. This claim is articulated within a fictional documentary, which itself attempts to represent today's Beijing. The generic choice itself, deliberately hovering between fact and fiction, between the real and the imagined, attests to the sheer impossibility of 'truly' capturing the changes of Beijing. This self-reflexive gesture comes from a Hong Kong filmmaker, for whom Beijing quite likely represents a mixed space of, on the one hand, possibilities for creativity in its thriving creative scene, and, on the other hand, impossibilities, as it hosts the new authoritarian government that has ruled his own city since 1997. Following the thrust of this fictional documentary, the imagination of the city is bound to be multivocal, complex, contradictory, and, above all, infinite. But is it really infinite? We believe it is not.

By now, over 60 per cent of the estimated 3.5 billion Asian population is living in cities (ADB 2008). It would be naïve to claim, however, that one can thus speak of 2.1 billion different experiences of the city. The experience of a city is intimately intertwined with existing and newly emerging imaginations of the city. One can trace recurring imaginations of the Chinese city in art and popular culture. At times, the Chinese city operates as a space of alienation in which unexpected, intimate relationships may emerge; Taipei for example, in the movies of Tsai Ming-Liang. At times, the city serves as a dystopian space, saturated with memories of a time past, like Shanghai in Lou Ye's *Suzhou River*. But we may also encounter the more lush, cosmopolitan and open imageries of Shanghai in the 1940s in Ang Lee's *Lust, Caution*. Or the city signifies a space of hope on which a bright future is mapped, as we can see in the propaganda material of the Chinese Communist Party. Yet, for visual artist Cao Fei, the future city, which she terms *RMB City*, is one that is already in decay, one driven by relentless speculation. These imaginations are indeed multivocal, complex and contradictory, but, contrary to Bono Lee, they do not seem to be infinite.

As Appadurai rightly claims, 'imagination has become an organised field of social practices, a form of work (in the sense of both labour and culturally organised practice), and a form of negotiation between sites of agency (individuals) and globally defined fields of possibility' (1996: 31). Given the social power of imagination, there is an urgent need, in our opinion, to seriously engage with the rapid circulation of imaginations of the Chinese city, which is what this book does. Aiming to steer away from an exclusive focus on Mainland China, our adjective 'Chinese' has a cultural meaning and includes places like Singapore, Taipei and Hong Kong. Imaginations of the city are not just mere reflections of a material reality, mirroring the assumed actual cityscape; rather, they are forces that *both* display and construct. Images provide an important symbolic toolbox, they are non-human actors with their own agency, following Bruno Latour's Actor-Network Theory. In the words of Yomi Braester (2010: 13): 'It is not the city that gives rise to movies; the cinema is not even merely the continuation of the city by other means, as David Clarke proposes. It is rather films – in direct interaction with political decisions and architectural blueprints – that forge an urban contract and create the material city and its ideological constructs'. Aside from cinema, other cultural forms, such as contemporary art, popular music, fiction and television, also hold such power and agency. The imaginations of the Chinese city in art and popular culture that this book explores are thus not taken as merely mirroring or reflecting 'reality'; on the contrary, they are part and parcel of the construction, destruction and deconstruction of that 'reality'. As such, these imaginations are enmeshed in the social, material and political realities that produce Chinese cityscapes.

Having explained our take on the subtitle of this book, a second question that comes up is related to its main title: why 'spectacle'? What is spectacular about the Chinese city? If we, for a moment, ignore Guy Debord's *The Society of the Spectacle*, it is not so difficult to think of Chinese cities as spectacular sites. The hyper-urbanity of Hong Kong, the futuristic skyline of Shanghai's Pudong, the sensational designs of Singapore's skyscrapers, the Japanese-style streets in Taipei, the sheer size of Beijing, the speed of changes, the subway lines that multiply year by year, the massive crowds, the 24-hour mega-bookstores: all these are spectacular sites, far removed from the picturesque, quaint and quiet cities of Europe that the authors both grew up in.

For global star architects, China seems to operate as the ideal playground for architectural excesses, be it Herzog and Meuron's national Olympic Stadium, also known as the Bird's Nest, or Rem Koolhaas' CCTV building in Beijing. Koolhaas' own theorisation of the 'generic city' – the place outside of culture in which identity dissolves, a space he baptises as full of new possibilities – takes the Pearl River Delta as its inspiration, as this is the site where new cities can emerge within the time span of only a decade (think of Shenzhen); an example that testifies to the dialectical relationship between imagination and construction.

It is tempting to join the chorus and celebrate the Chinese city, in reading these cities as signifiers of a new future that has shaken off the burdens of the past (Maoist, colonial, or feudal) and that present a line of flight out of the archaic, static and slow cityscapes that characterise Europe. This book resists this temptation. Instead, it searches for more critical, more careful and less celebratory understandings of the Chinese city. While the idea of including *spectacle* in its main title was merely inspired by a more intuitive, and maybe even romanticised, understanding of the Chinese city, as it turns out, this book is more indebted to Guy Debord than we had initially envisioned.

Guy Debord writes of the society of spectacle, driven by the forces of global capitalism. The latter has proved to be a much more malleable and flexible force than he may ever have imagined back in the 1960s, given that in China today, an official commitment to communism can so smoothly be merged with an even stronger commitment to capitalism. The spectacle of the city offers and manipulates modes of longing and belonging and feeds into a machine of perpetual desire. Contemporary Chinese cities evoke a sense of nationhood and cultural belonging, in conjunction with a sense of cosmopolitanism and world citizenship. This is all the more intense when the Chinese city is turned into a spectacular site, such as during mega-events like the Olympic Games of Beijing in 2008 and the Shanghai World Expo of 2010. It comes as no surprise that both of these mega-events were above all visual spectacles. Indeed, the idea of the spectacle itself is intimately linked with the visual; as Debord writes, 'The spectacle is not a collection of images, rather, it is a social relation between people that is mediated by images' (1995 [1967]: 12). What role do visual cultural forms then play in the society of the spectacle? As the opening quote of this introduction already indicates, Debord is highly critical of the separation between art and everyday life; he writes that:

> as soon as art – which constituted that former common language of social interaction – establishes itself as independent in the modern sense, emerging from its first, religious universe to become the individual production of separate works, it becomes subject, as one instance among others, to the movement governing the history of the whole of culture as a separated realm. Art's declaration of independence is thus the beginning of the end of art. (1995 [1967]: 132-133)

This helps to explain the Situationists' desire to transform everyday life through its realignment with art in its broadest sense. Taking this as a starting point, we wonder, how is the city-as-spectacle visualised and thus imagined and reimagined, if not contested, in art and popular culture? What are the possible escape routes from a completely commodified cityscape? How to realign artistic expressions of the spectacle with everyday practices?

Before probing these questions, however, we would like to emphasise that when we claim that cities are scopic machines saturated with the latest fashion designs, neon lights, billboards, shop windows, architectures – all fuelling desires that are rooted in the visual – we are not ignoring the importance of other senses in the experience of the city. In fact, by including an essay on sound and one on smell, we made a modest attempt to counter the occularcentrism that may be conjured by the term 'spectacle' (Jay 1994). The cityscape is a tactile space that immediately and constantly arrests our senses. Take, for example, the experience of arriving at an airport and taking a taxi to the hotel in the city centre: we are immediately entangled in a complex web of connections, between ourselves and the taxi driver, ourselves and the car (its smell, sound, image, and feeling), ourselves and the billboard that quickly passes by, ourselves and the music playing on the car radio, ourselves and the memories or expectations we have of this place; and these connections endlessly multiply and mutate, involving *all* our senses. In short, the city penetrates us even before we realise it consciously; it engages us in a complex web of connections.

In this sense, we may view the city as a 'haptic machine', in Deleuze's and Guattari's notion of the machine as 'a system of interruptions or breaks' where connections and (subsequently) subjectivities are produced. Deleuze and Guattari want to steer away from the notion of identity as bounded wholes, to resist a mechanical, deterministic way of thinking and instead zoom in on the importance of connections; connections that are by definition unstable, never fixed.

Cultural Studies and Area Studies

The chapters in this book navigate between different disciplines, in particular urban studies, area studies and cultural studies. The latter provides the general thrust of the work presented in this book, and is driven by the basic question posed by Lawrence Grossberg when writing about cultural studies. Grossberg claims that the major task of cultural studies is to simply ask ourselves, 'what is going on?'. He writes:

> The project of cultural studies is to tell better stories about what's going on, and to begin to enable imagining new possibilities for a future that can be reached from the present – one more humane and just than that promised by the trajectories we find ourselves on. Cultural studies then is a form of conjunctural analysis, which re-describes a context, often viewed with some sense of pessimism and even despair, into one of possibilities, by rejecting all forms of simplification and reduction, and embracing the complexity, contradiction and contingency of the world. (2010: 241)

In order to tell better stories about what is going on, it is of utmost importance to carefully contextualise any analysis, both in terms of time and in terms of space. But these contexts are always dynamic, and ridden with power relations. To quote Grossberg again, 'contexts are active and even in part self-producing formations, [...] the relations that comprise them are each overdetermined and transitive. Moreover, contexts are always structures in and of difference, or, in more humane terms, structures of power' (2002: 368). The context of Singapore is not quite the same as the context of, say, New York. This is a trivial statement, indeed, but it is one that is too often ignored.

The issue of locality has rapidly gained importance over the past decades due to the intensified processes of urbanisation. As Lindner argues,

> The recent 'global turn' in cultural theory and critical urban studies has highlighted the growing impact on the life and development of cities, from new trends in architecture and design, to new patterns of migrancy and Diaspora, to new techno-informational networks of communication and power. At a time when more than half the world's population lives in cities (for the first time in human history), the relationship between global processes and local conditions is one that positively demands increased scrutiny. (2010: 1)

In particular, economic, social and political lines of inquiry dominate research; but, as the other works in this volume attest, this balance is gradually changing. It has by now become a cliché to claim that globalisation results in localisation.

The global is embedded in the local; they are intimately intertwined and mutually reinforce each other. Taking this position helps to analyse, for example, how the national desire to produce architectural icons that represent the glorious and harmonious future of the nation is directly linked to a global network of star architects, as was the case when China assigned the Swiss duo Herzog and Meuron to design the Bird's Nest. It also helps us to analyse how such projects produce new classed spaces, or what Hemelryk Donald terms the 'dirty non-places of declassed workers in China's harmonious society' (2010: 134). Underneath the spectacular images of today's global cities, new ideological fault-lines produce new and increased inequalities that are both local and global. And, as some chapters will show, both art and popular culture help to probe these new inequalities that authorities are so keen to push backstage. Over the past two decades, the nation-state has returned with a vengeance, and it has done so by actively engaging in the reproduction of the cityscape.

What is often lacking in disciplines located outside area studies is a sensibility to the importance of place, resulting in an implicit claim to universalism. In other words, given the dominance of Western cities in urban studies, as well as the Anglo- or Eurocentrism that haunts cultural studies, this book aims to align both disciplines with area studies. It does so not through claiming the unique particularity or essential difference of China or 'Chineseness', but rather, through exploring the constructed-ness of place; or, to use Appadurai's words, by exploring the production of place. It is our contention that area studies (if discussing urban areas) needs the theorisations of both urban studies and cultural studies, just as the latter two need area studies' sensibility to spatial and cultural context; hence our attempt to traverse these three disciplines simultaneously in this book. In doing so, we aim to resist the denial of coevalness, as Johannes Fabian puts it (1983), that often creeps back in analysis of places outside 'the West'. Shanghai is *not* on a teleological march towards a form of modernity like that, say, seen in New York, nor is Shenzhen the ultimate laboratory for the future city. Instead, we choose to read these cities as manifestations of alternative, or partly overlapping, modernities, whose materiality changes with the shifting socio-economic and political context: whether driven by local forces, such as the People's Republic of China's (PRC's) ruling authoritarian regime, or by global forces, such as neoliberalism and economic globalisation.

Spectacle and the City

In the opening essay of this volume, **Ackbar Abbas** connects the notion of the spectacle to the issue of speed. In particular, he uses the later work of Debord, in which the earlier difference that was made between 'diffuse' and 'concentrated' forms of spectacle merges into the 'integrated spectacle'. For Abbas, this presents us with a paradox: 'It is a spectacle that is no longer spectacular, a spectacle that has reversed itself in that it is more covert than overt, a spectacle that is secret'. The work of Zhang Yimou and Jia Zhangke is used to explore the non-spectacular spectacle and its mutations in today's China. In chapter 2, **Chua Beng Huat** scrutinises how Geylang, the red light district of Singapore, is 'spectacularised' in artworks by artists who celebrate the district as the truly Bohemian part of the city. He takes the artists to task for using the district as a trope to critique the project of Singapore, by not only aestheticising and 'humanising' the sex workers – 'as if their humanity were ever in doubt' – but also by blatantly ignoring the abusive labour conditions that perpetuate Geylang. In the subsequent chapter, **Robin Visser** starts by mapping out Debord's theorisations on the spectacle, connecting this to two artistic works that have recently received global attention: the novel *Brothers* by Yu Hua and the virtual artwork, *RMB City*, by Cao Fei. She argues that the novel, in particular, uses tactics of *détournement*, a term referring to the fluid language of anti-ideology, as 'the narrative implies that the spectacle, regardless of its aesthetic form, necessarily conceals the violent power relations upon which it is constituted'.

Whereas Visser suggests that *RMB City* is subsumed by the urbanist spectacle rather than critiquing it, **Yomi Braester** argues that 'the focus on architectural imaging suggests a more self-reflexive intentionality on Cao's part'. Braester juxtaposes contemporary Chinese art and cinema with the recurrent use of architectural scale models. Whereas the latter present a utopian city, in which the nation-state, with the close cooperation of internationally renowned architects, celebrates urban growth through new architecture, both art and cinema help to leverage that uncritical neoliberal celebration by exploring dystopian or antitopian strategies that 'challenge the mimetic relationship between the model and the material city'. In chapter 5, **Jeroen de Kloet** analyses how the government's policies to promote the creative industries have turned the art zone 798 in Beijing into a spectacular site, where artists exhibit their work in what is assumed to be an atmosphere of criticality and freedom. In search of alternative versions of criticality that are less complicit with the authorities, the chapter engages with contemporary Chinese artwork, including, again, Cao Fei's *RMB City*. It is argued that not only the works as such, but in particular their rhizomic distribution through the Internet, allows for new and alternative meanings to proliferate that have the potential to disrupt the spectacle.

In chapter 6, **Jeroen Groenewegen-Lau** engages with sound artists from China and explores how they record the sound of the Chinese city, and why and how these sounds matter so much for the way in which we experience these cities. His chapter not only presents an overview of musical cultures in China, but also explores their experimental edges. He shows how important these are to recording and recuperating the sound of the city, as a tactic against the occularcentrism of our times. In his search for the role of the city in chapter 7, **Stefan Landsberger** presents a historical overview of propaganda posters in China. The absence of the city is often more striking than its presence. On a few occasions, namely during the Beijing Olympics and the Shanghai Expo, the city did feature prominently, indicating China's entrance on the global stage. As it turns out, the countryside, rather than the city, signifies revolutionary success, which is why the Chinese state relies more on rural images to communicate its messages to its citizenry. In the subsequent chapter, **Gladys Pak Lei Chong** opts for a genealogical approach to Beijing as an Olympic City. In her chapter, she analyses how the past is reinvented in the Qianmen shopping street in Beijing, how the present is produced through the construction of the Olympic Green, and how images of a new and hyper-modern Beijing are used to construct a prosperous future. Her chapter attests to the role of the nation-state in managing time and memory. This leads to her question how alternative memories can be rendered possible in the midst of all the symbolic promotion (if not violence) produced by the authorities.

In chapter 9, **Gregory Bracken** moves further south, to Shanghai, to explore how the built environment of this city is being represented in literature and cinema. Shanghai's past is increasingly being mobilised to mark the road towards the future. In this chapter, Bracken uses the traditional Shanghai alleyway house as an example to warn us of the dangers of nostalgia, as the preservation of these houses may in fact destroy the very thing it seeks to retain. In the subsequent chapter, **Margaret Hillenbrand** further theorises the nostalgia 'movement', which has 'bathed the East Asian cultural realm in the rosy glow of yesteryear'. Like Bracken, she also warns of the dangers of a commodified, recursive nostalgia, but shows that cultural productions like the cinema of Miike Takashi and Wong Kar-wai hold the potential to cling to, or conjure up, 'real memories' that are attached to a 'real city', thus helping audiences to feel deeply for the places of their past. In chapter 11, **Lena Scheen** discusses two Shanghai bestsellers portraying gendered subjectivities in a cityscape that is in a state of constant flux and moving towards a high capitalist mode. She scrutinises how the protagonists negotiate these changes, and how this negotiation intersects with gender. In her chapter, the novels serve as paradigms of the society of the spectacle – which in Shanghai is primarily a spectacle of consumerism and frantic growth – to explore the tensions imposed on the individual by this society, focusing in particular on gender, self-searching and agency.

In chapter 12, Beijing cultural activist, curator and blogger **Ou Ning** forcefully critiques the relentless processes of urbanisation that are sweeping China. He points to the devastating consequences for both the countryside and the cityscape. Taking his inspiration from protest movements across Greater China, such as that formed around the destruction of the Star Ferry/Queen's Pier in Hong Kong, he explores possibilities for protest and resistance. His contribution not only attests to the voices of protest that can increasingly be heard within China, but also offers glimpses of hope for a better and more sustainable future. In the final chapter of this book, **John Nguyet Erni** forges a connection between cultural studies and law. He analyses the environmental implications of the slow but steady destruction of the harbour in Hong Kong and argues that juridical sensitivity to the sensory consequences of what he terms the 'harbourcide' of Hong Kong, in particular smell, may help in the development of counter strategies.

We opened this introduction with quotes from Jacques Rancière and Guy Debord. Whereas the latter claims that art's declaration of independence signifies the beginning of the end of art, that art only appears 'as dusk begins to fall over life', the words of Rancière offer more hope; a hope with which we would like to conclude this introduction. Art and popular culture hold the power to inspire change, just as they hold the power to support the ideological status quo. In this book, we explore both roles and possibilities. It may come as no surprise that it is our hope that the arts may help us to imagine a better, more fair, more sustainable, more humane and more liveable city. That they help, in tandem with academic work, to tell better stories about how to live life in a time of rapid urbanisation. It may seem naïve, but we do hope that this collection of essays reflects that critical thrust; and even more so, we hope that this collection will inspire more work on the Chinese city that refrains from either univocally celebrating or critiquing the present, but instead straddles both in the search for a better future.

References

Appadurai, Arjun. *Modernity at Large: Cultural Dimensions of Globalization.* Minneapolis: University of Minnesota Press, 1996.
Asian Development Bank. *Managing Asian Cities.* Mandaluyong: ADB, 2008.
Braester, Yomi. *Painting the City Red: Chinese Cinema and the Urban Contract.* Durham: Duke University Press, 2010.
Debord, Guy. *The Society of Spectacle.* New York: Zone Books, 1995.
Fabian, Johannes. *Time and the Other: How Anthropology Makes Its Object.* New York: Columbia University Press, 1983.
Grossberg, Lawrence. 'Postscript.' *Communication Theory* 12, no. 3 (2002): 367-70.
—. 'On the Political Responsibilities of Cultural Studies.' *Inter-Asia Cultural Studies* 11, no. 2 (2010): 241-47.
Hemelryk Donald, Stephanie. 'Global Beijing: "The World" is a Violent Place.' In *Globalization, Violence, and the Visual Culture of Cities*, edited by Christoph Lindner, 122-34. London: Routledge, 2010.
Jay, Martin. *Downcast Yeyes: The Denigration of Vision in Twentieth-Century French Thought.* Berkeley and Los Angeles: University of California Press, 1994.
Lindner, Christoph. 'Globalization and Violence.' In *Globalization, Violence, and the Visual Culture of Cities*, edited by Christoph Lindner, 1-14. London: Routledge, 2010.
Rancière, Jacques. *The Politics of Aesthetics.* London: Continuum, 2004.

1. Speed and Spectacle in Chinese Cities
Ackbar Abbas

When we think of Chinese cities today, nothing comes more obviously to mind than 'speed' and 'spectacle': the speed at which urban construction takes place, giving rise to hyperbolic terms like 'urban frenzy' or 'Shenzhen speed'; and the way speed conjures into being, as if by magic, spectacular skylines – the Pudong area in Shanghai being the most often cited example. However, what is most obvious can also be most elusive. Rem Koolhaas has speculated amusingly that it might be the 'mutant figure' of Chinese architecture ('one-tenth as many architects have to build ten times as much for a tenth of the honorarium') that accounts for the speed of construction. But this is to forget the many bureaucratic delays that the Chinese architect has to put up with, and the sense, derived from bitter political experience, that the rules can change without warning; so that if you want to do something, you have to do it fast, before the rules change again. There is a paradoxical relation, therefore, between speed and slowness.

The spectacle is equally paradoxical. The best known theorist of the spectacle is, of course, Guy Debord, but if his notion of the spectacle is still relevant today, it is because in his last book, *Comments on the Society of the Spectacle* (1988), he radically revised his earlier position, arguing that a mutation in the form of the spectacle has taken place: from the 'diffuse' and 'concentrated' forms found in earlier capitalist and authoritarian societies respectively, to a recent merger of the two forms into the 'integrated spectacle'. If what integrates global society are information networks, then another word for integrated spectacle might be 'information'. Moreover, because of the speed with which it moves, information does not necessarily take on a visual form. This is tantamount to saying that the integrated spectacle confronts us with something of a paradox: it is a spectacle that is no longer spectacular, a spectacle that has reversed itself in that it is more covert than overt, a spectacle that is secret. In *The Society of the Spectacle* (1968), Debord had postulated two critical historical shifts in ethical and social life. The first involved a 'downgrading of *being* into *having*', when what you have becomes more important than what you are, the moment of the 'acquisitive society'; the second involved 'a generalized shift from *having* to *appearing*', when what you appear to have is more important than what you actually have, the moment of the spectacle. Today, we will have to postulate a third shift: from appearing to *disappearing*, a shift to the non-spectacular form of the spectacle, to its secret informational form.

In the case of China today, what underlies these paradoxes and mutations of speed and spectacle is a twist in social space, exemplified above all in the phrase 'a socialist market economy'. What does the phrase mean? Are we dealing with the life or death of socialism, or with something else more elusive, its *afterlife*: with a posthumous socialism whose emblem might be Mao's embalmed body lying in state in Beijing, like a preserved building? Socialism in posthumous form can have a vitality stronger than ever before. A spectre is haunting China today, we might say, and it is the spectre of socialism. And in its wake, we find a social space so contradictory and dense that, like a black hole, it cannot be observed directly, only deduced from the effects it produces; effects that we call cinema, architecture, information, and so on. These media do not *represent* space; rather, they *perform* space. And it is the contradictions and anomalies accompanying the performance – the parapraxes – that allow us to retain a sense of history that might otherwise threaten to disappear with the spectacle: a spatial history.

To give some substance to these speculations, let me now turn to two very different ways of performing space. The first is the Beijing Olympics Opening Ceremony, under the overall direction of fifth-generation filmmaker Zhang Yimou. It was an event broadcast live to a global audience; an instance, perhaps, of the return of spectacle with a vengeance? The second is the film *Still Life* by sixth-generation filmmaker Jia Zhangke; a film shot, like all his films, in an antispectacular, documentary style. However, as I shall try to show, it is possible to understand the spectacle as a kind of documentary, and the documentary as a kind of spectacle, insofar as Jia's documentary-style film, as much as Zhang's spectacular production, also makes use of cinematic special effects and shocking exaggerations. The two performances may be different, but they take place in the same social space.

Doubtless Zhang Yimou was given the assignment because, with the popular success of a film like *Hero*, he is regarded as a master of the spectacular effect. *Hero*, we may remember, also had a blatantly ideological theme. The story is about an assassin commissioned to kill the first Emperor of China, because of what seems at first to be the cruel and ruthless way in which he governs the country. However, when the two antagonists finally meet, the Emperor convinces the assassin that order and control are necessary to prevent the country from descending into chaos. In the Olympic Opening Ceremony, we do not find an explicit ideological statement; rather, what we see is the *performing* of order and control, most obviously in the way the movements of 15,000 performers are choreographed and synchronised. But even more important is the fact that unlike older spectacles that relied on the disciplining of bodies (like the synchronised dancing of the Tiller Girls that Siegfried Kracauer analysed in *The Mass Ornament*), here control is achieved through technology. It is as if each performer has been transformed into a dot or pixel on a high-definition TV screen. In fact, what is most memorable for most viewers of the Opening Ceremony is the advanced media technology used to produce the spectacular special effects, including the world's largest LED screen, the size of a football field. This suggests that in spite of the presence of 15,000 material bodies on the ground, what is central is the virtual space created by lighting and electronics, an immaterial space that is much more malleable and controllable than actual space (like lip-sync singing). In this space, 15,000 years of Chinese history can be presented to a world audience in a seamless narrative as a media event. This is the performance of nationhood on an epic scale.

The question we might now ask is: when was the last time China had a comparable media event that riveted the world's attention? And the answer would have to be – the tragedy of Tiananmen in 1989. Tiananmen was bloodshed and atrocity, played out live on television screens all over the world. But with hindsight, and in no way meant to condone the massacre, Tiananmen was also the first confrontation in Chinese history between two forms of power: the old power of military force and state control, and the new power (which the students knew how to wield) of information and global networks. While the People's Liberation Army (PLA) had guns and tanks and a whole state apparatus behind it, the students had telephones and fax machines, *Newsweek* and CNN, as well as 'world opinion' on their side. In this confrontation, the old state power was made to look awkward and gauche because it had little understanding of new media, relying only on old-fashioned violence as a means of re-asserting control; hence the massacre, which was also an example of the state *losing* control. With the Olympic Opening Ceremony, however, Tiananmen has come full circle. No longer is the state opposed to and suspicious of new media; it has learnt, with the help of filmmaker Zhang Yimou, to appreciate it, and to perform with confidence in this new space.

The space of the Opening Ceremony is the space of the 'global cultural salon', where cultural biennials and triennials proliferate, the main purpose of which is to put a city or a nation on the cultural map. This is both an acknowledgement of the importance of culture and its instrumentalisation. On the other hand, the link between the Opening Ceremony and Tiananmen that I am proposing introduces a more complex spatial history, and raises the question of cultural memory and forgetting. It shows us that forgetting is also a matter of *remembering as something else*; that is, forgetting is additive, not subtractive. The Tiananmen Massacre has not been and cannot be excised from history, but the function of an integrated spectacle like the Olympic Opening Ceremony is to give us something else to remember.

Let us now move to my second example, Jia Zhangke's *Still Life*. We might take this opportunity to briefly discuss the relation of documentary film to a problematic space: how does such cinema 'perform' space? It can do so only by changing the basis on which documentary is made. In spite of theoretical doubts, we see today not just the persistence, but also the growing importance of the documentary form, especially in experimental filmmaking. Why is this the case? An explanation might go as follows: we know that documentary, like translation, is always a betrayal. But if this is the case, we must start with the fact of betrayal, with the betrayal of fact, not with 'objectivity'. In a relatively stable space, we can try to 'seek truth from fact' (Deng); in an erratic space, we may first have to 'seek facts from lies'.

With these considerations in mind, let me now turn to Jia Zhangke's *Still Life*. The film is set in a small town called Fengjie on the Yangtze River that, because of the building of the Three Gorges Dam, is about to be demolished. The film is usually read as a critique of ruthless modernisation that does not weigh the human costs, and a celebration of the persistence, courage and resourcefulness of ordinary people: hence the Chinese title, *The Good People of the Three Gorges* (三峡好人), with its Brechtian overtones. But such a reading of *Still Life* as social documentary with humanist overtones does not do justice to the film's spatial history. First of all, space is not neutral; people disappear in it, or better still, it *disappears* people. The twin plot deals with a coalminer looking for his wife and child, who left him sixteen years ago, and a woman looking for a husband who went to work on an urban reconstruction project two years ago, and has not been heard from since, as if he had fallen through some wormhole in space. These holes in space are suggested by another feature: in a film that adheres, for the most part, to a realist documentary style, certain anomalous details intrude. For example, the characters look up at the sky and see what appears to be a UFO, and in the midst of a town under demolition, we see – incongruously – a newly-constructed building that suddenly takes off like a rocket being launched. It is as if behind the 'still life' pictures, beneath the surface, the spatial grids and coordinates are changing and twisting.

These spatial twists are always accompanied by a twist in temporality, and nowhere is this alluded to more clearly than in the changing meaning of nostalgia. We usually think of nostalgia as a strong desire to hold onto the past in the face of a confusing present. But what becomes of past and present, as distinct moments, when time is speeded up? What happens to nostalgia when the present instant so quickly becomes the instant past?

When he arrives in Fengjie, the middle-aged coalminer Sanming strikes up an unlikely friendship with Mark, a young local hoodlum. As they exchange phone numbers, we hear the different ringtones on their cell phones. Sanming uses the old song 'Bless the Good-Hearted People', redolent of a long-gone Communist era. Mark uses the theme song from the popular Hong Kong movie *A Better Tomorrow*, and likes to quote the line, 'Present-day society doesn't suit us because we are nostalgic'. Through this juxtaposition of Sanming and Mark, nostalgia begins to take on novel characteristics. It is no longer a generational phenomenon: not only are the old with a past nostalgic, so too are the young, who lack much of a past, as if the young had become old before their time. Second, nostalgia does not just belong to the individual; there can be large-scale mass nostalgias, such as the curious nostalgias that China has been experiencing in its globalising phase. One bizarre example is nostalgia for the Cultural Revolution, seen in a brief vogue for Cultural Revolution memorabilia and the appearance of restaurants serving atrocious Cultural Revolution food. When this vogue died down, another took its place: nostalgia for the 1980s, the period that marked the end of the Cultural Revolution, when universities, conservatories and art academies were re-opened. But the fact that there can be nostalgia *both* for the Cultural Revolution and for its demise; the fact that nostalgia can be so arbitrary; the fact that *both* Sanming and Mark can be subject to it, suggests that what we are dealing with is more like a form of hysteria when time itself is twisted, and history is experienced as hysteria, including the history of socialism itself.

One of the most interesting aspects of *Still Life* is the way it relates to new media, something Jia Zhangke has in common with Zhang Yimou. The film was shot in high-definition video, which gives the images great clarity and precision. At the same time, such technology also enables images to be spliced together seamlessly, so that anything can be connected to anything else, and that which can be imagined – such as UFOs and buildings-as-rockets – can be made visible; in short, the brave new world of Photoshop and the fake, the world of the spectral image. There is, however, a crucial difference between Photoshop and Jia Zhangke's use of this tool. The former is a kind of deception or hoax; the latter, by contrast, is a *provocation* to thought, opening up the possibility that the real is not the true, that the visible is not the intelligible, and the intelligible is not the visible. The Photoshop-like images in *Still Life* allow Jia Zhangke's cinema to work in the gap between the visible and the intelligible, as if it were only by means of spectral images that the spectral history of socialism could be evoked.

2. Planned Demi-monde and its Aestheticisation in Singapore

Chua Beng Huat

Brand Singapore

From the point of arrival at Changi Airport, Singapore impresses the visitor: it is, possibly, the easiest and fastest clearance through immigration and customs a visitor has to face at any international airport. A queue of taxis awaits to ferry the visitor through wide highways, gaily planted with lush green trees and colourful – orange, purple, fuchsia, white – tropical bougainvilleas, passing an endless parade of high-rise housing estates, the clean pastel walls signifying a high level of maintenance, into the city in less than half an hour. This city is served by an efficient infrastructure of highways, roads and a mass rapid transit system that is still adding new lines and stations. The cars that fill the roads are all of recent vintage; heavy taxation on automobiles discourages the keeping of cars beyond ten years.

In the city, the financial and corporate district is packed with tall, grey corporate buildings. The colonial commercial district along the Singapore River has been completely rebuilt, with some of the more monumental colonial buildings restored and reused, nestled among the skyscrapers. Singapore River itself is another symbol of the new Singapore; a ten-year clean-up effort has cleared it of debris and the clean, gleaming water is now a reservoir, unlike the rivers in other Southeast Asian cities that are choked with waste. The iconic buildings in the financial district are not the banking towers but the centre for performing arts, the Esplanade – Theatres on the Bay, and the six-star Fullerton Hotel, a beautifully restored colonial edifice that used to be the central post office. Across the bay stand the three glass towers topped with the sky-park of the Marina Bay Sands casino-convention hall-hotel-shopping complex. The glitter of this downtown area is exhibited to its extreme during the F1 Grand Prix, when all of the building's lights are switched on, augmented by the spotlights on the circuit; the city literally sparkles.

Next to the Esplanade is Marina Square, which marks the end point of a long line of shopping complexes that stretches inland to Orchard Road; Singapore has been likened to an endless pedestrianised shopping mall. All the needs and desires of local and foreign consumers, from mass to exorbitant, from poor taste to aesthetically sophisticated, can be found in the shops on Orchard Road; a flâneur's paradise? This pervasive affluence is only disrupted by the occasional wheelchair-bound vendor of lottery tickets or packs of tissues at inflated prices, which are purchased by passers-by more as an act of charity than of need. There is no other evidence of poverty along the curbs of roads or in the parks, or anywhere; poverty, as it exists, is well hidden. Economic success is part of the identity of individual Singaporeans and, collectively, of the nation. This story of economic success and its physical expression is the image that is projected to the world in globally circulating magazines and on television stations by all of the state agencies; not just the tourist promotion board, for example, but also the Economic Development Board, which uses this image of success to entice multinational corporations to invest in a 'Singapore that works!'.

Indeed, Singapore the city advertises itself.

Geylang

> We don't advertise prostitution. But every Singaporean knows there's a Geylang and things going on there. We would demean ourselves on our tourist brochures if we advertised the seamier aspects. It is beneath us.
> – George Yeo, Minister of Foreign Affairs, Singapore

Geylang is the most liberated space in Singapore, according to a foreign liberal-minded academic colleague who loves the place; he took everyone who visited him during his two-year academic sojourn in Singapore to Geylang. Geylang Road is a very long road with side-roads branching from it perpendicularly on both sides. These side roads, called *'lorongs'* in Malay, are numbered consecutively, from 1 to 42, with even numbers on one side and odd numbers on the other. In the early reaches of the street, from Lorong 1 to 13, is a continuous row of Chinese 'hotpot' restaurants. Beyond Lorong 13, almost every shopfront of the two-to-three-storey terraced houses, locally called shophouses, is an eatery, a coffee-shop, selling different styles of ethnic Chinese food. The hotpot restaurants compete for patrons among the huge influx of lower-end labourers who have migrated from China into Singapore in the last five years. They face some degree of public antagonism as a result of this influx, despite having the same ethnicity as the overwhelming majority of Singaporeans. In 2010, one quarter of the population of just over 5 million was composed of migrants of various social-economic backgrounds from all over the world, ranging from sex workers to domestic maids, from construction workers to front retail staff, and from computer engineers to CEOs of multinational corporations. Only lower-end migrants are routinely found in Geylang.

In the even-numbered lanes, a different scene unfolds. Many of the shops have blaring, gaudy neon signs of scarlet red, sunshine orange and cool turquoise, announcing that the place is a bar or a karaoke lounge. From inside the lanes, shards of purple colour from neon lights that ring the outline of the multi-storey love hotels extend to the main road. The colour palette of all these lights is one that any highly cultured art school would be unlikely to encourage. Instead of the conventional open front, these shophouses are walled up with closed doors that open into dimly-lit caverns. Inside, women loiter around or sit hidden behind cubicles with patrons of the establishment. Outside, packages of cigarettes lie on pieces of cloth, on the floor or on plastic chairs, under the sheltered eaves (colloquially called the five-foot way of the shophouses), seemingly free for the taking. The owners or vendors stand somewhere near the contraband, blackmarket merchandise, stepping forward only when a customer makes a purchase.

Unmistakably, loitering along the main road and lanes, seated in the coffee shops (*kopitiams* in Hokkien dialect), or standing in the sheltered five-foot way, are women; no longer young, adorned in skimpy clothes and high-heeled shoes and excessively made-up, waiting to be accosted or actively accosting men who walk by. Entering the lanes that emit the ghostly purple light, one sees more women standing in the dim streetlights. Some of the units among the rows of low-rise terraced houses, the original buildings of the place before some of them made way for the high-rise love hotels that rent out rooms by the hour, hang a red or pink light under the overhang of the roof, publicly announcing the presence of a brothel. These brothels have been losing business to the freelance streetwalkers who come from all over Asia – China, Indonesia, Thailand, Malaysia, Vietnam, India, Sri Lanka, and Bangladesh.

Men are everywhere. They take up more of the public space than the women, but no one pays them any particular attention; all of the attention is focused on the women. The main road is heavy with traffic and sections of it, between Lorong 12 to 20, slow to a crawl because cars are double-parked off the curb and male drivers slow down to take in the street scene. The sidewalk of the main road is crowded with male loiterers, forcing pedestrians to walk around them. The tables and chairs of various *kopitiams* that are strategically located at the corners of buildings spill onto the sidewalks, filled with idling men in groups, drinking beers and coffee. The lanes are filled with more men, often surrounding tables, gambling in the dark alleys at the back of shophouses. Some of the loitering men are the lookouts paid by pimps and gambling organisers to watch out for police. Most of the loitering and idling men evidently have nowhere in particular to go; most are voyeurs who take pleasure in ogling women, while a minority is in search of procuring sex (Ng 2010).

Planned Nation/Planned Demimonde

Singapore is an unlikely place to build a nation. Indeed, nationhood was thrust upon its citizens. The island-nation is constrained, if not cursed, by land scarcity, an absence of natural resources and a small population. Due to severe scarcity, all available land is husbanded for capitalist national economic development. This translates into a set of land-use practices: (i) comprehensively planned high-rise, high-density residential housing estates are of sufficient scale to enable services such as education, public transport, shopping and facilities for all daily necessities and amenities to be provided efficiently within the estate, to reduce the residents' need to travel; (ii) industrial estates and districts for higher-order commercial services, such as banking and tourism districts, are separated from residential estates to avoid traffic congestion and environmental pollution; (iii) the two types of development are linked by a network of rapid mass transit trains to discourage private automobile ownership, which is further discouraged by very high import duties and annual road taxes; (iv) the greening of the entire island by the ornamental planting of imported flowering plants to create an environment conducive to enticing investments by global enterprises.

The highly-integrated physical urban planning and governance of the island thinks of Singapore in the singular: one small island-nation constituted as one single planning unit, governed by a single-tier government, in the hands of an absolutely dominant single-party government, or party-state (Chua 1997). In the voluminous atrium space that is the grand entrance of the Urban Redevelopment Authority, the master planning authority, this comprehensive plan is on symbolic display, made visible in a three-dimensional model of the island built to scale, as the central planning agency sees it. Every inch of the island is accounted for, filled with existing buildings or designated for development. Pockets of vacant land signify either land reserved for future development or for nature, which could be converted into development sites with one stroke of the planner's pen; ironically, nature requires planners' permission to exist in Singapore. The government controls more than 80% of the land, meaning that the state owns – and thus controls – practically all public spaces (Wong and Yeh 1985).

As in urban planning, economic development has been turned into a singular, multifaceted technical problem to be solved on an ongoing basis by a group of well-trained and well-meaning professionals, including highly-educated politicians. To get the system going, and to then sustain its constant growth, requires a very highly integrated system helmed by a small group of individuals – politicians and top civil servants. All the top civil servants and politicians enjoy long careers under the dominant single-party-state of the People's Action Party (PAP), working together to execute long-term plans in relative insulation from the public, but always in the name of the public good. Furthermore, civil servants and politicians are interchangeable, with civil servants being drawn into political elections and becoming cabinet ministers, and retired politicians being appointed to head statutory boards and government-linked enterprises. Liberal conceptions of different viewpoints, different needs, and different desires on the part of individuals and groups, are kept out of politics and public administration by government-erected obstacles to hinder group formations, such as the obligation to apply for permits from the police department for the registration of associations. Such insulation is the dream of every civil service and government, although few have the ability to realise it. Singapore has thus been characterised as a nation that has become an administrative state, in which politics has disappeared (Chan 1975). This state of affairs is the consequence of the political history of Singapore's independence.

The history is one of the ascendancy of the PAP, from its social democratic beginnings through to its authoritarianism and uninterrupted occupancy of parliamentary power, from 1959 until the present day, and conceivably for the future two decades. In 1961, the left faction was expelled from the Party. The faction that inherited the Party re-designated itself as a moderate faction. This was followed by the violent repression of those that opposed the Party: the de-registration of leftist labour unions, the detention without trial of unionists and alleged communists and their sympathisers, culminating in the similar detention of expelled ex-PAP leaders. This dark age in Singapore's political history continues not only to be remembered, but also to cast long shadows of fear over Singaporeans, deterring them from speaking out against the ruling regime, despite the fact that political detention is a thing of the past. No one has been detained for political subversion since 1987; only Muslims who have alleged connections with terrorism are now imprisoned. This history of political repression has caused the single-party dominant state, a phenomenon that is in itself not unusual in post-World War II Asia, to retain its label as an authoritarian state.

However, the idea of a state without politics is inconceivable, and simply labelling the PAP 'authoritarian' fails to account for the overwhelming majorities that the PAP consistently wins in periodic general elections. These electoral successes suggest that the PAP has genuine popular support. Thus, I would argue that the depoliticisation is a displacement of contentious politics and its replacement by a hegemonic moral order based on the massive improvement of the material life of the entire population. The material well-being of the general 'Singaporean' population has generated voluntary acquiescence to the ruling regime. The people's apparent 'disinterest' in politics is therefore not a lack of political will or desire on their part. It is rather an expression of the fact that the majority of Singaporeans are happy with what the PAP party-state is doing on their behalf, namely, building a very secure and stable environment to indulge in the generalised and greatly expanded consumer culture that characterises global capitalism. These are as good reasons as any for enfranchised citizens to support the ruling party in which the hegemonic party-state is seen as providing moral leadership for the citizenry, as conceived by Gramsci (1971: 57-59).[1]

The PAP government's total control of all public spaces holds a politically sinister implication: it is a control of all space-requiring, physical rights of expression. No public activities can take place, whether these take the form of graffiti on walls, demonstrations on the streets, basking in parks or performing on any street corner. All of these conventional public activities are sanitised: graffiti is moved indoors into museum spaces and alleviated as 'art' (sadly with the complicity of impoverished artists, in a financial if not an aesthetic sense); public demonstration is confined to an allocated 'free speech' corner of a city park; and would-be street performers must first audition at the Ministry of Information, Communication and the Arts and given a license to practice.

Control is vested in the hands of the police force's Public Entertainment Licensing Unit (PELU); no activities, particularly those of a political nature, can take place without the written permission of the Unit, which can reject any application without having to provide reasons for doing so. Political dissidents have been routinely charged with 'disturbing the public peace' for making speeches on the street or demonstrating silently and peacefully in front of government buildings. The most recent 'move-along' law empowers the police to order loiterers or demonstrators to move along rather than stay put in one location; if they refuse to do so, they risk being arrested and criminalised. Control of space is thus a critical element in the arsenal of administrative instruments of the party-state of Singapore.

Thus, it is obvious that rather than blighting a landscape of success, Geylang, where PELU and the police seem to have abandoned any responsibility for administering the law, has the permission of the nation's planners and administrators to exist. The irritated Minister George Yeo's statement, cited above, attests to this. Indeed, Geylang is a planned component of the nation. In the immediate years after political independence from British colonialism in 1959, the PAP mounted a campaign against 'yellow culture', the code-word for everything 'Western' and libertine, including youth culture, drugs, rock-n-roll, and sex. However, it quickly came to realise that attempts to erase prostitution merely dispersed the practice spatially and drove it underground. In its pragmatism – the Party's unwavering ideology – it created Geylang in the mid-1960s, into which all the brothels in the island were relocated. For the single party-state, such a district is no less than an efficient means of regulating the sex trade. Thus, while the scene on parade in Geylang may be a great puzzle to the foreign visitor who, reading the government's rhetoric, perceives Singapore to be a straight-laced society, the demimonde of commercialised sex trade is merely an unavoidable necessity. Indeed, this control strategy is unexceptional and can be found in many cities around the world (Hubbard and Sanders 2003), perhaps the most notorious being the red-light district in Amsterdam. The only miscalculation, if it is such, is that the massively expanding wealth of Singaporeans has brought the influx of foreign workers, including street-walking sex workers, spilling onto the roads rather than discreetly conducting their trade within the walls of licensed brothels.

Politics of Pathos

Geylang, like all red-light districts around the world, is a Foucauldian heterotopia, an open space that does not restrict anyone from entry; a place that is similar to, but different from, the mundane everyday life outside it. Geylang is very much like any residential district: there are residents of all ages and gender/sexuality; there are retail businesses, in which workers make a living, catering to the everyday needs of consumers, whether local residents or passers-by; and places of worship for all major religions. However, all these mundane everyday people and events fade, and are rendered invisible, as the sex workers, around whom all the other businesses on the main street swarm, become the only visible signifying icons of the place. It is this iconic difference that is captured visually as spectacle, for locals, tourists, and artists.

That sex workers may be muses to artists is hardly new. Such artists range from the world-famous, such as Van Gogh and Gauguin, to artists of lesser fame, such as Dennis O'Rourke, an Australian filmmaker who became very involved with the Thai sex worker who was the main character in his film, *The Good Woman of Bangkok* (1992).[2] Similarly, artists in Singapore, foreign and local, professionals and amateur, portray the sex workers or Geylang as their subjects in a wide range of media. There are short video clips shot with mobile phones, documentaries, mainstream television drama serials, movies, paintings, pop music, and academic research reports. Movies and television dramas are perhaps, by their very visual and narrative characters, the media that take the greatest license in this spectacularisation, while painting is a quieter medium. For example, in the movie with the risqué title *Pleasure Factory*, which we will analyse further below, a young ethnic Chinese woman in a bright red dress, the top half of her body sticking out against the chassis of an open-roof convertible car, pumps her body rhythmically on a man in the back seat of the car, in a back alley flooded with amber street light. Geylang might be a lightly policed space for the sex trade, but the police, who are constantly present, do not tolerate such public sex (Ng 2010). The different media are different modes of looking in on the sex workers and their milieu; voyeurism is quintessentially a spectator sport. I would now like to look at two genres of spectacularisation of Geylang: painting and feature films.

Painting Geylang

The American artist, Joan Marie Kelly, taught drawing and painting at Nanyang Technological University in Singapore in 2005. She characterises herself on her blog as:

> coming from the chaos and anarchy of New York in the 1980s and Baltimore in the 1990s. (1980s I lived in NYC on 55th and 8th Ave., Hell's Kitchen. The introduction of crack cocaine to NYC and the crime that came with it, graffiti was taking off, Keith Herring [sic], Our flat was robbed every year in October, the Hari Krishna's lived across the street, I have nine false teeth in my mouth as a reminder of a single night some guy came up from behind me and whacked me in the face with something. My Mother lived in Baltimore, a nurse for the rape crisis centre at Mercy Hospital, she has been mugged 3 times, 2 at gun point.) Of course the fear of crime in the States was always frightening but I thrived on the chaos.[3]

Little wonder that the 'orderly visual setting and comfort with consumerism of Singaporean society was a shock'.

Then she discovered Geylang:

> Because this was the only setting that I felt I could relate to so far, I decided to bring my paints and easel there the next weekend. I began to do small portrait paintings at the same location the next week. The Indian named 'John' [the man she met the very first time she sat down in a *kopitiam*] proved he was a pimp. He brought the female sex workers to me to paint their portraits. I brought a friend Phillip with me. He is gregarious and likes to have a few beers, perfect for this occasion. The place was chaotic. People were crowded around me. I tuned much of it out and would focus on the scrutiny of the model and my painting. The light on the subjects was challenging. There was a blue light coming from one direction and a pink from the opposite and every time the cars along the street braked the red brake lights would illuminate the face. It was fun and got me out of the stifling routine of the Singaporean life where nothing happens unexpected or spontaneously.

Kelly writes, 'I began to understand the lives of other foreign workers in Singapore',[4] implying a claim to understand the pimps and sex workers who were her 'models'. Her presence in Geylang caught the attention of local mainstream media; 'My work was published in the Straits Times where in the headlines the question was asked "Why are they painting all these ugly people?" The attitudes of class stigma and class separation in Singapore began to come to the forefront through the process of the work'.

We can make an immediate observation regarding Kelly's narrative of her artistic activity in Geylang. Take the throwaway line that Geylang 'got me out of the stifling routine of the Singaporean life where nothing happens unexpected or spontaneously'. Singapore is an 'orderly visual setting and comfort with consumerism' – physically well-planned, clean, no litter, no logjam traffic and, one might add, no evidence of poverty. Instead, there are miles and miles of shopping complexes, signifying global capitalist consumerism in full glory. Socially and culturally, this Singapore is a bureaucratised society in which every possible strand of spontaneity of the spirit is bred out of its citizens. The Singaporean middle-class way of life is one of deferred gratification, with its years of intensely competitive schooling in preparation for long working hours, just to join the work-to-consume race for competitive advantage in consumption through displays of positional or status goods. As the former prime minister once put it during a national-day celebration speech, 'For Singaporeans, life is not complete without shopping'. Much like the Singapore government's anxiety, expressed in likening national economic expansion to a marathon without end, middle-class Singaporeans live in deep apprehension of being unable to afford a middle-class lifestyle, and thus rationalise their alienating long hours of bureaucratic and professional work as a necessary condition of contemporary life in late capitalism (Purushotam 1998).

The Singapore that is a globally marketed brand – a success story in global capitalism beyond any reasonable expectations, with its hardworking and hard-saving expanding middle-class population, a putative 'model' for many governments and peoples in developing nations – holds little interest for an artist who is in search of adventure. By contrast, Geylang is chaotic, coloured in hues of 'blue', 'pink' and 'red', offering instant gratification in legally ambivalent, if not outright illegal, activities, and, ultimately, fun. Recall here my academic friend's proclamation that Geylang is the most liberated place in Singapore. For the voyeurs, intellectual or touristic, the 'chaos', the 'spontaneity' and the 'fun' is humanity as it should be. In these intellectualised commentaries, Geylang is more than just a red-light district. Geylang is the critique of mainstream Singaporean lifestyles.

Pleasure Factory

The film *Pleasure Factory* was directed by Ekachai Uekrongtham, a Thai national who has lived in Singapore for more than 20 years. He is better known locally as the founder of a theatre group, Action Theatre, which produced the successful musical *Chang and Eng*. This musical was built around the lives of the Siamese twins Chang and Eng Bunker, who were born in Thailand (Siam) in the early 19th century and eventually married and settled down in the US, after having been exhibited by a British man as a curiosity in a world tour. *Pleasure Factory* had initial co-funding from the Singapore Film Commission, a government statutory board, but the director did not use the funds. The film was eventually entirely funded through private investments. The film was selected for the 'Un Certain Regard' section of the 2007 Cannes Festival, one of the few films from Singapore to receive this honour.[5]

The film tells three parallel stories that are stitched together by their co-presence in Geylang. The first revolves around two young men who are suggestively presented as homo-erotically inclined, if not involved. One of them is a virgin heterosexually, and they go to Geylang to help him lose his virginity. He picks up a sex worker from China who is gentle with him and discovers that he enjoys heterosexuality, which leaves his gay friend devastated. The second narrative revolves around a young woman who is at risk of being inducted into sex work by her own mother, while a young man who is smitten with her helplessly tries to save her from her fate. The final narrative is of a sex worker who, at the end of a night's work, pays a street musician to play her a special song and ends up taking him home with her. The stories unfold amid scenes of food served in restaurants, catering to the post-coital needs of patrons and purveyors.

In an interview, the director said that he was initially repulsed by Geylang, but subsequently came to find it 'a very vibrant world because different things co-exist'. Furthermore, he claims that he 'didn't make the film to expose the dirty side of Singapore', but that he wanted to make a film 'about human connections in a place that is the last place you'd think this would happen'.[6] Indeed, he has. In the three stories, the sex worker from China and the young man who experiences heterosexual sex for the first time with her are projected on the screen as establishing care, concern and intimacy in their encounter. Moreover, this sexual encounter turns him into a straight man, leaving his gay friend angry and alone. The Chinese sex worker and the street musician cosy up to each other tenderly on her bed, with no suggestion of subsequent sexual activity. The young girl is saved from sex work after the male client, who physically abuses her when her attempt to give him oral sex causes him pain, is smashed on the head by the girl's mother; the very last frame of the film shows the girl, fully clothed, sleeping soundly in the bed of the smitten young man at daybreak. At the end of the day, all of the protagonists in the three stories end up with warm human connections. The loneliness, alienation, and suffering of sex workers, local and migrants, are smoothed away by their ability to establish connections with other lonely individuals, needing and finding each other, thus humanising all the main characters and normalising the marginalised.

Filmic Representation as Political Critique

Filmic representation of the marginalised in feature films and in photography is a common practice in Singapore. One could say that the practice has been perfected by Eric Khoo, who is regarded as Singapore's leading arthouse filmmaker. Khoo caught the attention of the international film-festival circuit with his very first film, *Mee Pok Man* (1995), in which a lonely young noodle cook in a coffee shop, who is in love with an unavailable sex worker who operates out of the same space, gets his chance to be with her after they meet with an accident, and he takes her home to nurse her in his dingy, one-room public housing flat. She subsequently dies, and necrophilia is hinted at. The film garnered this review from *Time Magazine*:

> To the rest of the world, Singapore appears to be sparkling clean and thriving. At film festivals from Montreal to Fukuoka, *Mee Pok Man* – a highly praised first feature by a 30 yr-old presents a startlingly different perspective, portraying Singapore's seamy underside, with its alienated and outcast. Khoo evaded an all-out government ban, but the film has a RA (Restricted Artistic) rating [...] nonetheless, adult Singaporeans are packing theatres where it is playing.[7]

Since then, Khoo has produced three other feature-length movies featuring marginal Singaporeans (Chua and Yeo 2003). In every one of these films, Khoo is a master at selecting the most depressing sites on the island to shoot his scenes. His production company has also produced Royston Tan's feature film *15* (2006), about a group of teenage school dropouts who go around looking for a suitable tall building for one of them to commit suicide, facing a bleak future in a competitive society in which the uneducated are condemned to a marginal life amidst all the material prosperity. The film was widely circulated among international film festivals. Another illustrative example is the short film by the Singaporean documentary filmmaker, Martyn See, ironically entitled *Nation Builders*, an honorific title for the first generation of PAP leaders. The short film, which was posted on YouTube, features a population composed entirely of old people engaging in marginal occupations – street musicians, tissue vendors, beggars, collectors of waste cardboard and soft-drink cans – seeking out a meagre living.[8] If narratives around marginalised individuals were ready-made for such visual representations, imagine the rich pickings that an entire district such as Geylang holds for filmmakers and other visual artists.

Against the backdrop of the triumphal story of economic success that is constantly being projected by the single-party-state to both its citizens and the outside world, and upon which its legitimacy rests, it seems easy to critique Singapore's long-ruling PAP government by simply showing the underbelly of the city-society and exposing the lie that all Singaporeans are beneficiaries of capitalist economic success. Thus, these films try to put a chink in the triumphal economic success story of Singapore; a story one loves to hate, especially with its history of political repression and its ongoing illiberal party-state. That all these films attract international audiences is in no uncertain measure because they are read as illustrations of a mode of political critique in or of Singapore (Khoo 2006).

Aesthetics of the Pathetic

From an aesthetic point of view, the socially marginal have their own texture. Ironically, in contrast to the understatedness of the respectable middle class, the marginalised share with the rich an excess of texture. However, no one is likely to mistake one excess for the other. The textured opulence of the rich is constructed through layers of rich fabric, accessorised by glittering jewellery, colour-coordinated bags and shoes and a smoothed-over, coloured, made-up face. The socially marginal lie at the other visual extreme: a tattered patchwork of different designs of cheap fabric, often with a plastic sheen, and sometimes layered for warmth; for clothes, inexpensive sandals on bare feet; and a naked face etched with life's experiences. Nowhere is this contrast of extremes more obvious than in fashion, where the two excesses are sometimes intentionally crossed in the hands of fashion designers. The late Alexander McQueen was said to be able to draw inspiration from the clothes of the homeless, clean up the lines and present them on the runway. The enigmatic Moschino 'Cheap and Chic' label 'tarts up' expensive designer clothes, so to speak. On a lower fashion register is the common practice of wearing dirty, torn jeans by youth as a sign of rebellion against middle-class propriety; even this does not escape the purveyors of high fashion, as upscale designer-jeans are produced that feature original tears. Such gestures signify the romanticising of poverty, the rich playing the poor (at a comfortable distance, of course).

The texture of the streetwalker has been much caricatured in different media, particularly by films: stiletto shoes, short skirts, tops showing too much cleavage, costume jewellery, excessive make-up, all obviously inexpensive goods to even untrained eyes, finishing with bouffant, dyed hair. Perhaps the most famous such streetwalker on film is Julia Roberts in the Hollywood movie *Pretty Woman* (1990). Caricatures rely on real references, and this constellation of exaggerated elements of adornment is in fact commonly found among sex workers who parade themselves by the road. They stand out in the sea of visual ordinariness of others who mill around them. The excesses of the sex workers' bodies are, of course, intentional, the better to make themselves easily identifiable for those in search of their services. So, too, are their bodily gestures; whereas direct eye contact between strangers is generally accidental and immediately broken, such contact is a necessary gesture of the sex trade, as sex workers scan the males present to lock eyes with them. The excessively textured bodies are aestheticised and spectacularised through an intensification of their cheapness in visual representations, including films. This artistic overemphasis on cheapness draws the audience into a shared pathos for the pathetic, who is presented as normal and human just like everyone else, and who thus does not deserve her present fate as sex worker. This affirmation of Geylang as 'life' and 'humanity' is sustained from a privileged bourgeois intellectual position, where to slum it in the margins is a luxury of choice; it is not a position afforded to those who have to make a living in Geylang. Thus, artists like Kelly could just decide 'to bring my paints and easel there the next weekend' and 'began to do small portrait paintings at the same location'. Films like *Pleasure Factory* also belong to a genre that, according to

American film critic A.O. Scott, is motivated by humanism, the content of which is 'concerned with the lives of the rural peasants or the urban proletariat, movies that emphasise the social situations of their characters and whose representation is realist' (Khoo 2006: 93).

From a sociological point of view, the socially marginal are easy targets of voyeuristic attention, intellectual or otherwise, as proved by the number of ethnographic studies that have been elevated to the pinnacle of classics in urban anthropology as an academic discipline (Liebow 1967). Much like the natives encountered by foreign anthropologies, the socially marginal have very little means of shielding themselves from the public gaze and prying eyes, in contrast to the rich, who are able to screen themselves off and control their exposure to the public. In this instance, sex workers in Geylang are on the street, fully exposed as necessitated by the trade, unable to prevent anyone from photographing them, especially with inconspicuous, ubiquitous mobile-phone cameras. In the above-mentioned short documentary, *Nation Builders*, there were many shots in which those who are being filmed look up, unable to comprehend why the camera is recording their activities and too surprised to object to being captured for a few seconds.

The intrusiveness of the camera and the filmmaker behind it is plain to see. However, artists, both professional and amateur, may become insensitive to their intrusiveness. Indeed, armed with their self-justifying sense of pathos, even social injustice, they feel that they have a duty to paint or film marginal people, on the grounds that subsequent exposure of their subjects will prick the conscience of society and bring some assistance to the latter. It is therefore for the own good of the marginalised that they participate in artistic projects, even involuntarily.

Ironically, moments of discursive slippage belie the often shallow nature of this sense of humanism and social justice. The American artist Joan Marie Kelly proclaims that she 'always had a political commitment focusing on minority and marginalised communities'. Included in her description of the denizens of Geylang are

> older men [who] were coming down there to have just a little bit of happiness, their wife would be passed away (yeah, right [...]), they were living on their CPF [the Central Provident Fund, a mandatory savings and social security plan in Singapore] or social security money. Now their 'tool' wouldn't be functioning up to prime and the women were taking advantage of this, while at the same time these men were paying good money. She would be taking them and squeezing them between her legs instead to putting him inside! I had to laugh.[9]

The absence of self-reflexivity on the part of one who claims to have sympathy for the marginalised is indeed staggering; or is it that the pathetic old men who are still buying sex deserved to be laughed at? The humanism takes an equally hypocritical turn in the case of *Pleasure Factory*'s filmmaker. His condescension is reflected in his proclaimed change of attitude towards Geylang, from one of repulsion to one of seeing the human connections in such a place! His discovery of human connections in Geylang only belies his own ignorance of the daily lives of all the people who inhabit Geylang, especially the sex workers who are embedded in a network of mutual support and exploitation in order to earn their living (Ng 2010). They do not need the filmmaker to try to erase the humiliation of sex work to recover their humanity.

Beyond Liberal Humanism

The red-light district of Singapore, Geylang, has been used by artists, filmmakers and other intellectuals as a foil for the social and political critique of the economically successful single-party-dominated city-state, under an illiberal government that continues to restrict many of its citizens' liberal rights, including rights to public assembly. The relatively chaotic street scenes of double-parked cars on the street, pedestrians (including sex workers and men, mostly from the lower end of the social strata) thronging the sidewalks or idling collectively in local coffee shops, with the sex trade and other illegal activities ubiquitously taking place in the side roads and laneways, render Geylang as a space of freedom in contrast to the generally well-disciplined street scenes in the rest of the island. This relative freedom becomes a point of contrast, thus creating a discursive space for simultaneous celebration and critique of the socially and culturally conservative and politically quiescent middle-class individuals and their lives in the rest of Singapore. In addition, the sex workers emerge as figures to elicit our sympathy, as they become the main protagonists in aesthetic projects of visual and performance art. The aestheticisation process tends to suppress, if not deny, the reality of sex work and how it differs from other means of earning a living, by ostensibly recovering the humanity of the sex workers, as if their humanity were ever in doubt. This move to normalise sex work ironically exposes the bourgeois sentimental humanism of the artists themselves.

Apart from the shallowness of the artists' commitment, what is even more insidious in this liberal humanism is the need to constantly reproduce its object for sympathy. The politics of pathos in liberal humanism quickly reaches its critical limit because, with very few exceptions, those who labour in the low-end sex trade, including the pimps who live off the prostitutes' labour, are all reluctant participants in the business. These individuals could do without the 'chaos' and the 'fun' and the nightly display they put on as icons of libertine pleasure and immediate gratification to the voyeurs, whether they are intellectuals, artists, or tourists. These workers' unarticulated critique of society lies elsewhere in the capitalist economy that makes sex work necessary and that makes sex workers out of them. Yet, in these days of post-real-socialism in which ideological liberalism is hegemonic, and in the cornucopia of capitalist consumerism that seems to satisfy the desires of all, few will speak out for those who aim to make sex work unnecessary; namely, the volunteers and paid staff of non-governmental agencies who investigate and bring to trial those who traffick people into the sex trade.

Notes

1. The ability of the state to provide affordable housing for the entire population is a cornerstone of the PAP's ability to generate popular political support. For a political analysis of Singapore from the perspective of ideological hegemony, see Chua (1995).
2. This film generated much controversy in the Australian Cultural Studies community. See Berry et al. (1997).
3. All quotes are from her website: http://joankelly.blogspot.com/2009/01/beginning-shikahdas.html, accessed 2 February 2011.
4. She 'visited the "containers", the living quarters of the Bangladesh construction workers, 5 rooms, 25 men, no kitchen, no laundry and 1 bathroom'.
5. Among the other Singapore films that have received similar honours are 12 Storeys (1997) and Sandcastle (2010).
6. See: www.nytimes.com/2007/05/25/arts/25hit-singfest.1.5863686.html?_r=2, accessed 2 February 2011.
7. See: www.zhaowei.com/mpmrev.htm, accessed 10 February 2011.
8. See: http://www.youtube.com/watch?v=T463nFtg3tg, accessed 10 February 2011.
9. All grammatical errors are in the original.

References

Berry, Chris, Annette Hamilton and Laleen Jayamanne. *The Filmmaker and the Prostitute: Dennis O'Rouke's The Good Woman of Bangkok*. Sydney: Power Institute of Australia, 1997.

Chan Heng Chee. 'Politics in an Administrative State: Where has All the Politics Gone?' In *Trends in Singapore*, edited by Seah Chee Meow. Singapore: Singapore University Press, 1997.

Chua, Beng Huat. *Communitarian Ideology and Democracy in Singapore*. London: Routledge, 1995.

—. *Political Legitimacy and Housing: Stakeholding in Singapore*. London: Routledge, 1997.

Chua, Beng Huat and Yeo Wei Wei. 'Singapore Cinema: Eric Khoo and Jack Neo: Critique from the Margins and the Mainstream.' *Inter-Asia Cultural Studies* 4, no. 1 (2003): 117-25.

Gramsci, Antonio. *Selections from Prison Notebooks*. Edited and translated by Quintin Hoare and G.N. Smith. London: Lawrence and Wishart, 1971.

Hubbard, Phil and Teela Sanders. 'Making Space for Sex Work: Female Street Prostitution and the Production of Urban Space.' *International Journal of Urban and Regional Research* 27, no. 1 (2003): 75-89.

Khoo, Olivia. 'Slang Images: On the Foreignness of Contemporary Singaporean Films.' *Inter-Asia Cultural Studies* 7, no.1 (2006): 81-98.

Liebow, Elliot. *Tally's Corner: A Study of Negro Streetcorner Men*. Boston: Little Brown (1967).

Ng, Hui Hsien. *Moral Order Underground: An Ethnography of Geylang*, unpublished MA thesis, Department of Sociology, National University of Singapore, 2010.

Purushotam, Nirmala. 'Between Compliance and Resistance: Women and the Middle-Class Way of Life in Singapore.' In *Gender and Power in Affluent*

Asia, edited by Krishna Sen and Maila Stevens. London: Routledge, 1998: 127-66.

White, William Foote. *Street Corner Society: The Social Structure of an Italian Slum*. Chicago: University of Chicago Press, 1993.

Wong, Aline and Stephen H. K. Yeh, eds. *Housing a Nation: 25 Years of Public Housing in Singapore*. Singapore: Housing and Development Board, 1985.

3. Coming of Age in RMB City

Robin Visser

From the start of the book, where Li Guangtou spies on Lin Hong's buttocks, to his real father's death by drowning after also spying on women in the public toilet, to the ferocity of Li Guangtou's sexual desire and his early maturity, to his virgin beauty contest, his promiscuity, his vasectomy, the peddling of hymens, the obscenity of the cigarette-smoking factory manager, to Song Gang selling virility pills and breast-enhancement cream, to the blacksmith Tong visiting prostitutes, all the tales of the cripples, idiots, mutes and blind people at the social welfare workshop – all this is disguised as an ironic exposé of reality, but in fact it is only an enticement of the grossest kind. The book simply panders to the tastes of the lower type of reader for spectacle and voyeurism.
– Cang Lang, *Pulling Yu Hua's Teeth*

The spectacle is capital accumulated to the point that it becomes images.
– Guy Debord, *The Society of the Spectacle*

The 'Integrated Spectacle'

As Cang Lang's fury mounts, he creates a spectacle. Readers cannot but be entertained by the critic's breathless litany of the titillating events he lambasts in Yu Hua's bestselling novel, *Brothers* (兄弟, 2005a: 2005b). Funnier still is his frustrated attempt to extricate himself from the voyeuristic practices of spectacular society. As Guy Debord remarked in 1988, reflecting back on his 1967 opus, *The Society of the Spectacle*, 'That modern society is a society of spectacle now goes without saying [...] What is so droll, however, is that all the books which do analyze this phenomenon, usually to deplore it, must sacrifice themselves to the spectacle if they're to become known' (Debord 1998: 5).

In *The Society of the Spectacle* Debord analysed the transformation of societies organised around production into those organised by the late capitalist consumption of 'an immense accumulation of spectacles'. 'Spectacle' for Debord was a complex term that referred to a media society organised around the consumption of images, commodities, and staged events and to the vast institutional and technical apparatus that relegates subjects to passivity. Debord's basic claim is that what we *see* in the world – how the world is architected – is a reflection of triumphant ideologies (Gilman-Opalsky 2010: 120). Society as spectacle is the material realisation of a particular ideology, 'a weltanschauung that has been actualised' (Debord 1994: 12-13). Spectacle is the discursive content of the appearance of capitalist society; it does not control its subjects by force but through manipulating the consensus of collective desire. Surface appearances effectively control people, in Debord's account, because they render the rational techniques that manufactured them invisible, and what remains is the desire to possess the signifier of the sign.

Debord's understanding of media was influenced by Marxist notions of capital, whereby labour mediates between a worker's body and nature until its expropriation and reification into a commodity turns capital into the agent of mediation, with ideology consolidating the capitalist's power. He rejected the Marxist theory that capitalism inevitably destabilises itself, instead arguing that the technology that emerged after World War II enabled new mechanisms of control that could guard capitalism from any internal or external crisis that might give rise to revolution. Debord's 'situation', then, accepts a Gramscian paradigm of hegemony where mediation involves dynamic engagement with forces of capital. Capital in this sense is neither absolute nor antihuman, because its hold must be continuously rearticulated by social actors.

In this paper I consider Cang Lang's dilemma, namely, the possibility of critiquing the spectacle without simply reproducing or being subsumed by it. Central to Debord's original understanding of the spectacle is the idea that the spectator passively consumes discursive images without understanding their coercive constitution. His manifesto called for Situationist tactics of *détournement*, urban practices aimed at disrupting the spectacle in order to liberate subjectivity from the hegemony of advanced capital. Debord never precisely defined *détournement*, which literally means 'a turning away', but described it as 'the fluid language of anti-ideology' which 'mobilises an action capable of disturbing or overthrowing any existing order' (1994: 146). The term *détournement* has since been applied to international social movements against global capitalism and neo-liberalism, such as the 1989 uprisings in Venezuela against the International Monetary Fund and the widespread demonstrations throughout China in 1989.

Such 'disruptions' were quickly contained by media representations, underscoring the significance of one of Debord's central theses in 1967 (42): 'The spectacle is the moment when the commodity has attained the total occupation of social life. The relation to the commodity is not only visible, but one no longer sees anything but it: the world one sees is its world'. Because Debord's early theory of the spectacle assumed the priority of the visual and mind-body duality of Cartesian epistemology, Situationist *détournement* through corporal interventions in urban space could be understood to critique the spectacle. By 1988, however, Debord's discourse on the hegemony of the spectacle no longer privileged the ocular and the discursive; instead, 'the empty debate on the spectacle – that is, on the activities of the world's owners – is thus organised by the spectacle *itself*' (Debord 1998: 6).

It is in this sense that Debord theorised the later stage of the spectacle as the 'integrated spectacle', a new form of capitalist hegemony reinforced by technoculture such that the very conditions for creating meaning may already be prescribed and contained by it. Debord's central thesis in *Comments on the Society of the Spectacle* (1988) is that earlier forms of 'diffuse' spectacular power (American commodity capitalism) and 'concentrated' spectacular power (German fascism, Soviet Stalinism, Chinese Maoism) have been displaced by the 'integrated spectacle' (pioneered by Italy and France in the 1970s), which 'is established through the rational combination of these two, and on the basis of a victory of the form which had showed itself stronger: the diffuse' (Debord 1998: 6). The increasingly global 'integrated spectacle' expands the diffuse form (commodification of culture) while intensifying the falsification and secrecy of the concentrated form (which characterised authoritarian regimes). Jodi Dean has theorised the convergence of media culture with technologies of control in the digital age along similar lines to Debord, characterising techno-culture as an ideological formation that uses the rhetoric of democracy, creativity, access, and interconnection to produce subjectivities of communicative capitalism (Dean 2002: 103).

Anne-Marie Broudehoux also follows Debord in characterising Olympics Beijing as dominated by the 'integrated spectacular', although her hyperbole, ironically, reinforces spectacle by masking more subtle and global workings of power in urban China, and the fact that the integrated spectacular manifests in other political formations (2009: 52-62). Indeed, if we follow Debord's formulation, then the victory of the integrated spectacle results in the eradication of historical knowledge such that 'contemporary events themselves retreat into a remote and fabulous realm of unverifiable stories, uncheckable statistics, unlikely explanations and untenable reasoning' (Debord 1998).

Debord's late-20th-century analysis of media society suggests that agency (to alter the 'activities of the world's owners') is no longer possible; means are indistinguishable from ends as communication, culture, the state, and technology are deployed ideologically in the service of capital (Debord 1994: 150). Although Debord's later position rejects a Cartesian episteme of space, media critics such as Mark Hansen contend that digital media not only produces a radically new spatial regime, but that direct engagement of humans in artifice, unmediated by representation, radically enhances agency. Yomi Braester (in this volume), extrapolating upon Hansen's view that new media results 'from the displacement of visual (perceptually apprehensible) space in favour of a haptic space that is both internal to and produced by the viewer's affective body' (2004: 15), locates the critical potential of the virtual artwork *RMB City* in its aesthetic liminality: it immerses the subject *corporeally* in the virtual environment while replicating familiar *visual* landmarks.

According to these scholars, a more fully embodied, dynamic experience of the world, interactively mediated via olfactory, tactile, kinesthetic, and aural senses, fundamentally alters representational notions of art based upon verbal/visual experience and subject/object positions. Jeroen de Kloet, in his chapter in this volume, reminds us that it is increasingly ineffective to locate criticality in the text, or object, given that 'images are not so much representations as they are *things* that travel and circulate globally'. Yet the idea of images as things that circulate may reinforce Debord's position rather than challenge it. Surprisingly, Scott Lash and Celia Lury's formulation of culture, cited by de Kloet, has echoes of Debord's integrated spectacle: 'in our emergent age of global culture industry, where culture starts to dominate both the economy and the everyday, culture, which was previously a question of representation, becomes thingified' (Buck-Morss 2007: 4). If post-human digital media culture, where art is no longer mediated through representation, directly engages the body in artifice, then the human body, rather than labour, is also 'thingified'. Labour, as a commodity, is increasingly irrelevant. That is, it no longer mediates between the human body and nature in a Marxist sense; after all, 'mediation by representation is quite other to the mediation of things' (Lash and Lury 2007: 8).

In this chapter, I examine the question of whether it is possible, under conditions of 'new media' where mediation itself is problematised, to critique the spectacle through *détournement*. Lash and Lury, of course, refer to 'mediation' in its sense as power, agency, and instrumentality. Yet is it possible to create new meanings, or critiques, under conditions of cognitive capitalism, where immaterial assets such as ideas, social relations and affects constitute the core of participatory platforms in a digital age? What aesthetic techniques render visible rational techniques of capital accumulation masked by spectacle? Is visibility a necessary condition for disruption of hegemony, or does it further reinforce the hold of capital via an illusion of transparency and choice? I will suggest possible answers by analysing two examples from contemporary Chinese media culture.

The novel, *Brothers* (2005) and the virtual artwork, *RMB City* (launched in 2008) are interesting cases in that their promotion, reception, and critique are constitutive of spectacular society while the 'meaning' generated from the works themselves can, arguably, be interpreted as disrupting the spectacle. Unlike urban novels such as *Shanghai Baby* (上海宝贝, 1999), which was not only promoted and globally circulated as spectacle but also constitutes spectacle textually through humourless self-referentiality and seamless self-exoticisation, Yu Hua's narrative self-consciously manipulates the reader's voyeuristic desire in ways that call attention to the conditions of its constitution. Readers find themselves propelled forward by instinctual, conditioned responses to graphic descriptions of sexuality and violence strategically mitigated by moments of comic relief. The narrative patterns reader desires such that, not unlike surfing the Web, distinctions between thought, visualisation, and sensation become obfuscated. The narrative construction inhibits conscious reflection while reading; only later, when the reader is plagued by a vague sense of unease, does she suspect she may be complicit in the spectacle. This uneasiness is reinforced when the text occasionally frustrates readers' expectations. The best-selling novel materialises the moral of its own story, namely, the superior rationality of accumulating capital by circulating desire-inducing images rather than creating an *objet d'art*.

As a second case I consider Cao Fei's *RMB City*, an urban planning project launched in the participatory virtual platform, *Second Life*, which challenges its users to 'transform the cityscape'. In question here is how manipulations of the cityscape in 'second' life might alter 'first' life manifestations. Debates over how cyberspace fosters or constrains agency have given rise to the field of presence studies, which theorises dynamics between 'virtual' and 'material' worlds. Debord's notion of the integrated spectacle is germane to presence theory in that it does not foreclose possibilities for *détournement* in cyberspace, yet suggests that the alternative possibilities enabled by haptic experience remain subject to the spectacle. In a sense not dissimilar to *Brothers*, criticality in *RMB City* emerges by moving liminally between a representational aesthetics based in a Cartesian spatial paradigm and the space of flows within which the images of global digital media culture circulate.

Brothers: Coming of Age through the Gaze

Spanning the Cultural Revolution to the mid-2000s, the hyperbolic *jouissance* exhibited by the once traumatised protagonist of *Brothers* reveals a pervasive cultural logic informing contemporary Chinese urbanism. The collective protagonist is identified in the novel's opening line as 'we, the people of Liu Town', residents whose small-town values are transformed along with the rags-to-riches *bildungsroman* of the town's premier tycoon, Baldy Li. The two-part structure of the novel implies that the irrational exuberance fuelling the extreme makeover of Liu Town (Part II), a metaphor for China's frenetic post-socialist urban development, is compensatory for the collective trauma and deprivation suffered during the Cultural Revolution (Part I). Rife with violent spectacles made all the more horrifying by the hilarity of their 'packaging', *Brothers* is a sadly compelling epic of Chinese subject formation from Mao to the Millennium (Yu 2005). No mere national allegory, however, the novel manifests the dissimilation of power that constitutes media.

The narrative of *Brothers* is set in motion in Part I by 'a peep that sells'. After fourteen-year-old Baldy Li 'snared five butts with a single glance' by peeking at women under the partition of the public latrine, he deftly parlays aesthetic pleasure into bowls of 'House Special noodles' by fetishising the 'just-right butt' of Liu Town beauty, Lin Hong, through storytelling. In this early stage of the spectacle Baldy Li capitalises on his audience's assumption that media (here, verbal descriptions of images) represent reality. Although they were willing to pay for the images, they nonetheless insisted on evaluating the 'signifier' relative to the 'signified': 'when Baldy Li described the shape of Lin Hong's buttocks, his audience listened rapt with attention, their mouths hanging open, not even aware that they were drooling. But when he finished, they would look thoughtful and say, "It sounds a bit off"'. (19). By the time postmodern simulacra dominate Liu Town, however, commodity fetishisation has clearly advanced to the point that critical distance collapses altogether. Part I of the novel opens with the narrator, from his 21st-century vantage point, exuding ironic nostalgia for the high modernist aesthetics of the Cultural Revolution in contrast to the integrated spectacle of global media:

> Nowadays the world is filled with women's bare butts shaking hither and thither, on television and in the movies, on VCRs and DVDs, in advertisements and magazines, on the sides of ballpoint pens and cigarette lighters [...]

> It used to be that women's bottoms were considered a rare and precious commodity that you couldn't trade for gold or silver or pearls. To see one, you had to go peeping in the public toilet – which is why you had a little hoodlum like Baldy Li being caught in the act, and a big hoodlum like his father losing his life for the sake of a glimpse. (4)

Baudrillard's description of the successive phases of the image unfolds in a mere 40 years in Yu Hua's narrative, from Baldy Li's father, who would 'lose his life for the sake of a glimpse' (the image 'signifies reality'), to the son who barters his story-telling of a glimpse (the image 'dissimulates reality'), to the ubiquitous appearance of the once-taboo object of desire (the image 'bears no relationship to reality'). We recall that Baudrillard considers this precession of simulacra to be a fatal process in that 'there is a definite immanence of the image, without any possible transcendent meaning, without any possible dialectic of history [...] an exponential unfolding of the media around itself' (Baudrillard 1987: 29-30). Yu Hua, like Baudrillard, parodies the supposed superiority of earlier representational forms of the image, rejecting Baldy Li's nostalgia for an age when human mediation (the act of gazing) ostensibly allowed the spectator to experience 'the Real'. The meta-narrative of *Brothers* reveals, instead, how the absent object of desire is manipulated by mediation itself, whether high modernist (Part I) or postmodern (Part II), in order to accumulate capital. Further, the narrative implies that the spectacle, regardless of its aesthetic form, necessarily conceals the violent power relations upon which it is constituted.

Part I suggests that the illusion of representational aesthetics is concealed by appealing to the 'Real', or, as is particularly germane to Chinese epistemologies, by accurate representations of History. This lengthy quote, which takes place after Baldy Li is caught in the act of peeping, suggests that while the spectacle is interactive, that is, under negotiation by multiple social agents, its meaning remains constrained, and preconditioned, by abstracted forms of power:

> Liu Town's two Men of Talent flanked Baldy Li, proclaiming they were just taking him to the police station. There was actually a police station just around the corner, but they didn't want to take him there; instead they marched him to one much further away. On their way, they paraded down the main streets, trying to maximise their moment of glory. As they escorted Baldy Li down the streets they remarked enviously, 'Just look at you, with two important men like us escorting you. You really are a lucky guy'.
>
> Poet Zhao added, 'It's as if you were being escorted by Li Bai and Du Fu [...]'.
>
> It seemed to Writer Liu that Poet Zhao's analogy was not quite apt, since Li Bai and Du Fu were, of course, both poets, while Liu himself wrote fiction. So he corrected Zhao, saying, 'It's as if Li Bai and Cao Xueqin were escorting you [...]'.

Baldy Li had initially ignored their banter, but when he heard Liu Town's two Men of Talent compare themselves to Li Bai and Cao Xueqin, he couldn't help but laugh. 'Hey, even I know that Li Bai was from the Tang dynasty while Cao was from the Qing dynasty. How can a Tang guy be hanging out with a Qing guy?'

The crowds that had gathered alongside the streets burst into loud guffaws. They said that Baldy Li was absolutely correct, that Liu Town's two Men of Talent might indeed be full of talent, but their knowledge of history wasn't even a match for this little Peeping Tom. The two Men of Talent blushed furiously, and Poet Zhao, straightening out his neck, added, 'It's just an analogy'. (7)

Historical knowledge, in this passage, informs society's 'realistic staging' of a contemporary spectacle. Performance, of course, is a constitutive component of the oral story-telling that formed the origins of Chinese narrative fiction, and antecedents of the folk tradition continued to inform aesthetic norms under Maoism (Idema 1974). Such long-standing traditions of interactivity of spectators with performance media suggests that spectacle may negotiate its discursive formations with consumers in ways quite other than passive onlookers at a Platonic remove from a mediated 'truth'. Theories of media that ignore the haptic fail to recognise, in particular, that 'people both become and come-to-be situated as participants within articulatory spaces when they encounter or embody any media conceptually and/or material imbued or manifested by an icon's or iconic event's affective presence' (Reynolds 2009: 24). Human subjectivity is formed, in part, through mediated associations with icons.

The question that arises from this textual example is whether the hegemony of media (here, culturally dominant stories of historical literary figures) fosters a consensus of collective desire that precludes alternative formations of meaning. The 'appropriate' affective presence to be enjoyed by the spectacle is preconditioned by media, yet its negotiated articulation by spectators disrupts subject-object relationships. Baldy Li's agency in Part I, along with Yu Hua's, is facilitated by manipulating collective desires for an aesthetics that lays claim to accurate historical representations. By rearticulating the discursive formation of his performance to co-opt cultural perceptions of the Real already formed by media, Baldy Li is no longer the object of the spectacle but its subject, and the Two Men of Talent blush furiously. Part I of *Brothers* underscores the fact that the entertainment value of spectacle governed by high modernist aesthetics is enhanced through interactive processes evoking the affective presence of historically iconic figures.

With the precession of simulacra under postmodern aesthetics, historical and representational distance collapses, and celebrity culture takes priority. In Part II the spectacle is constituted via mediated associations with contemporary icons such as Baldy Li. Liu Town's theatrics culminate by orchestrating a frenzy of hymen reconstruction surgeries prior to hosting a national virgin beauty contest in which the grand prize is sleeping with the town tycoon/buffoon. As Lash and Lury point out, 'icons need not be attached to objects at all [...] brands, working through the intensities of their iconography, are one way in which contemporary power works' (2007: 15). Thus Yu Hua parodies the proliferation of simulacra in a scene where itinerant scam artist, Wandering Zhou, hawks domestic Lady Meng Jiang artificial hymens and imported Joan of Arc artificial hymens in Liu Town prior to its First Inaugural Virgin Beauty Contest:

> Because Poet Zhao wasn't married, Wandering Zhou called out to Song Gang, 'Song Gang, what brand of artificial hymen did your wife use last night?'
>
> 'An imported Joan of Arc one, of course,' Poet Zhao replied on Song Gang's behalf.
>
> Wandering Zhou asked Song Gang again, 'Last night when you made love, how did your wife feel?'
>
> Again it was Poet Zhao who replied, 'She cried out in agony!'
>
> Wandering Zhou nodded with satisfaction, then asked, 'How did you feel?'
>
> Again, it was Poet Zhao who replied, 'Broke out in a cold sweat'.
>
> This response, however, displeased Wandering Zhou. He frowned and said, 'It should have been warm sweat from all that happy exertion'.
>
> Poet Zhao immediately corrected himself, 'First it was a cold sweat and then – *a-one, a-two, a-three* – three seconds later, it turned into warm sweat!' (504)

Yu Hua's farcical narrative is an all-too-transparent spoofing of the endless circulation of self-referential signs theorised by Baudrillard: 'When the real is no longer what it used to be, nostalgia assumes its full meaning. There is a proliferation of myths of origin and signs of reality, of second-hand truth, objectivity, and authenticity' (Reynolds 2009, 11). Liu Town's (Baldy Li's) frenetic pursuit of sexual union with a 'virgin' is mediated via Poet Zhao's second-hand authentication of Song Gang's simulated sexual experience with the long-fetishised town beauty, Lin Hong. The spectacular completely circumscribes experience, which occurs by proxy. In this sense, Yu Hua narrates the cultural turn characterised by Baudrillard as 'the transition from signs which dissimulate something to signs which dissimulate that there is nothing' (Baudrillard 1983: 10-11). The illusion of critical distance grounded in the Real collapses as historical quotation replaces historical depth.

Although Lin Hong is never directly mentioned in the above passage, her affective presence, initially mediated through Baldy Li's (and Yu Hua's) storytelling, continues to produce collective desire (in Liu Town; in readers) and capital (for Baldy Li; for Yu Hua). Not only does Poet Zhao utterly divest authentic experience, namely that of Lin Hong's husband, Song Gang, of all agency, but his second-hand account of simulated ejaculation through an artificial hymen generates far more capital than a bowl of House Special noodles (the townspeople clandestinely purchase the artificial hymens by night). More revealing still is that fact that although the character of Lin Hong is clearly meant to function as an empty signifier of the absent object of desire in the story, her sudden moral demise (she ends up running a brothel in Liu Town) provoked a palpable sense of outrage among Chinese literary critics and readers. Cang Lang speaks for many when he lambasts Yu Hua for refusing to perpetuate the deception of the virginally pure Lin Hong, and by extension, a modernist aesthetics of the sublime:

> Perhaps we can forgive the intimacy between Li Guangtou and Lin Hong, the beautiful personification of the spirit, but why does Yu Hua turn her into a prostitute? Where is the immortality of her soul?
> [...]
> Art itself may be a lie, not truth, but it should bring us closer to truth. Literature reveals the emotions of people, but at the same time should improve the emotions of people. Without the support of faith, mankind can never attain eternity, and a writer can only sink into a world of filth, chaos, stench and blackness, without the slightest scrap of dignity.
> Cang Lang (2009: online)

What I am suggesting here, in contradiction to Cang Lang, is that what Yu Hua conveys as corrupt is not so much a specific representation but representation itself. In other words, to quote Lyotard, he 'puts forward the unpresentable in presentation itself; that which denies itself the solace of good forms' (1984: 81).

Yu Hua's decision to corrupt Lin Hong, apparently without narrative cause, that is, in violation of mimetic necessity, foregrounds the constructed nature of an aesthetics generated via the absent object of desire. Xiaobin Yang argues convincingly that Yu Hua's ironic historical narrative is generated by lack, namely, through attempts to attain the barred subject, or *object petit a* (2009). Informed by Žižek's Lacanian analysis of postmodernity, Yang argues that the entire novel, set in motion through voyeuristic gazing at women's behinds, is constructed by an attempt to fill the void in a Symbolic order constructed by desire. This explains the narrative's progression to a point, but fails to account for its framing, namely, Lin Hong's abrupt demise and the novel's uncanny conclusion (its opening line), which describes the tycoon Baldy Li contemplating a trip on a Russian spacecraft: 'Perched atop his famously gold-plated toilet seat, he would close his eyes and imagine himself already floating in orbit, surrounded by the unfathomably frigid depths of space. He would look down at the glorious planet stretched out beneath him, only to choke up on realising that he had no family left down on Earth' (1). The postmodern waning of affect is uncharacteristically subverted by narrative tropes such as Baldy Li's (Liu Town's) brief yet haunting acknowledgement that 'authentic experience' (embodied by Song Gang) and 'aesthetic sublimation' (embodied by Lin Hong) are no longer. These can be considered narrative instances of *détournement* in that Lin Hong's uncharacteristic acquiescence and abrupt degeneration, Song Gang's bizarre emasculation and tragic suicide, and Baldy Li's momentary desolation constitute what Debord called 'the antithesis of quotation', calling into question ideologies, such as the Real, that circulate as common sense (1994: 145-146).

These narrative disruptions invite the critical work of re-contextualising and re-historicising the implicit social, cultural, political, and economic vectors of valorised cultural narratives to better understand what makes them appear to be meaningful and true (Murray 2009). Song Gang's emasculation and graphic suicide is so peculiar it calls attention to the cultural assumptions valorising the violent ethics of the 'successful man' (成功人士) represented by his ruthlessly utilitarian stepbrother, Baldy Li. Similarly, Lin Hong's utter submission to Baldy Li (she succumbs in ecstasy after he brutally rapes her for hours on end) is so exaggerated it underscores the powerfully emergent sexist discourse of domination by China's new elite male. If interpreted along these lines, Yu Hua's narrative aesthetics suggest that spectacle is not merely an artefact of capital but a site of contestation via media manipulations. The desolate aesthetics of the novel haunt the reader even more because she is vaguely discomfited by her complicity in them. Why did she laugh immediately after passages of horrendous abuse, and why did she keep on reading? Should she blame or thank Yu Hua for desensitising her to the violence of representation by entertaining her? To be exposed as unwitting voyeurs, not in culturally sanctioned spaces for passively consuming visual images, but rather by actively producing them through our imaginations, is unsettling at best.

RMB City: Liberating Possibilities for Domination

If works such as *Brothers* disrupt the spectacle by revealing the mechanisms by which media images manipulate and indulge desire, do they do so only to reinforce these mechanisms? How might a viewer's awareness of her complicity in spectacle liberate her from it? Even if one establishes that control of capital generated via mediascapes is continually negotiated, how does that foster actions that do not reproduce the violence of representation? In *Brothers*, for example, Baldy Li colludes with the county government to destroy and rebuild the town in ways that materialise a profit-maximising ideology. The townspeople remark that Badly Li 'was like a B-52 bomber, carpet-bombing the formerly beautiful town' (429) and replacing it with high-rise apartments, department stores, and wide concrete roads. They add 'There is a saying that *rabbits will spare the grass growing next to their burrow*. But Baldy Li was really rotten to the core and had chomped down on every last blade of grass around his home, given that all of his profit was extracted directly from his fellow townspeople' (429). In fact, Baldy Li goes so far as to isolate every commodity market in the Town, providing 'those of us in Liu Town with everything, from what we ate to what we wore, from where we lived to what we used, and from birth to death' (430).

If *Brothers* challenges the ideological formations of the spectacle that manifest themselves in urbanising China, it also underscores its hegemony. As I argue elsewhere, turn-of-the-21st-century urban art in China was dominated by hegemonic images with both fanciful and historical referents, yet the increased *presence* (to borrow Saskia Sassen's term) of artists, activists, migrants and other subalterns has also altered the city's image and enhanced political agency (Visser 2010: 67-76; Sassen 2003: 25). Similarly, researchers in presence studies, a field that studies the science, technology, and social impact of digitally mediated interactions, contend that liberating possibilities for subjectivity and agency are enabled by virtual experience.

To better understand how the haptic experience of virtual reality might enable criticality, I examine *RMB City*, a *Second Life* city planning project undertaken by Chinese artist Cao Fei's online avatar, China Tracy. *Second Life* is a virtual world launched in 2003 by the U.S.-based company Linden Lab that enables its users (through avatars) to socialise, create and trade virtual property and services with each other, and to travel through the world. First presented at the 10th Istanbul Biennale in 2007 and shortlisted for the Solomon R. Guggenheim Foundation Hugo Boss Prize Award in 2010, Cao Fei describes her project as a 'condensed incarnation of contemporary Chinese cities with most of their characteristics; new Chinese fantasy realms that are highly self-contradictory, inter-permeative, pan-political, extremely entertaining, and laden with irony and suspicion'. She populated her *Second Life* property with iconic images from Chinese cities, and invited participants into her open-ended project 'to create a rich program of projects and events that will, in the process, transform the cityscape' (Cao 2008a).

Can presence in the virtual city actually transform cityscapes, as Cao Fei's utopian project imagined? What happens, one wonders, if we start manipulating cultural/city icons in virtual space? How does it feel to 'throw' the government's slogan, 'Harmonious Society', into the sea, or to set Rem Koolhaas' CCTV building on fire? Does designing a rusting Olympic Bird's Nest affect our experience of the city? Do we start acting differently? Does the city change as a result? In a 2007 interview between Jiang Jun, editor of *Urban China* (城市中国), and Hu Fang, the artistic director of Cao Fei's studio, Vitamin Creative Space, the consensus was rather pessimistic. Jiang Jun conceded that:

> although art is exploring reality, the latter often surpasses the former in unbelievable ways in terms of speed, quality and weight [...] Multiple forms of 'self-mimicking' are made possible by information technology, but in the future artists must be experts in certain aspects of real life (from politicians to hackers) in order to create art in a more profound way. (Cao 2008b)

What Jiang Jun finds most interesting about the social spaces in China presented by *RMB City* is 'how a reality controlled by powerful order and state apparatus managed to produce a kind of hyper-reality which seemingly loses control, and the way in which virtual reality simulates reality on a more profound level' (Cao 2008b). Hu Fang, in turn, insisted that *RMB City* (RMB stands for *renminbi*, which means 'people's money') goes beyond simulating reality to mediating fundamentally new ways in which capital circulates and people socialise: 'social networking itself becomes a new form of capital accumulation' (Cao 2008b).

Despite the liberating promises of participatory entrepreneurship, capital ac-

3.1. Cao Fei, *RMB City* (still from *Second Life*). Courtesy: RMB City 2012

cumulation in *Second Life* is subject to the same logic of First Life; namely, the necessity of venture capital. Cao Fei had to secure a financial backer in Uli Sigg in order to contract Avatrian, a Philippines- and San Francisco-based company specialising in Second Life content design, to build most of *RMB City*. She then needed connections to promote it. As Brian Droitcour, a journalist for *Art Forum International* who was 'present' as an avatar for the Grand Opening of *RMB City* in January of 2009, states: 'It's hard to think of a single work – let alone a work in progress – that got more play in 2008 than *RMB City*' (Droitcour 2009). In fact, however, the hyped interactivity of *RMB City* is an illusion. It took turns on display in (physical) exhibition spaces around the world in 2008, and an animated tour was available on Cao Fei's YouTube channel, but users could only access the inner city during the Grand Opening in 2009 and are again largely confined to its outer limits. Cao Fei has, however, parlayed virtual transactions into real world ones by offering development opportunities in *RMB City*. These are offered at rates analogous to those in Beijing, but translated into the fractional currency of Linden Dollars. At Art Basel, she sold a building unit in *RMB City*, taking her exploration of the impact of the virtual upon the real, and then linking it to very real references to real estate.[1] More recently she has used advertising space in *RMB City* to raise money, which she donated toward the rebuilding of New Orleans.

Cybertheorists such as Sherry Turkle or Jeffrey Schnapp celebrate participatory platforms as breaking with previous forms of media culture that constrain agency.[2] Mark Hansen insists on the radically new spatial regime of new digital media due to its constitution in haptic space 'that is both internal to and pro-

3.2. UliSigg Cisse (SL avatar of Uli Sigg, 'First Mayor of RMB City') inaugurates AlanLau Nirvana (SL avatar of Alan Lau) as 'Second Mayor of RMB City,' with China Tracey (Cao Fei's SL avatar) in the background. Courtesy: RMB City 2012

duced by the viewer's affective body' (2004: 15). Lori Landay insists 'we have a high degree of agency in *Second Life*; we can build things *out of nothing* [italics added], shape ourselves and our environment how we wish, and our choices are almost limitless' (2009: 21). Rather than understanding digital media culture as a radically different form of image-making, I have argued that, to the contrary, spectacle has always been constituted by audience participation. The question is to what extent new meanings can be formulated as global power increasingly constellates around capitalism. While de Kloet (in this volume) cites Buck-Morss, who argues that unprecedented access to images 'guarantee[s] the *democratic* potential of image production and distribution' (Buck-Morss 2004: 2), I would argue that the social conditioning of meanings associated with such images already restricts the possibility of fully liberating oneself from more abstract power formations. Participatory platforms such as *Second Life*, for example, are not simply about facilitating regimes of meaning production and circulation, but also about extracting value out of meaning.

Ganaele Langlois points out that 'while the characteristic common to all participatory platforms is to invite everybody to express themselves, the management and channelling of the communicative data produced by and for users is specific to the given context and goal of a platform' (2011: 23). As participatory platforms increasingly restrict user choices via interface technologies, generating alternative meanings, or critique, is increasingly difficult:

> It is much easier to click a 'share' button on a social network platform than it is to embed a hyperlink on an HTML page; however, HTML gave much more freedom to users to design and customise their Web pages [...] Semio-technologies serve not only to organise perceptions of the communication process and its possibilities, but also to ensure that there is no disruption to the constant production and circulation of meaning. (Langlois 2011: 23)

3.3. Avatars party in *RMB City* during rare access to its inner city (January 2009). Courtesy: RMB City 2012.

While one is able, for example, to design one's avatar in *Second Life* from a dazzling array of body-type choices that allow for double chins, single or double eyelids, flabby arms, beer bellies, and the like, in actuality one sees very few avatars that fail to conform in some way to media images of sexuality or beauty. Does awareness of choice in fact reinforce the consensus of desire all the more? Of greater concern, perhaps, is that while Linden Lab aggressively advertises a unique policy for allowing participants to own the intellectual property rights to the 'inworld' content that they create, a recent class action lawsuit contends that Linden Lab 'lured consumers [...] to invest real money into (*Second Life*) by [deceptively] promising those users that they would own the virtual land and property they purchased as well as the content they created' (McCarthy 2010: online).

Michael Ian Borer cautions theorists of cyberspace who reify and valorise it as a liberating alternative space, by invoking Guy Debord's claim that 'wherever representation takes on an independent existence, the spectacle re-establishes its rule' (cited in Borer 2002: online). Institutional structures of surveillance may have dissipated within the fragmentary space of the Internet, yet cyberspace has become increasingly panoptic for the sake of consumerism. What is peculiar about this phenomenon is the explicit complicity it requires of the subject, because for the surveillance to properly function it requires 'an element of participation on the part of the subject' (Cambell and Carlson 2002: 591). Thus while digital humanities manifestos celebrate the liberating power of play, business technology manifestos celebrate the seductive power of play. To cite but one example, this business model explicitly utilises panoptic technologies to extract information by 'letting customers play':

3.4. This still from *RMB City* Grand Opening (January 2009) evokes an uncanny sense of 'harmonized violence' (or 和谐下的暴力). Courtesy: RMB City 2012

> In the end, our model is a call for using the power of panoptic technologies for developing creative forms of multilayered customer relationships from which both the organisation and the customer benefit. The informational panopticon, in some sense, has to dissolve into a fast-moving game of catch. The history of individualising relationship management has become a conceptual liability for progressive customer management in computer-mediated environments. *Letting customers play might just be the formula of success in the 21st century.* (Zwick and Dholakia 2004: 232)

In this sense, Yomi Braester's suggestion (in this volume) that *RMB City* mocks the urban utopianism of scale models parallels my interpretation of *Brothers*; both Yu Hua and Cao Fei spoof claims to the representational sublime. Just as Cao Fei's cyberspace adventures mimic architectural practices that would abstract the building as a disembodied work of art, so, too, do Yu Hua's textual adventures mimic prevalent critical practices that would sublimate media images. However, if, as Maurizio Lazzarato has argued, following Lefebvre, global capitalism is 'no longer a world of production, but the production of worlds' (Lazzarato 2004: 96), then it is difficult to conceive of criticality as located in space and time, as Jeroen de Kloet suggests in his chapter. If space is no longer 'neutral' territory but is itself produced by cognitive, or virtual, capitalism, possibilities for *détournement* are virtually eliminated. While *RMB City* and *Brothers* have the potential to disrupt the spectacle, the temporal and spatial traces of critique become so quickly subsumed by the spectacle that it no longer has the power to haunt us. Resistance, in a Debordian account, depends on how comprehensive the power of the spectacle is understood to be. If a 'science of situations' in which participation overcomes spectatorship is to be possible, then the spectacle has to be understood as dominant in social life while leaving some interstitial spaces from which action can be organised. If, however, the spectacle has absolute control – as Debord seems to suggest in *Comments on the Society of the Spectacle* – then resistance takes on an oppositional stance in which the totality is confronted (Campbell 2008).

Notes

1. *Magazine électronique du CIAC* (2008), 13 April 2010, www.voyd.com/texts/LichtySLCI-ACWhyVirtualArt.pdf
2. In his 'Digital Humanities Manifesto', Jeffrey Schnapp, for example, declares that 'The 20th century left us with a vastly expanded set of spectacles arranged for our viewing pleasure. 21st century networks and interactions reengage the spectators of culture, enabling them to upload meaningfully, just as they download mindfully'. www.stanford.edu/~schnapp/Manifesto%202.0 (accessed 13 April 2010).

References

Baudrillard, Jean. *Simulations*. New York: Semiotext(e) Inc, 1983.
—. *The Evil Demon of Images*. Sydney: The Power Institute of Fine Arts, 1987.
Borer, Michael Ian. 'The Cyborgian Self: Toward a Critical Social Theory of Cyberspace.' *Reconstruction* 2, no.3 (2002). http://reconstruction.eserver.org/023/borer.htm (accessed 19 October 2011).
Broudehoux, Anne-Marie. 'Images of Power: Architectures of the Integrated Spectacle at the Beijing Olympics.' *Journal of Architectural Education* 63, no. 2 (2009): 52-62.
Buck-Morss, Susan. 'Visual Studies and Global Imagination.' www.surrealismcentre.ac.uk/papersofsurrealism/journal2/acrobat_files/buck_morss_article.pdf (accessed 28 January 2010).
Campbell, David. 'Beyond Image and Reality: Critique and Resistance in the Age of Spectacle.' *Public Culture* 20 (2008): 3.
Campbell, John Edward, and Matt Carlson. 'Panopticon.com: Online Surveillance and the Commodification of Privacy.' *Journal of Broadcasting & Electronic Media* 46, no. 4 (2002): 586-606.
Cao Fei. 'The Weight of the Unbearable Lightness in Reality: A Conversation on skype about RMB City Between Jian Juan and Hu Fang.' In *RMB City*. Guangzhou: Vitamin Creative Space.
Cang Lang 苍狼. *Pulling Yu Hua's Teeth* [给余华拔牙]. Beijing: Tong Xin Chubanshe, 2006. See translation by Eric Abrahamsen. 'Pulling Yu Hua's Teeth.' 29 March 2009. http://paper-republic.org/ericabrahamsen/pulling-yu-huas-teeth/ (accessed 13 April 2010).
Dean, Jodi. *Publicity's Secret: How Technoculture Capitalizes on Democracy*. New York: Cornell University Press, 2002.
Debord, Guy. *Comments on the Society of the Spectacle*. London: Verso Books, 1988.
—. *Comments on the Society of the Spectacle*. Translated by Malcolm Imrie. New York: Verso Books, 1998.

—. *The Society of the Spectacle*. Translated by Donald Nicholson-Smith. New York: Zone Books, 1994.

Droitcour, Brian. 'Virtual Reality: RMB City Second Life.' http://artforum.com/diary/id=21839 (accessed 16 January 2009).

Gilman-Opalsky, Richard. 'Why New Socialist Theory Needs Guy Debord: On the Practice of Radical Philosophy.' In *Crisis, Politics, and Critical Sociology*. Eds. Graham Cassano and Richard A. Dello Buono. Leiden: Brill, 2010. 109-134.

Hansen, Mark B.N. *New Philosophy for New Media*. Cambridge, Mass: MIT, 2004.

Idema, Wilt. *Chinese Vernacular Fiction: The Formative Period*. Leiden: Brill, 1974.

Landay, Lori. 'Virtual Kinoeye: Kinetic Camera, Machinima, and Virtual Subjectivity in Second Life.' *Journal of eMedia Studies* 2, no. 1 (2009): 1-33.

Langlois, Ganaele. 'Meaning, Semiotechnologies and Participatory Media.' *Culture Machine* 12 (2011).

Lash, Scott and Celia Lury. *Global Culture Industry: The Mediation of Things*. Cambridge: Polity Press, 2006.

Lazzarato, Maurizio. *Les Révolutions du Capitalisme*. Paris: Les Empêcheurs de Penser en Rond, 2004.

Lyotard, Jean-François. *The Postmodern Condition*. Translated by Geoff Bennington and Brian Massumi. Manchester: Manchester University Press, 1984.

McCarthy, Caroline. 'Class Action Lawsuit Targets Second Life.' *CNET News*, 3 May 2010. http://news.cnet.com/8301-13577_3-20004004-36.html (accessed 19 October 2011).

Murray, Stuart J. 'Editorial Introduction: "Media Tropes".' *MediaTropes e-journal* 2, no. 1, 2009. www.mediatropes.com.libproxy.lib.unc.edu/index.php/Mediatropes/article/viewFile/5342/2243 (accessed 13 April 2010).

Reynolds, Bryan. *Transversal Subjects: From Montaigne to Deleuze After Derrida*. New York: Palgrave Macmillan, 2009.

Sassen, Saskia. 'Reading the City in a Global Digital Age: Between Topographic Representation and Spatialized Power Projects.' In *Global Cities: Cinema, Architecture, and Urbanism in a Digital Age*, edited by Linda Krause and Patrice Petro. New Brunswick, NJ: Rutgers University Press, 2003.

Visser, Robin. *Cities Surround the Countryside: Urban Aesthetics in Postsocialist China*. Durham, NC: Duke University Press, 2010.

Yang, Xiaobin 杨小滨. 'The Subject of Desire and Spiritual Residue: A Psychopolitical Reading of Yu Hua's Brothers' [欲望"主体"与精神残渣：对"兄弟"的心理 - 政治解读]. Tsinghua Journal of Chinese Studies [清华学报] 2, no. 39 (2009).

Yu Hua. *Brothers*. Translated by Chow Eileen and Carlos Rojas. Pantheon, 2009.

Yu, Hua 余华. *Brothers*, Part 1 [兄弟·上部]. Taipei: Maitian Chubanshe, 2005a.

—. *Brothers*, Part 2 [兄弟·,下部]. Taipei: Maitian Chubanshe, 2005b.

Zwick, Detlev and Nikhilesh Dholakia. 'Consumer Subjectivity in the Age of Internet: The Radical Concept of Marketing Control through Customer Relationship Management.' *Information and Organisation* 14 (2004): 211-236.

4. The Architecture of Utopia: From Rem Koolhaas' Scale Models to RMB City

Yomi Braester

Scale models are the architectural equivalent of science fiction: they seem to relocate the viewer immediately into a better future. Their utopian claims are compounded by the fact that Plexiglas-and-Styrene models are giving way to computer-generated 3D simulations, and the digital image is fashioned as a vehicle of social transformation. Lev Manovich writes: 'new media technology acts as the most perfect realisation of the utopia of an ideal society composed from unique individuals' (2001: 61).[1] In the face of such hyperbole it is worth exploring how architectural practices, and digital technology in particular, can facilitate the representation of utopia or, conversely, allude to its breakdown. This chapter looks at a pivotal moment in the history of architectural simulation, namely the introduction of Rem Koolhaas' practices and thoughts in the People's Republic of China (PRC). I compare the work of international architects and government-supported planners with indigenous responses in installations, film, and digital art that use scale models and digital imaging to advance and critique utopian visions.

4.1. Models of the CCTV tower, at content exhibition. Courtesey: Rory Hyde under Creative Commons.

Utopia with Chinese Characteristics: From Conceptual to Figural Models

On 20 December 2002, Rem Koolhaas' Office for Metropolitan Architecture (OMA) won the bid for the Central Chinese Television (CCTV) Tower in Beijing. The complex (chief architects: Rem Koolhaas and Ole Scheeren) includes the CCTV Tower, a double-tower structure joined at the top by cantilevers, as well as the Television Cultural Centre (TVCC). (The TVCC caught fire on 9 February 2009, shortly before its planned completion, leading to an indefinite delay in the complex's inauguration.) The CCTV project and other brand-name building projects timed to coincide with the Beijing Olympics came to symbolise China's entry into the global market. Little attention, however, has been paid to the attendant shift in visualisation practices and transformation of utopian discourses in China.

Awarding the CCTV project to OMA in the high-profile bid supervised by the government should be attributed not only to the buildings' aesthetic attributes, but also to Rem Koolhaas' status as a vocal proponent of hyper-urbanisation. Koolhaas has backed up his construction projects with prolific writing, published in graphically rich books. Fredric Jameson commends Koolhaas' books for reintroducing utopia into the postmodern discourse of a 'windless present' (2003). In China, even more than elsewhere, Koolhaas' ideas have become influential in both professional circles and among decision-makers. Koolhaas' prosclytising vision of the Generic City – 'liberated [...] from the straitjacket of identity' (Fairs and Koolhaas 1995) – is getting ever closer to materialising in Beijing. Koolhaas has famously lamented the 'discrepancy between the acceleration of culture and the continuing slowness of architecture' and touted the solution in the Chinese practices of speedy construction. The CCTV project allowed Koolhaas to tout 'architecture as a fast medium' (Mattern 2008: 878). Koolhaas emphasises three elements, the interlinking of which is crucial to understanding the dominant discourse of government-supported urbanism in China: a utopian drive to transform skylines and cityscapes, an insistence on instantaneous transformation, and the use of elaborate visualisations, notably scale models, to promote these visions.

Koolhaas has endorsed an explicitly utopian agenda of the high modernist kind: 'only through a revolutionary process of erasure and establishment of "liberty zones", conceptual Nevadas where all laws of architecture are suspended, will some of the inherent tortures of urban life – the friction between program and containment – be suspended' (Fairs and Koolhaas 1995). The vehicle of the revolution is the skyscraper. In *Delirious New York* (1978), Koolhaas defined the skyscraper as a 'utopian device for the production of unlimited numbers of virgin sites on a single metropolitan location' (1994). His recent attack on the skyscraper as a 'corrupted' and 'exhausted' type, under the headline 'Kill the Skyscraper' (2004), is driven by an equally utopian impetus to eradicate evil and open new paths – in the form of yet bigger skyscrapers such as the CCTV Tower. Koolhaas kills the skyscraper only to build it anew. It is hard to see Koolhaas' change of opinion as more than a self-serving strategy, taking advantage of the client's inexhaustible funds to build the extravagant cantilevers and gain prestige. The return to the skyscraper, the shift to uncritical utopian vocabulary (in contrast with Koolhaas' earlier constructivist anti-modernism), and the use of glitzy design seemed a worthwhile sacrifice.

In describing the CCTV project, Koolhaas stresses that the design facilitates utopia here and now. He touts the TVCC as 'cake-tin architecture' (2004), a frame into which architectural elements can be poured as easily as instant cake mix. A new city can be erected in no time through such readymade modules. The Generic City is an updated version of the futuristic architecture of the mid-20th century, which promoted, for example, Archigram's Instant City (1971) – a 'travelling metropolis, moving in the country to provide local, provincial town[s] with an instant, shocking experience of metropolitan life'.[2] Koolhaas' 'cake-tin' takes the concept of the instant city a step further: the international architect brings in his carry-on moulds for reconstituting, in the shortest time possible, the urban experience of the first world.

The Generic City borrows from the 'instant city' not only the utopian drive and the idea of immediate transformation, but also the focus on variable configurations of modular building blocks. Koolhaas conceives of the city not as a concrete place, but rather as a space of potentiality. His architecture exists in disjunction from the history and even topography of the construction site; the material building is a thought experiment. In the words of Albena Yaneva, who has studied OMA's practices, 'rather than being a *terminus*, a building stands next to its models, coalescent and coterminous with them' (2009: 83). The completed structure is not the blueprint's realisation, but rather an instance of a higher ideal, an example of a concept that is best preserved in texts, sketches, and scale models.

The Generic City, and its supreme exemplification in contemporary Beijing, is directly linked to the role of scale models in Koolhaas' studio. Koolhaas follows Peter Eisenman's emphasis on the design process. OMA uses many models, representing each stage in its variants. Yaneva notes that OMA's exhibition 'Content' (2003) marked a 'revival of the importance of the scale models as objects that are to be viewed and appreciated in their own right' (2008: 83). Koolhaas' utopian claims hinge on the model: it is the enunciation of an ideal desire that is privileged over its material fulfilment in the completed structure. OMA has reinvented the scale model as the prime subject of architectural discourse.

In the course of the bid for the CCTV Tower, however, the function of the scale model underwent a dramatic, if unacknowledged, transformation. The mutual reinforcement of Koolhaasian utopianism and the PRC's urbanistic policy may be traced to OMA's change of strategy on the eve of the project presentation.

To understand Koolhaas' about-face, it is important to distinguish between scale models of different forms and different functions. OMA's design process makes extensive use of rough foam models, as a conceptual tool intended for in-house consumption. These stand in opposition to the detailed, figural scale models, which fetishise the final product. The final phase is that of presenting the project to the client. OMA has kept at a distance from figural models. In rare cases, Plexiglas models or computerised visualisations are commissioned, but, unlike the foam models, they are produced outside the offices by a separate company. The professionally made models are intended not for the designer, but rather for presentation to the client, and for this purpose include flashy devices such as interior lighting.

In the case of the CCTV Tower, however, Koolhaas' vision was attached to the figural model. As Carol Patterson of OMA explains, the politically appointed jury could not understand the beauty of the conceptual model. Despite its aversion to detailed maquettes, OMA ended up supporting its case with a polished video presentation and a realistic model, made by the local firm Crystal CG (Yaneva 2004: 41).[3] The many rough models ('Content' had over 50 designs of the Tower on display) were pushed aside. Instead, polished renderings of the Tower appeared in Chinese media and even on the streets around the construction site.[4] Public discussion took place under the impression that Koolhaas' utopian urbanism is best represented in these figural models: the new city emerges in finished form, without the context of previous planning, ready for immediate implementation. Arguably, in ceding to the exigencies of the CCTV bid, OMA exposed the limitations of Koolhaas' vision. In the case of the CCTV project at least, the conceptual and figural models complemented each other: the modular design ultimately facilitated disregard of the local context.

For all intents and purposes, Koolhaas' approach was indistinguishable from that of other international architects working in China at the same time. Beijing's future was envisioned in slick architectural simulations, made highly visible in the public realm. Notably, drawings of the National Opera House (completed in 2007) accompanied a heated debate in daily newspapers about the controversial process of choosing Paul Andreu's submission, derogatively nicknamed 'the huge egg', over domestic entries. Even less high-profile projects have entered the collective consciousness – artistic renderings of commercial projects are not only used for the explicit commercial purposes, but are also published as part of recording trade practices and collected as applied art.[5] Large maquettes have become a lynchpin in project launches and a standard fixture in sales centres. The CCTV project was a prominent element in this new visual environment. By the end of the first decade of the century, OMA's utopian ideas and use of scale models had penetrated the Chinese market and influenced planning circles.

Koolhaas' approach has established an enduring presence in China. In March 2010, Ole Scheeren, a former OMA partner and co-designer of the CCTV Tower, opened his own office in Beijing. Yet earlier, Neville Mars, quit OMA in 2003 and set up the Dynamic City Foundation (DCF) in Beijing, self-described as a 'research and design institute focused on the rapid transformations of China's urban landscape'.[6] Mars (who also goes by the Chinese name He Xincheng, or 'What New City') also propagates his message through installations and writings, including the 784-page tome *The Chinese Dream* (2008, co-authored with Adrian Hornsby). As Mars explains, the book was his entry card to the Chinese market, not only proving his knowledge of and commitment to Chinese urbanism, but also imparting the results of his research in a way that would encourage architects and policymakers to abandon their engineering-driven approach in favour of paying attention to the process of planning.[7] The book defies the authorities' announcement that four hundred new cities would be built between 2001 and 2020. Mars and the government planners seem to agree on little, with the exception of one matter: time is of the essence in the race for a sustainable Chinese urbanism.

In Koolhaasian fashion, Mars seeks to reduce the time between the perception

4.2. BBT model and projection. Courtesy: Neville Mars under Creative Commons.

of need and completing the architectural product: 'speed is also the main redeeming force of Dynamic Density. A force that only China can apply at any serious scale, at least if it sets its mind to it before the window of opportunity has shut'.[8] Mars follows Koolhaas in seeing China as a paragon for architecture at large: 'At hyper-speed China can be enjoyed as a laboratory for urban growth' (Mars and Hornsby 2008). Mars is especially interested in how '[t]he building blocks of China's cities are designed in days; the ensuing mud configurations then fixed for decades'. Based on model projects, architecture in China defies the temporal parameters of architectural practice worldwide and, for that reason, provides an object for emulation. Mars couches his vision in utopian claims: 'I set up the Dynamic City Foundation to produce architectural utopias in sculptures, movies and essays'.[9]

To drive home his point, Mars has presented, at least as a thought experiment, Beijing Boom Tower (BBT, designed with Saskia Vendel), a dense compound of high-rises (12,500 residents on 6 hectares) 'responding to all future demands'.[10] Mars has produced thousands of images, in print and online, including artistic renderings and computer-generated images of the compound, as well as drawings

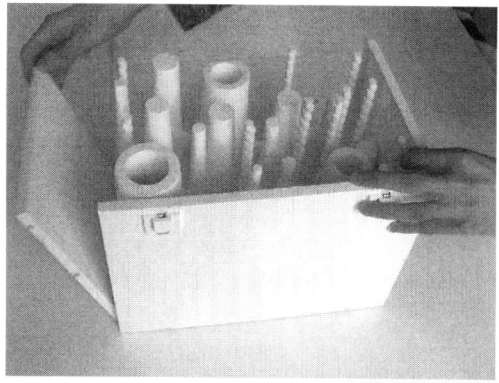

4.3. BBT case. Courtesy: Neville Mars under Creative Commons.

THE ARCHITECTURE OF UTOPIA

ranging from technical transportation schemes and the expected social structure in the towers to more impressionistic and abstract schemata.[11] The most comprehensive visualisation was a multimedia installation exhibited in galleries, including a large-scale model of BBT and three videos. One video was projected onto the model, turning it, in Mars' words, into a giant diagram. Two additional videos, describing life in the Tower, were screened on the adjacent walls.[12] The city – or at least its model – is literally turned into a movie screen.

Two objects made by Mars are perhaps even more telling. One is an all-white maquette of BBT that can be assembled and carried in a briefcase-like box, about a foot long. This model-turned-artwork illustrates, according to Mars, his problem-driven approach, yet it also emphasises the status of the scale model as a transportable abstraction that cannot be reduced to any single material construction. The other object is Mars' imaginary vessel, freeze. Part of a project that fast-forwards the viewer into the future, to illustrate what might befall China by 2020 if planners do not act upon Mars' ideas fast enough, freeze is a spaceship that has taken over the earthbound, no-longer-sustainable cities (in this capacity, it may be seen as a contemporary version of the Instant City dirigible). Annotated as a 'dream solution or counter-revolutionary nightmare', freeze shows utopia and dystopia contained within a single vessel, which is itself only available in the form of a scale model, more of an abstract sculpture than a viable blueprint.

Koolhaas and Mars imagine a malleable city, as if one can take each building and squeeze it between one's fingers. In multiple drawings, Mars shows a 'make your own BBT' kit and fashions the buildings as clay shaped with a potter's hands. DCF takes to the extreme OMA's idea of the architect's ability to hold out the utopian offering in his hand, so to speak: a palm-sized model that makes the material, full-scale city redundant.

Although Koolhaas, Mars, and other Western architects often present their practices as remedial to the habits of official planners, their utopian drive, combined with an insistence on modular, speedy construction and ignorance of cultural heritage, plays into the hands of administrators hell-bent on rapid hyper-urbanisation. Slick models have been part of government propaganda at least since the Ten Great Buildings project of 1958. As I have detailed in my book, *Painting the City Red*, theatre productions have incorporated scale models as stage props to allude to painless modernisation. Notably, the climax of *Forsaken Alley* (*Gala'r hutong*, 1993) features a scale model at centre stage. It is through this model that the district bureau chief makes a solemn promise to residents evacuated to make room for a new development. The onstage manipulation of the maquette glosses over historical rupture and presents the future in the form of manageable building blocks (Braester 2010). Practices that within the architecture profession are common and even necessary means of self-promotion turn in post-socialist China into complicity with top-down planning, predatory market manipulation, and a reductive historical perspective.

Whereas Koolhaas values the conceptual model as the material form of the design process, in China the figural model has come to carry an ideological undertone. Detailed scale models are often regarded simply as a professional tool for communicating the architect's ideas to non-specialist clients, builders, and sponsors (Yaneva 2008; Frampton and Kolbowski 1981). They may also imply predictability and control of the design (Böck 2008). Yet in post-socialist China, scale models present readymade utopia. The government seems to believe that the ideal city is made of modular pieces and that its vision is rendered incarnate in maquettes.

The extensive use of scale models by Chinese developers, and especially by Chinese local government, should be understood in this light. Illustrations and 3D models appear on billboards around construction sites and in long-term exhibits in completed compounds. The most visible displays are in the mushrooming municipal and exhibition halls. The urban planning exhibition halls in Shanghai (opened 2000) and Beijing (opened 2004) feature models stretching over hundreds of square meters. The Beijing hall includes vistas into the future, in the form of maquettes of the capital's suburbs and Central Business District as they will look in about a decade. A temporary exhibit at the same hall featured scale models of bids for the Olympic village (photos continue to be available on the website of the Beijing Municipal Commission of Urban Planning).[13] The Beijing hall also screens three films (including one in 3D and one in 4D) that include computerised animations of the city in different periods. The multimedia presentation comes as close as possible to a bodily experience transporting the visitor into the city past, present, and future – or at least to their idealised versions. The official use of scale models on a grandiose scale promotes an urbanistic utopia, a neoliberal apotheosis of the consumerist city, a harmony at the converging fields of politics, economics, and planning.

Antitopia: Scale Models as Points of Contention

The proliferation of architectural simulation in the public realm also provides an opportunity for criticism, or at least ridicule. Unlike the official policy, which few dare to directly attack, scale models are icons ready for manipulation in oblique manners, immune to censorship. Films, installations, and digital artwork have created alternative constructions using the same materials as official displays. Insofar as in the dominant practice, scale models promise the realisation of urban utopia in nearby locations and in the foreseeable future, the artworks discussed below place the ideal beyond reach. They neither offer an alternative utopia nor point to dystopia, but rather create *antitopia*: a space/time matrix that cancels out utopia.

A prominent example is found in the recent films of Jia Zhangke. *The World* (世界, 2004) is set in a Beijing theme park that includes downscaled replicas of architectural monuments from around the world, such as the Pyramids of Egypt, St. Mark's Square in Venice, and the Eiffel Tower. Whereas the Generic City offers the international traveller almost identical sites worldwide, the World Park is its flipside: a chance to visit unique world landmarks without travel. The protagonists, who work in the park, are not in it for leisure; they suffer from geographical and social immobility, and they often resort to escape fantasies, presented in the film through the virtual modelling of flash animation. In setting his film among miniature models of world architecture, Jia gives the lie to the official utopia of establishing of Beijing as a 'world city'. Whereas Beijing has turned into a theme park of world architecture, decoupled from indigenous architectural idioms, *The World* shows the World Park to be an extreme exemplar of the unsustainable claims made through scale models.[14]

In *24 City* (2008), Jia includes scale models in their more mundane form. The documentary follows the dismantling of a Chengdu factory and the construction of the high-rise compound 24 City in its place. The camera lingers on the billboards that surround the site, as well as on the maquette at the sales centre. Given the ubiquity of such models in the past decade, it is not surprising that they appear in films; for example, *Big Movie* (大电影, 2006) and *Crazy Racer* (疯狂的赛车, 2009). In *24 City*, however, the scale model's brief onscreen appearance is more pointed, its slickness emblematic of the material and social costs of real estate development criticised by the film.[15]

Installations and video art have been more explicitly scathing of the utopian pretentions of the dominant architectural discourse. A poignant example is found in the exhibition 'Merging–Emerging: Art, Utopia, Virtual Reality', at the Museum of Contemporary Art (MoCA) in Shanghai (2009), which established an implicit dialogue with the architectural visualisations at the adjacent exhibition, 'Recent Construction in Shanghai, 2006-2010' (上海城市近期建设, 2006-2010) at the Shanghai Urban Planning Exhibition Centre. In both cases, scale models presented a vision of the coming city, but with diverging emphases.

Both exhibitions were timed to precede the 2010 Shanghai Expo, which precipitated development and brought about the proliferation of visual representations. Contending urbanist visions were displayed side by side on the city's streets. The municipal government and other official units inundated public spaces with large signs proclaiming 'Better City, Better Life' – the Expo's motto. The signs, bearing images of the city and artistic renderings of the Expo pavilions, were uncompromisingly upbeat.

The exhibitions accentuated the contrast between the utopian 'better city' and reality on the ground. The exhibit at the Shanghai Urban Planning Exhibition Centre, toeing the official line, offered much visual information about the coming Expo, including plans for the different proposals for the Expo layout, artistic renderings, and scale models of the Expo and other affected areas. Multiple maquettes were dedicated to the China pavilion. The 'recent construction' on display included rejected blueprints as well as buildings that would not have been completed until 2010. Like the permanent scale model of the city in the same museum, these exhibits situated the visitors – laymen, planners, and political leaders – as observers from above, overviewing and controlling the structures that existed for the time being only in Plexiglas.

The Exhibition Hall also made use of advanced digital imaging. Computer screens displaying images, videos, and data were ubiquitous. Three videos were screened: a run-of-the-mill collage of scenes of Shanghai daily life and architectural landmarks, reminiscent of Zhang Yimou's 2001 promotional piece for the Beijing Olympics bid, and two tours of Shanghai and the Expo, which used computer-generated imagery (CGI) graphics to move in and around the buildings.

4.4. Zhong Kangjun, *City* 'detail'. Courtesy: Yomi Braester.

4.5. Zhong Kangjun, *City*, MoCA. Courtesy: Yomi Braester.

The second of these videos, located toward the exhibition's end and intended as a climactic conclusion, was a 360-degree, multiscreen, panoramic display under the title *A Magical Tour of Shanghai* (上海神奇之旅). Guided by an updated, hip version of the comics and film character Sanmao, the video introduced each planned site. The video foregrounded digital imaging and fashioned it as a tool for creating not just the video, but also the city itself: the cityscape emerges first in glowing outline out of a screen of green-on-black digits, ripping off the familiar image from *The Matrix*. *Magical Tour* presents the city in its future ideal form as magic, born out of digital models. The heavy reliance on digital modelling brings to mind W.J.T. Mitchell's warning about the new technology, which he regards as 'the convergence of techno-science with [...] new forms of totemism, fetishism, and idolatry' (2008: 15).

THE ARCHITECTURE OF UTOPIA

Coincidentally, artists' responses to the dominant practices were displayed at the MoCA, situated inside the People's Park just north of the Urban Planning Exhibition Centre. The exhibition, aptly named 'Merging-Emerging: Art, Utopia, Virtual Reality', emphasised the links between visions of the future and the media through which they are presented. Urban utopia is explicitly contradicted in the centrepiece, Zhong Kangjun's *City* (城, 2008). The installation, comprised of 24 large pieces (each up to 0.75m2), presents a modern cityscape. It is a composite of urban landmarks, featuring iconic structures such as the Bank of China tower in Hong Kong and the Taipei 101 tower. The most prominent are easily recognisable structures from Mainland China, including the Olympic Stadium (aka the Bird's Nest) and the National Aquatic Centre (aka the Water Cube), the Shanghai Oriental Pearl TV Tower, the Jin Mao Tower, and Koolhaas' Beijing CCTV Tower. Any sense of grandeur or futuristic promise is immediately thwarted: the monuments are arranged helter-skelter, without any spatial logic (Waibaidu Bridge leads, against Shanghai's topography, to the Pearl of the Orient TV Tower); the urban space is congested with traffic; a plane is about to crash into a skyscraper, while a helicopter rescues people from the top of the 93-story Shanghai World Financial Centre. The city is impregnated with the sense of a post-9/11 doom.

The artistic scale model stands in direct contrast to the slick professional presentations in the Urban Planning Exhibition Centre. It is made of rusted iron, with visible coarse soldering marks. There are gaping holes in the iron boards, as if the model is in the process of deteriorating. Some structures are made of *objets trouvés*. Moreover, *City* challenges not only the aesthetics of professional scale models but also their spatial and temporal logic. The models at the Urban Exhibition Centre are cordoned off, placing the structures in an idealised realm and the viewers in a position of visual control. In contrast, Zhong Kangjun's artwork is comprised of separate plates set on the gallery floor, level with the viewers, inviting them to walk into the exhibit and observe the material stitch lines from up close. Whereas the Exhibition Centre frames the model and distantiates the visitor, *City* shows that the scale model can also subscribe to haptic aesthetics that requires the visitor's active participation.

Unlike professional scale models, Zhang's *City* is not geared toward evaluating human movement inside simulated spaces by imagining miniature people inside them, but rather focuses on the movement of gallery visitors, approximately as tall as the buildings, who become part of the artwork. The videos in the adjacent Exhibition Centre conjure an out-of-body experience of unhindered flight among the structures; by contrast, the iron installation calls attention to the relationship between the rusted buildings and the human body. Against maquettes made for selling real estate, for explaining the principles of construction, or for planning the building's end use, Zhong's artwork refers primarily not to the represented structures, but rather to the viewer's experience of the scale model.

The self-referentiality in *City* may be informed by another artwork at the 'Merging-Emerging' exhibition, namely Zhang Tianxiao's 'Intersection' (交叉, translated at the exhibition as 'Cross'). Zhang's video art narrates in cartoonlike fashion the cross-cultural experience of a Shanghai person in Paris. The encounter is represented through replacing Shanghai landmarks with Paris monuments, achieved as a large human hand enters the image and plucks out one building after the other. The city is reduced to modular, toy-like building blocks manipulated by hand. Zhong's *City*, however, is more explicit in its challenge to architectural practices. The text introducing the installation says: 'The utopian city and the real world in which humanity exists conceal within them a severe admonition to sophisticated society. Humanity is the vehicle on which each message and every scar are etched. Man, the constructor! And the destroyer?'[16] The artwork exposes the scars left by utopian constructs and material structures alike. The hubris of the planners at the adjacent Exhibition Centre is exposed through a scale model that is at once a piece of construction and destruction. The MoCA exhibition contests the verbal and visual vocabulary of the official line and contrasts the transportability of a readymade city with virtual constructions that defy the utopian rhetoric.

Virtopia: *RMB City*

The MoCA exhibition challenges the official approach to visual representation and urban utopia, yet Zhong Kangjun's artwork shares a key element with the professional scale models: the reification of architectural space. The space in which the human body encounters the built environment is fashioned as a precondition for thinking about the coming city, whether existing or imagined, represented or unrepresentable. In other words, *City* assumes the prediscursive status of space that enables the utopianism of the dominant discourse, as generated by both professional architects and government planners.

The possibility of a structure that reinvents space and redraws around itself the boundaries of discourse is presented in *RMB City*, an entire town in cyberspace, in the realm of Second Life (SL). The place is an island on which architectural landmarks are heaped helter-skelter: the Three Gorges reservoir gushes out of the Tiananmen rostrum; Shanghai's Pearl of the Orient TV Tower, slanted like the leaning tower of Pisa, looms over Beijing's Olympic Stadium ('the Bird's Nest'), rusting in the ocean spray. In the words of its creator, Cao Fei, '*RMB City* will be the condensed incarnation of contemporary Chinese cities'.[17]

Even before creating her portion of SL, Cao Fei had made the video artwork *I • Mirror* (2007), in which she (as her SL avatar China Tracy) roams a city that spoofs the real-estate speculation-driven Chinese city. High-rises, existing only in contours delineated by the words 'for sale', resemble Beijing's gentrified compounds. *I • Mirror* turns the filmmaker into urban planner and real estate developer, and the city into an artwork that can be constructed anew, possessed, and copyrighted by the artist.[18] In *RMB City*, launched in 2008, Cao takes a step further in turning the viewer into an active participant who tours virtual space as an avatar.

RMB City exemplifies the unique experience offered by new media, and by virtual environments in particular. Mark Hansen, responding to Manovich's utopian claims about virtual imaging as a post-cinematic medium, has claimed that the digital image establishes an altogether new mode of perception, whereby cinematic framing disappears and experience is channelled through the viewer's body (2006). New media are truly new because the haptic cannot be reduced to the cinematic. Hansen's test case is Virtual Reality (VR), where telepresence renders the simulated space dependent not only on vision but also on the physical attributes of the virtualised body. *RMB City*, in which every visitor produces her own movie, so to speak, by following the peregrinations of her online avatar (one can choose between point-of-view and over-the-shoulder views), exemplifies how the new media unframe the gaze and immerse the subject corporeally in the virtual environment.

Through the familiar landmarks rebuilt like scale models in cyberspace, *RMB City* criticises prevalent spatial and architectural practices. Cao suggests that *RMB City* is a 'new land', an alternative to the overloaded material cities. Like Rem Koolhaas, Neville Mars, and Zhong Kangjun, she uses a simulated construct of her making, implicitly privileged over material space and alluding to the limitations of architectonic representation. Yet *RMB City* transports the viewer in time – without the utopian horizon of Koolhaas' work or the dystopian undertones of Zhong's *City*. Robin Visser, in her chapter in this volume, suggests that *RMB City* is subsumed by the urbanist spectacle rather than critiquing it. Yet the focus on architectural imaging suggests a more self-reflexive intentionality on Cao's part: *RMB City* pushes the idea of the scale model until it implodes into self-reference and is left to exist only within a patently virtual realm.

Within the parameters of VR, *RMB City* enjoys a liminal status between construction site and scale model. The SL space foregrounds the building process, featuring a cement mixer, cranes, signs proclaiming the area as a construction site, and a high-rise-size hardhat.[19] Cao's avatar China Tracy and her friends don shovels at the ceremony of laying the foundation stone for *RMB City*. *RMB City* is advertised like any realty, through ubiquitous billboards and a promotions centre (modelled after the Beijing Grand Theatre, with a ceiling identical to that of the Great Hall of the People). Yet the site also shows traces of modular outlining. Cao Fei makes explicit the affinity between *RMB City* and scale models. As Cao explains in an online video,[20] *RMB City* was designed with imaging software for architects. Cao Fei's extensive but entirely non-material architectural design lies somewhere between the avant-garde whimsy of László Moholy-Nagy and the fantastic visualisations in Koolhaas' books.

The extent to which *RMB City* frustrates definitions of materiality is evident in the SL site's relationship to its own scale model. Cao Fei has created a plastic-and-aluminium model of *RMB City*. Part of a multimedia installation tailored for art galleries, the model (120 x 130 x 120 cm) allows the visitor at the exhibition a convenient overview. Unlike the cheerily coloured SL site, the model is all in white, underlining its function not as a makeshift version of the site but rather as a practical architectural device. But whereas architects usually employ scale models to offer advance views of constructed space, the gallery model for *RMB City* seems superfluous, an eerily sterile object. The real model for *RMB City* may be said to be the SL site itself – both a visionary simulation and a quasi-material structure.

RMB City's liminal status, both as a cinematic image and as a scale model, is a symptom of a more fundamental unresolved tension: that of the utopian sign. Insofar as *RMB City* represents the future Chinese city, and even the future of urbanism, it shows that future to depend on the redefinition of space and vision in the age of digital imaging. *RMB City* does not offer a grand synthesis of the utopian dialectic, but it defines the discursive boundaries for reassessing the stakes in spatial simulation. It holds a critical mirror to the architecture of utopia, but it may not justify the assertion made by the cyber-critic Zafka (Zhang Anding), who finds in SL 'virtopia' – a utopian 'overturning' of reality through virtual space. At best, *RMB City* suggests a change in the visual regime that sustains utopian claims.

RMB City and the other artworks I have discussed leverage the discourse on architectural imaging against the rampant practices of the Chinese real estate market. The national and municipal governments have been advancing neoliberal policies of urban growth through architectural technologies of visualisation. In contrast with the professional and official practices, the artworks show the unsavoury consequences of the scale model as a self-sufficient totality: a totally modular city that can be freely taken apart and reassembled. The artists embrace an antitopian strategy that challenges the mimetic relationship between the model and the material city; they envision and visualise the future city as a spectacle that both depends on its encapsulation in model-like form, and acknowledges its inherent inviability.

The various modes of adapting and responding to architectural practices are indicative of larger urbanistic and cultural trends. Global astonishment at China's hyper-urbanisation not only reveals an anxiety about keeping up with construction demands and social change. The artworks addressed in this chapter also expose utopian architectural designs as signs of a particular anguish, a crisis of representation: the absence of tools to imagine the coming city and a breakdown in the perception of time as a measure of spatial transformation.

Notes

1. Manovich and Hansen alike use emancipatory rhetoric to describe the digital image. Manovich claims: 'Today, as media is being liberated from its traditional physical storage media – paper, film, stone, glass, magnetic tape – the elements of printed word interface and cinema interface, which previously were hardwired to the content, become liberated as well' (2001: 73). Hansen describes Jeffrey Shaw's art as aiming 'to counter the subordination of the body to the cinematic image and to liberate the space beyond the image' (Hansen 2006: 52).
2. http://parole.aporee.org/work/hier.php3?words_id=676&spec_id=12959&res_id=1323 (accessed 20 January 2010). The term reappeared in China in the 1990s, where 'instant cities' denote the mushrooming new urban centres striving to become 'world cities'. See Lau et al. (2000: 103-116).
3. I am also grateful to Zhu Tao, who patiently and passionately shared with me his knowledge and opinions on Koolhaas' thought and practices.
4. See images at http://asiatime.blogspot.com and www.skyscrapercity.com/showthread.php?t=179084&page=5 (accessed 20 January 2010).
5. See for example, the yearbooks of real estate and architectural imaging.
6. www.dynamiccity.org/summary.php (accessed 20 January 2010).
7. Author's conversation with Neville Mars, 28 January 2010. The author wishes to thank Mr. Mars for his cooperation.

8. http://burb.tv/view/DCF_BLOG?_session=j08r0q7dkpsq89tb8l4guip6h4 (accessed 20 January 2010). (Large parts of *The Chinese Dream* are available online; for the reader's convenience, I cite the online version.)
9. http://burb.tv/view/DCF_BLOG?_session=tzcuaahcm (accessed 20 January 2010).
10. BBT is not without its critics. A blogger commented:
    'Antithesis to Beijing Boom Town. Elizabeth Hickocks Jell-o Francisco. Earthquake resistant and deliciously edible. The only corporate sponsorship comes from Jell-o, and there's a Gelatin Valley busily producing millions of tons of colloidal gel. You have to dress in white in this city, and you can never lean against a wall.
    Boom Tower uses a very holey structure for maximum window surfacing and minimum pity for people living with vertigo. What's in those dark bottomless pits? Just streams of moving humans and products on conveyors? Speciated [sic] people with extra ears and no eyes? Sunlight never reaches down there, and most of the city is just wallowing in its own shadows. Like a landscape of whitewashed smokestacks or enormous albino lipstick tubes, you'd have to floodlight this city to make it livable [sic], and every other floor would be a tanning salon to deter depression. Only the penthouse suites atop the uppermost rings get anything like a country boys sun quota'.
    http://bldgblog.blogspot.com/2005/12/beijing-boom-tower.html (accessed 20 January 2010).
11. Images and texts on BBT are available at Mars' website: http://burb.tv/view/Beijing_Boom_Tower, and partially reproduced in *The Chinese Dream*, pp. 250-285. Extensive slide shows are uploaded at http://www.flickr.com/photos/dcf_pics/sets/.
12. For Mars, the imaginary project was a way to get his message across without facing the bureaucratic hurdles associated with real construction, yet the installation was so successful in literally projecting the future that visitors began asking how they could buy apartments in the compound.
13. See: www.bjghw.gov.cn/forNationalStadium/indexeng.asp (accessed 9 February 2008).
14. For more on *The World*, see Braester (2010: 298-303).
15. The scale model is the only photographic image included in the American version of the film poster.
16. Retranslated from the Chinese (another English version was available on site).
17. Cao Fei, 'RMB City – Online Urbanisation'. http://rmbcity.com/about (accessed 5 February 2010).
18. Cao has offered pieces of *RMB City* for sale for as much as $120,000: Moxley, 'Do Avatars Dream of Electric Streets?'; in *Painting the City Red*. I point out that *I • Mirror* exemplifies how artists can facilitate and even initiate what I call 'the urban contract' – in this case, calling on the viewer to enter a binding contract by logging on, signing in, and assuming an avatar identity (Braester 2010).
19. See, for example, http://vimeo.com/5404021, http://vimeo.com/5503207, and http://vimeo.com/4290970 (accessed 8 February 2010).
20. See: www.youtube.com/watch?v=mgSVfKW2dno (accessed 20 January 2010).

References

Böck, Ingrid. 'Imaginary Architecture and Spatial Immediacy: Rem Koolhaas and Experimental Conditions of Architecture.' In *Die Realität des Imaginären: Architektur und das digitale Bild*, edited by Jorg H. Gleiter, Norbert Korrek, and Gerd Zimmermann. Weimar: Verlag der Bauhaus-Universität Weimar, 2008.

Braester, Yomi. *Painting the City Red: Chinese Cinema and the Urban Cinema*. Durham: Duke University Press, 2010.

Fairs, Marcus. 'Rem Koolhaas.' In: *ICON* 013, June 2004, www.iconeye.com/index.php?option=com_content&view=article&id=2715:rem-koolhaas--icon-013--june-2004 (accessed 18 September 2011).

Frampton, Kenneth and Silvia Kolbowski. *Idea as Model*. New York: Rizzoli, 1981.

Hansen, Mark B.N. *New Philosophy for New Media*. Cambridge, Mass: MIT, 2006.
Jameson, Fredric. 'Future City.' *New Left Review* 21 (2003): 65-80.
Koolhaas, Rem. *Content*. Cologne: Taschen, 2004.
—. *Delirious New York: A Retroactive Manifesto for Manhattan*. New York: Monacelli, 1994.
Koolhaas, Rem and Bruce Mau. 'Imagining Nothingness.' In *S, M, L, XL*, by Rem Koolhaas and Bruce Mau, 198-202. New York: Monacelli, 1995.
—. *S, M, L, XL*. New York: Monacelli, 1995.
Lau, Stephen, Mahtab-uz-Zaman, and So Hing Mei, 'A High-Density Instant City Pudong in Shanghai.' In *Compact Cities: Sustainable Urban Forms for Developing Countries*, edited by Mike Jenks and Rod Burgess, 103-116. London: Spon, 2000.
Manovich, Lev. *The Language of New Media*. Cambridge: MIT Press, 2001.
Mars, Neville and Adrian Hornsby. *The Chinese Dream: A Society Under Construction*. Rotterdam: 010 Publishers, 2008.
Mattern, Shannon. 'Broadcasting Space: China Central Televisions New Headquarters.' *International Journal of Communication* 2 (2008): 869-908.
Mitchell, William J.T. 'Back to the Drawing Board: Architecture, Sculpture, and the Digital Image.' In *Die Realität des Imaginären: Architektur und das digitale Bild*, edited by Jorg H. Gleiter, Norbert Korrek, and Gerd Zimmermann, 13-20. Weimar: Verlag der Bauhaus-Universität Weimar, 2008.
Moxley, Mitch. 'Do Avatars Dream of Electric Streets? A Virtual Fantasia of China.' www.walrusmagazine.com/articles/2008.09-field-notes-avatars-dream-electric-streets-mitch-moxley-second-life (accessed 20 January 2010).
Yaneva, Albena. *Made by the Office for Metropolitan Architecture: An Ethnography of Design*. Rotterdam: 010 Publishers, 2009.
—. 'Obsolete Ways of Designing? Scale Models at the Time of Digital Media Technologies.' In *Die Realität des Imaginären: Architektur und das digitale Bild*, edited by Jorg H. Gleiter, Norbert Korrek, and Gerd Zimmermann, 83-91. Weimar: Verlag der Bauhaus-Universität Weimar, 2008.
Zafka (Zhang Anding). 'Here Comes Metaverse: A New Existential Manifesto.' http://rmbcity.com/2008/09/here-comes-metaverse-a-new-existential-manifesto (accessed 5 February 2010).

5. Imagining a Disappearing and Reappearing Chinese City

Jeroen de Kloet

So this is the glass I see – still a stone, but no longer solid.
Still a flame, but never again warm.
Still water, but never soft nor passing on.
It is a wound but never bleeds,
it is a sound but never passes through silence.
From loss to loss: this is glass.
Language and time are transparent, we pay a high price.
– Ouyang Jianghe, from 'The Glass Factory'[1]

Perpetual Disappearance

Since the closing of the *Yuanmingyuan* art village in the mid-1990s, a quite basic discourse has haunted the appearance and disappearance of art villages in Beijing: they are zones of freedom and creativity, usually located on the outskirts of the city, and always under the threat of demolition by an authoritarian state that cannot and will not accept artistic voices of discontent. This discourse of appearance and subsequent disappearance resurfaced in 2010 when the authorities announced the planned destruction of the *Caochangdi* art village, the village with Ai Weiwei as its unofficial yet highly prolific mayor. Huang Rui, artist and one of the founders of art district 798 in Beijing, wrote a piece titled 'A City that Abandoned Artists', which was posted on an e-mail list of which the accompanying text claims that 'the destruction of the artists villages continues' in China (MCLC list, 1 May 2010).

Somehow, this alleged cyclic appearance and disappearance of art districts in Beijing resonates well with a number of basic assumptions about art as a potentially subversive cultural form and the Chinese nation-state as an authoritarian state that does not and cannot allow such forms to proliferate freely. Such narratives all too easily ignore changes that have taken place over the past decade in urban planning in China, as well as in its art world. Driven by a desire to become a global player, the Chinese state has gradually formulated policies that are directed towards the strengthening of its creative industries, so as to be able to move from a 'made in China' image towards a 'created in China' image (Keane 2007). Apparently the work of Richard Florida has globalised even into the premises of

Zhongnanhai. This turn towards the creative industries took place around 2004-2008, the same time that the value of the work of Chinese artists skyrocketed on the global art market. This was also the period during which the capital prepared itself for the Beijing Olympics, a project that involved massive urban reconstruction, part of which included the further development of creative zones like 798.

Around the turn of the century, this former electronic-appliance factory complex morphed into an art zone. The discourse of demolition that surrounded 798 was then slowly replaced by a discourse on 798 as an example of the intense commercialisation of the Chinese art world. Many critics and artists alike believed this to have resulted in the production of an artistic theme park that only vaguely resembled the zone of artistic freedom and experimentation that it claimed to be. One of the first inhabitants was female artist Chen Liyun. She told me about the first years in 798: 'There were only a few people at the beginning. We moved there because it was convenient. The houses there were higher, and the prices were cheaper. The venues were convenient in terms of traffic and it was close to the city. The factories houses were large enough to make big paintings. Because of this, many artists started to move in'. Many people express a sense of nostalgia about the early days of 798, claiming that it was more subversive and less commercial. They include the architect Li Wenjun, who told me that 'seven or eight years ago, several artists came there and enjoyed their life, their friendship and the time to paint. Now everybody wants to get there to be seen, it is crazy, such a pity. I don't want to be there any more'.

Rather than retreating into a romanticised narrative about the innocent and pure past, I want to trace the possibilities of criticality in a less innocent and pure present. Inspired by the discourse on the appearance and disappearance of art zones, and the concomitant critique of their (loss of) criticality, I started to wonder if the metamorphosis of 798, for instance, is a question of the objects of art it hosts, or the time and space it occupies. In the midst of speed, fluidity and volatility of time-space relations in urban life, I aim to understand the criticality of art not only in art itself, but also in connection with time and space. In other words, I argue for a need to relocate criticality from text and language to time and space. Conventionally, criticality is located in the text or the object, it is the meaning of the work of art, or the ways the object speaks to us, that allows for change. In addition to what may be termed such 'representational modes of criticality', some of which will also surface in my own analysis, I would like to think of an additional method that focuses on reading criticality in connection with time and space.

In this chapter, I will show how creative urban zones have become part and parcel of the Chinese state's attempt to slowly change China from being a country of production into a country of creation. In these urban zones, global capital, the art world and the nation-state are conflated. Drawing on Rey Chow, I will show how both the articulation of ethnic difference as well as the voices of resistance and protest that are often articulated in such zones can be seen, regardless of the intention of the maker, as complicit with this creative industry-nation-state nexus. This does not erase the possibility of criticality, but it makes it more difficult.

Perhaps part of the criticality of 798 lies not so much in the artworks that are on display, but more in the ways 798 frequently resurfaces in the discourse of appearance and disappearance. 798, along with other art zones, such as *Caochangdi*, features in popular discourse not only as an art district but also as a battleground. These are spaces that are wrestling with time. Such battles are symbolic for the more general reconstruction of the Chinese cityscape.

I will subsequently show how the *Glass Factory* exhibition presents artworks that critically engage with the commercialisation of China and its art world, as well as with the reconstruction of the city. These representational modes of criticality are confined by the space itself. The reflexive aesthetics of the exhibition are ironically simultaneously constitutive of the art world itself. Yet, the space itself also enables different ways of engaging with art. In 798, people come and go; a visit has become part of the tourist itinerary, squeezed in between Tiananmen Square and the Summer Palace. Hence the ubiquitous presence of cameras, artworks become just another backdrop for pictures, they are appropriated and become props in the personal narratives of the spectators. The works serve not only as markers of space (I have been *there*) but also as markers of time (I was there *then*). They are visual reminders of the passing of time. The space, 798, along with the artworks that are on display, thus inflects time; it is a nostalgic warehouse of the contemporary, just like the Forbidden City conjures up fantasies about a grand history.

For Cao Fei's *RMB City*, a work I analyse in the final section of my chapter, it is rather the process of time inflecting space that opens up a space of potential criticality. The work constantly mutates over a period of two years, just as its mode of circulation enables the emergence of constantly changing visual alliances. Her work explores a different China, a different city, in constructing a virtual future of the present, the work offers lines of flight out of the present, ironic lines, that do hold the potential to become political. Being rooted in game culture, *RMB City* is a place where life waits to happen; it is a surreal place, spinning around endlessly, as if the city were a conveyor belt in a factory. It is also a post-human space; the absence of human life makes it an eerie place that at the same time allows human life to proliferate – if only we could imagine a way to colonise the future. In particular the mode of circulation through the Internet, and the related availability of the images, increases the yet unrealised criticality of the work.

Welcome to Creative China[2]

Located in North-east Beijing, just outside the fourth ring road and close to the IKEA megastore, the abandoned factory area 798 has changed, within only a few years, from a controversial artistic zone into a showcase of an allegedly new, creative and open China. The site is rooted in architectural culture; it is a massive, solid and monumental space, evoking memories of a bygone communist era. Built in Bauhaus style, 798 was established in the early 1950s as a joint venture between East Germany and China, as one of the very first steps in the strenuous process of nation-building. A staggering 150 million RMB was invested in the

5.1. Pace Beijing gallery in 798. Courtesy: Jeroen de Kloet.

military factory complex (Huang 2004: 2). As Luo Peilin, the head engineer of 798 in its construction phase (1951-1956), remarks, it 'contributed enormously to China's industrial growth and prosperity and the country and its people put to good use the goods produced there. [...] All of the loudspeakers at Tiananmen Square and on Chang'an Avenue were produced during the glorious years at Factory 798' (Luo 2004: 13). The suggested link between the factory and Tiananmen Square – the most politicised space in China, a space saturated with historical significance – is emblematic of the factory's importance to the nation-state.

The jump in time from the early 1950s to the early 21st century is dramatic, and indicative of the changes China has undergone. It is tempting to insist on the historical significance of 798, in particular its roots in a utopian, trans-communist project and its embedding in the building of the nation-state. Now, 50 years later, it continues to help maintain the nation-state, but linkages are no longer sought to fellow communist regimes, but to a probably less utopian (but not less brutal) global capitalism. In my interviews with critics, artists and architects in Beijing, my interviewees would frequently conjure up comparisons with districts like SoHo in New York. To think of 798 as a project solely born out of communist nostalgia is inadequate, as Dai writes: 'The choice for and reconstruction of 798 is not out of cultural nostalgia or to memorise a special and heated age, it was to copy and import an international and American way of artistic life to China – a SoHo art and living zone with a loft lifestyle' (2007: 35). But in my view, the nostalgic linkage to the past, as well as the gesturing towards a cosmopolitan lifestyle, do not contradict each other, but are instead closely intertwined. The production of locality is part of global capitalism.

The references to the communist past of 798 constitute a specific articulation of 'Chineseness'; not one related to China's assumed long history, nor its mythic rural origins (Chow 1998b: 146), but one connected to its recent past. A past that sells on the global art market in the form of Andy Warhol-like pop artworks, saturated with references to Mao Zedong and other emblematic revolutionary figures and styles. The best-known protagonist from this pop art style may well be Wang Guangyi, who mingles icons of Western capitalism, such as the Coca-Cola bottle, with posters from the Cultural Revolution. This conflation of the space – 798 – with the work, both of which evoke a feeling of communist nostalgia, imbues the creative zone with a peculiar sense of Chineseness. Indeed, the communist past is ubiquitously present in 798 – be it the factory space itself, the creations of Wang Guangyi, the porcelain statues of Mao, the numerous communist gadget-as-souvenirs, or simply the names of galleries such as *The Long March Gallery*.

Nostalgia works not only by conveying a sense of loss and melancholy; as Chow argues, it 'also works by concealing and excluding the dirty and unpleasant elements of social hardships' (1998b: 148). This is the case in 798, where the hardships of communism are displaced by a highly commodified theme-park rendition. The nostalgia evoked by 798 and the works on display turn the place into a global creative zone with Chinese characteristics. In other words, communist nostalgia has become a structure of feeling employed by the nation-state in conjunction with the artistic field to produce what is allegedly a uniquely Chinese creative zone. This change is indicative of a policy shift. In 2006, the national government endorsed a creative industry policy (Keane 2007), aiming to transform China into a country of innovation rather than manufacturing. In doing so, the post-socialist state has, through its complicitous coexistence with the market, 'rejuvenated its capacity [...] to affect the agenda of popular culture, especially at the discursive level' (Wang 2001: 71; see also Fung 2008; Pang 2012; Zhao 2008).

Underwriting this shift is the vested material and symbolic interests offered by the broad global reach of Chinese art. Chinese works easily carry a price tag from € 10,000 up to € 9,700,000 (Pang 2012: 139). While in 2002, there was only one Chinese artist among the world's top 100 artists, in 2008, there were 34 (against, for example, 27 European artists – computed by leading art market consultancy Art Price on the basis of auction revenue). Indeed, in 798 the works are invariably priced in European and American currencies instead of Chinese Yuan, just as the gallery owners all speak English. Preparing for the ultimate spectacle of the Beijing Olympics, 798 is to showcase an open, advanced and progressive China to the world. It has become a prime tourist spot that is used in the marketing of Beijing, an area through which figures like President Sarkozy of France are escorted. Global brands, like Nike, open their 'museums'. As Cheng Lei remarks, 'other visitors include important political figures, the elite of business and many celebrities. Creativity square has recently opened as the largest public space in 798 which will allow more internationally famous names to enter the area and increase the reputation of 798 as an international landmark' (2008: 83-85). Numerous photographs support his text, not only of the buildings and the artworks, but also of the celebrities that have visited 798, among them 'the richest man in the world, Warren Buffet's son, Peter Buffet' (Cheng 2008: 85).

It thus comes as no surprise that the cooptation and commercialisation of 798 have triggered critical voices within and outside China. In an interview with me, filmmaker and curator Ou Ning explained how the government can only think in terms of capital, rather than creativity:

> Nowadays, when talking about the 'creative industry', the government always means something that is linked to culture – animation, filmmaking, galleries and auctions – and how to covert that culture into more GDP. [...] I am reluctant to go to 798 if I have no business to do there. 798 actually reveals all of the problems occurring during the over-marketisation of Chinese contemporary art. I'm tired of those things. I leave a city when it is full of such annoying stuff.

It is, however, not my primary goal to critique an alignment of the nation-state with contemporary art; nor do I wish to discuss the intentions of Chinese artists. What 798 teaches us is how political and critical works can be mobilised in the production of a specific creative zone that serves as a showcase for a new and open China. The global art world has joined forces with the Chinese authorities to produce this zone of alleged freedom and resistance, with Chineseness as its selling point. Ethnicity and cultural difference have become part and parcel of the regime of global capitalism. Rey Chow (2002) has made a similar argument in her discussion on Chinese political dissidents, who have become commodities that can be freed in the name of human rights in exchange for improved business relationships. She draws on Weber's work on Protestantism and capitalism to question the assumed criticality of the human rights discourse, and shows how 'precisely this narrative of resistance and protest, this moral preoccupation with universal justice, is what constitutes the efficacy of the capitalist spirit. Resistance and protest, when understood historically, are part and parcel of the structure of capitalism; they are the reasons capitalism flourishes' (Chow 2002: 47, see also de Kloet 2010).

This, then, begs a similar question with regard to the criticality one encounters in 798. How to be critical in a zone that is so much a part of the intertwined logics of global capitalism and the Chinese nation-state? The ethnic difference is performed through works of art that often evoke a sense of resistance and protest – and, as explained by Chow, resistance and protest are very much part of the logic of capitalism. The global art world demands ethnic difference to authenticate and differentiate the artwork, haunting Chinese artists with the spectre of Chineseness (Maravillas 2007). The problem of the ethnic supplement drives the production of contemporary Chinese art; the artists are required to explain, justify and interrogate their work in relation to its geopolitical context. This 'vicious circle of discriminatory practice' (Chow 1998a: 5) is often mirrored in China itself, where an obsessive involvement with Chineseness and with an assumed essential difference from the West dominates intellectual and artistic circles.[3] The texts accompanying exhibitions in 798 frequently reify an East-West binary. For example, in a show curated by Hu Jiujiu, entitled *West to the East – Aesthetic Context of Intellectuals*, the curator writes, 'the intellectual artists have taken on a distinctive cultural position. All of them have studied Western cultures as well as have carried out artistic practices conditioned by the tradition and reality of China'. Examples abound from exhibitions that are framed by a fixed East-West binary and the geopolitical burden of representation.

To summarise, the ethnic card as played out in 798, as articulated through a sense of communist nostalgia – both in the factory space itself and the works on display – in conjunction with a discourse of protest and resistance, is part and parcel of global capitalism. Particular versions of Chineseness are commodified that propel the proliferation of contemporary Chinese art on the global art market. Its underpinning discriminatory logic is deeply intertwined with the structure of capitalism as well as with the maintenance of the Chinese nation-state. This state-global creative industry nexus is built on the remnants of a utopian transnational communism, dating back to the early 1950s when East Germany worked together with China to construct 798. The deserted factories now supply artworks that circulate with high economic value in a global economy of art, one that emerged in the 1970s and 1980s 'as part of a general financial revolution. Along with hedge funds, international mortgages, and secondary financial instruments of all kinds. [...] Contemporary art [...] expanded globally along an ever-increasing circuit of biennials and international exhibitions' (Buck-Morss 2004: 4). Yet, the works are not 'only' commodities, nor 'just' individual artistic expressions; they are also symbols in the process of nation-state maintenance, symbols that capitalise – literally – on ethnic difference, operating as signs for the authorities to articulate a China that is ready for the 21st century. The Bauhaus-style factories are still productive today, not as the heavily guarded suppliers of advanced electronic equipment for the army, but as the producers of what is assumed to be a new, open and economically prosperous China, a nation-state that aspires to become a creator rather than a manufacturer, a nation-state that operates in the midst of the workings of global capital.

Glass Factory

The analysis thus far runs the risk of getting stuck in what Deleuze might term an overcoded language featuring terms like 'resistance' and 'global capitalism' – as if these are known and stable categories that mean the same everywhere. When attending a discussion on how and whether art can be critical in the Iberia Centre for Contemporary Art on 4 May 2010, artist Lin Yilin explained how to him, the word 'critically', celebrated in art circles and often translated in Chinese as pipan (批判), is fraught with bad memories of the Cultural Revolution, when the same term had profoundly violent implications. It serves as a rather basic anthropological reminder, if not truism, of the need to be careful with the terms we use. In a similar vein, to characterise 798 as a district in which global capitalism, the art world and the Chinese nation-state are conflated runs the danger of reifying a binary in which the global is equated with capitalism and the local with the nation-state – whereas both are, as I argued earlier, intimately intertwined. The Iberia Centre is financed by a Chinese-European businessman, Gao Ping, who set up

5.2. Migrant labour protest in front of the Iberia Centre, June 2008 ('return my blood-sweat-earned money'). Courtesey: Gladys Pak Lei Chong.

the International Art and Culture Foundation in Spain to promote contemporary Chinese art and cultural exchange – another buzzword in the creative industry discourse. The centre often hosts exhibitions that engage with social issues. In 2008, while inside the centre, an installation work critiqued the lack of labourers' rights in China, ironically, outside the centre we ran into a demonstration by migrant workers who had gone on strike as they had not been paid (see figure 5.2).

This schism between the criticality of art and the social politics of the space itself is indicative of the question that was posed above, on how to be political in a sanitised zone such as 798. To look for an answer, I would like to focus on one exhibition, *Glass factory – Art in the new financial era* (15 April 2010 – 7 May 2010), which uses aesthetic reflexivity as its prime method, and then move on to the post-human aesthetics employed in Cao Fei's *RMB City*.

According to curator Sun Jianchu, the title of the exhibition is taken from a poem by the contemporary poet, Ouyang Jianghe. The curator explains the title as follows: the poem

> opens with the metaphor of sight: the conceptual penetration of the visual through matter which gives physical shape to everything originally abstract and spiritual. Glass factory symbolises a fairy-tale imprisonment of our culture of consumption (fashion window and the shimmering glass wall of sky scrapers), also suggests a new way of viewing typical of this age (camera, video camera and TV). Glass, once a characteristic representation of the medieval church myth, now is building a secular legend with fashion windows for the consumption era. It is exactly glass born from a young urban civilisation that is structuring consumptive psychology. (Sun 2010: 3)

Sun points to the importance of sight in today's cityscapes, and how new technologies facilitate new ways of seeing. His critique of the religion of consumption is translated into a selection of works that critique the commercialisation of the art world itself.

For example, in the work of Yang Zhenyong, who reproduces the work of some of the most famous photographers, as found on the Internet and printed actual size. The work thus highlights the reproducibility of works of art, and helps question the global system through which these works gain economic value. A conceptual work by Chen Shaoxiong involves the establishment of The Bank of Chinese Contemporary Art (BOCCA). The work resembles the kind of lounge one would find in a bank or real estate company. The slick white sofas, big flat-screen TVs and banners with graphs all mimic the corporate world to such an extent that it is easy to believe that this bank is real. The work comments on the auction and investment culture that has emerged around the Chinese art world. When visiting the Beijing Art Fair of 2010, numerous magazines were on display, all with titles like 'Art and Investment' and 'Art and Value' – outnumbering the magazines that dealt with the art itself. Art has become a lucrative business that is treated much like a stock exchange (when I mentioned to curator Pi Li the title of a book by Hans Abbing, *Why Are Artists Poor?*, he replied to me that in China, the title should be, *Why Are Chinese Artists Rich?*). What counts is not the work of art itself, but rather, the calculation of the best moment to sell the work again.

Chen Shaoxiong's bank claims that

> our service combines art work with investment opportunity in one unique package, providing a potentially low-risk and high-return fund that specialises in investing art works by well-established artists in the Chinese contemporary art market. [...] The BOCCA blue-chip fund is designed to cater to the need of investors who would like to invest in both critically and commercially recognised Chinese artists.

The conflation between the critical and the commercial resonates with Rey Chow's observation that the narrative of resistance and protest is an integral part of capitalism. The BOCCA initiative pokes fun at the Chinese art world, by mimicking its discourse of investment and quick turnover. It helps to counter the hegemony of the financial, yet at the same time, it risks falling back on a narrative in which commercialisation is perceived as incompatible with art.

The work of Ni Haifeng also critiques the investment culture of the Chinese art world, translating the work of Bourdieu into artistic practice. The work, entitled *Reciprocal Fetishism*, consists of a video in which we see an iron door; a door that, as the text explains, guards the collection of an art collector. The door is meant to protect the value of the work. The video underlines the immobility and static character of the collection: nothing moves, everything remains frozen in time and space. On display in the other part of the installation are items randomly taken from the apartment of the art collector, ranging from his Prada shoes, his plant, his books and a knife. The accompanying text explains the Bourdieudian rationale behind the work: 'the relation between an object and its symbolic image is inverted: the image does not represent the product, but, rather, the product represents the image. In this condition, a product of art is reduced to represent the symbolic power, the aura and lifestyle of the owner, institutional power, or in some cases, of the prestige of the very producer himself'. The work thus interrogates the relationship between a collector and his collection, as well as between the collector and the artist. More so, it questions the aesthetic value of art, which is replaced by its symbolic value, a value that does not need to be seen, as long as it is known to exist. The objects that are to be seen are the everyday objects that fill the collectors apartment, and what remains is to put these on display, so as to keep the collection itself protected and available for the art market. The work thus questions the fetishism of the art world, in which artworks are imbued with rapidly increasing cultural and, above all, economic value.

But what about the city, and the spectacle? The work of Ni Haifeng engages with the latter; it offers a critique of the society of the spectacle in which artworks have become commodities used to accumulate cultural and symbolic value. It shows how the spectacle does not always require visibility; what matters is the knowledge of the collection, more than the collection itself. The visual reigns, even when it is rendered invisible. The city itself, the place that is increasingly turned into a spectacle, with artistic theme parks and shiny glass skyscrapers, is not just a backdrop; it is the context that produces social relationships, that articulates subjectivities and that offers visions of both the past and the future. The work of Wang Youshen engages with the history of Beijing; it does so by washing photos of the city in water, thereby questioning the effects of time and the issue of remembering. Ironically, one of the works displayed in *Glass Factory* consists of two images, first a picture of the burned-down part of the CCTV building, and second, the same image after the process of washing. The irony in this image is that the building that once signified a hope for the future, a future in which China would become a global power, has turned into a quite different symbol: a symbol of decay, a symbol of failed supervision, as well as a symbol of censorship, given that Xinhua immediately tried to block all news of the fire, much to the dismay of many bloggers. A symbol of a lost future further disintegrates in the hands of Wang Youshen. What remains are some traces of a building that once expressed hope for the future; the building has become history before it has even been used. This disappearance of the future city, as displayed in the work *Washing Beijing*, stands in sharp contrast to the narratives of progress and prosperity that characterise dominant discourse in China, narratives that are drenched in a strong sense of nationalism. Wang Youshen shows that such narratives involve a selective remembering as well as a selective way of envisioning the future. His work shows the effects of time on a cityscape that is already disintegrating.

Yet, the circularity of the *Glass Factory* exhibition, with the art world that reflects upon the art world in a space that is located in the prime art zone of Mainland China, undermines, in my view, the point it tries to make. To critique the occularcentrism of our society by displaying visual works of art requires a great leap of faith. To critique the commercialism of art in an art zone that is so profoundly commercialised makes one also wonder how powerful such a critique can be, as Robin Visser also argues in this book. Does the space itself not overrule the works on display? The curators' vague statement that 'this exhibition attempts to embark in an art institution from an internal survey of art ecology' harks back towards itself, towards the art world. The self-reflexive and ideological aesthetics of *Glass Factory* risk reifying rather than challenging the art world and art zones like 798 – despite the works that are being displayed.

In other words, the representational mode of criticality runs the danger of being overruled by the space of representation itself. This, however, does not exclude the possibility of criticality, but maybe more than in the works themselves, these possibilities may be found in the uses of the space by the spectators. When walking through art zones like 798, two observations testify to the omnipresence of the visual in today's society. The spectacle of 798 is, above all, a visual spectacle. Below we can see three pictures taken on just one short walk in 798 (figure 5.3). The first picture is a photo shoot, most likely for a fashion magazine. The second picture, somehow even more bizarre, is a wedding photo shoot; here, the bride and groom are dressed as members of the Red Guards. The third picture of a racecar is emblematic of the convergence between art and capital (coupled with the freedom to flaunt the latter publicly), whereas the fourth picture is another wedding photo shoot. In particular, the re-enactment of the Cultural Revolution in a space that itself conjures up memories of a transitional communist utopia attests to the contradictions at work in 798. Communism and global capitalism can literally go hand in hand, so it seems. Indeed, the rise of creative China produces urban zones that are spectacles in which the visual reigns, presenting an ideal backdrop to photograph the modern, contemporary affluent self. No wonder that the camera is the one device carried by nearly all visitors.

5.3. A walk in 798, April 2010. Courtesy: Jeroen de Kloet.

This camera is also used inside the galleries; in a cheerful and carefree attitude towards copyright, visitors are generally allowed to take pictures of the works on display. This helps to undermine the sacredness of art and draws the work into the everyday lives of the spectators, who now collect pictures of art, along with other holiday pictures of, for example, Tiananmen and the Temple of Heaven. This appropriation of the work of art in everyday life becomes even more interesting, in my view, when we observe the ways in which pictures of art are taken. Very often, it is not the work of art being photographed, but a person together with the work of art (which resonates with the general habit of almost always

5.4. Mimicking art in 798, 2008. Courtesy: Jeroen de Kloet.

taking pictures with people, rather than of landscapes or buildings only). This person often tries to mimic the poses portrayed in the artwork, an act of mimicry that further helps to undermine the aura of the work of art (see figure 5.4).

This act of banalisation further turns 798 into a theme park of the contemporary, rather than a sacred art district. But instead of simply critiquing this, I think we can also point to its subversive potential, as it challenges the dominant modes of displaying works of art and thus of ways of seeing. It comes as no surprise that it is often galleries such as the Pace gallery from New York that eagerly retreat to the dominant practices of displaying art, strictly forbidding photographs of the works on display. Indeed, the staff followed me anxiously to prevent me from taking any pictures inside.

In other words, sight is the sense that predominates in 798; yet, despite the occularcentrism that permeates contemporary societies (cf. Jay 1992), the ways in which both the space 798 itself and the artworks that are on display are ingrained into the tourist experience can also help to subvert and undermine the aura of art. The possibilities of technological reproduction, as analysed by Walter Benjamin, are now also in the hands of amateur photographers, for whom a work of art becomes just another visual element to be included in one's holiday reportage – serving as a reminder of a specific moment in one's life. Rather than lamenting this further evaporation of the aura of art, we may also read this as yet another step in the democratisation of art, enabled by technologies of digital reproduction in a cultural context in which copyright is not yet heavily guarded by the cultural industries.

RMB City

Two years earlier, in the same Iberia Centre, I encountered a work that, in its digital form, is better able to escape the confines of the space in which it is exhibited, as it can always retreat to the virtual. *RMB City* refers to a second life city-planning project undertaken by Cao Fei's online avatar, China Tracy. She explains, 'as a two-year open-ended project in Second Life, the city will admit all different kinds of intellectual participation – to create a rich program of projects and events that will, in the process, transform the cityscape' (Cao 2008: 27). *RMB City* is rooted in game culture; its light-hearted play on the images of the city and its ungrounding of the real city trigger the viewer's curiosity. *RMB City* involved the creation of a virtual city as well as an art platform in which interactive art exhibitions and events were held over a two-year period. It attempts to mimic the structures of real-world real estate and urban planning (see http://www.rmbcity.com/home.html). The city is supposed to be

> the condensed incarnation of contemporary Chinese cities with most of their characteristics: a series of new Chinese fantasy realms that are highly self-contradictory, inter-permeative, laden with irony and suspicion, and extremely entertaining and pan-political. China's obsession with land development in all its intensity will be extended to second life. A rough hybrid of communism, socialism and capitalism, RMB City will be realised in a globalised digital sphere combining overabundant symbols of Chinese reality with cursory imaginings of the country's future. (Cao 2008: np)

The catalogue comes with elaborate explanations – including a manifesto – on the alleged meaning of the artwork, replete with ironic references to China's communist past ('Hand in Hand, Move Forward, Make a Virtual Future!'). The work received extensive coverage (as also testified by this volume); many regard Cao Fei as one of the country's most promising new artists. This process of sacralisation is not only gendered, as it is often Chinese femininity that travels best globally, but also linked to her age: born in the late 1970s, she is seen as the exponent of the new China. In the words of curator and art critic Hou Hanru, she is a part of a post-1989 generation growing up in a society driven by urbanisation and consumerism.

> Culturally and artistically, they are absolutely open to all kinds of newness and inventions, without any inhibitions or taboos. [...] By calling themselves 'New New Human Beings', they align themselves with completely new forms of living, believing and behaving. At the end, they never hesitate to merge themselves into the new globalised world driven by consumerism and technology. (Hou 2008: 46)

Cao Fei links her own work in her blog to the upcoming Shanghai World Expo, as both signify a utopian aspiration. She writes:

> The theme of Expo 2010 BETTER CITY, BETTER LIFE shares the same implicit utopian urge incidental to any real and virtual society. In Shanghai as well as in *RMB City* history and the past blend with progress and the future, ancient values and traditions find their way amongst modern models and new standards of life and Chinese paradigms overlap cosmopolitan issues. (From http://rmbcity.com/category/blog/, accessed 24 October 2009)

Thus, in the artist's discourse as well as in the reviews of the critic, we see how a rhetoric of the new is appropriated to position the artist and her work, and how alliances are forged with a state-sanctioned project such as the Shanghai Expo. In other words, the positioning of the work can be considered an example of the state-global creative industry nexus, as discussed above. But that, in my eyes, would do injustice to the work itself. It is tempting to read Cao Fei's words as articulations of the meaning of the work; in other words, to take the intentionality of the author as the authenticator of her work, and hence as the expression of its true meaning. However, visual works are to be seen as objects in themselves, objects that travel and circulate. The object itself also speaks back to its audiences (cf. Bal 2002). Following Bakhtin, we can push this even further by pointing at the danger of positioning a work *only* in its time and place. As Bakhtin writes about the study of literary texts, 'it is impossible to study literature apart from an epoch's entire culture, it is even more fatal to encapsulate a literary phenomenon in the single epoch of its creation, in its own contemporaneity, so to speak' (1986: 3). In the following paragraphs, I would like to explore the work, and its criticality, in terms of its imageries, tracing its representational mode of criticality, as well as in terms of its mode of circulation, focusing on the spatial and temporal modes of criticality.

First, the work itself: it presents the city as if it were a factory, a constantly moving, self-sustaining utopian machine that, at the same time, is permeated with its referent: China (including Hong Kong). We see Tiananmen Square, recognising the statue and the walls of the Forbidden City, yet the square has become a swimming pool, with palm trees and deck chairs. What was once the prime signifier of the political has morphed into a space of fun and leisure. A portrait of a panda replaces the portrait of Mao, as if the system has changed from authoritarianism into a new, cuddly mode of politics. It is a virtual world that transforms the real into the surreal, a magnification as well as a subversion of contemporary China. The most emblematic forms of urban pride – Tiananmen, the Oriental Pearl TV tower, Koolhaas' CCTV building, the Olympic Stadium, the National Grand Theatre, the Bank of China and the controversial Three Gorges reservoir – and at the same time, the small housing blocks, high-rise buildings and shabbier areas; all of these appear in *RMB City*, but are dislodged from reality, become surfaces whose 'original' materiality has evaporated in Second Life, to be replaced by a more playful, more ironic virtual materiality. The prime symbol of China's pride – the national stadium (the Bird's Nest) – is already in decay in *RMB City*: it is rusting away, standing in water, as if the nation-state that it used to signify has disintegrated. CCTV has become the people's entertainment television; it is hovering around the city, on the verge of being smashed against the ground or another building – with hindsight, a somewhat visionary image, given that part of it burned down in early 2009. The yellow stars have been removed from the red flag; instead, they are stars that keep the red flag floating freely in the sky. In the catalogue, the image of the flag is juxtaposed against the image of rock star Cui Jian, whose eyes are blindfolded by a piece of red cloth – a famous metaphorical critique on the system.

The work *RMB City* speaks back to the symbols that time and again appear to signify a new and prosperous China: it undermines and subverts them, transforms them into ironic and playful symbols of a both utopian and dystopian city that appears as a post-human factory. In the catalogue, 'RMB' is also linked to the word ReMemBering; the work expresses a politics of memorising the present in a different way. But at the same time, the title expresses how the work itself is enmeshed in processes of commercialisation:

> In this spectacular, extravagant and vehement manner, coupled with a great sense of humour and irony, a new China Town is born. Conceived as a kind of fantasy that only exists in 'lucid dreams' and mirage, or a kind of Calvino-style invisible city, it is nevertheless inseparable from reality in the First Life: it's named after the Ren Min Bi, China's national currency, and is for sale, with everyone welcome to invest his or her own money for the purchase and collection of buildings in the name of art. The actual exhibition of the work functions as a real estate agency and sales are targeted at the 'global art world'. (Hou 2008: 51)

The work is utopian in that it transforms signifiers that are loaded with political meaning into more playful ones; it transforms the real into the surreal, mocking the present and its obsessions with progress and the rhetoric of the perpetual new. It is dystopian in presenting the city as a post-human machine, parts of which are in decay, a city in which human life appears to be absent, or in which life is waiting to happen.

Indeed, in presenting the city as a machine, in its endless spinning and circulating, supported by the soothing tones of lounge music, the work also opens up the possibility of thinking differently; it presents a potential line of flight outside the current rush for urbanisation and progress: 'In this sense, all history is really the history of perception, and what we make history with is the matter of becoming, not the subject matter of a story. Becoming is like the machine: present in a different way in every assemblage, passing from one to the other, opening up one onto the other, outside any fixed order or determined sequence' (Deleuze and Guattari 1987: 347). In the manifesto of *RMB City*, Cao Fei declares that *RMB City* is 'a mirror that partially reflects; we see where we are coming from, discover some of the connections that fill the pale zone between the real and the virtual, the clues of which get disturbed, enriched, and polished. New orders are born, so are new strange wisdom' (2008: np). By transforming the project of urbanisation to a virtual realm, Cao Fei forges new possibilities of thinking and living the urban; her visual tactics playfully hark back to a reality that urgently requires an ethical repositioning. Instead of surrendering to the rhetoric of the perpetual new, she is looking for lines of flight, exploring a micro-politics that aims at difference, rather than newness, at different modes of becoming Chinese, or becoming wo/man, or becoming post-human. As she had already remarked in 1999, 'Oh, all you unfortunate men and women! If only you could alter your understanding and change your erroneous ways' (Cao 2008: np).

This brings me to the second point of the work: its mode of circulation. Alongside the official presentations at numerous biennales and museums, one can also participate through Second Life in making and buying parts of the work, and it is available on YouTube and other digital platforms. This raises important questions about works of art at a time of global digital circulation. According to Buck-Morss, 'images circle the globe today in de-centred patterns that allow unprecedented access, sliding almost without friction past language barriers and national frontiers. This basic fact, as self-evident as it is profound, guarantees the *democratic* potential of image-production and distribution' (2004: 2; italics in original). Images are to be seen as surfaces; the materiality of the image sends out two lines of force, one towards the viewer, and the other to the world:

> Lines of perception moving across the surface of multiple images traverse the world in infinite direction and variation. Cutting through space rather than occupying it as an object with extensions, image-lines are rhizomic connections – transversalities rather than totalities. These image-lines produce the world-as-image that in our era of globalisation is the form of collective cognition. (Buck-Morss 2004: 17)

Images are not so much representations as *things* that travel and circulate globally – which explains why Lash and Lury propose to speak of the mediation of things rather than of representations (Lash & Lurry 2007). 'In our emergent age of global culture industry, where culture starts to dominate both the economy and the everyday, culture, which was previously a question of representation, becomes *thingified*' (Lash & Lurry 2007: 4).

The circulation of images can constitute a political moment; one of the best examples may be that of the images from Abu-Ghraib prison. The circulation of *RMB City* may cause unexpected alliances, since images and clips generally appear in conjunction with other images that are more or less related. Google image and YouTube constitute a rhizomic warehouse in which new meanings proliferate due to unexpected connections. It may come as no surprise that politically, this threatens the nation-state, which explains why YouTube is blocked in China and why Google has worked with the authorities for many years to censor content. But the circulation of images can never be contained completely: 'the promiscuity of the image allows for leaks. Images flow outside the bubble into an aesthetic field not contained by the official narration of power. The image that refuses to stay put in context of his narration is disruptive' (Buck-Morss 2004: 24). The often unrealised potential of art lies in its global circulation and appropriation, its material power to provoke new sensory perceptions of the world; an insight that leads Buck-Morss to pose the question that concludes her essay: '*What kind of community can we hope for from a global dissemination of images, and how can our work help to create it?*' (2004: 28; italics in original).

Conclusion

This chapter has tried to come to terms with the possibility of criticality in an urban context that is fast, fluid and volatile, and caught in a continuous cycle of appearance and disappearance. At a moment when the Chinese authorities, the global art world and global capital have joined forces, at a time in which resistance and protest are part of the logic of capitalism, what possibilities of criticality are left? In addition to probing representational modes of criticality (through looking at the artworks themselves), I have tried to show the importance of including time and space in our analysis. By sensitising ourselves to what may be termed temporal and spatial modes of criticality in our analysis, we may be able to look and think beyond the work of art itself, or better, to look and think of the work or art in terms of its *not yet actualised* meanings and possibilities. The ways a space such as 798 features in discourses on the appearance and disappearance of the Chinese city, the ways in which it becomes a marker of the passing of time for spectators, a nostalgic signpost of the contemporary, as well as the ways in which artworks travel through time and space, enabled by new technologies: these all testify to the possibility of art – but not necessarily the works themselves – changing our lives, or at least, of offering a sense of hope for the future, in which both the city, as well as our lives within the city, may be configured not just differently, but also better. Or is that too romantic a belief?

Notes

1. Available at http://leiden.dachs-archive.org/poetry/translations.html, translation by Michael Martin Day, accessed 22 May 2010.
2. A different version of this section has also appeared as: 'Created in China and Pak Sheung Chuen's Tactics of the Mundane', *Social Semiotics* 20, 4: 441-456 (2010).
3. Apart from the more ironic pop art of Wang Guangyi (see Jiang 2007 for an analysis of the recurrent theme of the Cultural Revolution in contemporary Chinese art), Chineseness is often deconstructed, as in the work of Xu Bing (see de Kloet 2007), or playfully appropriated, as we will later see in the work of Cao Fei (*RMB City*). In general, the young generation of artists – coined the 'Gelatin Generation' (see http://www.shanghaidaily.com/sp/article/2009/200910/20091030/article_417876.htm) – is considered to be much less preoccupied with history and Chineseness than with contemporary, global pop culture.

References

Bakhtin, Mikhail. *Speech Genres and Other Late Essays*. Austin: University of Texas Press, 1986.
Bal, Mieke. *Travelling Concepts in the Humanities*. Toronto: University of Toronto Press, 2002.
Buck-Morss, Susan. 'Visual Studies and Global Imagination.' www.surrealismcentre.ac.uk/papersofsurrealism/journal2/acrobat_files/buck_morss_article.pdf (accessed 28 January 2010).
Cao, Fei. 'RMB City.' In *Journey*, edited by Fei Cao, 28. Guangzhou: Vitamin Creative Space, 2008.

Cheng, Lei. '798 and a Global Art Market.' In *Beijing 798 Now: Changing Arts, Architecture and Society in China*, edited by Lei Cheng and Qi Zhu, 72-93. Beijing: Timezone 8, 2008.
Chow, Rey. 'On Chineseness as a Theoretical Problem.' *Boundary 2* 25, no.3 (1998): 1-24.
—. *Ethics after Idealism: Theory, Culture, Ethnicity, Reading*. Bloomington: Indiana University Press, 1998.
—. *The Protestant Ethnic and the Spirit of Capitalism*. New York: Columbia University Press, 2002.
Dai, Jinhua. '798: Space Imprinting and Covering the History.' *Urban China* 23 (2007): 33-37.
de Kloet, Jeroen. 'Cosmopatriot Contaminations.' In *Cosmopatriots: On Distant Belonings and Close Encounters*, edited by Jeroen de Kloet and Edwin Jurriens, 133-54. Amsterdam: Rodopi, 2007.
—. 'Created in China and Pak Sheung Chuen's Tactics of the Mundane.' *Social Semiotics* 20, no. 4 (2010): 441-55.
Deleuze, Gilles and Felix Guattari. *A Thousand Plateaus: Capitalism & Schizophrenia*. London: The Athlone Press, 1987.
Fung, Anthony. *Global Capital, Local Culture: Localization of Traditional Media Corporations in China*. New York: Peter Lang, 2008.
Hou, Hanru. 'Politics of Intimacy.' In *Journey*, edited by Fei Cao, 45-52. Guangzhou: Vitamin Creative Space, 2008.
Hu, Fang. 'Once Again, We're on the Road.' In *Journey*, edited by Fei Cao, 113-120. Guangzhou: Vitamin Creative Space, 2008.
Huang, Rui. 'Sublimating Time.' In B*eijing 798: Reflections on Art, Architecture and Society in China*, edited by Rui Huang, 2-4. Beijing: Timezone 8 + Thinking Hands, 2004.
—. '1.2.3.4.5.6.798.' In *Beijing 798: Reflections On 'Factory' Of Art*, edited by Rui Huang, 2-11. Chengdu: Sichuan Fine Arts Publishing House, 2008.
Jay, Martin. *Downcast Eyes: the Denigration of Vision in Twentieth-Century French Thought*. Berkeley and Los Angeles: University of California Press, 1994.
Jiang, Jiehong. *Burden or Legacy: From the Chinese Cultural Revolution to Contemporary Art*. Hong Kong: Hong Kong University Press, 2004.
Keane, Michael. *Created in China: The Great New Leap Forward*. London: RoutledgeCurzon, 2007.
Lash, Scott, and Celia Lury. *Global Culture Industry: The Mediation of Things*. London: Polity Press, 2007.
Li, Rui. 'The 157th Democratic Republic Emerges from East Germanys Willpower.' In *Beijing 798: Reflections on Art, Architecture and Society in China*, edited by Rui Huang, 18-21. Beijing: Timezone 8 + Thinking Hands, 2004.
Luo, Peilin. 'Recollections on the History of 718.' In *Beijing 798: Reflections on Art, Architecture and Society in China*, edited by Rui Huang, 10-13. Beijing: Timezone 8 + Thinking Hands, 2004.
Maravillas, Francis. 'Haunted Cosmopolitanisms: Spectres of Chinese Art in the Diaspora.' In *Cosmopatriots: On Distant Belongings and Close Encounters*,

edited by Jeroen de Kloet and Edwin Jurriens, 253-82. Amsterdam: Rodopi, 2007.

Pang, Laikwan. *Creativity and its Discontents: China's Creative Industries and Intellectual Property Rights Offenses*. Durham: Duke University Press, 2012.

Sun, Jianchun. *Glass Factory: Art in the New Financial Era*. Beijing: Iberia, 2010.

Wang, Jing. 'Culture as Leisure and Culture as Capital.' *Positions* 9, no.1 (2001): 69-104.

Zhao, Yuezhi. *Communication in China: Political Economy, Power, and Conflict*. Maryland: Rowan and Littlefield, 2008.

6. Tuning Urban China

Jeroen Groenewegen-Lau

Sound art emerged in the People's Republic of China (PRC) around 2003. A substantial part of the scene makes abundant use of street sounds and other field recordings. These soundscape projects experiment not only with sound, but also with social engagement and critiques of urban transformation. I argue that Guy Debord's concept of the spectacle helps us to understand this under-researched scene, because Debord puts forward a question that also lies at the heart of sound art in China: is critique of the political system possible in contemporary societies?

The Revolution Will Not be Televised

> The whole life of those societies in which modern conditions of production prevail presents itself as an immense accumulation of spectacles. All that once was directly lived has become mere representation. (Debord 1994)

The Society of Spectacle radically opposes any kind of social separation. According to Debord, social separation lies at the root of inequality, suppression and

6.1. Flyer of the performance 'Rabbit Travelogue: Central Region' by the Hong Kong sound artist Edwin Lo. Courtesy: www.myspace.com/onsonicart.

alienation, it obstructs historical development (as defined by Marx) and in the final analysis, is an attack on life (cf. Debord 1994: Proposition 25: 171).

This fundamental problem is not only masked by the modern media; from the first proposition quoted above, the major contribution of *The Society of Spectacle* is its insistence on the fact that mass media and culture in general are structurally only capable of fueling social separation. In other words, Debord's notion of the spectacle pushes the Marxist adage of culture as the opium of the people to its logical extreme. He argues that since all culture is by definition divorced from reality (theatrically commenting upon, reenacting, escaping from, aspiring to reality), it is by definition part of the immense accumulation of spectacles. Even for critique, there seems to be no possible solution to this dilemma:

> In order to describe the spectacle, its formation, its functions and whatever forces may hasten its demise, a few artificial distinctions are called for. To analyze the spectacle means talking its language to some degree – to the degree, in fact, that we are obliged to engage the methodology of the society to which the spectacle gives expression. For what the spectacle expresses is the total practice of one particular economic and social formation; it is, so to speak, that formation's agenda. It is also the historical moment by which we happen to be governed. (Debord 1994: Proposition 11)

> Revolutionary theory is now the sworn enemy of all revolutionary ideology – and it knows it. (Debord 1994: Proposition 124)

But the mere fact that Guy Debord wrote *The Society of Spectacle,* and later made it into a film, suggests that he himself believes that mass-mediated critique is possible, even necessary. Just as the revolutionary organisation must strive towards its undoing in the revolutionary moment, along with all social separation (Debord 1977: 120), 'good' culture openly aspires to its own destruction:

> Art in the period of its dissolution, as a movement of negation in pursuit of its own transcendence in a historical society where history is not yet directly lived, is at once an art of change and a pure expression of the impossibility of change. The more grandiose its demands, the further from its grasp is true self-realization. This is an art that is necessarily avant-garde; and it is an art that is not. Its vanguard is its own disappearance. (Debord 1994: Proposition 190)

My hypothesis is that the simultaneous necessity and impossibility of anti-spectacular critique is the driving force behind Chinese soundscape projects.

Sound and Spectacle

The concept of the spectacle is biased towards the visual, potentially complicating my use of the concept with regards to sound. Debord's most succinct definition is:

> The spectacle is *capital* accumulated to the point where it becomes image.
> (Debord 1994: Proposition 34)

This conclusion of the first chapter refers back to proposition 18:

> The spectacle [...] naturally finds vision to be the privileged human sense which the sense of touch was for other epochs [...]; the most abstract, the most mystifiable sense corresponds to the generalized abstraction of present-day society. But the spectacle is not identifiable with mere gazing, even combined with hearing. [...] It is the opposite of dialogue. Wherever there is independent representation, the spectacle reconstitutes itself. (Debord 1977)

While Debord argues that vision presently has priority, he does not exclude other senses, such as touching and hearing, as methods of dialogue and representation. Moreover, precisely the fact that sound is less privileged makes it a suitable medium for anti-spectacular critique. Soundscapes challenge the dominance of the eye, a prerogative of the society of spectacle.

Strategies of Criticality

Two strategies that Debord and his fellow situationists have formulated are *dérive* and *détournement*. Debord:

> One of the basic situationist practices is the *dérive* [drift], a technique of rapid passage through varied ambiences. *Dérives* involve playful-constructive behavior and awareness of psychogeographical effects, and are thus quite different from the classic notions of journey or stroll. (Debord 1958)

Although a *dérive* may create chance encounters, its goal is rather the mapping and critiquing of spatially inscribed distinctions and hierarchies.

Whereas *dérives* take place in urban space, *détournements* do their comparable work in media and art. Like the pastiche and the ready-made, it is a recombination of pre-existing elements, which in this case is aimed at re-appropriating (popular) culture through guerrilla aesthetics and thus showing consumers that they can become active. The situationists *détourned* comics by changing the words of text balloons.

In the following pages I will evaluate how *dérive*, *détournement* and similar problem-ridden anti-spectacular strategies play out in Chinese soundscape projects. I will develop and test my hypothesis of Chinese soundscape projects' impossible anti-spectacularity by suggesting that they developed out of dissatisfaction with the spectacularity of other scenes; are interactive; aspire to criticality; and challenge social atomisation.

6.2. Flyer of Waterland Kwanyin (week 135) that reuses a picture of Mini Midi shot from the underground.

The Emergence of Sound Art in the PRC

2003 was the year in which the experimental electronic music scene emerged in the PRC. This is suggested by the four CDs of 'An Anthology of Chinese Electronic Music 1992-2008', published by the prestigious Belgium label Sub Rosa. These CDs furthermore suggest that the PRC has overtaken other Chinese-speaking regions since 2006. In addition, in 2003, the four-day Sounding Beijing (北京声纳) festival took place, for the first time offering Chinese musicians the opportunity to perform on the same stage as internationally renowned sound artists. Many of its participants have roots in the bands scene, which is true for most Chinese sound artists.[1]

In the PRC, as in other places, rock music's inclination towards drama and spectacularity threatens to encapsulate its subversive potential, making it come across as mere posing – a point that connects Jeroen de Kloet's discussion of rock mythology in China (de Kloet 2010) to Debord's analysis:

> The individual who in the service of the spectacle is placed in stardom's spotlight is in fact the opposite of an individual, and as clearly the enemy of the individual in himself as of the individual in others. (Debord 1994: Proposition 61)

Although additional fieldwork is needed to confirm this, I argue that in the early 2000s, a substantial number of Beijing rock musicians became aware of and even frustrated with rock music's limitations and looked for alternatives. This energy fuelled innovations in the scene, most notably the inclusion of parody and self-ridicule, and the emergence of new scenes around folksong and experimental electronic music (see Groenewegen-Lau 2011a).

This argument is exemplified by Yan Jun, who developed from rock critic via poetry and curating to become one of China's most influential sound artists. In the late 1990s he drafted the Declaration of Tree Village (树村声明) in which the rock scene collectively denounced being used as exotic props in a Hong Kong romantic film, marking the high-point of the underground scene and its stance against commodification (Groenewegen-Lau 2011b). In a recent interview, he looked back on the event:

> It was very easy to turn my face then. That was so hurtful for [director Mabel Cheung] and her team. Sorry! There was no argument between us before the 'Declaration'. Today I think it's always worth fighting against the spectacle machine: media, entertainment, mass will, political drama, etc. In the past I fought against it with the 'Declaration'. Today I fight against it by avoiding all kinds of declarations, since I have to end the logic of the dramatic illusion – which is the only thing you get from movements today. (Hudsucker 2011)

Yan Jun's activities in the 2000s can be seen as furthering his underground rock challenge to commodified rock and state rituals with other means. In 2003, he added the sub-label Kwanyin Records for experimental music to his label Sub Jam. Since 2005, he has organised the capital's sole weekly series of experimental electronic shows, entitled Waterland Kwanyin (水陆观音), as well as the annual open-air festival, Mini Midi.[2]

The emergent scene did not find support in Chinese conservatories, which stress spectacular virtuosity.[3] Although not entirely non-existent, connections with the dance music scene have also remained rather limited.[4] But sound art did relate to visual art, when in the 1990s, Li Zhenhua, Qiu Zhijie and others stumbled upon sound in their performance, video and digital art. Site-specific art has also proved an ally of sound art because of its explicit challenge to the spectacularisation and encapsulation of art in museums and galleries (Dal Lago 2000: 82).

But sound art's connections with the globally successful visual art scene simultaneously open up a different reading of its spectacularity. Whereas site-specific art ostensibly sought to get *out* of museums, sound art strove to get *into* the circuit of museums and art festivals. The double album, Music for Museums (美术馆音乐), with music by Yan Jun, Zafka and others was part of an exhibition at the Arnolfini in Bristol in 2008.5 In this light, sound art is a hip global idiom that enables former rock musicians and tech-savvy nerds to organise solo performances that spectacularly display the latest Western trends in China and vice versa.

Interactivity and Engagement

> The sound of the construction site at night. I know that at this moment two cities exist simultaneously. One is the birth of bustle and another is the dying out of silence. The sounds resemble both the crying of a newborn baby and the moaning of the end. I know all sound will cease one day. If that moment comes I wonder if I would feel at ease or lost. (Han Xu, Beijing, British Council 2008: 151)

> The elegant, quiet, serene and evocative bell sound. When I was a kid, I often took a walk with my grandparents on the street near the Liberation Monument. Surrounding chatting and merchant's hawking would drench us in hubbub. Only when the bell on the monument rang, I realized I had entered another world: a elegant, quiet and serene heaven induced by the bell's sound. Listening to this celestial sound became the joy of my childhood. My childhood memories were carved into that bell sound. (Wu Yu'an, Chongqing, British Council 2008: 160)

In these descriptions, Chinese locals engage with and reflect upon their sonic environment. They are taken from the 'Sound and the City' (都市发声) project, whose essence it is, paraphrasing the words of its organiser Colin Chinnery, to conceptualise a sense of place, identity, and society and communicate with the general public on this in open urban settings (British Council 2008: 4). I will now listen in on a number of specific soundscape projects, arguing that interactivity is one of the defining aspects of soundscape projects. Do these projects encourage participation to the point where social separation dissolves?

Sound and the City

Sound and the City was initiated by the British Council and took place in 2005 and 2006. It consisted of two parts, which are reflected in the two CDs that accompany the book *Sound and the City: City. Sound Environment* (都市发声：城市。声音环境) (2008). The first CD consists of field recordings in Beijing, Shanghai, Chongqing, and Guangzhou. Notwithstanding the fact that these cities are major hubs in their own right, the choice of Chongqing and Guangzhou marks an attempt to include a broader Chinese audience than that in the PRC's political and economic centres, Beijing and Shanghai. In addition, the sounds of the first

6.3. *Sound and the City* cover. Courtesy: British Council

CD were, in many cases, submitted by inhabitants and selected through relatively democratic procedures involving online voting and juries of specialists in the respective cities. In Beijing, 200 iPods were distributed as prizes for the most interesting submissions.

The second CD consists of commissioned works inspired by Chinese urban sound ecologies that were made by seven British sound artists, namely Brian Eno, David Toop, Peter Cusack, Clive Bell, Scanner (Robin Rimbaud), Kaffe Matthews and Robert Jarvis (links refer to side-projects inspired by the Sound and the City project).[6] As such, its sound is much more clearly manipulated, foregrounding it as the artist's reaction to the Chinese city rather than the Chinese city 'itself'. In other words, because of its intervention and mediation, it suggests more agency, as well as more critical distance and estrangement.

Nevertheless, these works also revolve around collective effort and interactivity, which occurs during creative processes that can inevitably be poorly represented by finished products such as books and CDs. A number of these seem to be inspired by the theory of the *dérive* or drift. For instance, *Sonic Bicycle Ride* consists of eight bicycles with loudhailers attached that follow different routes through a *hutong* area, creating 'chance combinations and bizarre sonic coincidences' in familiar neighbourhood settings (British Council 2008: 55). Whereas *Sonic Bicycle Ride* intrudes into public space quite aggressively, other works seek to establish contact in more subtle ways. Li Qiang, who accompanied Robert Jarvis in Chongqing, recounts:

> Robert played back the recording [we made during the day] to us in the nightclub. It was fantastic. All the notes have an uncertain quality to them, the bell, the phone, the trombone, the duck [...] but you could feel the emotional shifts.

Robert explained to us that he had employed a lot of modern technologies, such as splitting the original sound into numerous tiny little notes, dispersing them and putting them back together. I can't believe these are the sounds we encounter everyday, and that, with Robert's processing, these sounds can become so magical as to move beyond the usual sense of well-sounding. (British Council 2008: 116)

Despite drawbacks, such the audience's reluctance to lie down and immerse themselves in Kaffe Matthews *Sonic_Bed Shanghai* (British Council 2008: 138), *Sound and City* was successful in eliciting interaction between artwork and audience. At the same time, as a whole the project cannot entirely avoid the paternalism of teaching the Chinese to cherish their sonic and social environment.

Get it Louder

Yan Jun and others developed the interactivity of Sound and the City at the modern media festival Get it Louder, in 2007 under the supervision of curator in chief Ou Ning (www.getitlouder.com). The travelling festival brought Home Show (咖哩秀) and Moving Soundscape (听游记) to Guangzhou, Shanghai, Beijing and Chengdu.[7]

Since experimental electronic music generally only attracts small audiences, organising shows in people's homes is viable, which then enhances intimacy and invites participation (Liu Tianyun 2008). During a show in Shanghai in the home of Lu Chen, the lead singer of the improvisational rock band Top Floor Circus (顶楼马戏团), in a variation of *détournement* or re-appropriation, each participant was asked to bring one piece of dirty laundry. The home show would continue as long as the clothes were collectively being washed in a noisy washing machine that was standing in the middle of the cramped room, and that functioned as the centre of the shared improvisation. Due to the modest costs and their informal nature, home shows were not only able to explore new ways of interacting with audiences, but they could also travel beyond the obvious venues in coastal metropolises and into second-tier cities. Liu Tianyun claims that by 2008, in addition to eight shows in Beijing, home shows had been held in at least twelve cities, including Chengdu, Shenzhen, Dalian, Lanzhou, Hangzhou and Guangzhou, and Paris (a list can be found on Yan Jun's blog).[8]

Criticality

Soundscape projects seek to engage people in more direct ways than are commonly found in official media and at pop and rock concerts. This is illustrated by the fact that there often is no stage at sound art events to demarcate the hierarchy between performer and audience. But does this make soundscape projects democratic and critical? In this section I argue that soundscape projects are politically engaged, albeit in different and at times mutually conflicting ways.

Working-Class Neighbourhoods

The most obvious form of political engagement lies in the endeavour of soundscape projects to give voice to lower-class people. In a number of projects this endeavour is directly coupled to protest against demolition-and-relocation projects that threaten specific neighbourhoods.

Ou Ning initiated the Da Zha Lan Project as an art project to document a traditional *hutong* area at the southwestern corner of Tiananmen Square that was on the demolition-and-relocation list in preparation for the 2008 Olympics (www.dazhalan-project.org). The documentary *Meishi Street* (煤市街) (Ou Ning, 2006) sums up the context and purpose of this project. It shows how people in the area deal with this change: some count their blessings and leave, lamenting when they revisit its ruins, others get increasingly agitated in their frustrating attempts to stop what proves to be inevitable. The documentary fulminates and becomes melodramatic and voyeuristic when it zooms in on the pain suffered by the documentary's protagonist and most outspoken protester when the bulldozers pull down his small restaurant. Also part of this project, Yan Jun and Olivier Meys recorded 'sound documentations' in the area in 2005, which are available online.

The ex-band leader of AMK, Anson Mak, embarked on a similar but even more personal project in Hong Kong. She introduces the track 'Dawn Market' of her album *Going Home (Or Not)* (番（唔番）屋企) (2009) in the liner notes:

> Fuck the TVB story on dawn market that victimizes people by its usual unstylish yet cheesy dramatic ways of narrative for a seemingly objective documentary work. It narrowly and barely represents people's various dimensions in such markets. My observations and comments to the Kwun Tong dawn market, and as an ethnographic practice and a reflexive representation via soundscape, are very different than what the mass media represents. I realize the vibrancy and energy; the joy and green-life, the creativity and positive interactions in it. Instead of victimizing sellers/buyers as powerless and as the lowest spectrum of our society, I'd rather want to raise concern to other issues: due to the urban 'renewal' plan and property management-driven mentality, senior citizens (we also) may gradually lose the immense freedom for creative use(s) of street space (public space). Then, people's ways of lives, energy exchanges and many layers of social interactions and inter-relations will vanish. This is what most hurts them, by the admin-oriented, superficial and visionless Hong Kong Government rule.

The track is available at Re-records and on the website, A Map of Our Own: Kwun Tong Culture and Histories, where it is part of an ongoing effort to preserve this old Hong Kong neighbourhood and its social structure from demolition-and-relocation.[9] It is also a highly personal project, because Mak grew up in this area.

These and similar soundscape projects draw attention to the human cost of urban transformation by re-evaluating everyday life as something special, and as worth preserving and fighting for. They demand political participation, while at the same time they appeal to feelings of nostalgia for the relatively close-knit communities of the folk village or the *danwei,* the work unit that dominated social life in the PRC of the 1950s, 1960s and 1970s.

Fashion Soundwalk

Nostalgia and melancholia – also clear in the popular submissions to the Sound and the City project quoted above – are easily commodified in the society of spectacle. In other words, following Debord, nostalgic and melancholic strands threaten to neutralise the criticality of soundscape projects.

In 2008 the luxury fashion brand Louis Vuitton commissioned Stephan Crasneanscki of the New York-based new media company Soundwalk to create soundwalks in Beijing, Shanghai and Hong Kong. The website www.louisvuittonsoundwalk.com (now defunct, mirror site)[10] offers maps and three ten-minute audio guides through these metropolises with voice-overs by the well-known actresses Gong Li, Joan Chen and Shu Qi respectively, and the opportunity to purchase full 60-minute versions. This rare mainstream appearance of soundscapes targeted fashionable youths and encouraged them to take the tour while listening to these guides on their iPods. The soundwalks may resemble a *dérive,* but instead of critiquing spatially inscribed hierarchies, they reiterate them in order to fuel nostalgic longing and dreams of social mobility. The voice-overs are typically low, dry and near, and enhance intimacy by introducing themselves and consequently addressing the listener with 'you':

> Have you arrived at the Mansion Hotel? Find yourself a seat and sit down. Can you get me a cup of tea? Thank you. [pause, slow cello music] I am Joan Chen. I'm an actress, and also a director. I was born in Shanghai. I meet you today because I am going to tell you a love story, a beautiful story. Like so many love stories, it is full of hope and despair.

The narratives tell of romances that might once have developed in these locations, to which the music by Kubert Leung and Albert Yu adds a second layer that enhances sentimentality and drama. Sounds of the opening of doors, heels on the pavement, and people drinking in a café with high ceilings contrast with both the narrative and the music, because like old photographs, or rather documentaries, these street sounds foreground realism and the mimetic. These sounds, and soundscapes in general, draw the listener's ear by citing familiar sonic events.

De-valuating Sound

Nostalgia and melancholia are not the only threats that potentially neutralise the criticality of soundscape projects. On a more fundamental level, it is problematic to mobilise sounds for an argument or narrative, as the Shanghai-based sound artist Yin Yi suggests in a column for the magazine *Art World* (艺术世界):

Field recording (实地录音) does not exclude the other (没有排他性). [...] You could say a field recording is a sonic landscape (景观), a sonic field (场域). In this place that is constituted out of a series of sounds, no sound deserves more attention than any other. During aural evaluation, all sounds are of equal value. Precisely this concept of equal value in listening makes this whole sonic place vague, indecisive, uncontrollable and even chaotic. But at the same time what arises is multiplicity, variety, polysemy, surprise and the unfathomable. (Yin 2011a)

The Louis Vuitton Soundwalks are dominated by a verbal narrative, which reduces street sounds to illustrations that support the consumer's dream of detachedness. Laurent Jeanneau's *Soundscape China* builds an argument by juxtaposing, for instance, a talking calculator at a market with folk songs, but these sounds are only significant in as far as they contribute to Jeanneau's critique of China's modernisation. The Da Zha Lan project and A Map of Our Own also imbue sounds with meaning through framing narratives. Such citations differ from *détournement*, which does not organise its pre-existing elements in a smooth narrative or hierarchy.

The liberation of the ear from the terror of the eye that Yin Yi suggests also underlies Yan Jun's more radical slogan of Mini Midi 2008, 'Noise=Free' (www.yanjun.org/download). This liberation can be heard as a stand-in for the liberation of the individual from the terror of the spectacle. However, this line of interpretation cannot be made explicit in the soundscape projects, lest this narrative take centre stage in a spectacular way. And when the transference of human suppression onto the enslavement of sound is not articulated, the exploration of sound may become a goal in itself, beyond social relevance, and at a level of abstraction hard to relate to by general audiences. Yan Jun explains in his history of sound art:

> Whereas the visual arts first embraced abstraction and projection, the aural arts were much later. People would still be angry if we, like abstract painting, would offer sound's pitch, timbre and materiality without transmitting a so called meaning or when we, like film cameras, record and present reality's original sounds. Because that's not art. (Yan 2006)

In an exchange of e-mail, Yin Yi also hesitated between, on the one hand, acknowledging that sound art is inevitably art, that is, elitist and inconsequential; and on the other hand, that it has social responsibility and should therefore stay away from grand theory and the spectacle.

> Groenewegen-Lau: Do you want to make audiences aware of their environment?
> Yin: Besides realizing my own vision [sic], this was indeed my initial idea. But what I wanted urbanites to pay attention to was sound, their sense of hearing. Because, you know, China is dominated by visual culture. And this visual culture is disastrous. [...]

Groenewegen-Lau: Who do you think is your audience: the elite, the petty bourgeoisie, the People, the proletariat?
Yin: Personally I think my audience includes everyone. But I think that the only ones that can enter the discourse of my works are the elite – the cultural elite. Because what we make is art. [...]
Groenewegen-Lau: If I were to use Guy Debord's The Society of Spectacle to argue that China's sound ecology projects try to establish a new space and new human relations outside of the spectacle, would you think that I'm too political, too Marxist, even too spectacular?
Yin: Yes. I don't incline to any grand narrative. I start from myself. But this doesn't mean I don't care about the outside world. It's just that I doubt that art is a very efficient way of getting involved in (介入) society. [...] Should art be directly involved in politics? [...] China's artworks are getting bigger in size and scope, [becoming] grand narratives, aiming at the largest social effect. A friend argued that this is related to China's overall environment, how China as a nation comes into its own on the world stage. [This is illustrated by] the Olympics, World Expo, plans for ascending the moon, and so on. But ironically, although lots of artists on the surface resist this national consciousness, their own works hint at this ideology. Is that strange? Perhaps it's not. (Yin Yi, personal communication, 23 February 2011)

Zafka

As far as I can see, Yin Yi's portrayal of sound art as working-class-conscious and environment-friendly art for cultural elites (or: leftist intellectuals) seems justified. I will discuss one of his projects briefly below. But first I will take a short detour by exploring the tension between detached (and therefore potentially spectacular) political criticism on the one hand and the liberation of sound on the other, in relation to the development of Zafka.

Zafka received an MA in Political Studies from London's School of Oriental and Africa Studies (SOAS), and has been quite vocal in *The Sound and The City* (presumably written around 2006) and other early texts:[11]

> [close-listening] is firstly the destruction of the hegemonic ideological aesthetics – keep sound in its own position (本位主义), ears wide open and reconsider the hierarchical order hidden in your listening habits. (British Council 2008: 30)

As part of Get It Louder 2007, Zafka organised a team that focused on an area spanning both Beijing's *hutongs* and the city's Central Business District (CBD). Participants in Reinvent Your City, as the project was called, started recording sounds, taking notes, planning routes and creating works two months prior to the opening:

On one side of Dongdaqiao Road lie the relatively quiet embassy district and Ritan Park. The other side is littered with commercial districts that contain lots of apartments such as The Spaces International (尚都国际) and Soho Shangdu (尚都). In front of these residential buildings there are no flowerbeds, bicycle sheds or any other usable public spaces. So those old ladies and men can only play cards and chess or enjoy the breeze on the sidewalks. The constantly expanding CBD is kept on one side of the street by Ritan Park and the embassy district, but still it ceaselessly expands upwards and sideways, pressing against and swallowing neighboring residential spaces.[12]

Reinvent Your City can be understood as a *dérive*. But this reading is problematic because rather than a map that creates new possibilities, it offers an ethical and political evaluation of the transformations of the areas it scrutinises. By contrast, the album Yong Ø He (雍 Ø 和) (2006) signifies a change in Zafka's approach. As he explains in *City Pictorial* (城市画报):

> Yong He made me realize that my reevaluation of sounds as an observer or critic of city sounds had had cold moralist tendencies, such as criticizing a neighborhood for being too noisy. I started to rethink what an interesting urban sonic structure should be like, while avoiding basing myself in aural pleasantness or irresponsible nostalgia. The exploration of sound should return to life itself. (*City Pictorial* 2007)[13]

I interpret Zafka's otherwise vague vocation of 'life itself' in the light of Debord's qualification of the spectacle as being opposed to life, mentioned in the introduction. Zafka argues convincingly that offering a strong narrative framework threatens to defeat the purpose of soundscape projects, namely to reduce alienation and social separation.

Environmentalism and Social Atomisation

In the 1970s, R. Murray Schafer was the first to systematically describe the effects of modernisation on the sonic environment and argue that these changes are significant. Composer Barry Truax sums up his approach: 'The real goal of the soundscape composition is the re-integration of the listener with the environment in a balanced ecological relationship' (1996: 63). Through soundwalks and earcleaning, Schafer tried to overturn the trend fuelled by recording technology towards the splitting of sounds from their sources, which he called schizophonia. Concepts such as schizophonia, as well as the World Soundscape Project as it was originally conceived, seek to re-integrate not only human and nature, but also sound and source, and more generally, signifier and signified.

Although Schafer's stance against alienation seems similar to that of Debord, and Schafer's *Tuning the World* offers a powerful vocabulary to describe soundscapes, I have opted for Debord's approach throughout this chapter. In essence, R. Murray Schafer's position is that of a Romantic humanist, who longs for the time when the integrity of humans and their environment had not been corrupted by cities and machines. Whereas Schafer suggests a retreat into the countryside, Debord suggest taking over the streets and re-appropriating the machines – and this approach seems more suited to what is happening in contemporary Chinese soundscape projects. In addition, Debord is much more critical of the conditions for re-integration:

> Urbanism is the modern way of tackling the ongoing need to safeguard class power by ensuring the atomization of workers dangerously massed together by the conditions of urban production. [...] The effort of all established powers [...] to augment their means of keeping order in the street has eventually culminated in the suppression of the street itself. [...]
>
> But the general trend toward isolation, which is the essential reality of urbanism, must also embody a controlled reintegration of the workers based on the planned needs of production and consumption. Such an integration into the system must recapture isolated individuals as individuals isolated together. Factories and cultural centres, holiday camps and housing developments – all are expressly oriented to the goals of a pseudo-community of this kind. These imperatives pursue the isolated individual right into the family cell, where the generalized use of receivers of the spectacle's message ensures that his isolation is filled with the dominant images – images that indeed attain their full force only by virtue of this isolation. (Debord 1994: Proposition 172)

Do Chinese soundscape projects connect and disconnect people with their sonic environment? Do they challenge the social atomisation of the spectacle?

Conditioning Technologies

R. Murray Schafer deplores the urban acoustic environment and many contemporary publications focus on noise reduction, singling out specific industries, means of traffic, amplifiers and other machines as producers of particularly unwanted sounds. By contrast, most soundscapes have a relatively favourable attitude towards modern technology, and by extension towards urbanity. Inspired by Peter Cusack's project Your Favourite London Sounds (www.favouritelondonsounds.org), the Sound and the City project in China, and especially Cusack's spin-off album Favorite Beijing Sounds (最爱的北京声音) (Kwanyin 2007, recorded 2005), focuses on 'discovering what Beijingers [and other Chinese urbanites] find *positive* in their city's vast and rapidly changing soundscape' (Cusack, British Council 2008: 52; italics added).

In addition, the soundscape projects only came into being with the availability of cheap, portable recording devices and in general, sound art celebrates lo-fi technology of the kind that is responsible for many, if not all, of urban noises. From the washing machine in the Shanghai Home Show described above to FM3's Buddha Machine (www.fm3buddhamachine.com), which is inspired by a low-tech device that repeats Buddhist chants ad infinitum through its poor built-in loudspeaker: through the *détournement* of consumer electronics, these works draw attention to the mediation of technology.

The installation I/O Flows of the Hong Kong-based sound artist Cedric Maridet uses noises made by the artificial air management system of the Hong Kong Visual Arts Center. As Maridet explains in the exhibition leaflet available on his website, www.moneme.com:

> Developed to bring comfort and to ensure a high air quality independent from the outside climate, air-conditioning systems in buildings are artificial air management devices to renew and clean the air [...] Such a setting gives form to the idea of a closed space, and of the building as an autonomous entity [...] Sonic and spatial variations are mapped according to outside air quality indicators such as temperature and humidity, as well as the listener's presence functioning as air-processing bodies.

I/O Flows and its continuous flow question the compartmentalisation of urban spaces, and by extension the atomisation of human beings. It does so in terms reminiscent of those of the German philosopher, Peter Sloterdijk (2009). Sloterdijk's image-concept of foam offers an appealing metaphor for contemporary society as 'individuals isolated together'. Spaces such as the Crystal Palace of the 1851 World Exhibition, the aeroplane, the car and the apartment block show a trend towards an increasingly fleeting and transitional connection with specific locations and environments. In these foam-like structures, the outside world enters through windows and screens that are both transparent and difficult to penetrate. Air-conditioning is key to this atomised society, creating just enough pressure to stop the bubble from imploding or bursting and to create a sense of autonomy.

Getting There & Away

> Think of it as a trip. You only need to bring your ears and get in the car. You'll hear the vehicle humming (engine, tremors), the city breathing (the omnipresent surrounding noise), after that it's the artists' selection and creation. They

6.4. Moving Soundscape in Guangzhou

might collect sound bytes from the corners of the city, turn the scattered and sprawling street scenes into poetry to be recited, use new technology to extend the senses and imagination, or they might just produce noise. In a life filled with noise, what's better than experiencing noise anew?

This is Yan Jun's introduction of Get It Louder's Moving Soundscape project, inviting potential participants to enroll through e-mail for a 40-minute car trip hosted by sound artists. Descriptions and picture of Moving Soundscapes in various Chinese cities can be found on the Chinese Get it Louder website, from which this quote was taken. On his blog, curator-in-chief Ou Ning explains the use of the car, that paradigmatic symbol of 20th-century consumer society:

> When Yan Jun first suggested that we could use the car as a performance space, I thought we should develop it into a sound geography project [...] If we'd only use the driving car as a vehicle (载体) for performing sound art, and not for writing profound assemblages (结合) of urban landforms, the ecology of humans and phenomena, the state of affairs with transportation and the soundscape of the streets, then this project would merely pioneer a rather challenging new form of performing. [...] At exhibitions at Guangzhou, Shanghai and Beijing, we arranged for about six cars to be used by the sound artists (we took the matter up with BMW Mini Cooper and other car brands). [...] For the artists the crux was the delicate relation between 'moving' (seeing) and 'sound' (listening).[14]

A number of soundscape projects seek to *dérive* otherwise purely functional transitional spaces, such as train stations, airports, trains and cars. Project 1-24 records the sound at various locations around Shanghai's south railway station for a period of twenty-four hours.[15] Edwin Lo recorded sounds in and around Hong Kong's subway and train station between 2007 and 2010 for the project Rabbit Travelogue (see figure above, after introduction). The accompanying website (http://rabbit-travelogue.com) explains that the project seeks to destabilise official history and central concepts by using private and personal anecdotes. More than 1-24's Schaferesque call for environmentalism, Rabbit Travelogue's challenge to the centrality of power and its institutions has a political edge. However, the potential problem with Yin Yi's and Edwin Lo's projects, and also with Moving Soundscape, is that rather than re-connecting people with their sonic environment and empowering them, they fuel disconnection by taking sounds out of their direct contexts and thus enabling sonic tourism.

(Un)familiar Territories

> CHINA INCIDENTAL (Un)familiar Territories
> Headphone walks [in Manchester] by Yan Jun & Hitlike
> 24 May – 22 June 2008
> Chinese Arts Centre has teamed up with CHINA NOW, the UK's largest ever

festival of Chinese culture, to offer you a free trip to China [...] through sound. Yan Jun ([who recorded this work in] Shanghai) and Hitlike (Harbin) have each created a specially commissioned sound work that transports the listener to the streets of China as they follow a corresponding route around Manchester city centre. Taking in the bustling electronics market of Shanghai or main food sellers street in Harbin, the walks provide an entirely unique insight into life in China today. (www.chinese-arts-centre.org)

This official announcement by the Manchester-based Chinese Arts Centre promises an authentic Chinese experience. However, in an interview with Edwin Lo, Yan Jun – born in Lanzhou, based in Beijing – explains that he was interested in the opposite of representing Chinese modernity, namely in detaching sounds from their sociocultural meanings:

The Manchester curator [Matthias Kispert] wrote very international things: Shanghai, a hub of the Chinese economy, factory of the world, skyrocketing economy etc. [...] This time I wanted to cut away all social background, let's get rid of social backgrounds [...] for me that time in Manchester was interesting because I could relocate sounds to a different environment. However, for the curator the most important thing was the background of these sounds: where they come from, that economy and social science stuff (Lo 2009: online).

To make it even more difficult to decide whether this work connects people with their environment, the work that Yan Jun used for the soundwalk was not especially commissioned by the Chinese Arts Centre, but a spin-off from Get it Louder 2007 that, like the Da Zha Lan project, documents a working-class neighbourhood, now in Shanghai instead of Beijing. His description stands out as the most elaborate description of a *dérive* in Chinese sound art, which is why I quote it at length:

When I was in Shanghai in 2007, a friend introduced me to a place called Qiujiang Road. There were lots of secondhand markets, spread over seven or eight streets, dealing in computer accessories, electronic components, machine components, small devices, metal, large machines, audiovisual products and so on. Things were frighteningly cheap – some were used by others, pirated goods or cheap imitations that didn't even have a brand name. You can imagine that every day lots of people that are not so picky about quality come here to bargain. Even if [the people of Qiujiang Road] aren't wealthy, their lives cannot be divorced from electronics, machines, electronic products, computers and cell phones. At the fresh market over there you can also buy all sorts of fresh vegetables and fish, at throwaway prices. I have never spent over 10 RMB eating at a local restaurant. The dirty tables, floors and cutlery – all that feels completely natural (Yan 2008a: online).

Yan goes on to discuss spatially-inscribed class distinctions. The particularly striking contrasts between these distinctions at Qiujiang Road may well be what attracts Yan to this place. It confronts him with the question: on what side does he belong?

> Qiujiang Road is located where two high-speed train tracks converge. Seated in the trains are those youngsters, students and white-collar workers that of all of China know how to dress best. Watching down they see torn roofs, temporary shacks, crowds of people that dress in undignified ways. I don't particularly like these people. They spit whenever they feel like it, hit children, do the utmost to squeeze another penny out of me and sometimes sell me fake goods. Those that are dressed slightly better rudely order me to stop recording and leave their turf. Walking among them, from above, the thunder of the trains constantly comes down, while you are surrounded by all sounds you can and cannot imagine. Besides the sounds of production and exchange, there are those of daily life. Just like the Shanghainese like strolling in their pajamas, the people of Qiujiang Road play Chinese chess, wash chamber pots, make food, drink beer and cut hair in the street. In fact, in most places in China, the sounds of work and life are blurred into a mix. The blurring of the sounds from above and those from the surroundings in Qiujiang Road is something entirely different. Of this fact, everyone is both crystal clear and unknowingly muddled (浑然不觉) (Yan 2008a: online).

At this point in the narrative, Yan describes the route of his *dérive*, as well as its afterlife as a technical reproduction that both reconnects and estranges.

> Recording through the microphone of my headset, I started from a small laptop computer repair shop and wandered through Qiujiang Road. Sometimes I would turn my head to dodge motorcycles that pass by screaming. Sometimes I would stop to listen some more to the sound of dissembling junk. On the road I met people that sell cockroach poison and pornography, and I would attentively observe these strangers. Before I concluded my stroll, I turned around and followed a woman that sold cheap jewellery. She displayed pieces of zodiac-themed jewellery tied to a red rope: tinkle, tinkle. A few workers stood around watching for some time, but she didn't sell a single thing (Yan 2008a: online).
>
> This year in January I went back to Qiujiang Road. I recorded lots of new sounds, edited them into a CD entitled *Qiujiang Road* (虬江路) and had a thousand copies produced there. In Qiujiang Road I also found a rice-flour noodle shop, a DVD store, someone who sold computer accessories, someone who sold saw-cut CDs and someone who sold his own copies of popular songs, and asked them to sell this album. Jokingly I said that this is conceptual art, because all songs come from Qiujiang Road and return to Qiujiang Road. A friend said this piece documented China's reality as factory of the world, and that it then re-entered reality through its circulation as a consumer product. But perhaps the emphasis is not on this, because my vantage point

has always been the enjoyment of listening, in choosing the route and rhythm. This process is more like performance, and not like documenting reality. (Yan 2008a: online)

Abstraction and Virtuality

Debord presents mapping as the purpose of the *dérive*. However, the map is the penultimate example of the ambiguity of connecting and disconnecting people with their (sonic) environment. Maps are obviously site-specific and, for instance, the map-like nature of soundscape projects saves me from having to argue for the cultural specificity of these projects, something that can be challenging in respect to, say, pop music or abstract painting. But maps are also premised on the (social) separation of territory and representation and thus enable spectacular exploitation (i.e. neo-colonialism) and (sonic) tourism (i.e. free-floating globalisation). Debord also connects maps to the spectacle:

> Workers do not produce themselves: they produce a force independent of themselves. [...] All time, all space, becomes foreign to them as their own alienated products accumulate. The spectacle is a map of this new world – a map drawn to the scale of the territory itself. (Debord 1994: Proposition 31)

The Da Zha Lan project, A Map of Our Own, the Louis Vuitton Soundwalk, 1-24, Moving Soundscape including Reinvent your City, (Un)Familiar Territories: all of these soundscape projects make prominent use of maps. The China Sound Map pushes this to its extreme. Also part of China Incidental, at www.soundmapping.cn users can upload their own locally recorded sounds to a map of China and beyond. Sound artist Hitlike explains on www.hitlike.com that he initially recorded sounds in his hometown, Harbin in North China – the cracking of snow under his feet – and designed a website that represented these sounds on a map. People on Internet forums responded enthusiastically, and in 2009 Hitlike finished this nation-wide version together with Wang Changcun.

Such clickable maps point to an additional aspect of soundscapes projects, namely the extent to which they make most of the Internet. The Internet is a piece of technology that dwarfs distances and fuels disconnection with the immediate surroundings. This is especially true if soundscapes and maps are made of online or otherwise virtual worlds. Zafka's *I • Mirror* (Little Sound, 2008, recorded in 2007) consists of field recording in the online, virtual world of Second Life.[16] The album was published on iPod's Chinese sister v-Pod rather than on a CD, and formed part of the artist Cao Fei's Second Life Project, China Tracy, which premiered at the Venice Biennale in 2007.

Beyond Work and Self

'Plagiarism is necessary', writes Debord in proposition 207, plagiarising Isidore

Ducasse's *Poésies*. The 'knock-offs' (山寨) of Qiujiang Road and similar places seem to have taken his advice to heart. The Internet has revolutionised this co-creative process of the *détournement* to a point where the distinction between author and audience becomes porous. Users upload their sounds and enroll for collaborative projects on line. The website www.soundpocket.org.hk asks whether you want the website to respond to the sound in your surroundings, and if you agree, every sound becomes part of the composition. True enough, there is someone who sets the parameters, pays the hosting company, writes the software and so on, but the resulting work (if there is any) is even less the expression of one individual than it ever was. Agency becomes dispersed over the network. *I • Mirror* is undersigned by Zafka Ziemia, the Second Life avatar of Zafka, whose 'real name' is Zhang Anding (at least in alphabetic transcription).[17] To me, this is a vanishing point, where the atomisation of contemporary society and the pigeon-holing of my text reveal their inadequacy, and become vague and transcendental. Yin Yi explains in his column why he makes field recordings:

> Listening through a contact microphone to the wind swaying a fence surrounding a golf course, and through an underwater microphone in a fish bowl to the cruising of gold fishes between the currents; this gives me incomparable joy. This behavior as if facing formless sounds on the contrary gives me the intimate feeling of handiwork. This feeling makes me think of stacking blocks in my childhood and physical labor. Following these sounds, I become interested in all the 'matter' around me. Minuscule 'matter', floating around me, at my fingertips. […] all sounds in the headphone are infinitely enchanting. I try to catch every single one, but can't. These sounds are bustling with vitality (生气勃勃): they grow, prosper, fade away. As suddenly as they emerged, so mysteriously they leave. This feeling is like when I saw the sea at Xiamen or when I turned around to see the meandering path we took up into [the mountain region of] Shennongjia. I lose a kind of self-control. (Yin 2011c)

Concluding Remarks: Will the Revolution be Analysed?

Ultimately, I do not think that Chinese soundscape projects live up to Guy Debord's stringent demands. Just like the situationist movement of which Debord was part and to which *The Society of Spectacle* was a bible, Chinese soundscape artists create projects that are rife with contradictions.[18] Soundscape projects are both dissatisfied with rock music's spectacularity and eager to share in visual art's spectacular global success. They are participatory, but within parameters that are sometimes restrictive and hierarchical. Soundscape projects aspire to criticality, but may do so through spectacular protest, nostalgia and an insistence on art's autonomy. Finally, soundscape projects both connect and disconnect people with each other and their environment, thus tearing down, enhancing and adding spatially-inscribed social separations. According to Debord's analysis, these ambiguities and contradictions must ultimately mean that soundscape projects are wide open to tendencies that further the spectacular. Heard from this angle, soundscape projects exploit the working class, the proletariat and the everyday in new ways, by colonising the hitherto unproductive realms of the urban sound ecology, and living off of these sounds and the people that produce them by selling these projects to national and international art festivals, catering to increasingly global, urban elites.

This is also where I need to look closer to home; because writing this chapter has not quite put me into contact with the Dutch working-class neighbourhood in which I live and work. On the contrary, it helped me to shut out its noises, the conflicts of which are both crystal clear to me and unknowingly muddled. We remain isolated together, like foam.

Self-reflection is especially necessary because I believe I have successfully operationalised the concept of spectacle as a tool for producing knowledge about Chinese soundscape projects, industrial metaphor intended. In its avant-garde nature – in Debord's sense – soundscape projects constantly walk the thin line between 'good' self-effacing anti-spectacular critique and the 'bad' pioneering, charting and mining of areas where commodification hitherto had no method. If my goal is to offer a detached understanding of the Chinese soundscape scene, am I then not influencing the balance towards the latter? Is my narrative succeeding in anything else besides encapsulating and thereby neutralising the critical potential of these sounds and people? How is my analysis not spectacular – pointing out why the ostentatiously boring, endless recordings of familiar street sounds (is it even music?) are in fact exciting and heralding a new age (beyond music!)?

> The fact is that a critique capable of surpassing the spectacle must *know how to bide its time*. (Debord 1994: Proposition 220)

Here my narrative necessarily ends. These doubts seem inevitable and irresolvable in the Nietzschean aspiration for (self-)transcendence that Debord formulates. Critique is impossible yet necessary. In my failure, I hope to accumulate sounds to the point where someday something other than capital might appear.

Notes

1. Feng Jiangzhou (formerly the Fly), Dou Wei, Li Jianhong (Second Skin, organiser of the 2pi festival in Hangzhou, annually between 2003 and 2007) and later Jeffrey Zhang (Carsick Cars, White), Shenggy (Sheng Jing, White, former Hang on the Box), Zafka (Prague, Zhang Anding) and Wang Changcun (Torturing Nurse). In Hong Kong, Anson Mak was a member of the indie band AMK. Before Sounding Beijing, these experimental musicians seemed to focus on exploring the possibilities of their instruments, which seems natural given their years of band practice. However, Sounding Beijing drew attention away from (acoustic) input sounds and towards their (electronic and digital) manipulation and modification. Although the *guqin* (zither) was central to FM3's performances around 2003, they modified its sound by using laptop computers to create layers of resounding tones that interacted with the performance space, in the case of Sounding Beijing, The Loft (See also Yan 2004).
2. Cf. http://www.subjam.org/archives/category/releases, http://www.subjam.org/archives/category/events/wk and http://minimidi.cn/ respectively, accessed 20 October 2011.
3. Despite the efforts of Zhang Xiaofu (Central Conservatory of Music 中央音乐学院), Kenneth Fields (Central Conservatory of Music) and others.

4. In 'A Short History of Electronic Music' (中国"电子乐"小史) (2007), Yan Jun writes that 'since 2007, the artists of [the experimental electronic music label] Shanshui records have increasingly inclined towards dance tracks,' following a development that has been apparent since the early 2000s on the double album *Landscape*I&II (山水, 2003 & 2005) and in the work of Ronez, Sulumi, DeadJ, Hz (Huzi) and B6, among others. This development is important because it challenges the intellectual, elitist aura that sound art might otherwise have, and suggests a more directly physical way of interacting with the audience.
5. Cf. www.subjam.org/archives/81, accessed 23 October 2011.
6. For side-projects inspired by the Sound and the City project see http://blog.sina.com.cn/s/blog_54b6d6ab010000f4.html (David Toop),www.lcc.arts.ac.uk/60688.htm (Peter Cusack), www.clivebell.co.uk/news_12.htm (Clive Bell), www.scannerdot.com/music/2005/flower_echoes.html (Scanner aka Robin Rimbaud), www.musicforbodies.net/wiki/SonicBedShanghai (Kaffe Matthews) and www.robertjarvis.co.uk/installations.htm (Robert Jarvis), all accessed 25 October 2011.
7. www.getitlouder.com/blog/article.asp?id=142, accessed 20 September 2012.
8. Cf. www.xici.net/main.asp?url=/b783828/d56531906.htm(Beijing), www.emusic.com/album/11025/11025402.html (Lanzhou) and www.yanjun.org/blog/archives/387 (Paris). An additional list can be found on Yan Jun's blog, http://mu.subjam.org/yanjun/archives/1320, accessed 20 October 2011.
9. www.re-records.com/archives/re-on-002r/ and www.kwuntongculture.hk/en/home.php?op=cat&id=20&page=2, accessed 23 October 2011.
10. http://preprod-louisvuitton.clicmobile.com/travis/lv/Src/, accessed 30 September 2011.
11. Cf. www.post-concrete.com/blog/?p=176%20.
12. Reinvent Your City's website is http://soundscapes.blogbus.com. Listen to excerpts at www.diymusic.com/spacc/post/citypictorial/1750 or http://zafka.podomatic.com, accessed 30 October 2011. (Cf. Liu 2008: 34)
13. www.archive.org/details/Zafka-YongHe and http://blog.sina.com.cn/s/blog_539fbd8a010098mi.html, accessed 30 October 2011.
14. www.alternativearchive.com/ouning/article.asp?id=372, accessed 23 October 2011. Debord mentions the car and its influence on city planning in proposition 174. Ou Ning also relates this project to an earlier project he and Yan Jun worked on, namely www.alternativearchive.com/IOS/(China Power Station / Awakening Battersea), accessed 23 October 2011.
15. The project was recorded in 2009 by a team led by Yin Yi and was supported by 1mile^2 (www.square-mile.net), which in turn is mainly funded by the British government and whose mission it is to 'inspire communities to explore the cultural and ecological diversity of their neighborhoods through artistic engagement.' Additionally, 1-24 is highly interactive. Its website www.1-24.org shows a hand-drawn map with clickable locations that will then play the sounds recorded at this location corresponding to the hour of day at the user's computer.
16. www.post-concrete.com/vinyl/?p=12, accessed 23 October 2011.
17. Rather than works, Zafka glorifies *xianchang* (现场) 'the live, presence, scene' as sites of emergence and participation (www.gztriennial.org/shidai/zhinan/download/5.doc, accessed 21 October 2011, cf. Condry 2006). Yan Jun's Lamma Island Diary (re-records, 2009. www.re-records.com/discography/re-on-001r/, accessed 21 October 2011) can be listened to as an ego-document or individual travelogue, but the sounds of boats, water, wind and various announcements are not particularly revealing about Yan Jun, and are more productively listened to as recording moving through and stopping in an acoustic ecosystem of which Yan Jun briefly was a minor subroutine.
18. In the chapter Foam City, Sloterdijk presents Debord's fellow situationist Constant as the most important visionary and analyst of a second urban culture. Sloterdijk describes this second urban culture as consisting of radically artificial spaces that are above (and disconnected from) the traditional values of earth, labour and metabolism.

References

British Council. 'Sound and the City: City Sound Environment' [都市發声: 城市·声音环境]. www.britishcouncil.org/china-arts-music-satc.htm (accessed 20 December 2008).

City Pictorial [城市画报]. 2007: 1, Volume 170. Available at www.diymusic.com/space/post/citypictorial/1750, accessed 23 October 2011.

Condry, Ian. *Hip-hop Japan: Rap and the Paths of Cultural Globalization*. Durham: Duke University Press, 2006.

Dal Lago, Francesca. 'Space and Public: Site Specificity in Beijing.' *Art Journal* 59, no. 1 (2000): 75.

Debord, Guy. *The Society of the Spectacle*. Translated by Donald Nicholson-Smith. New York: Zone Books, 1994. Marxists Internet Archive. 'Society of the Spectacle.' www.marxists.org/reference/archive/debord/society.htm, accessed 23 October 2011.

Debord, Guy. 'Theory of the Dérive.' In *Situationist International Anthology*, edited and translated by Ken Knabb, 62-6. Bureau of Public Secrets, 2006.

De Kloet, Jeroen. *China with a Cut: Globalisation, Urban Youth and Popular Music*. Amsterdam: Amsterdam University Press, 2010.

Groenewegen-Lau, Jeroen. 'Asima, Her Pimp and a Melancholic Boss: On Chinese Rock Star Zuoxiao Zuzhou' in Norient, *Independent Network for Local and Global Soundscapes*. 2011a. http://norient.com.

—. *Tongue: Making Sense of Underground Rock, Beijing 1997-2004*. Lambert Academic Publishing, 2011b.

Hudsucker, Rudolph. 'Artist at Work: Yan Jun.' *Afterall Journal* (2011). http://afterall.org/online/artists-at-work-yan-jun/#cite5359, accessed 20 September 2011.

Kahn, Douglas. *Noise, Water, Meat: A History of Sound in the Arts*. Cambridge Mass, London: MIT Press, 1999.

Liu Tianyun 刘天韵. *The Characteristics of Dissemination and the Cultural Meaning of Sound Art: With a Part of the Sound Art at This Year's Get It Louder Festival as Case Study* [声音艺术的传播特点与文化意义 - 以年大声展声音艺术部分为研究范本]. MA thesis, Eastern Normal University [东方师范大学], 2008.

Lo, Edwin 羅潤庭. 2009. 與顏峻對談 - 《聽在》聲音藝術節 2009 (Interview with Yan Jun: Listening sound art festival 2009. Available at: http://www.soundpocket.org.hk/site/single_ajax.php?p=, accessed 23 October 2012.

Rolnick, Neil. 'Sound Travels: Neil Rolnick in China.' Arts Electric: Emf's Guide to Music, Sound Art, and Technology Worldwide (2008). www.arts-electric.org/stories/080818_rolnick.html, accessed 20 October 2011.

Sloterdijk, Peter. *Sferen: Schuim*. Amsterdam: Boom. 2009.

Soundpocket. *Around Sound Art Festival Booklet* [《聽在》聲音藝術節小冊子]. 2009.

Truax, Barry. 'Soundscape, Acoustic Communication and Environmental Sound Composition.' *Contemporary Music Review* 15, no. 1-2 (1996): 49-65.

Yan Jun 顏峻. 'FM3=Two Computers and a Carpet' [FM3==两台电脑和一张地毯], 2004. www.fm3.com.cn/site/?page_id=5, accessed 23 October 2011.

—. 'Backgrounds to Chinese Sound Art' [中国声音艺术的背景], 2006. www.yanjun.org/Words/03.html, accessed 10 October 2008.

—. 'A Concise History of Chinese "Electronic Music"' [中国"电子乐"小史], 2008. www.yanjun.org/Words/02.html, accessed 10 October 2008.

—. 'Qiujiang Road; Every Day The World in Stereo' [虹江路；每一天的立体声世界] , 2008a. Available at http://www.doucan.com/group/topic/4821792, accessed 23 October 2012.

Yin Yi 殷漪. 'Location Recording 1' [买地录音1: 一种对待声音的方法与态度], *Art World* [艺术世界], 2011a: 249.

—. 'Location Recording 2' [买地录音2: 买地录音的困境], *Art World* [艺术世界], 2011b: 250.

—. 'Location Recording 3' [买地录音3: 我为什么要做买地录音], *Art World* [艺术世界], 2011c: 251.

7. The City's (Dis)appearance in Propaganda

Stefan Landsberger

Even before the founding of the People's Republic of China (PRC) in 1949, posters formed a major component of the communication and propaganda strategy of the Chinese Communist Party (CCP). After emerging from the remote rural strongholds where it had gained strength over more than 15 years, it stands to reason that the CCP would devote considerable effort to swaying the population of the urban areas where it still had to establish its control. Paradoxically, this was not the case: while Party policy after 1949 drifted away from its previous fixation on rural China and focused on the urban, propaganda very much remained inspired by, and directed at, the countryside. (Re)construction and (re)organisation of the rural areas were stressed as desirable aspects of rehabilitation, modernisation and development, rather than urbanisation. Coupled with explicit policies to restrict internal migration, the rural was presented more frequently and as more desirable, in metropolises, provincial capitals, medium-sized cities, towns, townships, villages and hamlets.

As a result, the city-as-city served only as a stage, a backdrop against which a message could be presented, and only played a supporting role in the hegemonic visualisations of the future. Notably, on the few occasions a city did (or does) appear, it was (and is) Beijing, rather than Shanghai. The many posters devoted to the spectacles of 'The founding of the nation' (开国大典) and First of May Parades, or the song 'I love Beijing's Tiananmen' (我爱北京天安门) have less to do with Beijing as a city than with the symbolic and political centre of the nation, which happened to coincide with Beijing's Tiananmen. Likewise, the few posters that featured the skyline of Shanghai never focused on Shanghai as a city, but rather used it as a stage where other events were performed, such as demonstrations against American imperialism in Southeast Asia. But then, of course, Shanghai, with its colonial heritage, was a contested city grappling with problematic political issues and struggling to shed its image of a decadent Oriental version of Paris; its redevelopment did not really take off until the late 1980s (Abbas 2000).

With a few exceptions, the city only emerged as one of the *topoi* of propaganda after the reform policies took off, and the depoliticisation of society set in, in the late 1970s. Then the city came to signify China's new, open and globalised modernity. Zhang Yuqing's 'The bustling Nanjing Road' in Shanghai (1989) clearly serves as an illustration of the successes of the reform policies, which were a decade old by the time this image was published. Showcasing the successful outward development of the nation through cityscapes became a recurring visual element in posters of the 1990s. It is worthy of note that by then, the responsibility for producing these posters was no longer a central one, but one for the communities themselves. One could see them as efforts of self-promotion rather than as propaganda images. With a few notable exceptions, the posters appearing during the SARS crisis of 2003 interpreted it as an urban event.

Hypothetically, there should be a major exception to this prominent absence of the (capital) city from the propaganda of the early years of the PRC. This coincides with the Great Leap Forward movement (1958-1959): the task of (re)building Beijing in the form of the Ten Great Buildings was seen as proof of and testimony to the successes of the first decade of CCP rule. Likewise, 50 years later, in the run-up to the Beijing Olympics of 2008 and the Shanghai World Expo of 2010, the 'Economic Olympics' (Cunningham 2010), the city very much takes centre-stage. In both instances, the city represents the whole nation and functions as a stage where nationhood is enacted through grandiose architecture, whereas Shanghai in 2010 had also become the ultimate embodiment of China's great economic boom.

The first decade of the PRC

The first decade of CCP rule witnessed a concerted effort to educate the Chinese people in what the CCP leadership had in mind for the nation. Propaganda posters gave concrete expression to the many different abstract policies and grandiose visions of the future that the CCP propagated and implemented over the years. As China had many illiterates in the 1940s and 1950s, this method of visualising abstract ideas worked especially well to educate the people. That most of these illiterates lived in the countryside may account for the fact that the majority of the posters published from 1949 until the 1980s addressed rural topics for a rural audience, providing detailed, prescriptive and often very concrete information, clearly with the intention of changing attitudes or even behaviour; in turn, urbanites were exposed to urban-oriented messages, but also these tended to be communicated through other media, including radio broadcasts, newspapers (often read in communal reading sessions, for those unable to read themselves) and news reels. Posters did not have the same key function as in the countryside.

That being said, propaganda posters could be produced cheaply and easily, turning them into one of the most favoured vehicles to make government-directed communication more concrete and easier to understand. Because they were widely available, posters were able to penetrate every level of social organisation and cohabitation, and succeeded even in reaching the lowest ones: the multicoloured posters could be seen adorning the walls not only of offices and factories, but also of houses, schoolrooms and dormitories. An excellent way to bring some colour to the otherwise drab places where most people lived, people liked the posters for their colours, composition and visual contents, and did not pay too much attention to the slogans that might be printed underneath. This caused the political message of the posters to be passed on in an almost subconscious manner.

The most talented artists were mobilised to visualise the political trends of the moment in the most detailed way. Many of them had been designers of the commercial calendar posters (月份牌) that had been so popular before the PRC was founded in 1949. These artists were quickly co-opted and incorporated in the various government and party organisations that were made responsible for producing propaganda posters. These artists were, after all, well versed in design techniques and able to visualise a product in a commercially attractive way. The images they made were often figurative and realistic, almost as if photographs had been copied into the paintings. The aim of the idealised images they created was to portray the future in the present, not only showing 'life as it really is', but also 'life as it ought to be'. They were painted in a naïve style, with all forms outlined in black, filled in with bright pinks, reds, yellows, greens and blues; black-and-white imagery was avoided as much as possible, as it might turn off viewers. These works created a type of 'faction', a hybrid of 'fact' and 'fiction', stressing the positive while glossing over anything negative.

Although the CCP by necessity had focused its efforts during the Yan'an and Civil War years on the rural population, it was decided that the arts now also had to address the audience of urbanites who were still largely unfamiliar with, and potentially hostile to, the type of communism espoused by the Party. The CCP leadership turned to the Soviet Union for assistance in developing a style of visual propaganda that could be successfully targeted at city dwellers. Mao and other leaders were convinced that Socialist Realism, as it had been practised in the Soviet Union since the 1930s, was the best tool for this. The bright colours and the happy and prosperous atmosphere that radiated from Socialist Realist works were seen as a continuation of the essential features of the visual tradition of the New Year prints, while at the same time infusing the genre with new, modernised elements (Holm 1979).

Socialist Realism depicted 'life' truthfully and in its 'revolutionary development', not merely as an 'objective reality'. This tallied well with Party demands that art should serve politics (Shao 1993). In China, Socialist Realism would make it possible for '[...] Chinese artists to grasp the world of reality and to cure the indifference to nature which caused the decay of Chinese traditional art', while at the same time 'it was the most popular form of art, which was also easiest to grasp' (Ma 1959: 1). Socialist Realism, then, became the proscribed manner of representing the future and it was responsible for the politicisation and massification of all art genres.[1]

In the period between 1949 and 1957, many Chinese painters and designers studied Socialist Realism in Soviet art academies; the Soviet professors who came to teach in Chinese art institutes educated many others. Some of the artists who had been exponents of the commercialised 'Shanghai Style' that had been so popular in the urban areas – for example, Xie Zhiguang and the prolific Li Mubai – also tried their hand at this new mode of expression. They and many others were given the opportunity – or in some cases were forced by the Party – to study real life, 'to live with the people', and to spend time in factories and in the countryside, in order to produce images that were true to life. They did this with varying success, as their works were often criticised (Cai 1950: 1; Zhong 1950: 28; Shi 1950: 31).

Given this Soviet influence, careful analysis of available visual Soviet materials indicates that the inspiration the Chinese sought only covered artistic expression and did not include the subject matter of Soviet propaganda. In other words, Socialist Realism as a form of expression was studied, but the artists left the contents of Soviet 'revolutionary development' for what they were: although the Soviet Union, the first nation to have realised socialism, had had a head-start in depicting the new, largely *urbanised* socialist state, Chinese posters did not provide these links between development and urbanisation.

The Chinese working class, employed in the industries mainly located in the cities, formed a fertile ground for visual propaganda after 1949. Basically, two issues had to be addressed in the messages directed at them. The first was the awakening of their class-consciousness. By the time of the founding of the PRC, there were only some 1.4 million workers employed in what could be termed the modern industrial sector. Despite their relatively small number, they were to be imbued with the idea that they were the vanguard of the revolution: the group that had been exploited to such an extent in the past that it had become the most revolutionary. The second issue was to educate them about their responsibilities in building up state industry. This was all the more necessary as huge numbers of people from the countryside, most of them first-generation industrial workers, moved to the cities to enter the workforce. By 1957, the number of workers had risen to some eight million (Bergère 2002).

With the stress on industrialisation, tradesmen like construction workers, bricklayers and carpenters – in short, those people who were involved in changing the way Chinese cities looked – did appear as subjects. On the one hand, designers did not shy away from acknowledging the usefulness of the 'advanced Soviet example', although image 7.1 in the full color section does suggest imitation in the form of rebuilding the Moscow White House on Chinese soil. But most of the other building activities situated in urban areas, as featured in posters (image 7.2), were restricted to raising factories, not dwellings. And yet, the message these images presented was twofold: first, of course, it showed the hard labour that was changing the face of the city, but second, it provided glimpses of what the new and modernised China would look like.

On the other hand, the postered urban realities of images 7.3 and 7.4 are presented and obviously accepted as a given, without any attempt to imbue them with revolutionary significance, aside from the addition of political iconography, as in image 7.3. The images tell us more about social conditions (the presence of a radio and the number of children, for example) than about city life itself. The worker's family in image 7.3 has just moved into its new home in the work unit (单位), with the wider context of communal living visible through the window. While the city hardly seems to merit the interests of the poster designers, they lavish considerable attention on the great (material) life that awaits the workers in the work unit. Image 7.4 shows private entrepreneurship and the relative material wealth and spending power of a worker's family.

In short, the visual record for the first decade of the PRC shows abundant attention to the creation of a revolutionary countryside, but gives few clues about the revolutionary city. Many posters were devoted to rural campaigns, such as Land Reform and mobilisation for this cause, elections of representatives, the establishment of cooperatives and collectives and so forth, and these were consumed in cities as well. But there are no real poster equivalents for mass movements taking place in the cities. Thus, there are no posters showing the various stages of (re)construction that Beijing's Tiananmen Square underwent in the period 1949-1958, or the construction of the Monument to the People's Heroes on the same square (Wu 2005; Hung 2001). And most surprisingly, no posters were published about the preparations for and actual work on the Ten Great Buildings that were completed in 1959 as an urban – and more specifically, Beijing – component of the Great Leap Forward (1958-1960). There are numerous designs and artists' impressions of the finished constructions themselves, but little else.

The Ten Great Buildings

The preparations for the mass project designed to construct the Ten Great Buildings in less than a year's time to commemorate the tenth anniversary of the founding of the PRC started in September 1958 (Wu 2005; Zhu 2008). The structures consisted of the Museum of Chinese History, the Museum of Agriculture, the Military Museum, the Cultural Palace of the Nationalities, the National Art Gallery, the Beijing Railway Station, the Great Hall of the People, the State Guest House, the Hotel of the Nationalities and the Hotel of Overseas Chinese. Comparable to the construction fever surrounding the preparations for the Beijing Olympic Games in the period between 2001 and 2008 and Shanghai's makeover for the Expo in 2010, the project '[...] transformed the old Beijing into a new city by radically altering its orientation and appearance' (Wu 2005: 138).

The construction of the Ten Great Buildings was a major historical event that not only transformed a city (Beijing), but also the outlook of many of those involved, as well as the careers of great number of those who participated. One should not forget that the *political* career of the relatively moderate former Vice-Premier and chairman of the Chinese People's Political Consultative Conference Li Ruihuan, for example, took off once he was identified as a model carpenter (more specifically, as a 'young Lu Ban'[2] who modernised carpentry techniques) who took part in the building of the Great Hall of the People.[3]

Given the importance that the Party leadership attached to the undertaking and the close personal attention it paid to the designs – even Mao himself chipped in during the discussions over the proposals – and given the involvement of six major architectural institutes and universities, 34 building companies and the more than 10,000 experienced workers, artists and craftsmen that were mobilised to complete the buildings before August 1959 (Wu 2005: 113), the absence of visual propaganda surrounding the project is baffling. On all levels, a scheme as grandiose as this would have fitted well with the prevalent Great Leap Forward rhetoric of going all-out for communism, of 'working hard to make the country strong and to remake nature'. There is certainly no scarcity of posters produced at the time that urged people to construct backyard furnaces to produce more steel or grow ever bigger quantities of grain, giant fruits and vegetables. Moreover, the Ten Buildings was a project that included scores of 'revolutionary masses' actually involved in conquering the past and creating the new. A campaign like this would have been a great occasion to privilege the city in propaganda.

The 1960s

More than in the preceding years, 1960s propaganda posters actually started to pay attention to the urban environment. Coupled with a struggle to provide the people with food in order to survive the famine in which the Great Leap Forward ended, the period was marked by a return to predictable proceedings and the prevalence of order. Again, serious building activities were featured – both metaphorically and physically – to show that construction was back in the hands of the experts. The urban environment was clearly presented as a concrete result of revolutionary engagement, in a way that can be compared to the formation of the cooperatives, and later communes, in images featuring the countryside. What was missing was the visible engagement of political interest with the built-up area, a result of the subtle depoliticisation of society that unavoidably followed the hyped-up Great Leap.

Images 7.6 and 7.7[4] look very similar to the visual teaching materials that were used in schools; the nameless EveryCities represented here almost function like catalogues of development and modernity within existing urban or newly urbanised settings (the commune centre!), without the constricting and oppressive qualities of representing the capital. After the upheavals of the Great Leap, these images show that life is orderly again, that there are no mass movements, no overbearing slogans, and everyone is going about his or her own daily activities. If this is socialism, the message seems to be, it should look like this.

Image 7.8, situated on the banks of the Huangpu River in Shanghai, is of a more politically didactic and performative nature than the preceding images. As China was recovering from the Great Leap Forward famine in the early 1960s, an inner-Party power struggle was raging between the 'left' (revolution first, then prosperity) and the 'right' (economic reconstruction first, then revolution). While propaganda in general became more fierce and intense, it mainly addressed issues outside China itself: the struggle against international imperialism and the USA, against Soviet revisionism and the support for Vietnam. The choice of Shanghai in this poster seems obvious; there, the Art Deco-buildings along the Bund, the tangible remains of China's own humiliation under Western imperialism, serve as a counterpoint to the theme of the demonstration.

Cultural Revolution

Although the Cultural Revolution (1966-1976) started out as an urban campaign, the propaganda posters of the era focus primarily on people (Mao, of course, in great number;[5] other members of the leadership, including Lin Biao, but also those being physically taken to task as enemies; Red Guards; behavioural models; super-human proletarians smashing capitalist-roaders, and so forth), and, in the post-1969 period, on the nation as a rural Utopia in which harvests were bountiful and young urbanites were eagerly learning about revolution at the knees of the poor and lower-middle peasants (Huang 1998). While the so-called struggle posters were clearly designed for urban consumption, the later utopian ones were explicitly produced for national purposes.

A problem involved with researching the visual propaganda of the early Cultural Revolution is that quite a lot of the material produced in the early phase was clearly of local origin, produced for limited, local purposes. It has now become clear that even for these 'spontaneous', 'local' posters, the central levels often provided examples.[6] Nonetheless, we are left never really knowing what existed, when, and where.

The 'smashing-looting-beating' that marked the Red Guards' actions against the built-up area, while very much present in the photographic and documentary evidence of the Cultural Revolution, is by-and-large absent from posters. Image 7.9 recreates the revolutionary reality where old shop fronts were destroyed (as well as personal belongings that had been requisitioned and smashed) and replaced with more revolutionary alternatives. Other urban activities that became synonymous with the era, such as the mass rallies on Tiananmen Square in Beijing, People's Square in Shanghai, and elsewhere, and the numerous mass denunciation sessions, never made it to posters. A late and rather exceptional example of the mass character of the big-character-poster movement, simultaneously providing a glimpse of a city, is given in image 7.10, part of a series published in 1976 to commemorate the great achievements of the Cultural Revolution.

Towards the end of the Cultural Revolution, after the 1976 Tiananmen Incident, a renewed, rather small-scale mobilisation effort seemed to take place to support those associated with Mao. With Hua Guofeng anointed as the chosen successor, and with popular sentiments increasingly in favour of policies that were antithetical to their own, people like Jiang Qing and the other 'Gang-of-Four' members and sympathisers were increasingly forced on the defensive. Image 7.11, from August 1976, shows an Air Force man, peasants and minority representatives answering the call to support Mao (and presumably Jiang and her followers), on the verge of entering the Forbidden City, with one of the Ten Great Buildings, the Great Hall of the People, on the right. Here, the countryside (the peasantry) returns to the city, and the city returns to the poster, but it is the city as the *capital*, that is, the symbolic and political centre of the nation. This is the place where China's future will be decided. Thus, they have 'arrive[d] at Chairman Mao's side', but to accomplish what?

When Mao died in September 1976, posters focused on mourning the Chairman and 'carrying out his behest', but only for a relatively short time. This theme had to be cut short when designated successor Hua Guofeng assumed total power by arresting the Gang of Four and other opponents. After one month of official mourning, the propaganda apparatus had to scramble to spread a new message, intended to familiarise the people with their relatively unknown new leader.

Modernisation Days

From the perspective of propaganda poster contents, the city only really comes into play during the Reform and Modernisations era headed by Deng Xiaoping. While the adoption of the 'Four Modernisations' scheme in 1978 initially favoured the countryside, its main beneficiary was the city, leading to a growing developmental gap between urban and rural areas. In terms of poster representation, a reversal takes place that can be called almost complete: the predominantly rural-oriented themes and imagery are replaced wholesale by their urban counterparts. Propaganda's proclivity for urban China under Deng is illustrated below.

The urban area presented beneath Deng's words is clearly identified with pragmatic, hands-on government, that is, deeds rather than words (image 7.12), intended as a reversal of preceding practice. It is a modern city with high-rise buildings and (still rather empty) freeways, very much inspired by Western examples. As such, it can also be seen as a prelude to the later policy of urbanising the countryside in an attempt to stop the flow of labour from the interior to the metropoles on the Eastern seaboard. But more importantly, and in stark contrast to the recent past, this is an almost anonymous city, devoid of political symbols or activism played out in the streets. Similarly, China's Open Door policy (image 7.13), inaugurated in 1977 by the hapless Hua Guofeng, is very much associated with the city, even though the Special Economic Zones that profited most from the opening-up policy started out as mere villages. Shenzhen is the most famous case in point (image 7.14). The high-rise buildings visible through the newly opened doors have been designed in the modernist style (three wings, central elevator shaft) that was considered advanced in China and that would become very popular and widely replicated in the early 1980s.

But the Deng era is also associated with other aspects of urbanity. The depoliticisation of society allowed for various new forms of economic activity, such as (small-scale) private enterprise. In the early 1980s in particular, when the effects of the reforms were only slowly trickling down from the countryside to the cities, private entrepreneurship obviously needed to be promoted to appease the restive urban population, while at the same time to absorb the ever more problematic numbers of un- or underemployed urbanites. Image 7.15 clearly puts this exciting new economic activity on the same level as urban modernisation, with its modernist architecture in the background, but forms quite a contrast to the flower-seller of image 7.4 discussed earlier.

By the same token, given Deng's accomplishments in returning Hong Kong to Chinese sovereignty, the Special Administrative Region's famous skyline has become entwined with the image of the 'Great Architect' of the reforms. Image 7.16 juxtaposes the computer-manipulated 'images of China' (the Tiananmen Gate building, the Great Wall and others) that became so popular in 1990s poster art with the Hong Kong office of the Bank of China, designed by I.M. Pei and the new Chinese Foreign Ministry building. With Deng's image firmly anchored in the top half of the image, this conflation of Chinese tradition and Western-inspired modernity points to the CCP's new interest in employing Chinese history in the new nationalism as it has been constructed after the Tiananmen massacre of 1989. Mixing past, present and future remains a favoured technique, as Gladys Chong discusses in chapter eight of this volume on the imagination of the 2008 Beijing Olympics.

The urban orientation set in motion under Deng is nicely illustrated by two posters published to accompany the 2000 Census. The modern cityscape (Image 7.17) somewhat echoes Hong Kong's high-rise public housing schemes; it functions as an indication of the successes the reform and modernisation efforts will bring in terms of city planning and urban renovation and hints at the speed with which glimmering Central Business Districts (CBDs) will proliferate all over the place in the years to come. Even the countryside is promised its share of successful development in the form of urbanisation, as indicated by the two-to-four-storied housing dominating the village (image 7.18).[7]

Post-Deng China

When we consider the Deng era as the period in which visual propaganda's focus on the rural shifted decisively to the urban, it becomes self-evident that Deng's successors, Jiang Zemin and Hu Jintao, persevered on the course set by Deng. Where Deng appropriated the Hong Kong skyline as an icon of the modernity and national unity brought by his rule, Jiang Zemin identified himself as the advocate for the reinvigoration of his native city, Shanghai.

In the period immediately after the Tiananmen massacre, Jiang was still in the process of strengthening his position at the centre of power by forcing out the old revolutionaries and bringing in the younger, highly-educated technocrats from his own Shanghai/Jiangsu powerbase (Gilley 1998). Under his aegis, Shanghai, a relative latecomer to the reforms, was made the 'dragon head' of the modernisation and reform effort and its newly bustling commercial centre, made concrete by its most famous shopping street, Nanjing Road, was foregrounded to illustrate the glorious future that lay ahead (image 7.19) (Wu 2000; Ho and Ng 2008).

On the occasion of the 50th anniversary of the PRC in 1999, Jiang proudly and unabashedly presented 'his' Shanghai to the nation and the world against the backdrop of the Pudong skyline, including the famous landmark of the Oriental Pearl TV Tower (image 7.20). In taking the limelight, Jiang reverted to the practice of leader worship that his predecessor Deng had strongly discouraged after coming to power. But looking at the representation of the city laid out behind Jiang, the changes that took place in the ten-year period between the 1990 and the 1999 images are staggering (Abbas 2000: 779). It is no longer necessary to spruce up old imperialist-inspired landmarks like the Bund or the historic Nanjing Road. Instead, Pudong, 'the Manhattan of China' (Sun and Chen 2005), a whole new urban district and testimony to China's rise in the world, has come into being with an ample share of gleaming and reflecting fronts. In the same vein, the solid realities of modern city planning and construction, as exemplified in Shanghai, have superseded the fantasies of the future that the poster designers of days gone by created in their artworks.

City propaganda again took a different tack after Jiang left to be succeeded by Hu Jintao in the early years of the 2000s. With Hu's taking office, not only did state leaders once more disappear from visual propaganda,[8] but the actual practice of propaganda poster production also declined even further than it had during the preceding two decades. The main reason for this was the increased use of other, newer media for propaganda purposes (Landsberger 2009), including television and the Internet, coupled with a decision to produce less intrusive, *political* messages. Hence the intermittent but not overly loud stress on the formation of an ill-defined 'harmonious society' that has become the hallmark of the Hu administration. A second reason can be found in the new ways in which such propaganda was produced and disseminated, and this has a bearing on a new organisational form found in urban areas: the community (社区). Although the appearance of these communities can be traced back to the late 1980s, Hu must be credited with the fact that he ordered them to be allowed a degree of autonomy from direct local government intervention in their affairs (Xu 2008). This decision is widely interpreted as not merely a form of government reorganisation, but a process of deep reform with far-reaching consequences (Derleth and Koldyk 2004). Thus, with the communities responsible for providing social and welfare services and governing themselves in order to be able to better respond to the new demands raised by the emerging market economy, it becomes clear that the responsibility for propaganda has now become decentralised as well. This is illustrated by the appearance of posters produced by municipal districts as opposed to the municipal administration itself.

Images 7.21 and 7.22 are examples of this new development, publicising two aspects (development and the environment) that appear to be much on the minds of the administrators of Beijing's Dongcheng district. Note that development is interpreted here as high-rise urbanisation, considered to be a *sine qua non* for 'keep[ing] in step with the times'. The urban environment, a great concern for the ever-increasing numbers of urbanites all over the world, is credited by the Dongcheng administration with creating comfort and providing charm. The posters' meaning and intention is three-fold: on the meta-level, they call for the construction of a harmonious district in a cultured city, thus appeasing the higher levels of government; on the intermediary level, they show the district in all its environmental splendour and high-rise modernity; while at a subconscious level, they provide proof of good district governance.

Economic development, expressed in further urbanisation and a further improvement of the living standards of the population, remains a serious concern among Party and State leaders. It has become the government's and CCP's rallying cry that the people should achieve a 'relatively well-off' standard of living, and this state of material well-being is unavoidably linked to private home- and car ownership. Examples of propaganda, from the series *Spirit of the 17th Party Congress Propaganda Posters* published after the 17th CCP Congress in 2007, illustrate how this works and, more importantly, what it should look like (images 7.23 and 7.24).

Olympic Beijing, Expo Shanghai

Much has been filmed, said and written about the extreme makeover that urban Beijing underwent in the run-up to the 2008 Olympic Games, usually focusing on the construction of signature architectural designs (the Bird's Nest Olympic Stadium, Water Cube Aquatic Centre, the CCTV Building and Beijing International Airport Terminal 3), the demolition of old *hutong* and *siheyuan* neighbourhoods and the displacement of the original inhabitants.[9] As a multi-media mega-event, the preparations for the sports event figured prominently in visual propaganda, although it should be noted that the switch of media used to carry visual propaganda, from print to broadcast – a trend that has been discussed elsewhere in more detail (Landsberger 2009) – found its completion here.

This time around, the remaking of the political and symbolic heart of the nation *and* the capital was very much part of the PRC's efforts to demonstrate to the world that China had arrived. In a way that could be compared to the Ten Great Buildings Project of 1958-1959, the Olympics were to showcase China's greatness, its modernity, the creativity and wisdom of its people, and so forth. But as in 1958-1959, the *actual* process of the modernising makeover that Beijing had undergone since it was awarded the Games in 2001, the *actual* mobilisation of resources and people, remained absent from propaganda posters. This cannot be attributed to a lack of propaganda efforts: practically every aspect of human behaviour, from spitting and smoking in the street to learning English, from the clean clothes of the taxi drivers to the queues for busses, subways and trains, was didactically addressed in visual, printed or broadcasted propaganda (de Kloet, Chong and Liu 2008). But the rebuilding of Beijing, the construction of the landmark buildings, roads, subways, and so on, remained invisible. A possible explanation for this may be that this time around, the workers involved in construction were no volunteers whose enthusiasm needed to be whipped up, but migrant labourers who were paid for their efforts and sent home before the Games actually started. There were Olympic Volunteers, to be sure! They were the hospitality workers and general dogsbodies of the Games, interfacing with visitors, athletes, media representatives, organisers and events.

So where and how does the 2008 Olympic City feature in propaganda posters? Mostly in juxtapositions of the historical, 'eternal' China and the new image the Games had to present to the world; in other words, the juxtapositions of the Temple of Heaven and the Forbidden City on the one hand, and the Water Cube and the Bird's Nest on the other, as in images 7.25 and 7.26. In line with the decentralisation of the propaganda effort, many individual districts of Beijing came up with their own visual takes on the event; these districts included Dongcheng and Chaoyang. But none of these made use, or was allowed to make use, of images of the central Olympic structures: they have been turned into icons of modernity, belonging to the whole nation.

Image 7.27 further illustrates the iconic qualities ascribed to the Olympic structures (the Bird's Nest in particular) in their conflation with modernity (high-rise buildings) and internationalism.

Propaganda surrounding Shanghai's preparations for the 2010 World Expo seemed to be a largely local affair. Once 'Haibao', compared to a 'bit of squeezed out toothpaste to a Smurf with Chinese characteristics to a condom' (Wasserstrom 2008), was chosen as the event's mascot, it served as visual shorthand for nationwide use of these 'second Olympics'. Posters surrounding the event also were plastered all over Shanghai, but did not make it in large numbers to the city's eternal competitor, Beijing, or other parts of urban China. As soon as the China Pavilion was unveiled in February 2010, its image became the enduring national symbol for the whole exhibition, even though only 10% of the 73 million Expo visitors actually visited it.[10] In its symbolic sense, the Pavilion had the same function as the Bird's Nest.

Final notes

This chapter has looked at the role the Chinese city, and the capital city in particular, plays in the propaganda posters that have been published in the past 60 or so years. On the basis of ongoing analytical visual research, it was postulated that the city-as-city never appeared in a serious way as a signifier of revolutionary success or as an indicator of development until *after* the reform era started and the city came to signify China's new, open and globalised modernity. It was suggested that the major events in which city-building played a pivotal role – the Ten Great Buildings Movement of 1958-1959 and the construction of the Beijing Olympic City 2008 and the Shanghai 2010 World Expo – would form exceptions to this practice. This only partially seems to have been the case: although the concrete end results of the building activities (Great Hall of the People, the Bird's Nest and the China Pavilion, to name but a few) featured in these posters, only the Games and Expo projects have been linked explicitly to the discourse behind their construction; no longer necessarily as signifiers of revolutionary success, but as indicators of economic development, proof that China has arrived on the global stage.

Urbanisation has become noticeable in the countryside. In an attempt to stem the flow of migrant workers to the metropoles in the East, the government has designed plans to restrict the expansion of large cities while encouraging the growth of small towns. In 2006, Hu Jintao and Premier Wen Jiabao bundled policies to 'build a new socialist countryside' that seek to improve conditions for those who remain behind in order to reduce the pressures of urbanisation (Saich 2008). For a long time, clear ideas have existed about what this urbanised countryside should look like, as image 7.28 illustrates. Although there is no 'clarion call' to create an urbanised countryside, the link between further economic development, urbanisation and material well-being is being made here more specifically than at any previous time, including the early 1960s.

Notes

1. Interviews with Qian Daxin and Ha Qiongwen, Shanghai, 15 January 1998.
2. Lu Ban (507-440 BCE) was a legendary carpenter and inventor who became the patron saint of builders and contractors. See Ruitenbeek (1993).
3. See: www.chinavitae.com/biography/Li_Ruihuan/full
4. Zhang Yuqing (1909-1993), the designer of these two images, as well as other illustrations shown in this chapter, specialised in such panoramic representations. Many of his posters are New Year prints in the true sense: meticulously designed, they contain enormous amounts of visual information.
5. Geremie Barmé refers to estimates that 2.2 billion copies of the official portrait had been printed, in *Shades of Mao* (Armonk, etc.: M.E. Sharpe, 1996), p. 7-8. This number excludes the innumerable other posters that were devoted to Mao (or his sayings).
6. *A selection of revolutionary great criticism mastheads* [革命大批判报头选辑] (Hangzhou: Zhejiang renmin meishu chubanshe, 1970). Shui Tianzhong, 'What is Cultural Revolution Art?' [文革美术是什么?] *Century Art History Study* (http://cl2000.com/history/wenge/taolun/01.shtml, accessed 7 April 2003).
7. This process of rural urbanisation is well-described. See Chan, Madsen and Unger (2009: 288-375).
8. With one known exception: Hu appeared in a minuscule photograph reproduced on a poster detailing the government's steps in combating SARS in 2003.
9. Just a few examples out of many will be mentioned here: Ou Ning's documentary *Meishi Street*, on the re-construction of Dazhalan (2006); see also Broudehoux (2007: 383-399); Gottwald and Duggan (2008: 339-354).
10. 'Post-Expo plans set for China Pavilion', 30 September 2010, http://en.expo2010.cn/a/20100930/000006.htm (accessed 13 December 2010).

References

Ackbar Abbas. 'Cosmopolitan De-scriptions: Shanghai and Hong Kong.' *Public Culture* 12, no. 3 (2000): 769-786.

Bergère, Marie-Claire. 'China in the Wake of the Communist Revolution: Social Transformations, 1949-1966.' In *China's Communist Revolutions: Fifty Years of The People's Republic of China*, edited by Werner Draguhn and David S.G. Goodman,106-109. London: RoutledgeCurzon, 2002.

Broudehoux, Anne-Marie. 'Spectacular Beijing: The Conspicuous Construction of an Olympic Metropolis.' *Journal of Urban Affairs* 29, no. 4 (2007): 383-399.

Cai, Ruohong 蔡若虹. 'On the Creative Contents of New New Year prints' [关于新年画的创作内容]. *Renmin meishu* [人民美术], no. 2 (1950): 19-22.

Chan, Anita, Richard Madsen and Jonathan Unger. *Chen Village: Revolution to Globalisation*. Berkeley: University of California Press, 2009.

Cunningham, Maura Elizabeth and Jeffrey N. Wasserstrom. 'China Discovers World Expo Is No Olympics.' *YaleGlobal Online Magazine*, 17 August 2010 (accessed 18 August 2010). http://yaleglobal.yale.edu.

de Kloet, Jeroen, Gladys Pak Lei Chong and Wei Liu. 'The Beijing Olympics and the Art of Nation-State Maintenance.' *China Aktuell* 2 (2008): 7-35.

Derleth, James and Daniel R. Koldyk. 'The *Shequ* Experiment: Grassroots Political Reform in Urban China.' *Journal of Contemporary China* 13, no. 41 (2004): 747-777.

Gilley, Bruce. *Tiger on the Brink: Jiang Zemin and China's New Elite*. Berkeley: University of California Press, 1998.

Gottwald, Jörn-Carsten and Niall Duggan, 'China's Economic Development and the Beijing Olympics.' *International Journal of the History of Sport* 25, no. 3 (2008): 339-354.

Ho, Wing Chung and Petrus Ng. 'Public Amnesia and Multiple Modernities in Shanghai: Narrating the Postsocialist Future in a Former Socialist Model Community.' *Journal of Contemporary Ethnography* 37, no. 4 (2008): 383-414.

Holm, David L. *Art and Ideology in the Yenan Period, 1937-1945*, unpublished Ph.D. thesis, University of Oxford, 1979.

Huang, Chengjiang 黄成江. *Educated Youth in the Great Northern Wilderness* [北大荒知青]. Beijing: Zhongguo sheying chubanshe, 1998.

Hung, Chang-tai. 'Revolutionary History in Stone: The Making of a Chinese National Monument.' *The China Quarterly* 166 (2001): 457-473.

Landsberger, Stefan R. 'Harmony, Olympic Manners and Morals: Chinese Television and the New Propaganda.' *European Journal of East Asian Studies* 8, no. 2 (2009): 331-355.

Ma, Ke 马克. 'Political Propaganda Prints in the Ten years Since the Founding of Our Country' [建国十年来的政治宣传画]. *Meishu Yanjiu* [美术研究], no.1 (1959): 1.

Ruitenbeek, Klaas. *Carpentry and Building in Late Imperial China: A Study of the Fifteenth-Century Carpenter's Manual Lu Ban jing*. Leiden: Brill, 1993.

Saich, Tony. 'The Changing Role of Urban Government.' In *China Urbanises: Consequences, Strategies, and Policies*, edited by Shahid Yusuf and Tony Saich. Washington: The World Bank, 2008: 181-206.

Shao, Dazhen. 'Chinese Art in the 1950s: An Avant-Garde Undercurrent Beneath the Mainstream of Realism.' In *Modernity in Asian Art*, edited by John Clark, 76-77. Broadway: Wild Peony, 1993.

Shi, Lu 石鲁. 'Self-criticism of New Year Print Creation' [年画创作检讨]. *Renmin meishu* [人民美术], no. 2 (1950): 31.

Sun, Jiaming and Xiangming Chen. 'Personal Global Connections and New Residential Differentiation in Shanghai.' *China: An International Journal* 3, no. 2 (2005): 301-319.

Wasserstrom, Jeff. 'Red Shanghai: Blue Shanghai.' *The Asia-Pacific Journal* 50, no.2 (2008): 8

Wu, Fulong. 'Place Promotion in Shanghai, PRC.' *Cities*, 17, no. 5 (2000): 349-361.

Wu, Hung. *Remaking Beijing: Tiananmen Square and the Creation of a Political Space*. Chicago: The University of Chicago Press, 2005.

Xu, Feng. 'Gated Communities and Migrant Enclaves: The Conundrum for Building Harmonious Community/*shequ*.' *Journal of Contemporary China* 17, no.57 (2008): 633-651.

Zhong, Dianfei 钟惦棐. 'Looking at the Artistic Thought of New Year Print Makers on the Basis of this Year's New Year Prints' [从今年的年画作品看年画家的艺术思想]. *Renmin meishu* [人民美术] no. 2 (1950): 28.

Zhu, Jianfei. 'Beijing: Future City.' In *China Design Now*, edited by Hongxing Zhang and Lauren Parker. London: V&A Publishing, 2008: 138-147.

7.1. Zhao Yannian, Qian Daxin, 'The Soviet Union is our example' (苏联是我们的榜样), Huadong renmin meishu chubanshe, 1953.

7.2. Art Work Office of the Cultural Bureau of Jiangsu Provincial People's Government
Make sure that the proportion of the socialist component of the national economy steadily increases
(保证国民经济中社会主义成分的比重稳步增长)
Jiangsu renmin chubanshe, 1954.

7.3. Xie Zhiguang; Shao Jingyun; Xie Mulian, 'Moving into a new house' (搬進新房子), Huadong renmin meishu chubanshe, 1953.

7.4. Xie Zhiguang, 'A morning off' (假日的早晨), Xin meishu chubanshe, 1954.

7.5. Wu Yi; Guo Zhongyu, 'Develop socialism at a high pace' (高速度的建设社会主义), Shanghai renmin meishu chubanshe, 1960.

7.6. Zhang Yuqing, 'The new centre of the commune' (公社新邨图), Shanghai renmin meishu chubanshe, 1961.

7.7. Zhang Yuqing, 'The new look of traffic' (交通新貌图), Shanghai renmin meishu chubanshe, 1966.

7.8. Zhang Yuqing, 'An anti-American wave of rage along the Huangpu river' (黄浦江边的反美怒潮), Shanghai renmin meishu chubanshe, 1961.

7.10. Cultural Revolution Collective Painting Creative Group, 'Bombard the capitalist headquarters' (炮打资产阶级司令部), Shanghai renmin chubanshe, 1976.

7.9. Designer unknown, 'Scatter the old world, build a new world' (打碎旧世界, 创立新世界), c. 1967.

7.11. Pei Changqing, 'Arriving at Chairman Mao's side' (来到毛主席身边), Tianjin renmin meishu chubanshe, 1976.

7.12. Designer unknown, 'We should do more and engage less in empty talk – Deng Xiaoping' (多干实事, 少说空话 – 邓小平), Guangxi meishu chubanshe, 1992.

7.13. Sun Yi, 'Special Economic Zones – China's great open door' (特区-中国开放的大门), Renmin meishu chubanshe, 1987.

7.14. Tian Ying, 'The Shenzhen amusement park' (深圳游乐场), Zhejiang renmin meishu chubanshe, 1985.

7.15. Peng Ming, 'The age of smiling' (微笑的时代), Lingnan meishu chubanshe, 1988.

7.16. Wu Xiangfeng, 'The return of Hong Kong, One Country – Two Systems' (香港回归 一国两制), Hubei meishu chubanshe, 1997.

7.17. Office of the State Council Fifth Census Leading Small Group 'Report things as they really are, do a good job in the national census' (如实申报搞好人口普查), China Statistics Publishing House, 2000.

7.18. Office of the State Council Fifth Census Leading Small Group 'The national census benefits the nation and the people' (人口普查利国利民), China Statistics Publishing House, 2000.

7.19. Zhang Yuqing, 'The bustling Nanjing Road of Shanghai' (繁华的上海南京路), Shanghai renmin meishu chubanshe, 1990.

7.20. Design Institute of Wuxi Light Industrial College, 'Advance into the 21st century – Celebrate the 50th anniversary of the founding of the People's Republic of China' (迈向21世纪 – 庆祝中华人民共和国成立五十周年), Jiangxi meishu chubanshe, 1999.

7.21. Designer unknown, 'Establish a cultured city, construct a harmonious Dongcheng – Development, keep in step with the times' (创建文明城区, 共建和谐东城–发展, 紧跟时代步伐), publisher unknown, 2004/2005.

7.22. Designer unknown, 'Establish a cultured city, construct a harmonious Dongcheng – Environment, create comfort and charm' (创建文明城区, 共建和谐东城–环境, 塑造舒适美丽), publisher unknown, 2004/2005.

7.23. Wu Lei, Li Xiaoqian, 'The aim of the struggle is to let everybody attain moderate affluence' (奋斗目标全民小康), Guangxi renmin chubanshe, 2007.

7.24. Lin Yi, Li Xiaoqian, 'Improve the lives of the people, construct harmony' (改善民生共建和谐), Guangxi renmin chubanshe, 2007.

7.25. Designer unknown, 'One World One Dream' (同一个世界 同一个梦想), Beijing Organising Committee for the Games of the XXIX Olympiad, 2008.

7.26. Designer unknown, 'One World One Dream' (同一个世界 同一个梦想), Beijing Organising Committee for the Games of the XXIX Olympiad, 2008.

7.27. Designer unknown, 'Report census data accurately, provide a realistic picture of the economy – China Economic Census 2008 The Second' (如实申报普查资料, 反映经济全貌– 第二次全国经济普查标准试点), Office of the Leading Group of the People's Government of Beijing Municipality for the Second Economic Census, 2008.

7.28. Du Jiang, 'Build a prosperous and cultured new socialist countryside' (建设富裕文明的社会主义新农村), Sichuan meishu chubanshe, 1997.

8. Claiming the Past, Presenting the Present, Selling the Future: Imagining a New Beijing, Great Olympics

Gladys Pak Lei Chong

A new Beijing greets visitors to the 2008 Summer Olympic Games, a Beijing invigorated and transformed since it was awarded the Games seven years ago. The city has recovered its great cosmopolitan heritage as a meeting point for peoples, trade and ideas. Bold new structures have risen into the skyline. In the streets and behind closed doors, Beijing seethes with an economic and cultural ferment that makes it one of the most exciting cities on earth.
Foreword of the booklet *Olympic City* by the Beijing Foreign Cultural Exchanges Association[1]

The Olympics have made Beijing even more magnificent, so magnificent that I could not recognise it.
'The Beijing in the Olympics time', on the television programme *Hong Kong Connection* (11 August 2008)[2]

The city of Beijing features significantly in promotional materials for the 2008 Beijing Olympic Games. A telling example is the Beijing Olympics emblem, 'Chinese Seal, Dancing Beijing'. Its wide circulation during the Olympics has left an imprint on people's minds: whenever one sees the symbol, one is reminded of the Olympic City, Beijing. Beijing was not only a host city, it was also a symbol assigned with national significance. *The* Beijing that was connected to the Olympic moment intended to be a city that conjured up positive memories for Beijing residents and Chinese citizens, as well as the diaspora and the world at large.

A key Olympic slogan – literally 'New Beijing, New Olympics' (新北京, 新奥运) – indicated how the state envisioned the role of Beijing: a 'new' Beijing brought a 'new' Olympics that marked a 'new' Chinese era. Beijing needed to dress up, with new clothes, to present a new and fresh outlook to welcome the world to China. The English version of this slogan differs from its Chinese version: 'New Beijing, Great Olympics'. The reason for this is probably that it would be considered too immodest to claim to produce a 'new Olympics' in English. Suffice to say that by emphasising the word 'new' in its Chinese slogan, thus predominantly addressing the Chinese, the official material drew discursive power from a prevailing discourse in China that celebrated the idea of 'new' and progress (Zhang 2000; de Kloet, Chong et al. 2008). The idea of new in 'New Beijing, New Olympics', however, prompts us to ask the following questions: what is really 'new' about New Beijing; why is a New Beijing essential for bringing a New Olympics; what does a New Beijing mean for the state, the citizen, and the world; what defines 'new' (and 'old') about Beijing; and, most importantly, how is this New Beijing represented and performed?

'New Beijing' is not simply an official catchphrase, but a key moment of collective memory and identity formation. Memory formation in place-representation – comparable to an act of storytelling – is crucial in shaping identity. Representing a city is a performative act, involving strategies and tactics of 'selective remembering' and 'selective forgetting' (Chang 2005). What is to be remembered is rendered visible – to be 'on the map'; what is to be forgotten is forsaken and therefore rendered invisible – to be 'off the map'. Memory formation is not an innocent act that simply conserves the past; rather, it involves series of selection strategies that call the past into the present to cater for contemporary needs, and, intrinsically, shape the ways one anticipates the future. Thinking along these lines, one is prompted to ask: whose and what memories are selected and therefore deserve to be remembered? Similarly, whose and what memories are being denied and therefore forgotten, and what purposes do they serve? New Beijing is not only about making a new Beijing, but also about how the 'old' Beijing is being remade and then represented in the package of New Beijing.

This chapter examines how official propaganda – through place-representation of the Olympic City Beijing – shapes collective experience of the city. How did the state seize the Olympic moment to imagine and represent a Beijing that shaped people's views about the city, China and Chineseness? It is important to note that urban transformation related to mega-events has been extensively studied and the selective process of memory and representation involved in place-making has also been widely addressed (see, for example, Gold and Ward 1994; Gruffudd 1995; Zukin 1995; Chang 2005; Chang and Huang 2005; Davis 2005). My aim here is not to repeat what has been studied, but to demonstrate the way it was done through a case study of Beijing during the 2008 Games.

Concepts of disappearance, reappearance and appearance are central in discussing the city as a material and visual site of memory and identity formation. Driven by the emergence of the real-estate market, the rapid urban development in Beijing since the 1990s has generated a lot of discussion about the disappearance of the once familiar landscape, and the adverse impacts urban development has had (see, for example, Wu 2000; Fang and Zhang 2003; Visser 2004; Acharya 2005; Lai and Lee 2006). This discussion reached its height during the period around the Beijing Olympics, centring predominantly on the destructive aspects of the project to make China reappear in the global arena (see, for example, Broudehoux 2007; Marvin 2008). Theoretical insights from Abbas' analysis of (post-)colonial Hong Kong and 1990s Shanghai offer a way of rethinking the notions of disappearance and reappearance in the politics of memory production.

Ackbar Abbas (1997), writing against the backdrop of the imminent return of Hong Kong to China, examines the politics of cultural space of (post-)colonial Hong Kong through an analysis of architecture, cinema, photography and fiction. Central to his argument is the politics of disappearance that requires us to take the local context into consideration. In the case of Hong Kong, he asserts that the notion of disappearance is a multifaceted and dynamic one; to Abbas, disappearance is not simply about 'nonappearance, absence, or lack of presence' (1997: 7). Drawing on Freud's idea of 'negative hallucination', Abbas elaborates that disappearance should be understood as misrecognition: 'not seeing what is there' as well as 'recognising a thing as something else' (1997: 6-7). Disappearance is intimately related to representation. It is in representation that one sees how disappearance is manifested; to quote Abbas, 'many instances of this [disappearance] in cinema, architecture, and writing, where disappearance is not a matter of effacement but of replacement and substitution, where the perceived danger is re-contained through representations that are familiar and plausible' (1997: 8). One of the examples he gives concerns the preservation of Flagstaff House (a former colonial military base) in the form of a Chinese teaware museum. The historical building is preserved, but the associated colonial history is emptied out and substituted by something else; in this case, it is the appearance of Chinese culture – tea culture – that makes the colonial past disappear. The museum might have saved the building from being demolished, yet it emptied out the colonial past by replacing it with Chinese culture.

Abbas sees disappearance as something ambivalent and double-edged. For instance, disappearance associated with the politics of preservation presents a problematic side when preservation paradoxically erases cultural memories of the past (1997: 80). However, he also demonstrates that disappearance is not only a threat, it can also be a productive force: it was the imminent disappearing of Hong Kong that gave birth to a booming interest in Hong Kong culture and the identity of the Hong Kong people (1997: 14). In this light, disappearance offers the opportunity of potential change, as 'not all identities are worth preserving' (1997: 14). When one form of identity disappears, it is time for a new form of identity to be invented. In short, Abbas argues that what seems to be new in Hong Kong is always intimately linked to the conditions of disappearance. He writes that Hong Kong culture is 'a culture of disappearance' (2000: 777).

In contrast to Hong Kong, Abbas argues, the case of Shanghai exemplifies a culture of reappearance, 'a reappearance coinciding with China's re-inscription, after decades of closure, into the global economy' (2000: 779). Paralleling the construction of a new Shanghai – building new skyscrapers and new infrastructure – is Shanghai's booming interest in preservation since the 1990s. This keen interest in preservation is, Abbas believes, not about preserving 'cultural heritage'. Rather, it is driven by a strategic vision about Shanghai's future; in his words, 'the past allows the present to pursue the future' (2000: 780). Shanghai's reappearance is a reappearance that tries to capture its legendary past to boost its attractiveness. These preservation projects are crucial for the city's development in three ways. The first is the potential economic appeal: attractive historical sites draws tourists' money and improve the city's image for foreign competitiveness. The second is that preservation helps to revitalise and gentrify decaying urban areas; and, the third, which seems to Abbas to be the most important, is that through intervening with the municipality's urban policy and the city's future development, the state asserts its ruling authority, while, at the same time, finding an opportunity to meet the private sector's demand for economic growth. While Abbas' analysis is based upon the specific context of Hong Kong (1997) and Shanghai (2000), I will explore his politics of cultural space and memory production in a different context: *the* Beijing that was caught in the wind of the Olympics. Beijing, as the cultural and political centre of today's China, is in many ways different from Hong Kong, a (post-)colonial city struggling with the disappearance of its culture and identity, and from Shanghai, a re-emerging Chinese city attempting to recapture its past glamour after 40 years of disappearance.

My analysis draws on two sets of sources, together with my data collected during fieldwork (2007-2008). The first set consists of official representation tools published and sponsored by the Beijing Foreign Cultural Exchanges Association, the Information Office of Beijing Municipal Government, and the Beijing Tourism Administration. It includes two maps – *Map of Beijing: Beijing Welcomes You*, and a three-dimensional *Map of Beijing*[3]; three books on tourist information – *Beijing Official Guide*, *Olympic City* and *Get by in Beijing*; and a booklet, *Beijing Investment Guide* 2008-2009.[4] The second set of sources consists of four film clips about the city of Beijing produced by the Beijing Planning Exhibition Hall, entitled *The City of Eternity*, *Today's Beijing*, *2008 Beijing Olympics*, and *New Beijing*.

The analysis is structured according to three temporalities. The first section focuses on remembering the city: it shows how the past – through the preservation project of Qianmen – appears, and re-appears in the making of a New Beijing. The second section, re-inventing the city, shows how the Olympic City is built on disappearance. The notion of disappearance is to be understood from Abbas' idea of misrecognition, namely how the representation of the Olympic present is built upon a replacement or substitution of history. The Olympic Green is the focus of this analysis. The third section looks at how the future of Beijing is being imagined.

Re-membering the City

Walking in the city of Beijing on the eve of the Olympics, one could easily spot passers-by carrying a single-lens reflex (SLR) camera, taking pictures of a city that was in the midst of a great transformation. Some of them – including myself – wanted to capture *the moment* before the changes substituted and replaced what the site seemed to represent. Memory takes many forms; the most discernable two are individual memory and collective memory. In its most general sense, collective memory is about shared, sometimes imagined, experiences. The construction of a cultural identity needs collective memories; it is a way to bind people into an imagined community (Anderson 1983; Bardenstein 1999; Kong 1999). The act of constructing collective memories involves processes of 'selective remembering' and 'selective forgetting': members of a community assemble and interpret the memory of its own past and present that helps strengthen its community's own uniqueness vis-à-vis its alterity (Bardenstein 1999; Chang 2005). The act itself is a dynamic, negotiable and contested process: it can be performed as an act of resistance, like Palestinians' use of cultural symbols to counter their displacement (Bardenstein 1999), or like the invention of a Hong Kong identity in the face of Hong Kong's imminent return to China (Abbas 1997; or see for example, Fung 2001); or, it can be an act initiated by officials or other interest groups to shape an identity in order to achieve political and/or economic goals (see, for example, Bunnell 1999; Chang and Huang 2005). However, since an officially-sanctioned memory does not always suit the will of its initiator, the act of memory production is in fact a highly contested arena.

The making of a 'New Beijing' did not imply that everything in Beijing was built from scratch. Rather, this project was one that utilised the past – capitalising on the historical capital – in conjunction with the new and (ultra-)modern. Using the case of Qianmen (前门), the area south of Tiananmen whose *hutongs* were destroyed to make place for a shopping district with Chinese characteristics, I examine the role of preservation in the construction of New Beijing. I will show how the past appeared, or reappeared, to form a map of places with a bountiful history and facts that represented a New Beijing.

Preservation, in its general sense, is to protect something from falling apart or decaying. It is usually thought of as something 'constructive', as it helps to conserve a past that is otherwise destroyed and will be forgotten. It seemingly saves the memory of a people from being forgotten. However, on closer inspection, projects of preservation pertaining to urban development are not that simple (see, for example, Chang 2005; Chang and Huang 2005; Peleggi 2005). Just as with the case of Flagstaff House in Hong Kong, projects of preservation are often paired with disappearance (Abbas 1997: 65): a disappearance of a collective memory that is replaced by a more 'timely' one – Chinese culture in the Hong

8.1. Qianmen under construction was surrounded by paper walls with imaginary of a Qianmen-to-be; taken on 4 June 2008. Courtesy: Gladys Pak Lei Chong.

Kong case. In a different context, Shanghai, the thriving interest in preservation projects is a political project that seizes the glamorous past to pursue the future – in Abbas' words, not 'Back to the Future' but 'Forward to the Past' (2000: 780). Preservation assists Shanghai to reappear on the global stage. To put it succinctly, preservation is rarely an innocent nostalgia for the past and, as Abbas writes, 'preservation is selective and tends to exclude the dirt and pain' (1997: 66). In the context of Beijing-in-the-making, what does the preservation project in Qianmen reveal to us?

The 'preservation' of Qianmen was not an arbitrary choice. Quite the contrary; this preservation project, because of its historical connection and geographical proximity to the Forbidden City, played a key role in creating the imaginary of a New Beijing. This project was implemented in the name of preservation, a preservation that claimed to insist on 'renovation without demolition' (宁修不拆) and to restore its original look (古风貌),5 with a combination of traditional and modern elements. In practice, the project involved large-scale demolition of old *hutongs*, followed by a rebuilding, recreation and installation of cultural symbols. Preservation in this case is merely about preserving the surface, imagined or not: it is like an old box without its original contents. The preservation project officially started in 2006; after two years of construction, it was opened to the public two days before the grand opening of the Beijing Olympic Games on 8 August 2008. The area around Qianmen has been discursively portrayed as a place representing old Beijing (老北京).

Situated at the south side of the Forbidden City, Qianmen – which literally means 'the front door/gate' – is the gate to the imperial city, the Forbidden City. It is a few steps from the very heart of the capital: Tiananmen Square (see figure 8.2: map of the centre). Tiananmen Square is the power centre of a new China, symbolically marked by the moment when Mao declared the establishment of a new China in 1949 (Dong 1988; Wu 1991; King and Kusno 2000). Until today, most official ceremonies are held on this square. The Forbidden City is the imaginary that represents the cultural and imperial history of the ancient city. It is seen as the most suitable symbol for the historical development of Beijing: the Beijing Planning Exhibition Hall identifies it as the central object in telling the story of Beijing and China. The symbolic significance of these two sites is marked by their central location on any map of Beijing. Maps, as Doreen Massey writes, are means of representation; a map 'embodies a particular way of understanding, a particular interpretation of the place it is depicting' (1995: 20). Looking at the map of Beijing, one can easily identify this area as the centre point where the story of the city unfolds and where the significance of other places is measured.

Preservation projects like this do not conflict with or contradict the larger discourse of New Beijing. Similar to Shanghai, the zeal to preserve the old Beijing reflects the state's plan to capitalise the city's 'celebrated' old days and its assumed rich historical past for its contemporary use and future development. Preservation in Beijing – as part of the Olympic mega-project – marks the reappearance of Beijing and China in the global arena, after a 'century of national humiliation' (1842-1942) and Maoist China (1949-1976) (Callahan 2004; Ong 2004; Callahan 2006; Close, Askew et al. 2007; Brownell 2008; Xu 2008). Just

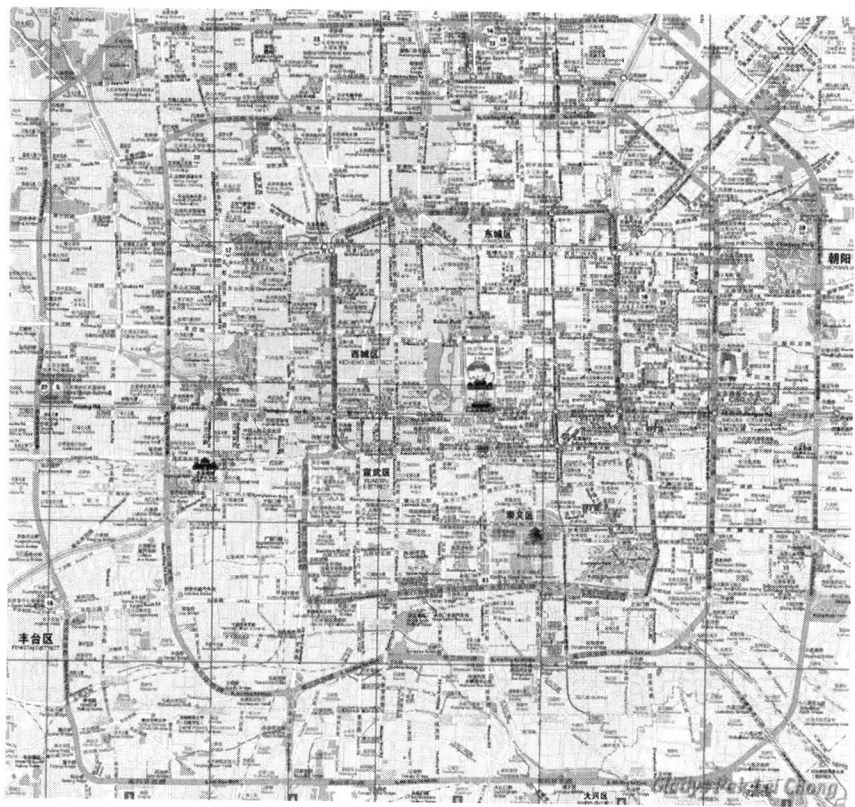

8.2. The centre of Beijing on *Map of Beijing: Beijing Welcomes you*.

like the representation of history is never solely about the past, preservation is also always about the past, present, *and* the future: the past captured in the present helps further the developmental plan of the New Beijing project.

Historical information – selected 'facts' – such as narratives of origin, past patrons, legends of the past, and images, are crucial to authenticate this site as a 'place in history' (Peleggi 2005: 262). Built in the Ming Dynasty, Qianmen is 'the first and the oldest commercial street in Beijing' (something mentioned in almost all the representation tools listed above). The use of these superlatives certifies its special place in history and its significance in collective memories of Beijing. Classified under the shopping section on the city maps and in the official guide, Qianmen is well-remembered for its connection with some of the well-known shops, '*laozihao*' (老字号; translated as 'time-honoured-brand' businesses). It presents itself as the birthplace of many well-known Chinese shops and the legendary stories associated with them. The Qianmen area was a prosperous place, where the ordinary Beijingers would eat (for example, at *Yuechenzhai* 月盛斋),[6] shop (for example, at *Qianxiangyi* 谦祥益 and *Ruifuxiang* 瑞蚨祥),[7] seek medical advice (for example, at *Tongrentang* 同仁堂)[8] and find their entertainment (for example, at *Guanghe Theatre* 广和剧场).[9] These narratives call for a sense of nostalgia linked to these shops, as each of them has its own legendary past and stories: for example, Emperor Kangxi visited *Duoyichu* (都一处)[10] and gave it the name it has now; Empress Dowager Cixi demanded the food from *Yuechenzhai* (月盛斋); and the famous Peking opera artist, Mei Langfang, performed at Guanghe Theatre. Collectively, these narratives are powerful discursive tools that enhance the place's historical heritage.

Qianmen-Dashilan is said to 'have reflected the city's sometimes turbulent history' (*Beijing Official Guide*: 97). This turbulent history is nonetheless not visible: it disappears in its representation. The history of this place is condensed into a few old photos installed on some buildings in the street. All these representations of the past are highly selective: a bit of Ming dynasty, a bit of Qing dynasty, and a bit of the early Republican Period (1911-1948/49) in the 1910s. The nonpresence of the period since the 1920s is an act of selective forgetting that breeds a collective amnesia. This collective amnesia/forgetting, to draw on Abbas' argument, is not about not remembering, but about 'remembering as something else; that is, forgetting is additive, not subtractive' (Abbas in this volume).

To create an atmosphere of 'Chineseness', cultural symbols and items, such as the pagoda, lampposts and flowerpots with 'Chinese characters' (see, for example, figure 8.3) and sculptures of historical people, are installed on the street: the past is reduced to a decoration of 'the centuries-old shopping street' (*Beijing Official Guide*: 97). In a similar way, the term *laozihao* is used in its promotion: *laozihao* has now become a decorative term extracted from its original meaning. The social relations associated with *laozihao* – loyalties and trust from the customers and a close relation with one's clientele – disappear in the preservation project. Some of the *laozihaos* reopened only after the renovation project had named them *laozihao*: they were sold and are now either state-owned or commercially exploited. *Yuechenzhai* is a case in point: the one in Qianmen today is '*Yuechenzhai at Zhengyangmen*' (正阳门月盛斋) and state-owned, the 'real' *laozihao* – renamed as 'The Ma Family's *Yuechenzhai at Hubujie*' (户部街马记月盛斋) – was actually reopened after the economic reforms in Houhai (后海; an area that is known for its nightlife).

The new Qianmen could therefore be called a 'mnemonic site' (Nora 1989), a site designated by the state to sell nostalgia as a commodity (Chang 2005: 250 and Peleggi 2005: 263). With the pagoda at the entrance of the street, the street arguably resembles the generic image of a Chinatown. It is, to use King and Kusno's words (2000), like an act of 'cut and paste': copying an urban architectural style to paste it into a different social and cultural context, with some editing here and there to construct the 'new' (King and Kusno 2000: 47). Today, the image of a Chinatown is comparable to Abbas' description of 'placeless' buildings that can be found in many cities. These Chinese neighbourhoods make use of similar 'ethnic symbols' like the pagoda, 'Chinese' symbols and items and Chinese street names to attract visitors (see, for example, Anderson 1987; Chang 1999; Christiansen 2003; Collins 2006).[11] It can be argued that the newly restored Qianmen looks more like a film set, a simulacra of the once-lived-in area (Baudrillard 1994). It is like a Disneyland, a theme park with a 'Chinese' theme that is actively promoted as the new trendy shopping street with its past glamour. The rent has

8.3. Street decorations with 'traditional Chinese' characteristics.
Courtesy: Gladys Pak Lei Chong.

8.4. Paper wall built to hide the less pleasant scene behind the Qianmen area.
Courtesy: Gladys Pak Lei Chong.

skyrocketed, and few old shops were able to return to their original sites; rather, the place has attracted many international brands such as Starbucks, Uniqlo, H&M, and ZARA; shops that one can find in any main shopping street or mall around the world.

The preservation project in Qianmen captured the larger global heritage-industry trend – the commodification of the bygone (Hewison 1987; Chang 1997; Chang 1999; Peleggi 2005) – to enhance the city's historical image in the making of a New Beijing. The past, accompanied by imagined memories of it, sells better than the present. The past does not exist until one claims its present: 'present pasts' (Huyssen 2000). Yet, this performance of a legendary past has been rather partial and, to a large extent, superficial: this area is next to a decaying local residential-cum-commercial area, an area that has been undergoing demolition. To make the less pleasant surroundings 'disappear', usually walls – either paper or concrete – were built to hide them from the scene (see figure 8.4).

Re-inventing the City (The Present)

In the opening ceremony of the Beijing Olympics, 29 giant firework footprints figuratively walked from Tiananmen Square, along the Central Axis, to the National Stadium (aka the Bird's Nest) in the Olympic Green. This performance symbolically marked a visible trail of China's development: from the centre of the Chinese civilisation of the past to the centre of global attention in the present. This performance resonated with the narrative sequences of Beijing in many official materials: the narration often starts with the Forbidden City and Tiananmen Square, then moves along the Central Axis, reaching the modern and joyous National Stadium on the Olympic Green (see, for example, 2008 *Beijing Olympics*, *Today's Beijing*, *New Beijing*).

The Central Axis is not a historical site like the Forbidden City or the Temple of Heaven; and, yet, because of its recent connection with the Olympic site, it was promoted as a landmark, a historical achievement with 700 years of history. The descriptions in English often state that the Olympic Green is 'located on the north end of the Central Axis of Beijing City' (2008 *Beijing Olympics*; *Beijing Official Guide*: 5); or, alternatively, the Central Axis stretches 'all the way to the Olympic Green' (*Olympic City*: 36). Interestingly, the description in Chinese says that the Central Axis ends at the Drum and Bell Tower[12] – not the Olympic Green. It seems logical: if the Central Axis has a 700-year history, it is quite unlikely that it ends at today's Olympic Green. The difference between the Chinese and English materials could very well reflect different emphases to cater to different audiences – the Chinese version emphasised the Chinese historical past, while the English version selected (or, to be more precise, summarised) what the producers believed to be important and sufficient for English readers. Suffice it to say, the Central Axis is presented as connecting the past with the present.

The present is the time period between the past and the future; it is 'the location, both source and product, of cultural memory' (Bal and Vanderburgh 1999:

8.5. The Olympic Green, taken on 23 August 2008. Courtesy: Gladys Pak Lei Chong.

3). The present represented here was a reinvention: it was a present that was built on disappearance – not implying absence or lack of presence – but, following Abbas, a form of misrecognition (1997: 7). The example of the Central Axis demonstrates how the meaning of a site can be altered and selectively (mis-)presented to mark its connection with other sites: the historical and cultural 'past' of the Forbidden City and the modern 'present' of the Olympic Green. The story of the Central Axis ends at its connecting point with the Olympic Green; what lies beyond it is rendered not important, therefore not represented – a vacuous space.

The Olympic Green was thus an emblematic site/sight of how a New Beijing was reinvented. Its importance is also projected on the three-dimensional map that directs the gaze towards three areas of significance: the political and cultural centre (the heart of Beijing), the financial and economic centre (the *Chaoyang* District), and the *new* political and cultural centre (the Olympic Green in the north). The Olympic Green is the (future) site of China's Olympic memory. Given its political significance, the area was designed to embody an actively promoted image of the New Beijing; an image of the present that represented progress, modernness and open-mindedness to set an example for a promising future. The Olympic Green has an area of 1,159 hectares. It is home to most of the Olympic venues, including the renowned Bird's Nest, the National Aquatic Centre (aka the Water Cube), the Olympic Village, the Main Press Centre (MPC) and the Olympic Forest Park. To this day, the charm of this Olympic legend has not faded; it keeps drawing visitors from different corners of China and the world.

Unlike the preservation projects of historical sites, the Olympic Green has been widely presented as something built from scratch, like drawing on a blank sheet. What the official promotion materials never tell us are the stories about the site: what was it before the Olympic Green was built? Questions related to urban removal and demolition are therefore selectively downplayed and replaced by non-stop positive stories related to the construction of Olympic venues.

The Olympic Green, with its spacious design that housed most of the attention-drawing venues, drew together a population of diverse groups during the Games. The area was comparable to a cosmopolitan space, a space in which individuals knew how to respect otherness (Abbas 2000; Appiah 2006). The joyous, carnival-like atmosphere seemed to live up to the cosmopolitan ideal promoted by the Olympic slogan, 'One World, One Dream'. For some curious reason, the global critical reaction to China's response to the Tibet demonstrations, and the subsequent tensions followed by global contestations, seemed to disappear; what was left was a sense of harmonious coexistence of differences. I argue that this cosmopolitan image associated with the Olympic Green was made possible by, first of all, selectively forgetting the efforts of the migrant workers who built the venues and managed to finish the projects on time. News about accidents related to the construction went largely unreported. Also, their presumably 'unpleasant' looks were believed to contradict the 'pleasant' look of the city; they were persuaded to return home or move to other jobs in other cities before the Games started. Second, it was made possible by censoring the news about strict visa requirements that deterred any potential demonstrators from entering the country. Third, the area was meticulously guarded by countless security checkpoints and security police; its cosmopolitan image was made possible by carefully securing its boundaries and stringent overall surveillance – practices that, to some extent, were rendered invisible to the general public.

Because of its strong association with place, architecture is wedded to a city's assumed identity (Crilley 1993; Abbas 1997; Charney 2007). The Beijing Organising Committee for the Olympic Games (BOCOG) and the Beijing Municipal Planning Commission (BMPC) seized on the global place-marketing trend by using architecture as advertising tools. Two telling examples are: the Bird's Nest, designed by Swiss architects Jacques Herzog and Pierre de Meuron, with the help of Beijing artist and cultural entrepreneur, Ai Weiwei; and the Water Cube, co-designed by PTW Architects and China Construction Design International (CCDI). Yet, this 'going-global' ambition was not without contestation: some argued that China had become 'the laboratory for foreign architects' and that it was losing its 'authentic character' (Ren 2008).

Interestingly, in highlighting the design features of the Bird's Nest and the Water Cube, the 'foreign' presence is replaced by an emphasis on Chinese tradition:

> [The] designs have adopted the traditional Chinese philosophy: the sky is round and the earth is a square [天圆地方]. The two stadiums, one is round symbolising the sky and the masculine, the other is square symbolising the femininity which perfectly caters to the Chinese spirit of the unity of the universe and the humans [天人合一]. (2008 *Beijing Olympics*)

Chinese tradition appears to have replaced foreign architecture. This selective forgetting of foreign architects is also found in media productions and official promotion materials; for example, in the documentary on the Bird's Nest, *The*

Bird's Nest Where A Dream Begins,[13] and in *Olympic City*. The focus is on how amazing the buildings are and how the construction projects were carried out; the architects' names are never mentioned. Cultural symbols representing 'tradition' and 'Chineseness' are installed around the Olympic Green, seemingly to tell the public that in pursuing modernity, Chinese tradition has not been forgotten and that both can co-exist harmoniously (Abbas 2000; de Kloet, Chong et al. 2008). This is also made clear in *Today's Beijing*: the film asserts that 'alongside the new development, the historical features of ancient Beijing will also be carefully preserved, and its cultural characteristics will be inherited to coordinate the past, the present and the future'. The accompanying image shows a few senior Chinese and a young Chinese boy practicing *tai chi* in a park, after which the image zooms in on the Bird's Nest and the Water Cube.

Mapping Beijing's Future (The Future)

The future is unknown, yet made foreseeable by plans and expectation. It is not yet memory, but memory in the making. The image of New Beijing is based upon Beijing's recent development. This becomes most clear in the short film *New Beijing*, in which the image sequence goes as follows: the Forbidden City, a carnival-like Tiananmen Square (with colourful air balloons flying above it), the National Theatre, Beijing's Central Axis, the Olympic Green, the Bird's Nest, the Water Cube, Petrochina Plaza, Keichun Plaza, Huan Run Plaza, Zhongguancun, New Capital Airport, Xizhimen Transportation Centre, the Financial Street, Xidan Bookstore, CBD, CCTV, and a panoramic night view of the city.

The New Beijing represented here is a clean, tidy, efficient, technologically-advanced city, and a somewhat mechanical one that does not have much human presence. It is strikingly similar to teasers promoting sales of real estate. It is important to note that the film was not made of 'real' photographic images, but was constructed graphically. It con-fuses the present with the future, on the one hand; and, on the other, it seems to convince us that a promising future is proceeding apace, as one can recognise the existing buildings in the city. Time and speed matter: the faster the development is, the brighter the future will look. This sense of speed is in tune with the general discourse of pursuing newness. Progress and change are wrapped in the larger discourse of the new. This discourse can be dated back to as early as the 19th century, when China fell prey to Western imperialism. Over the course of a century and a half, China has been caught up with this pursuit of speeding up the pace of modernisation in order to be on a par with the West; to quote Zhang (2000), 'time has become a space in the global arena waiting to be filled or conquered' (1000). The future of Beijing, and China, had to be one that succeeded in making a great leap forward – conquering time and making progress. In the anticipation of a promising future, the present was represented to be progressing towards a well-planned future. Just as Debord mentions in *The Society of the Spectacle* (1995 [1968]), contemporary social life can be understood, in his words, as 'the decline of being into having, and having into merely appearing' (17). The spectacle of the future presented here shows that what the future *appears* to be is more important than what it actually *is*.

To map out Beijing's future is to carve out a space to ascertain Beijing and China's reappearance on the world stage. Vision and planning – the focus of this section – are central in mapping Beijing's future. Having a good vision and planning for the future of Beijing, and subsequently, its projected (symbolic) significance for China, are important for the state to claim ruling legitimacy. It needs to demonstrate its competence, a competence to bring progress and prosperity, and to maintain stability and social order (Shue 2004). Being able to put visions onto a map of plans is a sign of power. It displays a set of productive power – 'biopower' – a systemic way of managing life and its reproduction (Foucault 1990; Foucault 2003).

The vision for Beijing's Future is to make Beijing 'a national capital', 'an international metropolis', 'a cultural city', and 'a liveable city' (*Today's Beijing, Olympic City, Beijing Investment Guide*). *Beijing Investment Guide* has a clear elaboration on how these four visions are to be achieved, and these four aspects of the future Beijing are also visualised in *Today's Beijing*. The vision of 'a national capital' has a bird's-eye view of Tiananmen Square. It is a status that needs to be maintained, rather than to be achieved. Its articulation serves as a reminder of its status, not a vision per se. The vision of 'an international metropolis' includes an image of skyscrapers with green in the forefront, an image resembling New York City (skyscrapers and Central Park). The idea of catching up with the (economically) developed others is the most prominent here. It is a vision to place Beijing in the league of world cities. Skyscrapers symbolise modernity and development. The green park represents an eco-friendly, relaxing leisure space. The message is that urban development does not harm the quality of the living environment. The vision of 'a cultural city' shows an image of the Forbidden City. Just like the preservation projects and the installation of 'Chinese' symbols mentioned earlier, it reassures us that in pursuing modernity, Chinese tradition has not been forsaken. A liveable city has an image of green and nature. It is as if a promise is being made to not sacrifice the environment in its pace of development. These visions together make up an imaginary of the future Beijing – a selective way of imagining the future.

An advanced transportation system and infrastructure feature prominently in these four visions and in Beijing's overall development plan. A well-developed transportation system symbolises mobility, a mobility that stands for modernity, progress and technology. It is a key aspect for an international metropolis. When talking about Olympic-led urban transformation, infrastructure is one of the first items to be mentioned: 'from wider roads and fresh taxi fleets to new parks and entertainment districts' (*Olympic City*: 5). The past is often drawn upon to make salient Beijing's progress today and its foreseeable future. In *Olympic City*, it says:

> Twenty years ago, bicycles ruled the roads in Beijing and private cars were virtually unknown. Economic development and the rise of an affluent middle class have transformed the urban environment. There are now more than three million cars in the city and the road network has expanded accordingly. (120)

The presence of bicycles suggests a less modern past; today, their disappearance is substituted by a positive discourse of economic development and, subsequently, a positive discourse of urban development. The appearance of 'three million cars' strengthens the image of a mobile future in sight. This is, however, in conflict with the environmental concerns mentioned in 'the Green Olympics' or the vision of 'a liveable city', and, needless to say, the endless complaints about traffic congestion in the city.

In the planned development of public transport, the project to expand the Beijing Subway occupied a key place. Subway line 10, tailor-made to cater for the Olympics, was opened on 19 July 2008. Its significance was revealed by its place in Beijing maps: all the maps published in the period around the Olympics had a Beijing Subway map, in addition to clear indications of subway lines marked on the city map. On some maps (photo 8-2), 'subway lines in construction' were also marked, clearly indicated on the map's legend. The construction projects of the Beijing Subway were often mapped onto the city's plans: 'By 2010, the length of the Beijing subway will be extended to more than 300 km; by 2020, there will be 19 subway and light-rail lines in Beijing, with a total length of about 660 km' (*Olympic city*: 121). In foreseeing the future, images like the city's subway map were used to help one to visualise plans; in Abbas' words, 'the more abstract and ungraspable space becomes, the greater the importance of the image' (1997: 69). The graphic image illustrating the plan to expand the subway demonstrates a ceaseless determination, technological advancement, well-thought-out plans and above all, progress.

Conclusion

This chapter has shown how the state government seized the Olympic moment to imagine and to represent a Beijing that shaped a collective memory of the city, China and Chineseness. The making of New Beijing displayed both the politics of reappearance and the politics of disappearance. Comparable to Abbas' analysis of Shanghai, the construction of a New Beijing showed a culture of reappearance, a reappearance that was driven by China's ambition to make its presence felt in the global arena. This reappearance echoed the popular discourse of a 'China Rejuvenated' circulated widely in the period around the Games. The slogans 'New Beijing, New Olympics' and, in particular, 'One World, One Dream (Chong 2012)', reflected China's long-term ambition to make progress and to be in the same league as 'the West' – an imagined Other that was more developed than China. The reappearance of a New Beijing in the global arena required the remaking and the imagination of the past, the present, and the future. The past, in the example of Qianmen, reappeared to fill people's imagination of the good old days. Its reappearance was made possible by the disappearance of the *old* social fabrics (*hutongs* and the social lives revolving around the area). Disappearance is usually perceived as a threat; however, Abbas' concept of disappearance illuminates a new way of looking at disappearance; it has a productive aspect. Paralleling the booming interest in discussing Hong Kong's cultural identity in (post-)colonial Hong Kong, the disappearance of the old *hutongs* in Qianmen has generated thriving interest in urban transformation, demolition and preservation in Beijing. Take, for example, Ou Ning's documentary *Meishi Street*, academic studies on urban change, countless journalistic reports on demolition, and the many who carried their SLR cameras to capture a disappearing Beijing; all of them attempting to write on the would-be-forgotten, and yet, precisely because of their actions, the disappearing reappeared in other social spaces. Another way of looking at the politics of disappearance, yet with much contestation, is that this preservation also allows the creation of a new image, a new possible identity – in this case, of an officially initiated project of place-making, it is a modern yet traditional Chinese identity that tried to shake off the out-of-date and shabby image of the past.

Likewise, the cosmopolitan image presented by, for example, the Bird's Nest, appeared to displace the negative and contested image of China revolving around the 2008 Games. China saw the Olympics as a crucial global spectacle to present a positive image of Beijing, China and Chineseness to the world. This positive image – through the image of openness and happiness associated with the Olympic Green – was made possible by the displacement of the relatively less celebrated 'facts' of, for example, the working conditions of migrant workers and the stringent security measures. In following Abbas' argument on disappearance and forgetting, these less-pleasant facts are not quite forgotten, but people 're-membered something as something else' (in this book). In this light, the Chinese government deployed this tactic of disappearance in a very timely manner. After the Olympics, a museum dedicated to narrate the stories of the migrant workers opened in the Olympic Green. Again, it shows that the migrant workers did not quite 'disappear' but that they were made invisible to make room for a pleasant, cosmopolitan image of the present. Likewise, the future plan of the city of Beijing is also not about what it will become but what it *appears* to become. A promising future is visualised through misrecognition – a displacement of narratives.

Two years after the 2008 Games, another mega-event, the World Expo 2010, took place in Beijing's rival city, Shanghai. Both the Expo and the 2008 Olympic Games displayed China's ambition to showcase its recent economic achievement to the world; both could be read as steps marking China's reappearance in the global arena. Like the Beijing Games, the preparation for the Expo entailed urban transformation on a massive scale, involving demolition and the relocation of local residents and industries from the chosen site. An area of 5.28 square km around the Huangpu River was dedicated to this six-month event; extensive infrastructure (e.g. subway lines, new taxis) was put in place. With a gathering of almost 200 different countries and 50 corporate organisations,[14] the Expo site displayed a strikingly similar cosmopolitan image to that presented by the Olympic Green. I believe this cosmopolitanness is the image that the Chinese government would like to present to its citizens and to the world. With the slogan 'Better City, Better Life', the Expo spelt out the national vision of 'the future'. It is a future made possible by technology and meticulous urban planning, which can easily be translated into modernity and progress, as also demonstrated by the Beijing case. Despite these similarities, however, the two mega-events and the two cities were not quite the same. In terms of global appeal, the Olympics seemed to draw more international attention than the six-month-long Expo. The majority who visited the Expo were Chinese from China; more importantly, the Expo hardly led to any global contestation. In terms of the cities' status, Shanghai is perceived as the financial centre, whereas Beijing is seen as the cultural and political centre. As a result, the roles assigned to them are different. In terms of urban development, preservation projects in Shanghai (e.g. *Yuyuan* 豫园) had taken place long before the Expo. Besides, a remarkable difference appeared in the way in which the two cities dealt with the issue of demolition. During the Olympics, the Beijing government chose to make neighborhoods disappear; yet, the Shanghai government had made deliberate efforts to make the demolished neighbourhoods reappear. For instance, a theatre show performed by 300 former residents of the Shangsteel district, called 'Homeland, an Impression of Shangsteel' (家园·印象上钢), was staged in the Expo, and efforts were made to show how preservation projects were carried out (for example, old factories were restored into exhibition halls). Viewed in this light, the Shanghai government seemed to have learned from Beijing's mistake of not dealing with the issue of demolition. Research into urban transformation in Shanghai precedes that on Beijing (Olds 1997; Abbas 2000). The Expo undoubtedly furthered Shanghai's ongoing plan of reappearance. For this reason, urban transformation pertaining to the Shanghai Expo deserves its own detailed analysis. Lastly, given the roles of these mega-events in Beijing and Shanghai, one is prompted to ask: how do other Chinese cities rival these two major, leading cities?

Notes

1. *Olympic City* is a booklet published and sponsored by the Beijing Foreign Cultural Exchanges Association, the Information Office of Beijing Municipal Government, and the Beijing Tourism Administration.
2. Hong Kong Connection is a weekly news documentary programme produced by Radio Television Hong Kong (RTHK). It is usually broadcast at prime time (between 7 p.m. and 8 p.m.) on the two major commercial television channels, Television Broadcasts Limited (TVB) and Asia Television Limited (ATV).
3. Both could be found online at Beijing This Month Publications, www.btmbeijing.com (accessed 10 August 2008).
4. This booklet is organised by the Beijing Foreign Cultural Exchange Centre, and sponsored by the Beijing Municipal Bureau of Commerce.
5. As Wang Shiren, a cultural relics expert participating in the renovation project, said in a press conference (*Time Out, Beijing*, 12-25 June 2008).
6. *Yuechenzhai* is a shop selling (*halal*) meat products. The shop was founded during the Qing Qianlong era in 1775.
7. *Qianxiangyi* and *Ruifuxiang* specialise in silk fabrics and silk garments. The former was founded in 1840 and the latter in 1862.
8. *Tongrentang* specialises in Chinese medicine. It was founded during the Qing Kangix era, 1669.
9. *GuangheTheatre* was the most famous theatre in Beijing during the Qing dynasty.
10. *Duoyichu* is a restaurant that dates back to the Qing Gianlong era (1742).
11. The image of Chinatown with a pagoda appeals to people's imaginary of Chinatown. The image has circulated so much in Chinatowns around the world, for instance in Amsterdam, that Chinese entrepreneurs, together with some members of the city government, have been discussing for years the building of a pagoda to attract visitors there.

12. It did not say exactly when the Drum and Bell Tower was built, but according to the description and the emphasis on the connection between the Central Axis and the Drum and Bell Tower, the latter was also built 700 years ago.
13. Produced by China International Television Broadcasting, it was broadcast by the Television Broadcasting company (TVB) in Hong Kong, on 7 August 2008.
14. Expo 2010 Shanghai China, http://en.expo2010.cn/pavilions/index.htm (accessed 19 January 2011).

Sources used

Beijing Foreign Cultural Exchanges Association, Information Office of Beijing Municipal Government, Beijing Tourism Administration (2008). *Olympic City*. Beijing. China Intercontinental Press. http://store.btmbeijing.com/pdf-books/o_city.pdf.

Beijing Foreign Cultural Exchanges Association, Information Office of Beijing Municipal Government, Beijing Tourism Administration (2008). *Beijing Official Guide*. Beijing. Beijing This Month Publications. http://store.btmbeijing.com/pdf-books/bog_e.pdf.

Beijing Municipal Bureau of Commerce (2008). *Beijing Investment Guide* 2008-2009. Beijing. Beijing This Month Publications. http://store.btmbeijing.com/pdf-books/big_e.pdf.

Beijing Foreign Cultural Exchanges Association (2008). *Get By in Beijing*. Beijing. China Intercontinental Press. http://store.btmbeijing.com/pdf-books/gbib.pdf.

Beijing Foreign Cultural Exchanges Association (2008). *Map of Beijing*. Beijing. Beijing This Month Publications. http://store.btmbeijing.com/pdf-books/3d_map.pdf.

Beijing Foreign Cultural Exchanges Association and Information Office of Beijing Municipal Government (2008). *Map of Beijing: Beijing Welcomes You*. Beijing. Beijing Publishing House. http://store.btmbeijing.com/pdf-books/o_map.pdf.

References

Abbas, Ackbar. *Hong Kong: Culture and the Politics of Disappearance*. London: University of Minnesota Press, 1997.

—. 'Cosmopolitan De-Scriptions: Shanghai and Hong Kong.' *Public Culture* 12, no. 3 (2000): 769-86.

Acharya, Shrawan K. 'Urban Development in Post-Reform China: Insights from Beijing.' *Norsk Geografisk Tidsskrift-Norwegian Journal of Geography* 59, no. 3 (2005): 228-36.

Anderson, Benedict. *Imagined Communities*. London: Verso, 1983.

Appiah, Kwame Anthony. 'The Case for Contamination.' *New York Times*, 1 January 2006.

Bal, Mieke, and David Vanderburgh. 'Editors' Introduction Passagen 2000: The City, Pace and Space.' *Parallax* 5, no. 3 (1999): 1-8.

Bardenstein, Carol B. 'Trees, Forest, and the Shaping of Palestinian and Israeli Collective Memory.' In *Acts of Memory: Cultural Recall in the Present*, edited by Mike Bal, Jonathan Crewe and Leo Spitzer, 148-68. Hanover: University Press of New England, 1999.

Baudrillard, Jean. *Simulacra and Simulation*. Michigan, Ann Arbor: The University of Michigan Press, 1994.

Berg, Van Den, Leo Erik Braun, and A.H.J. Otgaar. *Sports and City Marketing in European Cities*. Hampshire: Ashgate Publishing Ltd, 2002.

Broudehoux, Anne-Marie. 'Spectacular Beijing: The Conspicuous Construction of an Olympic Metropolis.' *Journal of Urban Affairs* 29, no. 4 (2007): 383-99.

Brownell, Susan. *Beijing's Games: What the Olympics Mean to China*. Maryland: Rowman & Littlefield, 2008.

Bunnell, Tim G. 'Views From Above and Below: The Petronas Twin Towers and/ in Contesting Visions of Development in Contemporary Malaysia.' *Singapore Journal of Tropical Geography* 20, no. 1 (1999): 1-23.

Callahan, William A. 'National Insecurities: Humiliation, Salvation, and Chinese Nationalism.' *Alternatives: Global, Local, Political* 29, no. 2 (2004): 199-218.

—. 'History, Identity, and Security: Producing and Consuming Nationalism in China.' *Critical Asian Studies* 38, no 2 (2006): 179-208.

Chang, T.C. 'Heritage as a Tourism Commodity: Traversing the Tourist – Local Divide.' *Singapore Journal of Tropical Geography* 18, no. 1 (1997): 46-68.

—. 'Local Uniqueness in the Global Village: Heritage Tourism in Singapore.' *The Professional Geographer* 51, no. 1 (1999): 91-103.

—. 'Place, Memory and Identity: Imagining "New Asia".' *Asia Pacific Viewpoint* 46, no. 3 (2005): 247-53.

Chang, T.C. and Shirlena Huang. 'Recreating Place, Replacing Memory: Creative Destruction at the Singapore River.' *Asia Pacific Viewpoint* 46, no. 3 (2005): 267-80.

Charney, Igal. 'The Politics of Design: Architecture, Tall Buildings and the Skyline of Central London.' *Area* 39, no. 2 (2007): 195-205.

Chong, Gladys Pak Lei. *China Rejuvenated? Governmentality, Subjectivity, and Normativity. The 2008 Beijing Olympic Games*, Media Studies, University of Amsterdam, Amsterdam. 2012.

Christiansen, Flemming. *Chinatown, Europe: An Exploration of Overseas Chinese Identity in the 1990s*. London: Routledge-Curzon, 2003.

Close, Paul, David Askew, and Xin Xu. *The Beijing Olympiad.The Political Economy of a Sporting Mega-Event*. New York: Routledge, 2007.

Collins, Jock. 'Ethnic Precincts as Contradictory Tourist Spaces.' In *Tourism, Ethnic Diversity, and the City. Contemporary Geographies of Leisure, Tourism and Mobility Series*, edited by Jan Rath, 67-86. London: Routledge, 2006.

Crilley, Darrel. 'Architecture as Advertising: Constructing the Image of Redevelopment.' In *Selling Places: The City as Cultural Capital, Past and Present*, edited by Gerry Kearns and Chris Philo, 231-52. Oxford Pergamon Press, 1993.

Davis, Jeffrey. S. 'Representing Place: "Deserted Isles" and the Reproduction of

Bikini Atoll.' *Annals of the Association of American Geographers* 95, no. 3 (2005): 607-25.

de Kloet, Jeroen, Gladys Chong, and Wei Liu. 'The Beijing Olympics and the Art of Nation-State Maintenance.' *Journal of Current Chinese Affairs* XXXVII no.2 (2008): 6-37.

Debord, Guy. *The Society of the Spectacle*. Translated by Donald Nicholson-Smith. Brooklyn: Zone Books, 1995 [1968].

Dong, Liming. 'Beijing: The Development of a Socialist Capital.' In *Chinese Cities: The Growth of the Metropolis since 1949*, edited by Victor. F. S. Sit, 67-93. Oxford: Oxford University Press, 1985.

Essex, Stephen and Brian, Chalkley. 'Olympic Games: Catalyst of Urban Change.' *Leisure Studies* 17, no. 3 (1998): 187-206.

Fang Ke and Zhang Yan. 'Plan and Market Mismatch: Urban Redevelopment in Beijing During a Period of Transition.' *Asia Pacific Viewpoint* 44, no. 2 (2003): 149-162.

Foucault, Michel. *The History of Sexuality, Vol. I: An Introduction*. Wiley Online Library, 1978.

—. *Society Must Be Defended: Lectures at the College de France, 1975-1976*. New York: Picador, 2003.

Fung, Anthony. 'What Makes the Local? A Brief Consideration of the Rejuvenation of Hong Kong Identity.' *Cultural Studies* 15, no. 3-4 (2001): 591-601.

Gold, John Robert and Stephen Victor Ward. *Place Promotion: The Use of Publicity and Marketing to Sell Towns and Regions*. Chichester: John Wiley & Sons Ltd, 1994.

Gruffudd, Pyrs. 'Remaking Wales: Nation-Building and the Geographical Imagination, 1925-1950.' *Political Geography* 14, no. 3 (1995): 219-39.

Hall, Coli Michael. 'The Effects of Hallmark Events on Cities.' *Journal of Travel Research* 26, no. 2 (1987): 44-45.

Hewison, Robert. *The Heritage Industry: Britain in a Climate of Decline*. London: Methuen, 1987.

Hung, Wu. 'Tiananmen Square: A Political History of Monuments.' *Representations*, no. 35 (1991): 84-117.

—. 'Zhang Dali's Dialogue: Conversation with a City.' *Public Culture* 12, no. 3 (2000): 749-68.

Huyssen, Andreas. 'Present Pasts: Media, Politics, Amnesia.' *Public Culture* 12, no.1 (2000): 21-38.

King, Anthony D. and Abidin Kusno. 'On Be(ij)ing in the World: Globalisation, Postmodernism and the Making of Transnational Space in China.' In *Postmodernism and China*, edited by Dirlik A and Zhang X, 41-67. Durham: Duke University Press, 2000.

Kong, Lily. 'The Invention of Heritage: Popular Music in Singapore.' *Asian Studies Review* 23, no. 1 (1999): 1-25.

Lai, Gina and Rance Pui Leung Lee. 'Market Reforms and Psychological Distress in Urban Beijing.' *International Sociology* 21, no. 4 (2006): 551-79.

Marvin, Carolyn. 'All Under Heaven – Megaspace in Beijing.' In *Owning the Olympics: Narratives of the New China*, edited by Monroe Edwin Price and

Daniel Dayan, 229-59. Ann Arbor: University of Michigan Press, 2008.

Massey, Doreen. 'Imagining the World.' *Geographical Worlds, The Open University, Milton Keynes* (1995): 3-51.

Nora, Pierre. 'Between Memory and History: Les Lieux De Mémoire.' *Representations*, no. 26 (1989): 7-24.

Olds, Kris. 'Globalizing Shanghai: The "Global Intelligence Corps" and the Building of Pudong.' *Cities* 14, no. 2 (1997): 109-23.

Ong, Ryan. 'New Beijing, Great Olympics: Beijing and Its Unfolding Olympic Legacy.' *Stanford Journal of East Asian Affairs* 4, no. 2 (2004): 35-49.

Peleggi, Maurizio. 'Consuming Colonial Nostalgia: The Monumentalisation of Historic Hotels in Urban South-East Asia.' *Asia Pacific Viewpoint* 46, no. 3 (2005): 255-65.

Ren, Xuefei. 'Architecture and Nation Building in the Age of Globalization: Construction of the National Stadium of Beijing for the 2008 Olympics.' *Journal of Urban Affairs* 30, no. 2 (2008): 175-90.

Roche, Maurice. 'Mega-Events and Urban Policy.' *Annals of Tourism Research* 21, no. 1 (1994): 1-19.

Shue, Vivienne. 'Legitimacy Crisis in China?' In *State and Society in 21-st Century China: Crisis, Contention, and Legitimation*, edited by Peter Hays Gries and Stanley Rosen, 24-49. New York: Routedge, 2004.

Visser, Robin. 'Spaces of Disappearance: Aesthetic Responses to Contemporary Beijing City Planning.' *Journal of Contemporary China* 13, no. 39 (2004): 277-310.

Wu Hung, 'Zhang Dali's Dialogue: Conversation with a City.' *Public Culture* 12, no. 3 (2000): 749-68.

Xu, Guoqu. *Olympic Dreams: China and Sports, 1895-2008*. Cambridge: Harvard University Press, 2008.

Zhang, Zhen. 'Mediating Time: The "Rice Bowl of Youth" in Fin De Siècle Urban China.' *Public Culture* 12, no. 1 (2000): 93-113.

Zukin, Sharon. *The Cultures of Cities*. Cambridge, MA: Blackwell, 1995.

9. Shanghai in Film and Literature: The Danger of Nostalgia

Gregory Bracken

Nostalgia is dangerous. While it may be important to know what has happened in the past, too fond a reading of it may well blind the viewer to possibilities for the future. Shanghai's history is justifiably famous, some would even say infamous; the city is very well-known, yet many people only experience it vicariously, either through watching a film or reading a book. How the city is portrayed tells us a lot about how people perceive it, whether it is the inaccurately slapdash imagery of *Mission: Impossible III* (J.J. Abrams) or the lavishly recreated street scenes of *Lust, Caution* (Ang Lee). Books too play a role in selling Shanghai; novels such as *When We Were Orphans* (Kazuo Ishiguro) and *The Song of Everlasting Sorrow* (Wang Anyi) are permeated with nostalgia for a vanished way of life – the upper-class glamour of the former contrasting with the down-to-earth everyday life of the alleyway house in the latter.[1] This emergence of nostalgia is something that some other commentators have also picked up on, notably Lena Scheen in her essay on Shanghai's *longtang* houses, 'Sensual, but No Clue of Politics' (Bracken 2012), and is something that I will be warning about in this essay.

There is something spectacular about a city like Shanghai. And, like its regional neighbours, Hong Kong and Tokyo, the city is seen a backdrop for international forces, where marquee architecture sets the scene for its global ambitions. In a rapidly globalising China, where there has been a wholehearted embrace of capitalism with Chinese characteristics, the city has become the site for another kind of spectacle: that of conspicuous consumption. Yet in order to make way for the new urban forms that facilitate this global growth, a long-established way of life is being swept aside.

Asia's explosive urbanisation has forced all eyes on the subject of the city. The city has, accordingly, become a recurrent theme in popular culture and art, which is part of the rising tide of consumerist culture submerging the reality of ordinary daily life. What are the aesthetic responses to this process of overall disruption in both individual and collective experience? As an urbanist who originally trained and practiced as an architect, my chapter will focus more on the built environment of Shanghai than on the cinematic or literary portrayals of it. I intend to show how nostalgia for a vanishing way of life can actually destroy the very thing it seeks to retain.

The renovated district Xintiandi, which I will come to at the end of the chapter, is a good example of this. Here we will see how an effort to retain something of the past can, thanks to too rose-tinted a view of it, actually destroy it all the more effectively. And what does this say about a city like Shanghai? Where efforts to retain two blocks of *shikumen*-style alleyway houses (in Xintiandi)[2] have actually left us with nothing more than shells.

Urban Disconnect

Seeing Shanghai included as one of the glamorous destinations in an action film like *Mission: Impossible III* places it alongside Berlin and Rome as the scene for fast-paced adventure, but the city is in fact nothing more than a backdrop to the film; we catch the occasional glimpse of the skyscrapers of Pudong, and we are shown a map of the Suzhou River in a sequence where Tom Cruise, as Ethan Hawke, is running to intercept a villain. The map may show the Suzhou River, but Cruise's character is actually seen running through Zhou Zuang, a city two-hours' drive from Shanghai. While this may seem a trifling point, and people who go to see something called *Mission: Impossible* do not necessarily expect a high degree of verisimilitude, including the skyscrapers of Shanghai in a film such as this means they can now be seen as having made it to the big time. Shanghai, as a global city, is now worthy of inclusion in an international blockbuster. However, it is enough merely to be included; juxtaposing it with images of Zhou Zhuang, a city with an entirely different character, undermines any attempt at a realistic portrayal of the city, something that would not be accepted if it were New York or London. Zhou Zhuang is, in fact, a city completely unlike Shanghai. It quite openly trades on its 'water village' credentials to attract tourists, with its ramshackle two-storey buildings linked by traditional 'moon' bridges that span pretty waterways. Shanghai's glittering skyscrapers eschew any such prettiness as they thrust their way into the future. To juxtapose these symbols of a city's globalising credentials with the low-rise, low-key city that clearly relishes its past shows a complete contempt for, or at least indifference to, what Shanghai is trying to achieve on the part of the filmmakers; or, worse, it shows a blissful ignorance.[3] Mario Gandalsonas, in his book *Shanghai Reflections*, has pointed out the futility of the attempts of China's Cultural Revolution to erase the country's past; he sees this as underpinning the relationship between preservation and development in a city like Shanghai, especially as it modernises. Gandalsonas sees Ackbar Abbas' questioning of 'where do we invest?' or 'how do we rule?' as masking the even deeper question of 'what will we remember?' (2002: 32). He also points out that memories are selective in Shanghai, but this is hardly unique to Shanghai: memories are selective everywhere. However, it is what Gandalsonas calls Shanghai's 'multifarious past and complex colonial history' that is presenting a unique set of problems today, especially with regard to the question of urban preservation. The preservation of the past in Shanghai, as a sort of symbolic capital, has, according to Gandalsonas, allowed the establishment of cultural differences that were previously blurred by colonisation. As a result, the question of nostalgia has become one of the forms through which this relationship between the past and the present is acquiring a presence within the physical and cultural context of the city today.

Ackbar Abbas sees preservation in Shanghai as being motivated by something quite different from cultural heritage, which, given the city's quasi-colonial past, has always been somewhat ambiguous. Abbas sees it as being motivated by anticipation of the role the new Shanghai will play in the world, and, as such, he sees it as rivalling its old self rather than harbouring any tender feelings for it (2002: 38). Preservation has a place alongside development, what Abbas likens to the city as a 'remake, a shot-by-shot reworking of a classic, with a different cast, addressed to a different audience. Not "Back to the Future", but "Forward to the Past"' (2002: 38). Abbas is right to dismiss the preservationists who take the moral high ground because they 'often do so by eliding the ambiguities of history' (2002: 41). Abbas also calls the glamorous architecture of the 1920s and 1930s 'a shallow kind of cosmopolitanism', 'a question of style imported from elsewhere' (2002: 42). As he says, 'The more complex the history, the more intricate the issue of urban preservation becomes, and few modern cities have had a more complex history than Shanghai' (2002: 41). This makes the film analogy, the notion of the city's heritage as a classic being remade shot-by-shot, even more appropriate. As the city was an artificial construct in the first place, something with no real grounding, then it is so much easier to maintain and reanimate it by cultural trickery, much like a cinematic special effect.

Representations Old and New

Ang Lee's film version of the Eileen Chang (also known as Zhang Ailing) novella *Lust, Caution*, shows Shanghai and Hong Kong in the 1940s, when both cities were under Japanese occupation. Full of period detail, like the Chinese having to salute the Japanese guards and Westerners having to wear armbands indicating their nationality, the film also contains some anachronisms, like the continued use of the rickshaw, which was banned by the Japanese on the grounds they were demeaning (which was, of course, ironic, as they had been invented in Japan).

Ang Lee's portrayal of the film's sex scenes, which at first glance may seem gratuitous, is in fact brilliantly daring, as it not only underscores the lustful nature of the relationship between Wang Chia-chih and Mr Yee, the man she seeks to entrap (and kill), but also shows the development of a power relationship so complex, so profound, and, ultimately, so beautiful, that she ends up sacrificing everything to save him. The fact that Mr Yee is, as the cliché goes, old enough to be her father, is also explained obliquely by the subtle references earlier in the film to Chia-chih's thwarted relationship with her own father, a man we see only in photographs. The most poignant moment in the film comes when, surrounded by Japanese soldiers and their geisha in a Japanese-style inn, Chia-chih sings 'The Wandering Songstress' to her lover; a classic Chinese love song, the pathos and poignancy of which is further enhanced by the evidence of the surrounding Japanese occupation. Interestingly, this is also the song that Bijou sings in *Shanghai Triad* (Zhang Yimou) to communicate to her lover, Song. The mistress of the Tang triad boss, Bijou uses this song as a secret signal to her lover, one of the boss' paeans. The characters in *Shanghai Triad* tend to refer to the song by its nickname *Moonlight*, which of course has other resonances in Chinese culture, but the song itself remains simply a more lushly orchestrated version of this popular classic.

These films make use of the real Shanghai as a location to conjure up a world that no longer exists; yet is this geographical verisimilitude any more real than the films that were actually made in the era? Take *Thank You, Mr Moto* (Norman Foster), a film that has all the usual ingredients: the seedy nightclub (including the figure who was to become *de rigueur* in subsequent portrayals of this era: the nightclub singer), illegal gambling dens, smuggling (albeit of jewels not drugs), Russian doormen, guns and gangsters. Yet apart from some stock footage of the Bund, this film consists entirely of scenes filmed in the Hollywood studios of 20th Century Fox. Yet in temporal terms it achieves a degree of verisimilitude that can never be matched by any current film. So which of them is more real? Are any of them real? Or are they all merely a sort of shadow play? What is interesting is that even as long ago as the 1930s, the same old tropes had begun to crop up, that and the fact that it was the skyline of the Bund that enabled a director to immediately situate their story. As a set piece, Shanghai needed no other introduction, in much the same way that Pudong is now used in portrayals of twenty-first-century Shanghai.

The Bund is also shown in the opening scene of *Shanghai Triad*, after the boy Shuisheng has arrived by boat to be met by his gangster uncle. M. Christine Boyer points out that as the boy's head moves from right to left, his eyes sweep the port, but he does this from a stationary point of view; we, as an audience, are denied the more usual panoramic or aerial shot of the cityscape that usually sets the scene. What we get instead is a backdrop seen across a river (2002: 69). When his uncle arrives to collect him, Shuisheng then spends the next few minutes gazing out from under the tarpaulin in the back of his uncle's lorry as it moves through the city. Again, we see only the boy's eyes as he stares at the off-screen city, his face coloured by its lights. Boyer sees these opening scenes as signalling to the viewer the fact that this film is going to be about the reflected image. Her highly detailed analysis of the film's scenes highlights the dexterity with which the device of reflection is used; and not just reflection: even in a scene ablaze with light (as in the exterior of the triad boss' house, or in the house's corridors, which are swathed in golden tones), the light emanates from interiors and not from the city itself.

As Boyer accurately points out, direct views of the city are blocked out. This she sees as a signal to the film's viewer that '[...] something has to be renegotiated: whether it is the relationship of the present to the past, or of the East and the West' (2002: 69). Boyer states that 'Whatever it is about the past that fascinates the gaze, it cannot be approached directly' (2002: 69). According to Boyer, Zhang Yimou has taken the glamorous nightlife of 1930s Shanghai and flattened it. Far from being a seductive, dazzling swirl of fascinating and ever-changing images, the scenes are mere tableaux. No shot of Shanghai is intended to directly lure or entrap the gaze; the nostalgic longing for modern Shanghai is retrospective. By presenting modern Shanghai as an image or object to be looked at, Boyer sees the spectator caught in a trap, and it is Zhang Yimou's efforts to deflect this trap that make him invert this gaze (2002: 69). This could lead one to believe that Yimou was clearly aware of the uses, as well as the dangers, of employing such a nostalgic *mise-en-scene* in his film.

The Alleyway House in Literature: *When We Were Orphans*

Kazuo Ishiguro's *When We Were Orphans* is set largely in Shanghai in the 1930s. This evocative and haunting novel explores themes of loss and longing. Kazuo Ishiguro's Shanghai is geographically accurate, which is more than can be said for a number of recent novels that have been set there (for example, *The Painter of Shanghai*). The only time there seems to be some confusion is when Ishiguro leads his detective into the Warren towards the end of the book – and this is clearly deliberate.

Christopher Banks' parents went missing when he was a child, so he returns to Shanghai as an adult to try and find them – which he does, but not in a way he might have liked. What Banks, his female friend Sarah Hemmings, and his ward Jennifer all have in common is they are the orphans of the book's title. Banks' attempts to reconstruct his childhood become increasingly unreliable; his detecting skills, normally so sharp and successful are rendered ineffectual when it comes to investigating his own past. He begins to realise that he may have remembered some things incorrectly; not only details of past conversations, but the context in which these took place. The clearest details of his childhood are the pranks perpetrated by his Japanese neighbour, Akira. The fear that these two small boys felt as they fretted over what would happen if they were caught seems to have seared these events most reliably into Banks' memory.

The trade in opium, a legal one in Shanghai at the time of the book's opening, is also one of the leitmotifs of the story, but Ishiguro's mentioning of 'the great trading company of Butterfield and Swire' (Ishiguro 2000: 24) seems to have angered this great *hong*, who subsequently sued the author for libel. In fact, both of Banks' parents' disappearances seem to have opium at the back of them, but this turns out to be, in the great detective tradition, a red herring.

The choice of Shanghai as a backdrop is interesting. The city at this time was teetering on the brink of ruin, a place whose days were numbered, because between 1937, when the Japanese took over Chinese-administered Shanghai, leaving the foreign concession as 'the lonely island', and 1941, when they took over the rest of the city, it gives a certain urgency to the narrative, an urgency which only highlights the contrasting fecklessness of the colonial inhabitants who fritter away their time in nightclubs and gambling dens. This tone becomes increasingly breathless and confused when Banks is wandering through the labyrinth of the Warren – the alleyway houses of Chapei (now Zhabei) – which was being reduced to an empty shell, thanks to Japanese bombardment. Banks ends up in this part of the city unwittingly; he does not even realise that he has passed beyond the safety of the foreign concessions and into the war zone until it is too late. Pursuing the chimera of his parents' hiding place he pushes ever deeper into the Warren, and danger.

Here the author's meticulously observed geography becomes nebulous, but it gives Banks, and the reader, a chance to take stock of the Warren, a place where foreigners rarely come, unless they are missionaries or communists. Banks finds it hard to believe that human beings can live like this; it looks to him like an ants' nest. The houses, intended for the poorest inhabitants of the city, have tiny rooms, and sit back-to-back, row after row. Looking carefully from his vantage point on top of an abandoned police station, Banks is able to make out the many alleyways, the 'Little alleys just wide enough to allow the people to get into their homes. At the back, the houses have no windows at all. The rear rooms are black holes, backing on to the houses behind' (Ishiguro 2000: 235). This is a sign of the alleyway houses' throwback to the traditional Chinese courtyard house (四合院), which had blank north-facing walls. (In fact, the fronts of Shanghai alleyway houses always face south if possible – in keeping with the precepts of *feng shui*.)

After being rescued from the nightmare of the Warren, Banks finds himself once again in 'civilised' Shanghai. The business of his parents' disappearance is explained in a suitably detective-like denouement by his 'Uncle' Philip. As incidents, these two events were unrelated, and both had more to do with sex than drugs. Banks' father had run away with his mistress, while his mother was kidnapped into the harem of a Chinese warlord. The notion of a spirited upper-class Englishwomen being forced into this sort of bondage strikes an almost comically lurid note at the end of the book (at least it would if it were not so sad). Added to this is the shocking revelation that gentle 'Uncle' Philip was the one who had orchestrated this shameful state of affairs (out of his thwarted desire for her). The irony of all of this is that the money that has enabled Banks to live the life of a gentleman has been provided by this Chinese warlord; yet another unsettling discovery that turns the hero's world upside down.

The Shanghai of *When We Were Orphans* is portrayed in an overwhelmingly negative light. This is probably because Ishiguro knew that he was portraying a society experiencing its death throes; a way of life was ending, one whose decadence had led it to this sorry pass. Christopher Banks, the celebrated detective, did find what he was looking for, but like so many who do, he must have wondered whether it might not have been better not to have done so. One of the most important lessons we can learn from a novel like *When We Were Orphans* is the danger of nostalgia. The past is the past, it forms us into the people we are today, but it does not necessarily benefit us to go back and rake it over; indeed, it may well be damaging.

The Alleyway House in Literature: *The Song of Everlasting Sorrow*

Kazuo Ishiguro's novel gives us a glimpse of the alleyway house as it is being destroyed by the Japanese. Wang Anyi's *The Song of Everlasting Sorrow* does something similar, in that it acts as an encomium for the vanishing way of life that was lived in these houses, which are now under an even more serious threat – that of economic redevelopment in reform-era Shanghai.[4] The novel's heroine, Wang Qiyao, is a fascinating character. An innocent in a city of sin, she would have led a much more traditional way of life had she been brought up in another part of the country. Shanghai, and the way of life that was lived there, seems to have corrupted her. A beauty, though not quite in the first rank (as is shown by her coming third in the pageant that takes place early in the story), Wang Qiyao was still attractive enough to represent the perfect embodiment of a Shanghai kind of beauty, one that was wholesome and connected to everyday life, one that reminded people of 'concepts like marriage, life, and family' (Wang 2008: 77).

Where Wang Anyi's writing really shines is in her rendering of the Shanghai alleyway house. This was something she was very much aware of, because when her American publisher wanted to delete the opening sequence, which describes the houses in lavish detail, Wang rightly insisted they be retained. The alleyway house features almost as a character in its own right; to have deleted these beautifully evocative descriptions would have been greatly to the book's detriment. These descriptions, coupled with such a remarkable heroine, as well as the historic sweep of the novel, make it one of the better books set in Shanghai; certainly it is far superior to most of the ones that see the city as a conveniently exotic backdrop for an otherwise generic plot.

Wang Anyi writes that 'This city has more energy than it knows what to do with' (2008: 73). She does more than just refer to the energy of the city; she describes it in loving detail by describing the people and the spaces of the alleyway houses. She calls them 'the backdrop of the city' (2008: 3). Always using the Shanghainese term *longtang*, she opens her novel with the lines: 'Looked down upon from the highest point in the city, Shanghai's *longtang* – her vast neighbourhoods inside enclosed alleys – are a magnificent sight' (2008: 3). From this point on she treats us to a step-by-step architectural description beginning with the *tingzijian*, the dormer window that protrudes from the alleyway house rooftop. These are described as 'showing themselves off with a certain self-conscious delicacy; the wooden shutters are carefully delineated, the handmade rooftop tiles are arranged with precision, even the potted roses on the windowsills have been cared for painstakingly' (2008: 3-4). Then, 'Next to emerge are the balconies; here articles of clothing hung out to dry the night before cling motionless like a scene out of a painting' (2008: 4), and 'After that come the cracked gable walls, lined with traces of green moss that look cold and clammy to the touch' (2008: 4). And finally 'The grease-stained rear kitchen window is where the *amah* gossips. Beside the window is the back door; from this the eldest daughter goes out to school and holds her secret rendezvous with her boyfriend' (2008: 4).

Eileen Chang made reference to the cramped spaces of the alleyway houses in *The Golden Cangue*, where she writes 'Lan-hsien said, smiling, "Second Sister-in-law is used to the houses in Peking, no wonder she finds it too cramped here"' (2007: 178). Wang Anyi goes even further, paying particular attention to the materials that go into the alleyway houses. She describes "Some of the gullylike alleys are lined with cement, others with cobblestone' (2008: 6), and notes the difference to the experience of an urban environment that materials can make: 'The cement alleys make you feel cut off, while the cobblestone alleys give the sensation of a fleshy hand. Footsteps sound different in these two types of alleyway. In the former the sound is crisp and bright, whereas in the latter it is something that you absorb and keep inside' (2008: 6). Nothing escapes her writerly gaze, from 'The cement on the balustrade peels away to reveal the rusty red bricks beneath' (2008: 4), to 'the iron-railed balconies of the newer *longtang* apartments where the sunlight is already striking the glass panes of the French doors, which refract the light' (2008: 4).

Wang Anyi also points to the subtle differences that obtain between different types of alleyway house: 'The trendy *longtang* neighbourhoods in the eastern district of Shanghai have done away with such haughty airs. They greet you with low wrought-iron gates of floral design. For them a small window overlooking a side street is not enough; they all have to have walk-out balconies, the better to enjoy the street scenery' (2008: 4-5). Whereas:

> On the western side of the city, the apartment-style *longtang* take an even stricter approach to security. These structures are built in clusters, with doors that look as if not even an army of ten thousand could force their way inside. The walls are soundproof so that people living even in close quarters cannot hear one another, and the buildings are widely spaced so that neighbours can avoid one another.

This she describes as being the 'security of a democratic sort – trans-Atlantic style – to ensure and protect individual freedom. Here people can do whatever their hearts desire, and there is no one to stop them' (2008: 5); which is, of course, the very antithesis of traditional Shanghai street life.

Then there are the slums, which Wang Anyi describes as being open-air and where 'The makeshift roofs leak in the rain, the thin plywood walls fail to keep out the wind, and the doors and windows never seem to close properly. Apartment structures are built virtually on top of one another, cheek by jowl, breathing down upon each other's necks' (2008: 5). This would, of course, be in the poorer parts of the city, rundown areas such as Chapei, which we have already seen in Kazuo Ishiguro's Warren.

Wang Anyi describes the people of Shanghai as being 'like water that finds its way into every open crevice' (2008: 286). But this water is drying up; the people of Shanghai are leaving the alleyway houses. What their fate will be remains to be seen. As Wang Anyi notes, 'Shanghai's *longtang* come in many different forms, each with colours and sounds of its own. Unable to decide on any one appearance, they remain fickle, sometimes looking like this, sometimes looking like that […] Actually, despite their constant fluctuations, they always remain the same – the shape may shift but the spirit is unchanged' (2008: 4).

Their spirit is changing now; it has been forced to change by economic circumstances. A robust and popular housing typology born out of economic necessity, yet managing to produce an effect of beauty, much like the streets and squares of the British Isles' Georgian era, where practical considerations for a purely speculative development resulted in an urban environment of elegant practicality. So, too, did the alleyway house manage to produce an urban environment that was rich and diverse, as well as having considerable architectural merit. It survived and thrived despite floods of refugees, the Japanese occupation,

World War II, and the horrors of campaigns such as the Hundred Flowers, the Great Leap Forward and the Cultural Revolution, only to find that it is with the influx of money that has occurred since the reform era that has seen the typology really begin to suffer. Rapid economic growth can be more damaging to an urban environment than mere disasters; this is certainly proving to be the case for the Shanghai alleyway house.

The Future of the Alleyway House?

If we now move from these different representations of the city to its actual materiality, we could do worse than look at an interesting example of Shanghai's rapidly changing urban environment in the Xintiandi complex, a two-block redevelopment of *shikumen*-style alleyway houses in the former French Concession between Taicang, Zizhong, Madang and Huangpi South Roads. Architects Wood and Zapata's development forms part of a larger redevelopment of the surrounding Taipingqiao area, which includes luxury hotels, office towers and extensive residential facilities. Since it opened in 2001, Xintiandi has become one of the city's most popular shopping and entertainment hubs. The architects managed to recreate an ambience somewhat reminiscent of Shanghai's Golden Age of the 1920s and 1930s through their extensive reuse of traditional building materials and by cleverly designing the pedestrian areas. The bars and restaurants, many of which are Western in theme, fit perfectly into the cosmopolitan image that signified Shanghai in the colonial era.

The reason Xintiandi is proving so popular is that the two different groups of people who use it see it in a very different light: foreigners think they are seeing the real China, while the Chinese see it as exotically foreign; a double misperception that works in the area's favour. As an image of Old Shanghai, it is undeniably successful, but it is what Peter G. Rowe would call 'allegedly local' (2005: 188). Its glamour is both seductive and illusory in that it is based on an overtly nostalgic reading of Shanghai's past. It is what Michelle Tsung-yi Huang calls 'a phantasmagoric Old Shanghai, in the manner of a Hollywood diva like Greta Garbo, which re-enchants the foreign investors and the local residents with a cosmopolitan past as not only a cultural heritage but also the foundation for the global city' (2004: 120). According to Robert Hewison, 'The impulse to preserve the past is part of the impulse to preserve the self. Without knowing where we have been, it is difficult to know where we are going' (quoted in Harvey 1989: 86), but it is invariably our own reinterpretations of the past that appeal to us; brand-new constructions, like the rebuilt *shikumen* houses of Xintiandi, are basically a fake.

Xintiandi has become something of a showcase for the much-vaunted capitalism with Chinese characteristics; a glamorously dressed-up version of the relatively humble housing typology, where one can find the world's luxury brands for sale. All the modern conveniences have been elegantly packaged with Shanghai's signature sophistication. The nostalgia we see here is nothing less than a purging of the past, a cleansing of any hint of dirt or grime or misery so that the newly scrubbed and polished version of the city's history can be repackaged for the global elite, so they sit and sip coffee in peaceful contemplation of just how pretty a place Shanghai can be.

One alarming aspect of this cultural cleansing is the rumour that security guards exclude shabbily dressed locals from entering the Xintiandi complex. This redevelopment may be seen as public space, but you are only allowed into it if you happen to be a member of the public it prefers. This is one very clear instance of how spaces of global capitalist accumulation are impinging on the everyday lives of those who call the city home. Michelle Tsung-yi Huang sees this as 'one of the effects of the capitalist space of globalisation which is to make everyone believe that this space is his or her own, regardless of the fact that the city was restructured based on the assumed needs of a small group of multinational service class people, the human agents of global capital' (2004: 110). In fact this has become something of a moot point; the exclusionary practices of security guards are no longer needed for the simple reason that people in the area do not even try to go to Xintiandi as they simply cannot afford to (they have perfectly pleasant – and cheaper – teahouses nearby). Of course this price barrier is still a form of exclusion; nothing so crude as a security guard barring the way, but just as effective.

Gentrification may well preserve some of an area's traditional houses, or at least facsimiles of them, but ironically it is the success of the Xintiandi redevelopment that has meant that neighbouring communities have been forced out of their homes due to an attendant rise in the value of the land these homes were built on. Arie Graafland has described gentrification as the process whereby 'the uneducated make way for more qualified residents in certain neighborhoods of the city' (Graafland 2000: 212), and this is what is happening here. Ironically, once these surrounding areas have been freed for development, many of the houses are then demolished so that other alleyway houses can be 'restored' using their bricks. This is a singularly appropriate example of Sharon Zukin's plain 'vernacular' being appropriated by capital and transformed into a desirable 'landscape' (cited in Abbas 1997: 88).

Ackbar Abbas makes the point that preservation is not memory; he states that 'Preservation is selective and tends to exclude the dirt and pain' (1997: 66). He mentions this while lamenting how so much of what passes for postcoloniality in Hong Kong actually only amounts to a form of kitsch. Xintiandi, too, is a form of kitsch, a kitsch that may well be enjoyable to visit once in a while, even wallow in occasionally, but we must always beware of the dangers of nostalgia. For the moment it is enough to be aware that we should not allow ourselves to be blinkered by the pretty kitschiness of places like Xintiandi, because such selectiveness of vision can blind us to the very real fact of some of the side-effects that result from bringing these places into being. According to Abbas, it is this same sort of denial that has made Hong Kong's (Kowloon) Walled City, 'with its traffic in drugs, prostitution, and human misery, look so glamorous' (1997: 66). This infamous (and now demolished) Walled City, like the Shanghai alleyway house, was really only glamorous 'after the fact' (1997: 66).

Michelle Tsung-yi Huang points out that when the former residents of an area are forced to make way for gentrification it is not a simple matter of 'renting a moving truck and getting on the road'. She is worried that 'being uprooted from the community one has been familiar with cannot be easily compensated for: what jackhammers and bulldozers demolish within minutes often takes generations to build' (2004: 114); or as Marshall Berman more colourfully puts it: 'buried under debris where their lives used to be' (Berman 1988: 79). This is what the alleyway houses are all about: the people who called them home. Cities are not buildings and streets; cities are people, and their networks of interaction: social, family, and commercial. The buildings of a city form a symbiotic relationship that is built up between a people and their environment, and it is one that undergoes an evolution from generation to generation. The changes we are seeing to the way of life in Shanghai's alleyway houses are less about changes in buildings' uses due to the forces of global capitalism, and more about the changes being wrought in Chinese society by, among other things, the One Child Policy. It is not the buildings, no matter how superficially pretty they are, that are interesting; it is the way of life they engendered, and that, in turn, they were engendered thanks to the symbiotic relationship humans have developed with their environment.

Yet, in Shanghai today, without the extended family and the tradition of social and community life it entailed, what future can there really be for the alleyway house? Not that the traditional Chinese family life was necessarily always perfect, or even good, or comfortable (or even desirable), but the relationship that it enjoyed with the alleyway house that sheltered it does seem to have been a surprisingly successfully symbiotic one, and one that is sadly lacking in Shanghai, where the alleyway house has become nothing more than a decorative shell for commercial developments (if it is lucky; otherwise it becomes the fodder for wrecking balls). I have no wish to over-idealise the life that was led in the alleyway house – it must have been pretty grim for the most part – but I do feel it is important to point out that a once-vibrant way of life (as well as the spaces that enabled it to exist) is being swept away by city authorities who are intent on massing the hardware of the global city without taking into account some of its potential casualties. Indeed, there hardly seems much point in retaining the alleyway house just so that international coffee chains can have interesting-looking outlets. Xintiandi, while a charming piece of urban regeneration, and a successful one, is preserving nothing more than a shell – an interesting and attractive one, but a shell nonetheless. The life that once made these places really interesting is gone, perhaps forever, and too nostalgic a reading of these spaces can ultimately do more harm than good.

Shanghai's Urban Environment: the Bund

Before ending, I would like to give one example of an unwittingly successful example of urban regeneration: the Bund. Here there was no effort at a nostalgic recreation of the past; the waterfront's spectacular buildings were in fact reused by people who felt a great deal of antipathy towards them. China's newly victorious Communist authorities were appalled at the monumental and bombastic architecture of the Bund when they came to power in 1949. They saw it as nothing less than the concrete signature of Western imperial power scrawled across their city. But they did not destroy it for the simple reason that they could not afford to. To indulge in such postcolonial vandalism would have drained valuable resources; they preferred to reuse the buildings, rather than raze them. Which means that the Bund we see today looks almost exactly the same as the one we glimpse in *Thank You, Mr Moto*.

The former Hongkong and Shanghai Banking Corporation is a particularly appropriate example. The headquarters of this pre-eminent British *hong* in the colonial era, it became the seat of Shanghai's city government during the Maoist era and is now home to the Pudong Development Bank. This fine neoclassical edifice has been the perfect representation of the driving force between Shanghai's different and very contrasting phases of development for the 90 or so years since it was built. The practical reuse of the Hongkong and Shanghai Banking Corporation headquarters had nothing decorative about it. The building was kept because it could effectively be used for new functions. Now it is home to another bank, one that is underwriting the development of the Pudong area, which faces it across the Huangpu. In this it is making no concession to history; each phase of the building's life has been primarily concerned with its current function, not with some decorative past. The irony is that this approach has saved the building for us today, and in a way that is far more effective and realistic than any mere museumification or pandering to tastes that run to a liking for colonial-era nostalgia.

Of course, the fact that these imposing edifices were constructed by the colonial-era power elite to signal to the city, and the rest of the world, that they were in charge has meant that they never had anything like the cosy, intimate everyday-type space of the Shanghai alleyway house. But that doesn't matter. What has happened to the magnificent buildings of the Bund since 1949 has not been the result of a nostalgia-driven agenda for their preservation – quite the opposite in fact – yet here they are, in all their muscular glory. What is more, they are still being used as banks, offices and luxury hotels, just as they were originally intended to be.

In its sheer practicality, the Communist government managed to preserve and protect something that can still be enjoyed today. Something that, for all the imagination the redevelopers of Shanghai's alleyway houses have been lavishing on recreations of housing enclaves like Xintiandi, are somehow missing. This focusing on the building as artefact, rather than as a means for the expression of a healthy social and cultural life, has stymied many an effort at the imaginative redevelopment of a housing typology that may well have outlived its usefulness. The Communist re-users of the Hongkong and Shanghai Banking Corporation building were practical, not nostalgic, yet they have managed to preserve the building almost perfectly. The redevelopers of alleyway houses are trying to imaginatively recreate a vanishing way of life, and in so doing are wiping it out all the more effectively. This is one of the worst dangers of nostalgia, because too nostalgic a reading of a city's spaces will concentrate the eye and the mind on the buildings and not the people, thereby missing the whole point of the buildings in the first place. It would be better if more developers and their architects were to beware of nostalgia.

Notes

1. Note, there are many different terms for what I refer to as the 'Shanghai alleyway house': *lilong* (the most commonly used Chinese term); *longtang* (the term invariably used in Shanghai); and *shikumen* (a specific type of house which takes its name from the stone-arched gate or door that forms its main entrance). There are at least four other terms, but it is the *shikumen* that is probably the best known. Actually, *shikumen* is rather a misleading example of the alleyway house, because it can be a stand-alone dwelling, whereas the typology is most famous for the intricate structure of the alleyways connecting the houses into clusters. I am hoping that a forthcoming monograph called 'The Shanghai Alleyway House' (which is scheduled for publication with Routledge in 2013) may bring some much-needed clarity to this issue.
2. The Xintiandi area happened to be mainly home to the *shikumen*-type of alleyway house and may indeed have done much to imprint it on the public's imagination as the best-known example of what is in fact quite a diverse typology.
3. Interestingly, this is something that also happened to Kuala Lumpur in 1999, when the May-December romance *Entrapment*, starring Sean Connery and Catherine Zeta-Jones, showed images of decrepit wooden buildings, again on a pretty waterway, artfully arranged (thanks to trick photography) at the foot of the Petronas Towers. Just as in *Mission: Impossible III* there is a total disconnect between these two groups of buildings, as these houses are in Malacca. The Malaysian government, after having provided evey assistance to the film-makers, were reported to be furious to see their glorious towers, the new symbol of their country's global ambitions, mired in this way.
4. This is also cogently analysed in Lena Scheen's 'Sensual, But No Clue of Politics: Shanghai's *longtang* houses' where she also highlights the pervasiveness of nostalgia for the vanishing alleyway house way of life as described in this remarkable novel. See Scheen (2012: 117-135).

References

Abbas, Ackbar. *Hong Kong: Culture and the Politics of Disappearance*. Minneapolis: University of Minnesota Press, 1997.

—. 'Play It Again Shanghai: Urban Preservation in the Global Era.' In *Shanghai Reflections*, edited by Mario Gandalsonas, 36-55. Princeton: Princeton Architectural Press, 2002.

Bracken, Gregory, ed., *Aspects of Urbanization in Asia: Shanghai, Hong Kong, Guangzhou*. Amsterdam: Amsterdam University Press, 2012.

Berman, Marshall. *All That Is Solid Melts into Air: The Experience of Modernity*. New York: Penguin Books, 1988.

Boyer, M. Christine. 'Approaching the Memory of Shanghai: The Case of Zhang Yimou and "Shanghai Triad" (1995).' In *Shanghai Reflections*, edited by Mario Gandalsonas, 56-87. Princeton Architectural Press, 2002.

Chang, Eileen. *Love in a Fallen City*. New York: New York Review Books, 2007.

Gandalsonas, Mario, M. Ackbar Abbas, and M. Christine Boyer. *Shanghai Reflections: Architecture, Urbanism and the Search for an Alternative Modernity: Essays*. New York: Princeton Architectural Press, 2002.

Graafland, Arie. *The Socius of Architecture: Amsterdam, Tokyo, New York*. Rotterdam: 010 Publishers, 2000.

Harvey, David. *The Condition of Postmodernity*. Malden, MA: Blackwell, 1989.

Huang, Tsung-yi Michelle. *Walking between Slums and Skyscrapers: Illusions of*

Open Space in Hong Kong, Tokyo, and Shanghai. Hong Kong: Hong Kong University Press, 2004.
Ishiguro, Kazuo. *When We Were Orphans*. London: Faber and Faber, 2000.
Rowe, Peter G. *East Asia Modern*. London: Reaktion Books, 2005.
Scheen, Lena. 'Sensual, But No Clue of Politics: Shanghai's *longtang* houses.' In *Aspects of Urbanization in Asia: Shanghai, Hong Kong, Guangzhou*, edited by Gregory Bracken, 117-136. Amsterdam: Amsterdam University Press, 2012.
Wang Anyi. *The Song of Everlasting Sorrow: A Novel of Shanghai*. Translated by Michael Berry and Susan Chan Egan. New York: Columbia University Press, 2008.

Filmography

Entrapment, 20th Century Fox Film Corporation (1999).
Lust, Caution, Buena Vista Home Entertainment (no release date).
Mission: Impossible III, Paramount Pictures (2006).
Shanghai Triad, Sony Pictures Classics (1994).
Think Fast, Mr Moto, 20th Century Fox Film Corporation (1937).

10. Nostalgia, Place, and Making Peace with Modernity in East Asia

Margaret Hillenbrand

Nostalgia is a notoriously slippery concept, and this, of course, is why people try so hard to theorise it in ways that hold fast. For Dai Jinhua, it is the ascendant fashion of the *fin-de-siècle* (1997: 8); whereas for Hao Zaijin it is a 'movement that dare not speak its name' (1996: 23). Svetlana Boym's seminal study makes the sentiment Janus-faced, sometimes 'restorative' and sometimes 'reflective' (2001), while in Fredric Jameson's rather more indignant schema, it is just corrupted memory (1991: 20-1). Alternately good, bad, modern, postmodern, an amnesiac, or an *aide-mémoire*, nostalgia is malleable in different hands; but in recent years, its most common fate has been a kind of exasperated censure. Nostalgia irritates its critics because it seems to harbour so much potential for an affective reckoning with the past – but more often than not elects to squander that promise in an excess of retro schmaltz. In a sense, then, it is the chimera of authenticity which fuels the critical fascination with the nostalgic mode, however the latter is defined. Is there a 'real' nostalgia? If so, what might it look like? And why, until recently, has there been so little of it around in contemporary East Asia?

The present chapter looks at these questions by attempting to theorise the nostalgia 'movement' which, for at least a couple of decades now, has bathed the East Asian cultural realm in the rosy glow of yesteryear. From the 'native place' parcel post catalogues that allow Japanese consumers to cherry-pick different flavours of 'home' to the Taiwanese 'golden oldie' radio station 'Taiwan Nostalgia' (台湾乡愁电台), the taste, sound, and look of the past has become paradoxically contemporary. As Hanchao Lu puts it of China, the very prefix 'old' now carries real capital:

> A good indication of the nostalgia in China today is the growing torrent of publications entitled 'old something,' most of which have appeared in series and always sold well: Old Photographs, Old Cartoons, Old Coupons, Old Houses, Old Customs, Old News, Old Callings, Old Cities, and many others. Apparently the word 'old' is appealing and marketable in the current social milieu (Lu 2002: 184).

Much of this nostalgia, moreover, carries a whiff of the phoney. Its bogus character derives, first of all, from simple marketability: the more daintily nostalgia is packaged – and the more it sells – the further it strays, almost as a point of principle, from the grit and grime of historical credibility. But equally significant, and rather less remarked upon, is the problem of what we might call mnemonic credibility in the East Asian nostalgia boom. Rather than being rooted in the dense fibres of memory, and thus able to cause the kind of unbidden pangs for the past that bear the ring of truth, a good deal of the nostalgia this boom has manufactured is for epochs – 1930s Hong Kong, Showa-era Japan, colonial Taiwan – of which the 'remembering' subject has no bodily recollection. This glut of disembodied nostalgias has certainly attracted attention in East Asian studies. But most critics have interpreted the trend in specific, linear, and faintly kneejerk ways: it is a retreat from time, and from a troubling socio-political present in particular.

But this nostalgic scene realigns its component parts into a different picture when we look at it via the comparative lens, and interpret it intertextually across the region. Realigning things in this way echoes Lawrence Grossberg's point that any context is always both spatial and relational – denoting both a 'bounded interiority' and also those transversal relations which bear on that bounded entity – and is thus best viewed in a multiperspectival way (Grossberg 2010: 30). And when seen through such a prism, it becomes apparent that East Asia's strange vogue for the unremembered past expresses not just a flight from time, but from place, too, and from one locale in particular. This abandoned site is the city of lived memory, a psycho-physical topos to which nostalgia has quite obstinately refused to stick. Underlying this reticence is the notion, both powerfully predictable and yet powerfully tenacious, that the 'really remembered' city is not a proper 'place': earthy, *gemütlich*, and thus worthy of our nostalgia. This notion persists across East Asia, and most especially in its literature and cinema, despite the plain fact that cities are ever more the region's primary site of dwelling. And behind this refusal to reconcile with the city as a place of home and hearth lies, of course, the same queasy trepidation about modernity that has both plagued and sustained cultural practice in East Asia and abroad.

More crucial to my argument here, however, is the particular developmental stage of modernity that nostalgia has tended to find uncongenial in East Asia. Ragtime, retro cities, as we will see, have proved very photogenic to the nostalgic eye, chiefly because the modernity they showcase is reassuringly done and dusted – so much so, in fact, that their neon and asphalt are even quite quaint. The cities we grew up with, by contrast, are a work in progress for the simple reason that we live through their every change; and it is precisely this messy and untameable character that has caused nostalgia, with its supposed affinity for what Simmel called 'uninterrupted habitations' (1950: 410), to recoil. In this chapter, I begin by trying to unpick the intractable relationship that obtains between place and the-city-we-know in 20th-century East Asian culture; and in the second part I look at some recent cinema which articulates an alternative aesthetic of nostalgia to bring about something of a rapprochement between the two. In particular, these films elaborate a visual language of incompleteness and imperfection which has a long local genealogy, and which aestheticises the 'flaw' so as to bring about this transition from anxiety to acceptance.

Nostalgia, Place, and the Soil

If the city of recent recall is not a 'place', then what is? The answer, needless to say, is the soil, and visions of place have clung quixotically to it throughout much of East Asia's modern cultural history. Ideologues and philosophers across the region have helped to ensure that roads lead back there, and literary representation has performed regular and ritualistic loyalty to it, from Shen Congwen's pastoralism and Shimazaki Tôson's elegies on provincial life to Taiwanese nativist (乡土) writing, post-Mao root-seeking (寻根), and the earth-writing of Zhang Wei. This attachment to the soil is well understood, and few would argue that it springs from the cracks of spreading concrete sprawl. Just as the West needed the East to define itself, so has the countryside played the necessary other to the city, ostensibly furnishing the fantasies of home it could not yet host; and, in this sense, romancing the soil is just the flip-side of decades of urbanisation. Both these relationships – East and West, city and countryside – depend upon the mediations of enchantment: just as Orientalism was the gauzy filter through which the West saw the East, so too has the city's vision of the countryside long been refracted through the prism of nostalgia for simpler, better days.

What is more, this yearning for the soil-as-place has drawn much of its strength and meaning from ephemerality. It is a will-o'-the-wisp sort of sentiment that can be grasped only fleetingly, and as Jennifer Robertson notes of Japan, many of its most familiar, most freighted symbols are either non-tactile or in other ways elusive: 'a rural landscape: dirt path, sky, fields, mountains; symbols of estrangement: train, train station, port, train whistle, soldier, letter' (1988: 496-7). Nostalgia for the soil, in other words, quickens precisely at the vanishing point, and it moves us for the very reason that we are resigned to – indeed, anxiously anticipating – its imminent loss. In a sense, then, this kind of nostalgia is not so much about Simmel's stable places as fugitive effects, and what might perhaps be termed the logic of the synecdoche. Certainly, it is a longing for a lost past of plenitude, but its favoured *leitmotivs* – a wisp of smoke, a half-caught sound, and so on – are often predicated on the fragmentary, imperfect power of suggestion. It is precisely through the 'part' that the 'whole' is glimpsed in ways that touch the heart, and this, paradoxically, gives the sentiment a sense of the *echt*. This relationship between place, nostalgia, and fugitive effects has, of course, deep roots. We see it in poems as disparate as Li Bai's 'In a Quiet Night' (静夜思), in which the poet catches a glimmer of the moon and yearns for home, and Bashô's 'Kyô nite mo' (京にても), where the passing cuckoo's cry is so evocative that it brings on that selfsame longing even though the poet is dwelling safely in his hometown.

Deep as these roots are, however, it is arguably only when the soil begins to suffer grave erosion that nostalgia for it really swings into gear. Hence the tremendous discursive care that intellectuals across East Asia begin to lavish on the soil, and its various epistemological offshoots, from the late 19th century onwards. Thus we have Shiga Shigetaka's paean to scenic Japan, *On the Japanese Landscape* (日本風景論 1894); Yanagita Kunio and the invention of folklore studies; and Ishida Eiichirô's assertion that Japan belonged to a 'rice-based cultural sphere' (稻作文化圈) (1969: 150-2), together with all the 'rice-based scholarship' it has helped to cultivate.[1] Republican-era China partakes of the same enthusiasms, despite all its strident intellectual chatter about reforming the benighted countryside. Haiyan Lee notes that 'Almost every prominent writer of the May Fourth era seems to have written homecoming narratives, whether or not he/she is known as a native soil writer' (2007: 12); and Prasenjit Duara observes that even Lu Xun, who was in some ways the anti-apostle of the soil, 'could not avoid a nativist cathexis, a poetics of identity' (2000: 33).

The tendency is perhaps even more vivid in China's essay and *belles-lettres* tradition, which reiterates the idea that place, the soil, and even culture itself denote one another in a sealed semantic equivalence. In his influential essay 'Place and the Literary Arts' (地方与文艺, 1923), for example, Zhou Zuoren writes that 'When we talk about place (地方) [...] we are simply venerating that force of the soil (土之力) which fosters individuality' (Zhou 1992: 214). By the time of Fei Xiaotong's treatise on the salt of the Chinese earth, *Earthbound China* (乡土中国, 1947), this relationship between place, soil, and culture had become something close to a civilisational creed, a true measure of Chineseness. The belief was only drummed home further by Mao's rural re-working of classic urban-based Marxism in the years that followed. But although this creed may have called itself 'Chinese', Duara has shown that soil-based writing – whether ethnographic, geographic, anthropological, or literary – was vigorously cross-pollinated in East Asia, particularly from Japan to China (2000: 16-23). The relationship between place, soil, and culture was one, therefore, that was mediated in a shared regional space, with implications for the meaning of nostalgia which filter down through time too.

All these discursive journeys are nostalgic in both itinerary and destination, since the literati who made them sensed all too clearly that they were witnessing the soil as something *déjà disparu*, and this intuition quickened their longing for the past. Ultimately, however, it is the inferences they make about culture that are most telling. As Zhou Zuoren sees it, there is an unbreakable link between the soil and the grandeur of the philosophico-literary muse itself:

> People nowadays [...] must jump back down to earth and let the breath of the soil and the taste of the mire flow through their veins and find expression in their writing. Only this is real thinking and real literary art [...] (Zhou 1992: 214)

This notion that cultural creativity requires earthy 'emplacement', and will indeed founder without it, sharpens nativist anxiety over modernity and its many uprootings. What will happen to nostalgia after urbanisation has had its wicked way with the countryside, when the soil is not just vanishing, but long gone? More precisely, what fate will befall culture when modernity turns people into offspring of the city – urbanites, born and bred – who have no bodily memory of the soil and the wistfulness it engenders? The received wisdom here is that the city robs urbanites of the right to nostalgia, leaving their loss to ache and tingle like the proverbial amputated limb. These are the pangs to which Dai Jinhua refers when she writes of the contemporary Chinese urbanite's 'ship of nostalgia which can find no berth' (1997: 11), a notion that itself echoes city-born Kobayashi Hideo's much earlier essay on 'Homeless Literature' (故郷を失つた文学, 1933), in which he grieves not for the loss of a rural hometown so much as for all the oddly sustaining sorrow – nostalgia, by any other name – which that loss brings. 'Born in Tokyo', Kobayashi writes in bewilderment, 'I cannot grasp what that might mean. I have the uneasy sense that, for me, there is no home' (Kobayashi 1967: 31).[2] But what really troubles him, is what will happen to 'culture' in an urban world where nostalgia only has itself to fantasise about. Indeed, Kobayashi's essay meditates in key ways, if unconsciously, on Zhou Zuoren's earlier piece, making an explicit connection between the loss of the soil, nostalgia cast adrift, and a literary enterprise on the ropes.

'Armchair Nostalgia': The Memory Market in East Asia

In a sense, then, Kobayashi's essay intimates that this vagrant nostalgia with pines for itself – this nostalgia for nostalgia – is essentially bad for culture. Possibly he was prescient in this regard. Because the truth is that nostalgia does not take the obliging route and simply evaporate when there is no longer a rural homestead to miss. And this, in its turn, duly begs the question: what, exactly, *do* city people do with their 'nostalgia for nostalgia', with this sentiment that surges even when its proper object has been displaced? Recent evidence, both in and outside East Asia, would suggest that they sell these feelings out, and allow them to be comprehensively commandeered by the 'memory market'. Thus in *Modernity at Large*, Arjun Appadurai writes of what he calls 'armchair nostalgia', an ersatz and all-too-often kitschy thrill that is visible, and purchasable, everywhere across the cultural landscape. Dispossessed nostalgia for place has been co-opted into a 'clever instrument of the merchandiser's tool-kit', a marketing ploy so brazen that it barely bothers to disguise itself (Appadurai 1996: 76-78). In common with many other instances of commercially colonised affect, it worms its way into unlikely corners, progressing from a sort of 'chintz and Chippendale' fondness for the well-heeled rural past to the sort of encyclopaedic recreations of gutted coal-mining towns that John Urry has noted of post-industrialised Britain (1995: 218). For all its brashness, though, 'armchair nostalgia' deserves its moniker, since at base it is emotionally sedentary: it takes no risks in its relationship with memory, and the past it recalls has been edited for all surprises. Small wonder that David Lowenthal describes it as 'memory with the pain removed' (1985: 8), although we might add that it is missing much of the pleasure too. Instead of what the Germans call *Heimat* – a bodily, almost pre-speech experience of hearth and its homeliness – 'armchair nostalgia' is about the ornaments on the mantelpiece and not the warmth of the fire itself.

This ersatz reproduction of the past-as-place is ubiquitous across East Asia too, and it has roused an animated response in East Asian studies. Examples of the trend over the last couple of decades are legion, and range as far and wide as 'red tourism' and the vogue for Maoist memorabilia; 'hometown-building'

(ふるさとづくり), a mythopoeic process in which a villagey feel is painstakingly re-created in just those places where it is on the wane; Edo/Tokyo studies and the fad for the 'low city' (下町): the run-down, traditionally lower-caste areas of the capital; the seemingly unstoppable boom for old Shanghai, which has also wended its way to Hong Kong in the form of the retro 1930s aesthetic retailed by designers such as Alan Chan and David Tang; other urban vogues for old Beijing, old Chongqing, old Xi'an, old Nanjing; Hong Kong's home-grown black-and-white advertising campaigns which lyricise the fishing village the territory once was; and the fashion for tea art houses and colonial-era hot spring resorts in contemporary Taiwan.

What would probably cause Kobayashi most angst, however, is the extent to which representation, too, seems to have been re-routed away from real, re-membered, muse-like places, if not simply hijacked for its monetary value. In the bluntest sense, this is simply because nostalgia has become big business in cultural production, and many highly successful texts of recent years ply the trade, consciously or otherwise: the Shanghai extravaganzas of Wang Anyi, Zhang Yimou and Chen Kaige, the homely Hengchun evoked in Wei Te-sheng's *Cape no.7* (海角七号, 2007), 1960s' campus life in a decent slice of Murakami Haruki's oeuvre, the 1930s' Hong Kong reimagined by Lillian Lee and later Stanley Kwan, and so on. Yet equally pertinent is what Fredric Jameson calls the 'art language' of nostalgia and its basic incompatibility with 'genuine historicity' (1991: 19). This aesthetic of the 'once upon a time' is all about worshipful attention to period costume, sweeping pans of well-assembled antiquarian objects, and sepia-tinted film stock; it is about snuff bottles, vintage Shanghai calendar posters (月份牌), and other collectible items; and it is so much about the quest to get everything just as it was and 'just so' that the past becomes a bit too picture-perfect to make poetry flow.[3]

Nostalgia-as-commodity has nevertheless proved an arresting theme, not least because it intersects pleasingly with other themes *du jour* in contemporary East Asian studies. Indeed, the nostalgia boom is almost always interpreted in locally-specific ways, and usually along the following lines: national trauma or transformation (the legacy of the Cultural Revolution, Japan's oil shocks, Shanghai's precipitous rise, the looming Hong Kong handover, Kuomintang rule on Taiwan) generates the desire to beat a retreat from the present as socio-political anguish or disorientation. 'Armchair nostalgia' then steps in to transport the consumer back to a time scrubbed clean of Jameson's 'genuine historicity', to a pseudo-epoch in which remembrance is so far removed from pain that it actually becomes analgesic, if not outright amnesiac. That it sells well is further grist to the mill. This reading is all well and good as far as it goes, and it certainly sheds light on part of the process; but it obscures the fact that nostalgia is never simply about time alone. Indeed, if we theorise these nostalgias in a comparative frame – as a set of emotional-cum-economic responses that share the same rough co-ordinates, and thus might be strung together in a different chain of meaning – then it is repetitive anxieties of place that are thrown into high relief.

The Real Crux: City Versus Place

Essentially, this anxiety stems from a reluctance to allow the place which so many producers and consumers of the East Asian nostalgia boom actually grew up in to be just that: a 'place'. The non-place in question is the city – or at least the city as it lives in memory – and the refusal to see it as rooted, homely, and worth the affective investment of nostalgia is consistent across national borders. Indeed, if we look across East Asian literature and film over the last two or more decades, it is striking how the 'really remembered' city – of the 1960s, 1970s, and 1980s – is represented. Generally speaking, it is the badlands, conceived in metaphors of debris, squalor, and social dislocation across an extraordinary span of cultural texts. This compares curiously with the region's various retro cities, which seem to gather nostalgic sentiment to themselves quite effortlessly. This process of alchemy occurs, of course, because the passage of time has allowed the retro city to become more place-like: time has mellowed its modernity, settling the rubble into the dignified stasis of museum relic, and this mitigation is the crux of the matter. The look and feel of newer built environments in East Asia, by contrast, feed a creeping sense of shame, since they are so visibly the matrices of a modernity that is very much in progress, playing postcolonial catch-up with powerhouses, glamour zones, and citadels elsewhere. As a consequence, the city of recent recall is almost never seen as a 'place': what Yi-fu Tuan so succinctly calls 'enclosed and humanised space', those 'centres of felt value where biological needs [...] are met' (2001: 54), and which provide some kind of shelter and succour against the levelling blasts of modern life.

Much recent study of place, both in East Asia and elsewhere, has focused precisely on its role as the last barricade against a space-time continuum that flattens all before it in ways that seem so perfectly epitomised by the hungry, homogenising advances of contemporary urban sprawl. This idea that place-sense and the city-we-know are irrevocably at odds finds perhaps its most compelling Western evocation in Heidegger's concept of 'dwelling' (1975: 145-161). For Heidegger, this utopian state, 'signifying the manner in which mortals are on the earth' (1975: 148), is elusive in the built environments of modernity. These spaces brutally diminish our capacity for dwelling, because they steal from the natural world rather than sparing it, and thus wrench us from our roots. Place-sense across East Asia is arguably still more conservative, where so much of the lexicon used to evoke a sense of deep-seated dwelling – 家乡, 故乡, 家园, 鄉土, 故鄉, ふるさと – has a recognisably rural lilt. As Yiyan Wang notes of China, 'the city marks a blind spot in critical studies' of native place, chiefly because the city's intimate alliance with Chinese modernity makes it *a priori* unhomely (2005: 9); but her observation can be extrapolated right across East Asia. Jing Wang notes the same kind of myopia in Taiwan's nativist ideologies, which set village and city up as spatio-temporal 'antipodes', with the former as both 'central scene' and reservoir of all value (1980: 48-9).

The bias is visible in Japan, too. Yoshimi Shunya, for example, observes that those who have grown up in the big Japanese cities since the 1960s lack an 'originary landscape' (原風景)[4] which can seep into the fibres of memory and stay there (1987: 352). In his study *Originary Landscapes in Literature* (文学における原風景, 1972), Okuno Takeo goes further, stating that the metropolis is 'entirely excluded' from Japanese images of native place, unlike in European culture (French cinema being his key example), where cities, rank and rowdy as they are, can always be 'home' (Okuno 1972: 72-73). Takahashi Yoshitaka, meanwhile, seems to flout the trend by writing on the palpable presence of the Honjo area of Tokyo – and particularly an enclave called Otakegura – in Akutagawa Ryûnosuke's writing. Otakegura is both the author's 'originary landscape' and his muse: 'it casts its shadow over all of Akutagawa's work', Takahashi observes, 'its soft voice, like a kind of baseline, sings out faintly across his writings' (Takahashi 1978: 31). Yet in *Honjo Ryôgoku* (本所両国, 1927), the travelogue/memoir in which Akutagawa himself describes the influence of Otakegura on his early life, it becomes clear that although the latter lies in the heart of Tokyo, it is nothing other than a rural proxy, a 'place' in the good old-fashioned sense of the word:

> [...] it was a patch of wilderness such as was rare to find in the city, with a grove of trees and a bamboo thicket, and there was even an ancient bridge with a ditch beneath it which ran into the river [...] it was Otakegura that first taught me the beauty of nature. (Akutagawa 1997: 11)

If there were any residual doubt, Akutagawa dispels it in an essay entitled 'Tokyo People' (東京人, 1923). 'As someone born, bred, and resident in Tokyo', he opines, 'I have no recollection of ever having much empathy with the idea of loving one's hometown (愛郷心)' (Akutagawa 1996: 164).

This notion, hinted at or expressly adumbrated over so many literary-critical writings, that an irreconcilable rift lies between 'enclosed and humanised space' and the city of lived memory is key to an understanding of the region's recent nostalgia boom. The point will become clearer if we sketch the picture which emerges when an intertextual, comparative gaze is levelled on East Asia's strange surfeit of faux-nostalgic texts and products. Most obvious are those which stage a blatant spatial escape from the city. The refrain of 'Oh, the good old days' (なつかしいな！) which provides the voiceover to *sake* commercials in which the camera pans over rolling rice paddies that most people nowadays only really recognise from the air-conditioned comfort of the bullet train instantly springs to mind. But the rural setting – indeed, the rural premise – of a film such as *Cape No. 7* makes much the same point about the 'really remembered' city and its basic inhabitability. More subtle, perhaps, are the nostalgias for retro cities cited earlier, which seem at first to buck the anti-urban trend, but which keep their affection largely gestural by reaching out to 'places' that have little meaningful life in the cellular memory of people now. The obsessions with 1930s Shanghai and Hong Kong, played out in countless period pieces, are the stand-out case studies. That said, the 'Old City series' (老城市系列丛书) brought out by Jiangsu Art Publishing House, which marries turn-of-the century sepia images to textual commentary by leading literary scions from each of the cities featured, is just as relevant.[5] But most peculiar of all, perhaps, is the penchant for what might be called 'transnational nostalgia', which is both a spatial and a temporal flight from the city of recent recall. A notable example here is Japan's yearning for the pristine rural idylls of South East Asia which came to the fore in the 1980s, although postcolonial East Asia's longing for the 1960s campus world of Murakami Haruki is just as mnemonically disembodied.

Collectively, these texts demonstrate that *ersatz* nostalgia is much more than simply an escape from the troubling present. On the contrary, it makes more solid sense when viewed as a retreat from precisely the place from where 'true' nostalgia is supposed to spring: the remembered past and, most particularly, that past as home. This trepidation about the 'really remembered' city is easy enough to understand. The razing of old districts, the high-rises built in a day, the haphazard, strung-out forays of the metropolis into the countryside: all, apparently, are anathema to nostalgia. They create spaces rather than places, amorphous zones and precincts in which, as Gertrude Stein so memorably put it, 'there is no there there' (Stein 1937: 289). Or as Rey Chow explains it:

> In the midst of [...] wrecking balls, bulldozers, pile drivers, air hammers, and power drills, how does one begin to be nostalgic? (1998: 135)

Cities exist – subsist – in a vortex of movement that spirals too fast for memory to keep abreast, and nostalgia for place is the inevitable casualty. Indeed, this is Chow's point when she argues that the 'unprecedented disintegration of stationary places' is so devastating that it has caused nostalgia to forsake place altogether and reconstitute itself in looping 'fantasies of time' (1998: 135). Certainly, Chow is right to note at least a partial displacement of nostalgic energies now that place has become such an inhospitable host for them, and perhaps nowhere more so than in the sprawling cities of industrialised East Asia.

Yet has nostalgia really given up entirely on the 'really remembered' cities of childhood, a decade ago, even yesterday? The Canadian poet Anne Michaels offers a beautiful rebuttal of this point when she writes:

> So much of the city is our bodies. Places in us
> old light still slants through to.
> Places that no longer exist but are full of feeling,
> like phantom limbs. (1997: 86)

This notion of cellular memory, and of a city so indelibly encoded into it that bulldozers and wrecking balls are just blunt instruments against its tenacity, is one that perhaps has resonance for the study of place in East Asia. More precisely, if nostalgia quickens at the vanishing point, then surely 'really remembered' cities should be the most nostalgic places of all, and on virtually every street corner. After all, every new high-rise is still the death of some lived memory, even if it is a short-lived one, and although every new highway may not concrete over the dirt paths of childhood it still takes the place of something. We see this in several recent documentaries from China which depict nostalgia as a sudden bodyblow which strikes urban dwellers as they endure experiences such as forced demolition and relocation (拆迁).[6] Often, the dwelling thus destroyed is a shack of recent construction; but this, if anything, only makes the sudden fact of homelessness all the more agonising.

Yet the reluctance to grant the city of lived memory its nostalgic aura remains entrenched. It stems, as suggested earlier, from the rift between the remembered city and 'place'; a rift which, in its turn, speaks of a deeper reluctance to admit modernity in all its rawness and rubble into long-hallowed visions of what 'dwelling' should be and do. If place is the final rampart of the anti-modern, then to acknowledge that the city – not of yesteryear, but of yesterday – is nostalgic is to demand a very different concept of 'enclosed and humanised space': one which is ready to bring the flawed, unfinished nature of modernity into its frame of reference, and call that modernity home. For cities on the rise, cities reaching out for globality – cities like Shanghai, Tokyo, Taipei – this notion of modernity as *acceptably* traumatic is, perhaps, a bit too awkward to countenance. And this is precisely why so much recent nostalgia treats the city of lived memory as a sort of flyover zone, a space skipped past with eyes averted on the journey from a chintzy past to a glossy, high-spec future. Ackbar Abbas makes just this point when he writes that 'The listed buildings on the Bund and the chaos of skyscrapers in Pudong do not so much confront as complement each other on either side of the Huangpu River; in a sense, both old and new are simply steps in the remake of Shanghai as a City of Culture in the new global space' (Abbas 2000: 782).[7] And as it is in life, so in art – and not just in Shanghai.

But is this really the job of culture? What about the victims of demolition, of gentrification in Taipei,[8] of urban 'renewal' in Tokyo, of slash-and-burn deracination right across the region? After all, these people do have feelings for the cities they hold in memory; these places do, indeed, live on 'in our bodies'; and they do evoke nostalgia, both acute and authentic, even – especially – when the sheer speed of change can make this nostalgia something of a hopeless affair. Margaret Farrar notes in a recent paper that nostalgia often waxes strongest 'in impoverished, marginal, out-of-the-way districts and corners' (2008). Paraphrase her observation slightly and it reads: nostalgia waxes strongest where modernity hurts the most, but – and this is the key point – there is also succour and meaning to be found amidst the grief. Moreover, it is precisely through this pleasure/pain that urbanites come to experience the city as place: as the 'enclosed and humanised space' that in its plainest formulation is nothing other than home. What is needed is a different kind of nostalgic art language, one which might enable some kind of 'working through', and transmute some of this trauma into solace.

An Alternative Aesthetic of Nostalgia: *Young Thugs* and *In the Mood for Love*

The remainder of this chapter focuses on a pair of texts from the last fifteen years – Miike Takashi's *Young Thugs: Nostalgia* (岸和田少年愚連隊 望郷, 1997) and Wong Kar-wai's *In the Mood for Love* (花样年华, 2000) – which do precisely this. These two films, although very different from each other, are at the same time critically alike in their exposition of an alternative aesthetic of nostalgia.

This alternative aesthetic works by transforming the imperfect, incomplete character of the 'really remembered' city – all its trauma, in short – into the crucial pre-conditions for a nostalgia which, to revisit the opening of this essay, exploits the ephemeral pleasures of synecdoche to mourn the passing of time. Cities in these texts are places only partially preserved in memory. Yet, and at the risk of being unfashionably biographical, they are sites to which their creators feel a bodily attachment, some cellular memory. And to return to the image of the amputated limb, these narratives have no truck with the prosthetic, and prefer, like the walking wounded, to carry their sense of loss openly. Meanwhile, the imperfection of the city of lived memory, its status as 'impoverished, marginal, out-of-the-way', whets this sense of poignancy. Imperfection dominates the physical landscape, the built environments, of these two films: modernity is tireless and exacting here, and the city is caught in its toils, constantly worked over into ugly, makeshift apparitions that the filmmaker does not baulk at showing.

As suggested earlier, this delicate relationship between nostalgia and an aesthetic of flawed or fugitive effects has long antecedents in East Asia. An early exposition of the dialectic comes in the meditations of the Japanese monk Yoshida Kenkô. In *Essays in Idleness* (徒然草, 1330-2) he writes:

> Are we to look at cherry blossoms only in full bloom, the moon only when it is cloudless? [...] Branches about to blossom or gardens strewn with faded flowers are worthier of our admiration [...] It is only after the silk wrapper has frayed at top and bottom, and the mother-of-pearl has fallen from the roller that a scroll looks beautiful [...] In everything, no matter what it may be, uniformity is undesirable. Leaving something incomplete makes it interesting [...] (1967: 70 and 115)

Crucial to Kenkô's sensibility here is an apprehension of how both imperfection and incompleteness provoke bittersweet rumination on the passing of time. Imperfection registers time as attrition, incompleteness acknowledges it as loss, and the two become bittersweet – and thus suggestively nostalgic – because of Kenkô's decision to celebrate the transience of life rather than cower from it. As Yuriko Saito notes, this predilection for the blemish reaches its high-water mark in the rituals of the tea ceremony, in which moss-covered stones were sought as stepping-stones for the garden, and cracked, roughly-shaped bowls were prized as utensils (1997: 378).

Historians of Chinese art would, of course, be quick to point out that this Japanese penchant for imperfection clashes with the pursuit of flawlessness that so often drove Chinese potters, especially those who crafted imperial wares. Such was the quest for perfection that even the most microscopic flaw could doom a piece, causing it to be smashed into pieces and buried in pits near the kiln site. Yet Chinese painting, and particularly the *xieyi* tradition, provides another genealogy for the aesthetic of incompleteness. We see this, most conspicuously, in the marked preference for visual synecdoche, exemplified by the many artists who have conveyed the perishable beauty of blossom by painting a solitary branch rather than the whole tree. But still more crucial, perhaps, is the concept of 'leaving a whiteness' (留白). This staple of the Chinese landscape style keeps parts of the canvas starkly bare, thus forcing the viewer to ponder pregnant spaces and the contrast between line and emptiness. A deliberate denial of the ethos of completion, leaving a whiteness marks the painter's grasp of the illusory nature of endpoints. As Michael Sullivan observes:

> We are often told that the Chinese painter leaves large areas of the picture space empty so that we may 'complete it in our imagination'. But that is not so [...] His landscape is not a final statement, but a starting point; not an end, but the opening of a door (1984: 156).

The salience of this for the representation of nostalgia needs little in the way of glossing, since the latter, at least in its more 'reflective' forms, is a sentiment that thrives at the threshold between memory and the more ungovernable, unknowable realm of the imagination. More critically, this long-held taste for both incompleteness and imperfection – which is, at base, a willed aestheticisation of loss and disenchantment – enables nostalgia to become the conduit to a reconciliation with the present and its travails. This is precisely what we see in the films by Miike and Wong, both of which bring this aesthetic of resignation back to life. In this pair of films, incompleteness and imperfection operate as textual tropes through which, above all else, a rapprochement with the city as place is articulated. This process of acceptance is aestheticised still further by linking nostalgia decisively to states of love, or, more precisely, lovesickness. Feelings of love course through these texts; and in ways which mirror the incomplete, imperfect city itself, these attachments are left unconsummated or somehow unrequited. The various protagonists of these texts view the urban world through the veil of heartache, but this filter is an infinitely softening one: so much so, in fact, that it brings into being a harmony – a sense of dwelling, even – between the urbanite and his or her environment. Thwarted love and the flawed city become parallel states of living and being, their essential equivalence drawn out by the mediating powers of nostalgia, which looks back and finds in the fabric of the city the imprints, scars, and traces of the feelings from that time. In this way, nostalgia also becomes a love affair with the city itself, and with the city precisely as a site of pleasure and pain.

Miike Takashi's *Young Thugs: Nostalgia* brings this process to life in startling ways. The tender prequel to his later rough-and-tumble treatment of juvenile toughs in Osaka, *Young Thugs: Innocent Blood* (岸和田少年愚連隊血煙り純情編, 1997), *Nostalgia* trains its focus on chief hoodlum Nakaba Riichi as a child. Riichi belongs to an impossibly dysfunctional family. His father is idle, ultra-violent, and bi-polar; his mother is hard-working, put-upon, and festering with rage; and his grandfather, comparatively the stable core of the *ménage*, is an eccentric rogue. As Miike puts it succinctly in an interview: 'they're a hopeless family, really, but so full of life (生き生きしている)'.[9] In his child-like way, Riichi adores them all – and also his pretty home-room teacher Miss Itô, who does her best to plead his cause, despite being physically assaulted by his father. Indeed, the film is brimming over with frustrated love, from Riichi's fierce crush on Miss Itô, to his much-tried affection for his parents, to their own harrowing but persistent attachment to each other. The vital backdrop to these entanglements is Kishiwada itself, the fishing district on the outskirts of Osaka in which *Young Thugs* is set. Grey and tired at first, Kishiwada soon imprints itself more persuasively on the visual fabric of the film. Plenty of outdoor shooting, in which the same locales are swept over time and again, allows the exteriors of the city to work steadily on the eye. The interiors, too, are appraised with the same kind of mounting deliberation. We know the film's theme from its title; but what discloses itself rather more subtly is the role that synecdoche – and its suggestion that the 'part' is more redolent with meaning than the 'whole' – plays in making the city a key focus for this nostalgia.

This process begins via Miike's creation of a pre-pubescent point-of-view in *Young Thugs*. Daily life for Riichi is essentially a process of ellipsis, by which I mean that much of the information he would expect to receive in order to make sense of his existence is denied him. In cinematic terms, most notably in the work of directors such as Ozu Yasujirô and Hou Hsiao-hsien, ellipsis works by substituting tenuous narrative links for the tightly-meshed, well-worn patterns of tension and *dénouement* that characterise conventional movie fare. In deft hands, ellipsis can cut to the chase of human dramas in ways that, according to Hou, are ironically 'more clear-cut and to the point' (Chiao 1995: 48) than full narrative disclosure. Ellipsis for Riichi, however, is not a mediated effect of viewing, but lived reality in the raw. Riichi never knows when one of his parents will disappear from the family home, nor when they might appear again; he has little inkling of why it is that drunken, half-naked women stumble through the door in the middle of the night, nor why – in the strangest moment in the film – his father submits to the most grotesque physical chastisement from his grandfather without the slightest demur. Riichi is forever trying to fill in the gaps of his patchy, pot-holed understanding; but the skill of Miike's evocation of nostalgia lies in how he turns these lacunae into deep wells of meaning. It is the very incompleteness of Riichi's schoolboy understanding, so well caught in the film's elliptical idiom, that makes its mood poignantly nostalgic, since the fragments which we glimpse, through the narrow prism of his point of view, are a reminder that nostalgia is all about acknowledging – and with a certain rueful pleasure – that the past is not just lost, but was never entirely ours to begin with.[10]

This sense of incompleteness works as a foil for Miike's visual rendering of the imperfect city in *Young Thugs*. The movie is shot within a battered industrial landscape of dented oil drums, piles of driftwood, burnt-out tyres, abandoned breeze blocks, rotting fishing nets, rusting junks, slab-sided concrete walkways, factories snaked over with tubes and drainpipes, gerry-built shacks, and squat grey residential blocks (団地) with corrugated roofs. This landscape is densely forested with pylons, railway signals, and telegraph poles. Almost the sole scrap of green, the strawberry patch cultivated by Riichi's neighbour, is so toxic that it kills a stray dog who forages there. The film's interiors – Riichi's home, the corner store, the local bordello, the barber's shop – take this slapdash modernity indoors, and they are littered with the bric-à-brac of mass-produced, low-budget life: tin teapots, mismatched crockery, chipped plywood *kotatsu*, and desolate-looking trinkets, such as the *maneki-neko* which gamely beckons good fortune from atop the Nakaba's TV set. The surfaces are greasy, the wooden fixtures are scarred, the lighting is strip style, and the palette of colours is streaked with grey and beige. Yet, and quite remarkably, the visual texture of this film is so dreamy and wistful that the imperfection of the urban world, and much of the misery of Riichi's life, seem to dissolve into a mirage of luminosity and hope. Indeed, much of this process is technically abetted by the uses of lighting in the film: Miike often shoots in the midday sun, and the heat, as it ripples and shimmers, acts palpably on the appearance of the shot, lending it a softer, dappled look. But as with Wong Kar-wai's later film, it is the veil of love which operates as the real diffusion filter in *Young Thugs*, casting its haze over Kishiwada and making it strangely radiant.

This aesthetic of incompleteness and imperfection finds its apotheosis in the recurring shot of the cratered terrain which lies in front of the Nakaba home. This stretch of ground is punctuated by three huge sinkholes dug in the dirt, as spectacular as meteor sites, and the camera pans over them with a slow, purposeful approach at several crucial moments in the film. Riichi and his grandfather are often to be found lying prostrate inside, pondering the world, either alone or together. The origin of these craters – who made them, and why – is a deliberate riddle in the film; but what their presence signifies most inescapably is a messy, half-hearted stab at modernity. These great circular cavities in the earth can only have been hacked out by bulldozers, yet the project these machines launched has never been completed, and the holes remain as open sores on the landscape – testimony to the district's 'impoverished, marginal, out-of-the-way' status, and its failure to secure sustained economic attention from the powers that be. It is just these sorts of forsaken places, however, which can breed the keenest longing for the past, and so it is in Miike's film. The sinkholes might look like urban blight; but Riichi's father declaims to his rapt infant son that 'Dad made this hole', and to the boy's grandfather, they are a symbol of 'our glory' (わしらの栄光). Riichi's love for his hopeless, feckless, yet endlessly watchable family finds perfect metonymic form in the craters, which are about as simple an indexical shorthand for incompleteness and imperfection as could be cinematically conjured. More importantly, the careful connection made by the camera between these holes and the few precious moments when Riichi communes properly with his father and grandfather enables *Young Thugs* to make a strong visual statement about the city, nostalgia, and the nature of place.

Wong Kar-wai's *In the Mood for Love*, his evocation of life among the Shanghainese community in Hong Kong during the early 1960s, illustrates this reconciliation in unexpectedly cognate ways. The film tells the story of Mrs Chan and Mr Chow, who rent rooms in adjacent apartments in a tenement block, and who discover that their respective spouses are having an affair. Left alone for days at a stretch, the pair slowly seek consolation in each other, but it is a romance which remains resolutely chaste. Eventually, Mr Chow invites Mrs Chan to leave for Singapore with him; but she arrives too late, and they narrowly 'miss' each other twice more before the film ends, inconclusively, at the ruins of Angkor Wat. This quiet drama unfolds against an intricately realised urban backdrop of newspaper offices, shipping companies, mahjong parties, and restaurant interiors which, as Stephen Teo observes, speaks unmistakably of Hong Kong, even though the film was shot in Thailand (2001). That the text is self-professedly nostalgic is signalled by its very title, 'The Age of Blossoms' (花样年华), a phrase that suggests the richness of time gone by. More significant, however, are the ways in which Wong uses strategies of synecdoche to link this richness to the city of lived memory.

The process begins with Wong's use of *mise-en-scène*, which offers an exemplary exposition of nostalgia as synecdoche. The film contains not a single establishing shot, not one panorama of any kind. Its action revolves around a tight cluster of locales – the two adjoining apartments in which the protagonists live, the cramped hallway that links them, a couple of offices, a short stretch of rainy street, the winding stairwell down to a noodle stall – each of which is filmed with the most stringent economy of angle and shot. The camera is often positioned in some kind of adjunct space, the hallway being the most telling example, and its habitual immobility means that interiors are glimpsed only in segments, sometimes slivers. Framing devices – partition walls, doorframes, cubby-holes, banisters, apertures, casement windows – are everywhere, with the result that the composition of space within the shot becomes both extraordinarily angular, and extraordinarily mediated. The lens of the camera is, of course, the first filter for the flow of images. But much of what we see is also trammelled through one or more of these edged boundaries, which constantly slice the screen into a collage of open and occluded spaces. These framing devices function as the visual syntax for Wong's nostalgic language. They tell us not only that the past can only be glimpsed in fragments – that much surely needs no repetition – but that the essence of nostalgia is our longing for what lies beyond the wall of what we can remember, our sense that there is so much more besides. In this sense, Wong's nostalgia is the very opposite of the 'listed buildings on the Bund', which present the past as glorious technicolour panorama.

This mood of incompleteness is complemented by the studied shabby imperfection of the lost city in Wong's film: Hong Kong in 1962. Wong's vision of urban space in *In the Mood for Love* is almost exclusively interiorised, and in ways that deliver a rebuff to the usual policies of urban preservation, which either channel their funds into the restoration of beleaguered civic structures, or create small, perfectly-formed, and somehow patronising enclaves of vernacular architecture. Wong's portrait of the city is textured in very different ways, with texture being, perhaps, the apposite term: his Hong Kong is a swirl of faded wallpaper, peeling paint, torn flyers, threadbare drapes, sun-bleached lampshades, battered filing cabinets, dusty wall maps, mottled mirrors, worn slippers, and gently fraying bedspreads. This kind of materiality jibes at 'armchair nostalgia', in which the restorability of the past becomes a kind of energetic fetish, a quest to get everything just as it was and 'just so', even though – as Zhao Jingrong notes – this lifelike reproduction simply kills the imagination (Zhao 2003: 86). The camera in Wong's film, by contrast, plays endlessly on these scruffy, pockmarked surfaces, immortalising their flaws with the indulgent eye of love, and leaning in towards the decrepit paintwork for the kind of close-up normally reserved for faces.

Significantly, it is the walls in Wong's film – just like Miike's craters – which become the centripetal point for this 'impoverished, marginal, out-of-the-way' nostalgia. In the first half hour of the film alone, the camera lingers on walls, with a sort of lazy intensity, at least a dozen times. At first, these long looks appear inadvertent: they seem to mark time as different protagonists move in and out of shot. But after a while, it becomes clear that the camera craves these walls, and returns to them with something like compulsion. One crucial, oft-repeated shot shows a rickety fuse box, an off-white Bakelite light-switch, and a patch of wall daubed with flaking paint in cream and brown. It borders the front door to the Khoo's apartment in which Chow and his wife are lodging, and we see it again and again as Mrs Chan approaches the door, with ever increasing emotion and intent, in search of Chow himself. The sheer repetitive deliberateness with which the camera links the battered wall – a metonym of defective modernity *par excellence*, with its fusebox and blistered paint – to Mrs Chan's febrile, lovelorn state (capturing her fingers as they slide along its grubby surface, framing her profile against the fusebox, panning over the paintwork at her eye level) allows Wong, just like Miike before him, to make a strong visual statement about the city, nostalgia, and the nature of place.

Both the battered wall and the world behind it evoke a longing for the past which works through synecdoche, and which thereby recognises, just as nostalgia for the soil did, that it is precisely an acceptance of hopelessness in the face of change which makes yearning for days past quicken. These devices of synecdoche – the dilapidated urban fabric and the slow, unconsummated love which blossoms between the two protagonists – fall under the same nostalgic aura in Wong's film, and its glow transmutes the city of memory into a place of dwelling. Wong knows that city life, and perhaps the Hong Kong life of personal memory in particular, is often spent indoors and in straitened spaces. But his longing is precisely for this cramped, flyblown world, for the mood of cabin fever that hits its zenith in the scene where, after a stolen conversation together, Chan and Chow find themselves walled up for hours on end in his room unable to leave because their landladies have begun a mahjong marathon next door. The scene is stultifying in one sense, as the two protagonists swelter in the heat and the tedium of waiting. But in another way, the episode renders the poetics of the city perfectly, since their proximity to one another, and yet the ineffable distance between them (also captured in the scenes where they shimmer awkwardly past each other in the hallway) create a vivid visual language for incompleteness and imperfection. Wong's willingness to allow the claustrophobic, slightly run-down Hong Kong that he remembers from childhood to become nostalgic in this way is an eloquent rejoinder to the neatly reconstituted nostalgias for unremembered times and places that have been circulating so freely around East Asia in recent years. But more importantly, his nostalgic city shows a rapprochement with modernity – not as an infatuation with the possibilities of the future, but as an acceptance of the past and its trauma – that enables a kind of 'working through'.

Andreas Huyssen has noted that 'nostalgic longing for a past is always also a longing for another place [...] temporality and spatiality are necessarily linked in nostalgic desire' (2006: 7). This is surely so; but what Wong's film, and Miike's too, reveal is the essential *reciprocity* between nostalgia and place, the dialectical bond that links them. Nostalgia is nothing but a floating simulacrum unless it is bedded down in ground that feels like home; but a sense of place, too, must inspire feelings of nostalgia if it is to seed itself in memory. Precisely because of this dialectic, it is not so much the physical site – the concrete 'where' – of the past that matters, but its hospitality to certain emotions; and this is why the linked entities of nostalgia and place can, to borrow Duara's term, 'cathect' themselves to objects other than the soil. Indeed, what Wong and Miike show, via their visual idiom of the aestheticised lack or flaw, is that the city of memory – ravaged or run-down as it may be – can play just as meaningful a host to this dialectical rapport. What is more, by showing nostalgia's evolution from a sentiment that was supposedly tied to the soil, through one that could cling to the retro city, to a yearning that pines – at last – for the city of recent recall, these two films also reveal that nostalgic art can be a potent gauge of modernity and its no-longer-discontents.

But more than this, these films may even be vessels for what Raymond Williams famously called 'structures of feeling': those social experiences that are '*in solution*, as distinct from other social semantic formations which have been *precipitated* and are more evidently and more immediately available' (1977: 133). Oftentimes, moreover, it is culture – literature, art, and perhaps pre-eminently cinema – that catalyses the reaction which converts solution into precipitate. And it is arguably when culture pre-empts society in this way, as opposed to the other way around, that it functions at its forceful and redemptive best. In this sense, and to modify Williams' metaphor, these two directors 'bottle' the vagrant, object-less nostalgia that Kobayashi Hideo and Dai Jinhua identified, and infuse it with a passion for the city-as-place in ways that both capture and also act upon the *Zeitgeist*.[11] By making films such as these, Miike and Wong both 'show' that the 'really remembered' city can be a place, and also work a kind of retrospective magic on our cellular memory that 'makes' this fact incomparably truer. As a result, nostalgia in their hands becomes not just *echt*, but salvational too; after all, most people want and need to feel deeply for the places of their past.

Notes

I would like to express my gratitude to Leung Ping-kwan, Michael Puett, Lena Scheen, and Hsueh-man Shen for their kind help in the preparation of this article.

1. Karatani Kôjin views all this in high deconstructionist style when he describes the comprehensive 'discovery of landscape' in Meiji- and Taisho-era Japan. See Karatani (1993: 11-44).
2. Okuno Takeo, also a Tokyoite, makes the same point more forcefully when he writes of the 'irritation and discomfort' he felt from childhood onwards whenever he heard the words '*kokyô*' or '*furusato*'. See Okuno (1972: 71).
3. Leung Ping-kwan makes this point incisively of Hong Kong's nostalgia cinema and its version of *la mode retro* (回顾的风格) when he notes that these films encourage us to view the past as a 'piece of theatre [...] decked out in an array of dramatic costumes', and with its temporality ostentatiously marked by 'faded photographs [...] and newspaper headlines which mimic a historical narrative'. The past thus evoked is 'neat and orderly [...] and harks back to the good old days when truth always triumphed'. See Ye Shi (1995: 38-46).
4. Oh Seon-Ah credits Okuno Takeo with the coining of this evocative term, stating that it

first appears in Okuno's aforementioned study of 1972, where it denotes a wild open space (原つぱ) that first imprints itself on the heart during early childhood. Oh notes the evolution of the term across the different disciplines of psychology, anthropology, geography, and architecture in the decades since, arguing that it has become something of a cultural keyword. See Oh (2001: 20-21).
5. In his preface to the volume *Old Xi'an* (老西安, 1999), Jia Pingwa refers to this process quite bluntly 'as using other people's experiences to write about the city'; and to hammer the point home he even admits, in a slightly embarrassed disclaimer, that he is not a 'born and bred' (土生土长) native of the city anyway. See Jia (1999: 1). In some ways, his apologia echoes comments made by Wang Anyi about her nostalgic novel of Shanghai, *Song of Everlasting Sorrow* (长恨歌, 1996). In a recent interview, Wang has remarked that she is less satisfied with the part of the novel which takes place in the 1940s 'because I have not experienced this period myself'. Public interview (by Lena Scheen) with Wang Anyi in the Rotterdam Library, 10 November 2009.
6. Telling examples are the recent documentaries by Ou Ning and Shu Haolun, entitled *Meishi Street* (煤市街, 2006) and *Nostalgia* (乡愁, 2006) respectively.
7. Chen Yihe and Wang Yanyun make a similar point when they note that the Shanghai nostalgia films of the 1990s are engaged in 'conspiratorial' relations with the city's contemporary cultural construction. See Chen and Wang (2006: 39-44).
8. Yomi Braester has done valuable work on this theme. See Braester (2003: 29-61).
9. 'Interview with Miike Takashi.' In *Young Thugs: Nostalgia*, DVD, 1998.
10. Benjamin Thomas puts it rather differently when he notes that the 'trick' of the film is 'its refusal of the melancholy, tinged with beatific idealization (of the past), that characterizes nostalgia'. See Thomas (2009: 149).
11. Braester notes in this connection that the 'city life and the cinema bleed into each other'. See Braester (2003: 54).

References

Abbas, Ackbar. 'Cosmopolitan De-scriptions: Shanghai and Hong Kong.' *Public Culture* 12, no. 3 (2000): 769-786.

Appadurai, Arjun. *Modernity at Large: Cultural Dimensions of Globalisation*. Minneapolis: The University of Minnesota Press, 1996.

Akutagawa Ryûnosuke 芥川龍之助. 'Honjo Ryôgoku'[本所両国]. *Akutagawa Ryûnosuke zenshû* [芥川龍之助全集], vol. 15, 3-39. Tokyo: Iwanami shoten, 1997.

—. 'Tôkyôjin' [東京人]. *Akutagawa Ryûnosuke zenshû* [芥川龍之助全集], vol. 10, 164-165. Tokyo: Iwanami shoten, 1996.

Boym, Svetlana. *The Future of Nostalgia*. New York: Basic Books, 2001.

Braster, Yomi. '"If We Could Remember Everything, We Would Be Able to Fly": Taipei's Cinematic Poetics of Demolition.' *Modern Chinese Literature and Culture* 15, no. 1 (2003): 29-61.

Chen, Yihe 陈犀禾 and Wang Yanyun 王艳云. 'Nostalgic Films and the Identity Construction of Shanghai Culture' [怀旧电影与上海文化身份的重构]". *Journal of Shanghai University* [上海大学学报] 13, no. 3 (2006): 39-44.

Chiao, Peggy. 'Great Changes in a Vast Ocean: Neither Tragedy nor Joy.' *Performing Arts Journal* 17, no. 2/3 (1995): 43-54.

Chow, Rey. *Ethics after Idealism: Theory, Culture, Ethnicity, Reading*. Bloomington: Indiana University Press, 1998.

Dai, Jinhua 戴锦华. 'Imagined Nostalgia' [想象的怀旧]. *Tianya* [天涯], no.1 (1997): 8-15.

Duara, Prasenjit. 'Local Worlds: The Poetics and Politics of the Native Place in Modern China.' *The South Atlantic Quarterly* 99, no. 1 (2000): 13-45.

Farrar, Margaret. 'Amnesia, Nostalgia, and the Politics of Place Memory.' Paper presented at the Western Political Science Association Meeting, San Diego, 2008.

Grossberg, Lawrence. *Cultural Studies in the Future Tense*. Durham: Duke University Press, 2010.

Hao, Zaijin 郝在今. 'A Tide of Urban Nostalgia' [都市怀旧情潮].' Lüye [绿叶], no. 1 (1996): 23-25.

Heidegger, Martin. *Poetry, Language, Thought*. Translated by Albert Hofstadter. New York: Harper & Row, 1975.

Huyssen, Andreas. 'Nostalgia for Ruins.' *Grey Room* (2006): 6-21.

Ishida Eiichirô 石田英一郎. *Nihon bunkaron* [日本文化論]. Tokyo: Chikuma shobo, 1969.

Jameson, Fredric. *Postmodernism, or, the Cultural Logic of Late Capitalism*. Durham: Duke University Press, 1991.

Karatani Kôjin. *The Origins of Modern Japanese Literature*. Translated by Brett de Bar. Durham: Duke University Press, 1993.

Kobayashi Hideo 小林秀雄. 'Kokyô o ushinatta bungaku' [故郷を失つた文学]. In *Kobayashi Hideo zenshû* [小林秀雄全集], vol. 3, Tokyo: Shinchosha, 1967.

Lee, Haiyan. 'The Other Chinese: Romancing the Folk in May Fourth Native Soil Fiction.' *Concentric: Literary and Cultural Studies* 33, no.2 (2007): 9-34.

Lowenthal, David. *The Past is a Foreign Country*. Cambridge: Cambridge University Press, 1985.

Lu, Hanchao. 'Nostalgia for the Future: The Resurgence of an Alienated Culture in China.' *Pacific Affairs* 75, no. 2 (2002): 169-186.

Michaels, Anne. *The Weight of Oranges / Miner's Pond*. Toronto: McClelland and Stewart, 1997.

Okuno Takeo 奥野健男. *Bungaku ni okeru genfûkei. Harappa dôkutsu no gensô* [文学における原風景. 原つぱ・洞窟の幻想]. Tokyo: Shueisha, 1972.

Robertson, Jennifer. '*Furusato* Japan: The Culture and Politics of Nostalgia.' *International Journal of Politics, Culture, and Society* 1, no. 4 (1988): 494-518.

Simmel, Georg. 'The Metropolis and Mental Life.' In *The Sociology of Georg Simmel*, edited and translated by Kurt H. Wolff, 410. New York: The Free Press, 1950.

Stein, Gertrude. *Everybody's Autobiography*. New York: Random House, 1937.

Sullivan, Michael. *The Arts of China*. Berkeley: University of California Press, 1984.

Takahashi Yoshitaka 高橋義孝. 'Genkôkei to genfûkei' [原光景と原風景]. *Shisô* □[思想], 653, 1978, pp. 27-35, p. 31.

Teo, Stephen. 'Wong Kar-wai's *In the Mood for Love*: Like a Ritual in Transfigured Time.' *Sense of Cinema* 13 (2001).

Thomas, Benjamin. *Le cinéma japonais d'aujourd'hui*. Rennes: Presses Universitaires de Rennes, 2009.

Tuan, Yi-fu. *Place and Space: The Perspective of Experience*. Minneapolis: University of Minnesota Press, 2001.

Urry, John. *Consuming Places*. London: Routledge, 1995.

Wang, Jing. 'Taiwan *Hsiang-t'u* Literature: Perspectives in the Evolution of a Literary Movement.' In *Chinese Fiction from Taiwan: Critical Perspectives*, edited by Jeannette L. Faurot, 43-70. Bloomington: University of Indian Press, 1980.

Wang, Yiyan. *Narrating China: Jia Pingwa and his Fictional World*. London: Routledge, 2005.

Williams, Raymond. *Marxism and Literature*. Oxford: Oxford University Press, 1977.

Ye Si (Leung Ping-kwan) 也斯. 'History and Gender in the Nostalgic Film Trend [怀旧电影潮流的历史与性别].' In *Hong Kong Culture* [香港文化]. Hong Kong: Hong Kong Arts Centre, 1995.

Yoshida Kenkô. *Essays in Idleness: The Tsurezuregusa of Kenkô*. Translated by Donald Keene. New York: Columbia University Press, 1967.

Yoshimi Shunya 吉見俊哉. *Toshi no doramaturugî : Tôkyô sakariba no shakaishi* [都市のドラマトゥルギー: 東京•盛り場の社会史]. Tokyo: Kobundo, 1987.

Yuriko Saito. 'The Japanese Aesthetics of Imperfection and Insufficiency.' *The Journal of Aesthetics and Art Criticism* 55, no. 4 (1997): 377-385.

Zhao, Jingrong 赵静蓉. 'The Three Faces of Modern Nostalgia' [现代怀旧的三张面孔].' *Literary Theory Study* [文艺理论研究], no. 1 (2003): 81-88.

Zhou, Zuoren 周作人. 'Locality and Literature' [地方与文艺].' In *Zhou Zuoren Sanwen (2)* [周作人散文 (二)]. Edited by Zhang Minggao 张明高 and Fan Qiao 范桥, 212-215. Beijing: Zhongguo guangbo dianshi chubanshe, 1992.

11. Femme Fatales and Male Narcissists: Shanghai Spectacle Narrated, Packaged and Sold

Lena Scheen

11.1. Wei Hui's *Shanghai Baby* and Ge Hongbing's *Sandbed*.

Wei Hui, *Shanghai Baby*	Ge Hongbing, *Sandbed*[1]
This street, which features in all the guidebooks to Shanghai for overseas visitors, follows international fashion closely, and prices are cheaper than anywhere else. […] Whenever I'm feeling down, like other girls I go to Huating Road, stroll from one end to the other, and buy up a storm. (85)	[…] whenever we passed Häagen-Dazs, Xiaomin would say we had to go in and enjoy a foreign sorbet; passing O'Malley's, we had to taste a pint of world-renowned Irish Guinness; while passing the Sea King Restaurant, both ladies would agree the Australian abalone tasted the best […]. (191)

Wei Hui, *Shanghai Baby*	Ge Hongbing, *Sandbed*[1]
YY's has two floors. The lower one, down a long staircase, houses the dance floor. The atmosphere in the room was joyous, full of alcohol, perfume, money, saliva, and hormones. (67)	Tonight they were playing *Trip-Hop*, such a bizarre sound that has the same uncontrollable effect as marijuana, making you crazy, delirious and boiling with excitement. (68)
The tip of his rum-soaked tongue teased my nipples, and then moved downward. He penetrated my protective labia with deadly accuracy, and located my budding clitoris. [...] I thought I could die and he would keep right on going, but then I climaxed with a sharp cry. (59-60)	My hand wandered from her shoulders over her collarbones, down the valley between her breasts, passing her smooth belly and further down to her pubic hair [...] Now I arrived into her secret core: in the midst of her trembling and shock I felt the deepest vibrations. (27-8)

Although we are taught not to judge a book by its cover, the covers of *Shanghai Baby* (1999) by Wei Hui (b. 1970) and *Sandbed* (2003) by Ge Hongbing (b. 1968) might move one to agree with cultural critic Zhu Dake's qualification of Ge Hongbing as 'a male Wei Hui'. The first thing that catches the eye is the women, with their similarly shaped eyes and mouths, slim faces, and half-naked bodies. Besides the suggestive titles ('sandbed' (沙床) seems to be a homophonic pun for 'go to bed' (上床)), the covers also seduce the reader with catchy sentences on love, sex and the city, such as 'A physical and spiritual experience from a woman to other women [...] an alternative love story set in the secret garden of Shanghai' (*Shanghai Baby*), and 'A mournful love experience; a sorrowful life story [...] Shanghai: my party of life and death, my secret grand banquet' (*Sandbed*).

The semi-autobiographies indeed share many similarities. In *Shanghai Baby* we follow the writer CoCo (after Coco Chanel) and her love affairs with the impotent drug addict Tian Tian and the married German businessman Mark; *Sandbed* tells the story of a terminally ill Christian, Professor Zhuge, and his love affairs with, among others, the student Xiaomin, widow Pei Zi and fitness instructor Luo Xiao. Both are set in Shanghai in 1999, and depict a globalising city in the midst of commercialisation and sexual liberation. Both portray hedonist characters delving into the modernising city, leading a cosmopolitan life of transnational sexual adventure and enjoying Western cultural products. Both largely take place in shopping streets, bars, nightclubs, bathrooms and bedrooms, making the city a sexualised space of intoxication and temptation that functions as a playground for sensory experience.

Contrary to the other works of art discussed in this volume, *Shanghai Baby* and *Sandbed* are evidently not political and/or critical works; rather than *disrupting* the spectacle of Shanghai – predominantly characterised by consumerism and frantic growth – they *reflect* the spectacle on many levels, as I will show in this chapter. '*Shanghai Baby* is spectacle,' Harry Kuoshu indeed argues, 'showing the advance of the McWorld in China, and indicating how a market-transmitted lifestyle is mounting the centre stage' (2005: 97). And Robin Visser, in her chapter in this volume, goes even further, stating that *Shanghai Baby* 'constitutes spectacle textually through humourless self-referentiality and seamless self-exoticisation'.

Taking *Shanghai Baby* and *Sandbed* as paradigms of the society of the spectacle, this chapter will scrutinise the tensions imposed on the individual by this society. How do the protagonists negotiate their identity in Shanghai's fast-changing cityscape that is moving towards a high capitalist mode? And how does this negotiation intersect with gender? Being subsumed by the ideologised space, do the protagonists merely behave as uncritical consumers whose lives are determined by fleeting coincidental events and thrills, or do they still act as self-determining agents? How do they deal with questions on moral agency? Are sex and consumption ends in themselves, or do the protagonists use sex and consumption as a means to the end of self-expression and/or searching the self?

Before addressing these questions, however, I will first briefly discuss the promotion and reception of *Shanghai Baby* and *Sandbed*, and then contextualise the novels' portrayal of the city as sexualised space in Shanghai's literary tradition, in which the trope of Shanghai as a seductive *femme fatale* is a recurrent trait.

Selling Her Body and Selling His Intellect

> When culture becomes nothing more than a commodity, it must also become the star commodity of the spectacular society.
> Guy Debord, *The Society of the Spectacle* (1967)

Interestingly, *Shanghai Baby* and *Sandbed* not only portray and reflect the society of the spectacle, they are themselves prime examples of cultural products *of* the society of the spectacle, in which bestsellers are produced by authors and publishers who effectively create an image of the novel and the author (her/himself) as part of their marketing strategy. For example, Ge Hongbing's novel was promoted as 'the first novel by a Stud Writer' (美男作家). Referring to this in an interview with Zhou Manzhen, Ge defensively claimed: 'I can understand the importance of promotion, in order to sell his melons a farmer still has to call out for customers, right?!' (2003: online). Moreover, Ge instigated a controversial public debate with Zhu Dake, who blamed Ge for 'running stark naked through the streets while bashfully covering his 'cheeks' (脸蛋) (note: not covering his 'private parts' (羞处)), 'proving' that all that was left of Chinese fiction was 'a spectacle of a fervent competition in taking off one's pants' (2003: online).

Wei Hui, meanwhile, created a big scandal during her novel's promotional tour in Chengdu: while wearing sexy clothing and blowing kisses to her male fans, she flirted with journalists and made provocative comments on established male Chinese authors. After one local tabloid published a picture of Wei Hui wearing a revealing dress next to an article that claimed Wei Hui had told the photographer to 'let them see the breasts of the Shanghai baby', the scandal escalated into a huge national media sensation, soon followed by her public catfight with the author Mian Mian over alleged plagiarism.

The sensation turned both novels into instant bestsellers in China, and *Shanghai Baby*, translated into 34 languages and having sold over 6 million copies in 48 countries, is one of the most-sold contemporary Chinese novels.[2] Moreover, the novels' conscious play with the blurring of the line between author and narrator fuels the sensation. The deliberate mystification starts with the covers of the novels, which define *Shanghai Baby* as a 'semi-autobiographical work' and *Sandbed* as a 'self-narrated biography'. As Carlos Rojas remarks on *Shanghai Baby*:

> This sense of being trapped in a fun-house of mirrors actually describes quite well the way in which both CoCo and the author Wei Hui find themselves sandwiched between layers of fictional identity: between their loosely autobiographical fictional protagonists, on the one hand, and the fictional extrapolations their readers make about the authors on the basis of reading their works, on the other. (2009: 275)

The various editions of *Shanghai Baby* all feature a picture of Wei Hui herself on their cover, reaffirming the biographical link with her novel and, arguably, the 'self-packaging' of her own body to sell her work.

Unsurprisingly, the novels' depictions of hedonism and promiscuity have often been criticised by readers, critics, and the authorities as a blatant celebration of transnational consumer capitalism. *Shanghai Baby* was soon labelled a 'slave to Western culture' and banned, 'with authorities burning 40,000 copies and instructing the state-media to never mention the author or the book again because of its sexually charged content' (Ian Weber 2002: 347). An established literary scholar himself, Ge Hongbing is criticised, in particular, by his colleagues from the academic world for succumbing to commercialism, displaying a lack of morality, and expressing a nihilist attitude to life. However, the discourse of domestic criticism strikingly shows how the gender of the author influences the perception of their works: while Wei Hui is said to be a bad example for Chinese women at large, Ge Hongbing is said to have tarnished the reputation of male *intellectuals*; while Wei Hui is accused of 'selling her body', Ge Hongbing is accused of 'selling his intellect'.

A Complicated Love Story: Shanghai and the *Femme Fatale*

'Me no worry, me no care, me go marry millionaire, if he die, me no cry, me go marry other guy', goes the rhyme 'Miss Shanghai', which children liked to sing during Shanghai's Treaty Port era (1842-1942). This provocative verse in 'Chinglish' is representative of the popular imagination of the 'modern girl' who emerged around the world in the first half of the 20th century. Just like her sisters in Tokyo, Paris, New York, or Johannesburg, Miss Shanghai was an independent, westernised, sexually and socially liberated young woman.

Since Shanghai is 'historically the most "foreign" Chinese city' and 'the quintessential symbol of modernity in China' (Lee 2005: 133), the Chinese version of the 'modern girl' or 'new woman' was readily identified as a woman from

11.2. The song 'Miss Shanghai', by cartoonist Friedrich Schiff (1908-1968; resident in Shanghai from 1930 until 1947). Courtesy: ®Pictures from History.

Shanghai, and even came to personify the city of Shanghai itself. Her fashionable clothes, open-mindedness, and wild lifestyle – all strongly influenced by foreign cultures – represented Shanghai's cosmopolitan image. However, as this openness was a side effect of colonial power, it simultaneously tainted the concept of the modern girl, giving it negative political connotations. In the words of Vivian Lee: 'In cinema, literature, and popular culture, images of women, especially those of liberated "modern girls", embody a modern sensibility informed by the complex, and sometimes contradictory, reactions of the Chinese toward foreign domination and the superiority of Western material culture in the colonial enclaves of China's treaty ports' (2005: 133).

One of the first works in which the modern city of Shanghai and the modern girl are fused is Wu Youru's (1839-1897) illustration series *One Hundred Shanghai Beauties* (1893), depicting beautiful Shanghai ladies in Victorian-style dresses, playing billiards or dining with knife and fork in a room with European furniture and fireplaces. The popularity of the series gave the modern girl a prominent position in commercial art, of which the 'calendar posters' (月份牌) are probably the most famous. As Madeleine Dong writes: 'While the Modern Girl was represented in advertisements as a beguiling icon of the glamour of modern life and happiness ostensibly achievable through consumption of industrial commodities, she also often appeared as a mystery and was seen as a threatening figure [...] a woman as baffling as the modern city Shanghai itself' (2008: 194-5). In addition, the images of these sexy women promoting cigarettes, silk or whisky came under attack from leftist intellectuals who strongly advocated the emancipation of women and fiercely condemned how commerce turned the modern woman into a commodified object of the consumer's gaze.

In short, the image of the modern girl was complex and contradictory: a symbol of colonial repression, a site of problematic modernity, or the mere embodiment of 'the promised pleasures of industrial society', in Tani Barlow's (2008: 288) words. However, in all these readings she evokes both fascination and anxiety in the spectator, who is unable to 'conquer' her either literally or figuratively. It is precisely this disturbing power that puts her squarely in the tradition of the classic *femme fatale*, about whom Elisabeth Bronfen writes:

> The *femme fatale* has resiliently preserved her position within our image repertoire precisely because she forces the spectator to decide whether she acts as an empowered modern subject or is simply to be understood as the expression of an unconscious death drive, indeed, whether we are to conceive of her as an independent figure or merely as a figure of projection for masculine anxiety. (2004: 114)

In Modernist Chinese fiction, particularly in the writings of the *New Perceptionists*, the seductive *femme fatale* became a recurrent metaphor of urban modernity. Take, for example, the narrator in the story 'Men Taken as Leisure Items' by Mu Shiying (1912-1940), who remarks: 'Rongzi, what a modern girl, thriving on stimulation and speed! You are a mixture of *jazz*, machinery, speed, urban culture, American flavor, modern beauty' (cited in Des Forges 2007: 148). The plots of many of these *New Perceptionists* stories are remarkably similar: first the male protagonist falls for the exotic, modern woman, but then she deceives him or simply remains unattainable, arguably revealing the writers' ambivalent attitude towards modernising Shanghai; they are intrigued by the speed and spectacle of the alluring city and pursue a cosmopolitan lifestyle, but at the same time, they see the city as a source of moral decay, where Western values threaten to erase traditional Chinese values.

When the cosmopolitan *femme fatale* – whose seductive power forms a constant threat toward men – made her comeback in 1990s Shanghai fiction, she was characterised by precisely these same features of foreignness and modernity. What is more, regardless of women's changed social status, these *femmes fatales* trigger responses that, intriguingly, are comparable to those that their sisters in colonial times received, ranging from their celebration as avant-garde feminist characters to their condemnation as empty-headed lust objects, selling their bodies for fame. As Dai Jinhua argues:

Facing rapid social changes during the transitional period and encountering the fetishism of money, desire, and survival and status anxieties, Chinese male writers and film-makers inadvertently adopted another strategy, once again transplanting their personal and social crisis and angst onto the female roles. The 'new' image of Women, which was once a sensation during the 1930s in Chinese urban literature, began to reappear in contemporary Chinese culture. (2002: 132; translation by Jonathan Noble)

However, Dai does not mention that nowadays, many female authors have themselves adopted the trope. Hence, the *femme fatale* is no longer exclusively a product of the male gaze, but is often the one who is observing and speaking. The author Wei Hui and her fictional personage CoCo are, of course, a telling example: 'I figured I'd already attracted the eyes of plenty men with my dancing – like a princess in a Middle Eastern harem, and a bewitching Medusa, too. Men are often desperate to mate [with] a bewitching female who will eat them alive, like a black widow spider' (68-9).

The Screaming Body of a *Shanghai Baby*

'I call her CoCo, as in the movie *Shanghai Baby*, because she was all herself in that movie.' Thus comments 'Weallhope?' on the weblog of the actress Bai Ling (b. 1966), who plays the role of CoCo in the movie adaptation of *Shanghai Baby*. Many approving comments of other fans follow, one of them quoting an 'Italian university blog': 'It is clear that *Shanghai Baby* is primarily a film on Bai Ling, a restless actress of sensual charm who has also managed to win many Western viewers. [Bai Ling] appears in an indissoluble identify [sic] with the heroine of the novel and literally gives all of herself to the spectator'.[3]

In an incessant, spiralling relation, Bai Ling is thus identified (and identifies herself) with the movie's character, CoCo, who is a representation of the novel's character, who is in turn identified with the author, Wei Hui, who in turn identifies herself with her own fictional characters; in other words, the 'original' has dissolved in its numerous 'counterfeits'. For example, even though Bai Ling is originally from Chengdu, she recurrently refers to herself as a 'Shanghai Baby' on her weblog, just like the author Wei Hui does, on whom Rojas notes: 'This process of recursive projection and identification is clearly evident, for instance, in the author's personal webpage, which combines aphorisms from Wei Hui's fictional works and pictures of the author herself in sexually provocative poses reminiscent of her own fictional protagonists' (2009: 275-6).

Notably, the sexually-charged nude pictures and 'live chat sessions' on Bai Ling's weblog portray an even more provocative and daring version of CoCo/Wei Hui. Likewise, at the movie promotion session in Cannes, Bai Ling created a remarkably similar scandal to that caused by Wei Hui in Chengdu, by wearing a dress which was even more revealing than Wei Hui's. In other words, as Wei Hui 'models herself on the larger-than-life fictional personas of her fictional protagonists', to again quote Rojas (2009: 276), one could argue that Bai Ling models herself on larger-than-life mimetic personas of Wei Hui/CoCo, accelerating 'this sense of being trapped in a fun-house of mirrors' (275) to the extreme.

In one of the pictures on her blog, the sexy, half-naked Bai Ling is surrounded by a crowd of male photographers – her sensual pose and smile reminding us of Miss Shanghai in the illustration of the old song (figure 11.2) – featuring as the quintessence of the seductive, modern woman turning herself into a spectacle for the male gaze. This is not to say, however, that she is no more than 'an encoded figure who exists only as the phantasmic emanation of others', as Bronfen (2004: 114) remarks in her discussion on the *femme fatale*, but 'rather a separate subject who has agency and is responsible for her decisions'. Likewise, one can read the mantric tagline of Bai Ling's weblog, Naked Seduction, as a (poorly written) expression of a Chinese immigrant struggling to survive in the American capitalist jungle, or as the voice of a desiring and empowering subject whose agency is not based on resistance or disruption of the system, but manipulation:

> Yes it's true this is what I do this is what I do the best to seduce you with the nakedness naked emotion naked heart naked mind and naked confession naked naked soul and naked compassion I seduce you with the pure naked me and my naked love I seduce you like a woman I seduce you like your best friend I seduce you like you I seduce you with the distance only on the other side of the computer [...] Seduce with the nakedness with danger [...] I am your mirror only reflects you [...].

By presenting herself as 'your mirror', Bai Ling attracts the eye of the spectator only to turn the objectifying gaze back to the spectator himself, who is now drawn into the 'fun-house of mirrors', where depth and meaning have disappeared for what Jean Baudrillard would call 'the sacred horizon of appearances' (2001: 152), and what he regards as the domain of seduction: 'Is it seducing, or being seduced, that is seductive? Yet being seduced is still the best way of seducing. It is an endless strophe. There is no active or passive in seduction, no subject or object, or even interior or exterior: it plays on both sides of the border with no border separating the sides' (163).

Inside and outside the novel, the movie and the weblogs, the game of seduction is played out on many levels: between the protagonist and her fictional male admirers, between the author/actress and their audiences, and also between the fictional characters and the city of Shanghai. Take, for example, the DVD cover of the movie *Shanghai Baby*, which shows the mini-skirted Bai Ling paired with the flickering neon-lit Oriental Pearl TV Tower; like two seductive bodies – one phallic, one ostentatiously feminine – competing for attention. The cover immediately reminds one of the closing scene of *Shanghai Baby's* second chapter, entitled 'Modern Metropolis':

> Standing on the roof, we looked at the silhouettes of the buildings lit up by the streetlights on both sides of the Huangpu River, especially the Oriental Pearl TV Tower, Asia's tallest. Its long, long steel column pierces the sky, proof of the city's phallus worship. The ferries, the waves, the night-dark

grass, the dazzling neon lights and incredible structures – all these signs of prosperity had nothing to do with us, the people who live among them. A car accident can kill us, but the city's prosperous, invincible silhouette is like a planet, in perpetual motion, eternal.

When I thought about that, I felt insignificant as an ant on the ground.

But the thought didn't affect our mood as we stood on the top of that historic building. As the sound of the hotel's septuagenarian jazz band came and went, we surveyed the city, yet distanced ourselves from it with love talk. I liked to undress right down to my bra and pants in the moist breeze from the Huangpu. Maybe I have a complex about underwear, or I'm a narcissist or an exhibitionist or something, but I hoped this would somehow stimulate Tiantian's desire.

'Don't do that,' said Tiantian painfully, turning his head away.

But I kept undressing, like a stripper. A tiny blue flower began to burn my skin, and that odd sensation made me blind to my beauty, my self, my identity. Everything I did was designed to create a strange new fairy tale, a fairy tale meant just for me and the boy I adored.

The boy sat entranced against the railing, sad but graceful, watching the girl dance in the moonlight. Her body was smooth as a swan's, yet powerful as a leopard's. Every feline crouch, leap and turn was elegant yet madly seductive.

'Please try. Come into my body like a real lover, my darling, try.'

'No, I can't,' he said, curling himself into a ball.

'Well then, I'll jump off the roof,' laughed the girl, grabbing the rail as if to climb over it. He caught her and kissed her. But broken desires couldn't find a way. Love was a miracle the flesh couldn't copy, and the ghosts defeated us... Dust covered us, closing my throat and my love's.

Three A.M. Curled up on the big comfortable bed, I watched Tiantian [...] Lying beside my love, again and again I used my fingers to masturbate, making myself fly, fly into the mire of orgasm. And in my mind's eye, I saw both crime and punishment. (13-15)

Significantly, the scene takes place on the rooftop of one of the symbols of old, cosmopolitan Shanghai, the Peace Hotel on the Bund, with the sound of the old jazz band playing in the background, and a beautiful view over the symbol of new, global Shanghai: Pudong with the prominent Oriental Pearl TV Tower landmark. Although the feminine purple 'pearls' of the TV Tower have often been cited as an example of Shanghai's feminine image, in CoCo's eyes the tower symbolises 'the city's phallus worship', seemingly critiquing Shanghai's patriarchal culture.

Michel de Certeau has famously described the 'voluptuous pleasure' and 'ecstasy' of viewing a cityscape from a high spot: 'It transforms the bewitching world by which one was "possessed" into a text that lies before one's eyes. It allows one to read it, to be a solar Eye, looking down like a god' (1988: 92). Looking out over the 'rapturous sight' of the New Bund, 'the only cityscape in China which really works', as journalist Christopher Lockwood has described it (cited in Jansson and Lagerkvist 2009: 34), CoCo portrays herself as 'madly seductive', like the city itself, and even tries to compete with it by enticing her lover Tiantian to turn his gaze from the skyline to her. In fact, on the first page of *Shanghai Baby*, CoCo already makes it clear that this is her main goal in life: 'Every morning when I open my eyes, I think of what kind of amazing thing I can do to attract the eye of people. I imagine myself one day in the future rising into the sky to burst upon the city like gorgeous fireworks. It has almost become my reason to live, the reason that makes it worth living on' (1999: 1). So, while the *femme fatale* CoCo represents the city itself, as the 'Shanghai Baby' of the novel's name, she tries to surpass its allure at the same time: 'the neon streetlights were no more dazzling than I, the ATMs no richer' (178).

Standing on the roof, however, CoCo is even more confronted with the absorbing power of the overwhelming and ever-changing city, making her feel 'insignificant as an ant'. CoCo tries to escape this feeling and to transcend the city by an exhibitionistic self-enactment. However, since CoCo's seductive performance is a reproduction of the popular image of Shanghai, which is itself already a reproduction of an image, she arguably transforms herself into an empty simulacrum, in the Baudrillardan sense, 'never again exchanging for what is real, but exchanging in itself, in an uninterrupted circuit without reference or circumference' (2001: 173).

CoCo has become such an intrinsic part of the capital-driven society that even a private act such as tempting her boyfriend to make love to her is changed into an advertisement show, in which she commodifies her own body by promoting it as a market product: 'smooth as a swan's, yet powerful as a leopard's', and later in the novel she tellingly says, 'I was like a credit card with a healthy line of credit which could be used now and paid for later' (178). Interestingly, CoCo's depiction of her own body almost seems a reference to Mu Shiying's depiction of Rongzi's body, in the earlier-quoted story 'Men Taken as Leisure Items': 'She has a snake's body, a cat's head, a mixture of softness and danger'.

So, on the one hand, the female perspective in *Shanghai Baby* converts the classic *femme fatale* from an object subjected to male desire and the male gaze to a desiring agent forcing the male gaze towards herself, while simultaneously herself gazing at men, something that is reinforced by Tiantian's 'unmanly' impotence. This is also what Sheldon Lu notes on the works of contemporary Shanghai writers:

> The body, sexuality, seductiveness, and manipulation are in part what endow the female characters with agency and power over the male. [...] In their erotic longings, the city is eroticised, men are eroticised. [...] She uses her wit, body, looks, and sexuality to seduce men, sleep with them, move into their apartments, live off their money, and control them. Men, Chinese or foreign, become their vehicles in the pursuit of capitalist consumption and entertainment. (2008: 176-7)

On the other hand, she is arguably still represented as an object to the consumer's gaze, albeit an 'active' object 'selling itself'. Instead of revealing her inner life or a vulnerable side of herself to Tiantian, CoCo turns herself into a spectacle, reproducing a clichéd image of female sexuality to such an extent that it becomes simulation, or, in the words of Baudrillard, 'the ecstasy of the real': 'Ecstasy is that quality specific to each body that spirals in on itself until it has lost all meaning, and thus radiates as pure and empty form' (2001: 190).

By writing her novel on Shanghai, which appears to be the novel *Shanghai Baby* itself, CoCo gains a form of control over the city and wants 'to create a separate reality, *more real* than the one we live in' (24; italics added), in her own words. Yet again, her 'passion of intensification, of escalation, of mounting power, of ecstasy, of whatever quality so long as [...] it becomes superlative' (2001: 190), to cite Baudrillard a last time, is expressed in her wish for her novel to 'explode like fireworks and give meaning to our existence' (64): 'There should be a road show with parties throughout China to promote the book. I'd wear a backless black dress and a grotesque mask. The floor would be littered with confetti made from my book, and everyone would be dancing madly on it' (66).

In the roof scene, we also see the spectacle embodied in CoCo when the narrator tells us that all she does is 'designed to create a strange new fairy tale', immediately switching to a fairytale style by changing from the first person to the third person, referring to 'the boy' and 'the girl'. In this way, the narrator transforms CoCo into an interchangeable flat, nameless character that has become an intrinsic part of the spectacle. One could argue, conclusively, that while CoCo laments that the city's 'signs of prosperity had nothing to do with us', in fact, she represents herself as one of these very signs.

Interestingly, the passage ends with CoCo's guilt about masturbating after her fruitless attempts to seduce Tiantian. The new female voice that has been given to the *femme fatale* has apparently not been able to free herself from the moral judgments once voiced by her male narrators and/or spectators. To make things worse, she even fails to sexually conquer her admirer, and has to settle for self-stimulation, which mirrors her previous performance. However, Tiantian is still 'fatally attracted' to CoCo, which is attested by his deadly overdose; or, in the narrator's own words: 'My life would always be a revolver of desire, capable of going off and killing at any moment' (248).

Whispering Souls on a *Sandbed*

The following passage in *Sandbed* is remarkably similar to the roof scene in *Shanghai Baby*:

> That evening Zhang Xiaomin came over, bringing some bread and fresh vegetables, and a six-pack of beer. After dinner we climbed up on the roof to drink our beer and chat.
> Thanks to Shanghai's 'from flat to pitched' roof-renovation project, my building's rooftop now had red colored tiles and they had even installed neon lighting. Sitting on the sloping roof, we viewed the pineapple-shaped dome of Shanghai Circus World's glowing orange in the distance. Nearby the elevated

highway of Gonghe Road meandered like a luminous ribbon past our feet.

There were no stars, but a pleasant wind was blowing. Watching the autumn wind wash over Zhang Xiaomin's body, now swirling her hair, now lifting her skirt, it might have been the beer talking, but I couldn't help laughing out loud: 'The wind is doing what I dare not!' Zhang Xiaomin absentmindedly smoothed down the hem of her skirt: 'You're not as sweet as the wind, I'll let the wind do things you can't.' (66)

Again, a woman's seductive body is placed against the backdrop of alluring Shanghai, the main difference being that this time, the male character is rejected by his seductress, albeit in a playful way. The young student Xiaomin is, in fact, in love with her professor, Zhuge, and tries to win his interest by lying that she has a boyfriend. Although Zhuge is just 30 years old, he repeatedly emphasises their age difference and speaks of 'people of your generation'. In this way, Xiaomin is represented as the young modern girl whose tempting flirtations remain innocent, although never completely free from potential threat: 'She was shy and reserved, but mischievous and cunning at the same time' (5).

Even though Xiaomin's position is subordinate to Zhuge's, she is still the one who takes the initiative and sets the limits. Remarkably, Zhuge does not seem to have any influence on the course of their relationship, as Xiaomin regularly comes to his home uninvited (climbing through his window when he is not at home), sleeping in his bed when she feels like it, and eventually staying for a long time until she decides for herself it is time to move in with her new boyfriend. Before Xiaomin leaves, however, she begs Zhuge to make love to her, because she wants 'to offer her virginity to the man she loves'. Zhuge refuses her wish, which is the only time throughout the novel he seems to make a decisive choice in their relationship.

This is a recurrent feature of *Sandbed*: the male-narcissistic Zhuge plays a rather passive role and all women – as true *femmes fatales* – seduce him. Eventually, however, the women turn into self-sacrificing admirers of Zhuge, which ostensibly casts him in the role of an *homme fatale*, albeit a passive one, whose fatal attractiveness is only enhanced by his passivity, or more precisely, his implicit, morally motivated hesitation to accept the offer they make of their bodies: presumably, this is meant to portray him as protecting them from himself.

This male-chauvinist view of sexual and love relationships in *Sandbed* is disturbingly common in contemporary Chinese fiction and cinema, and reflects 'the post-revolution and pro-market nature of China's gender politics', in the words of Zhong Xueping: 'Increasingly, women are shown as emotional beings whose reason for existence depends on whether or not men love them' (2007: 303). Indeed, the women in Zhuge's life are only portrayed from the perspective of their love and/or admiration for Zhuge. In their role as Other they do not function as equal, independent subjects, but merely as alter egos, each woman representing another side of Zhuge, who either complements or reaffirms Zhuge's self-image.

Whereas works by female writers in general, and *Shanghai Baby* in particular, have repeatedly been criticised for their narcissist tendency, the male narcissism of Zhuge that permeates Ge's entire novel is rarely mentioned. While I would argue that CoCo's own declarations – 'Narcissism is probably my dominant vice' (145) and 'I am falling in love with the "I" in my novel' (cited in Rojas 2009b: 275) – have a humorous, self-ironising side to them, Zhuge's self-love is matched only by his ostentatious self-hatred: 'A nothingness [like me] can never love another person; a nothingness that regrets everything and doesn't believe in anything. He also doesn't deserve to get anything, of course. The only thing he will get in the end is nothingness as well' (84). However, in the course of the novel, it becomes clear that Ge's self-contempt stems from the same origin as his self-love, as they are both manifestations of his self-obsession.

At the same time, however, I am aware of Bonnie McDougall's warning that 'self-projection in fiction by Chinese writers and their audience's tolerance for authorial narcissism' is a persistent feature in Chinese fiction, and that non-native readers therefore should be cautious in their understanding of sentiments such as 'self-justification, self-deception, self-pity, self-aggrandisement, self-importance, self-praise, self-satisfaction, self-deception, self-indulgence and self-glorification' (2003: 11 and 46). If we read the self in *Sandbed* 'not necessarily [as] the "self" of the individual but the "self" as a member of the particular social group to which they belong', to continue with McDougall's argument (2003: 95), the terminally ill character Zhuge arguably serves as an allegory for the struggle of Chinese intellectuals with contemporary society.

This reading could also explain Ge's choice of the uncommon two-character last name, Zhuge (诸葛; of which the second character *ge* (葛) is the same as Ge Hongbing's family name), which will remind any Chinese reader of the famous chancellor during the Three Kingdoms, Zhuge Liang (诸葛亮, 181–234). Not only is he regarded as one of the most accomplished military strategists and statesmen, but, more importantly, he is also specifically well known for his reputation as an intelligent and learned scholar. The protagonist's name can thus be read as an indication of both Ge Hongbing's identification with the historical figure and the protagonist's function as a representation of Chinese male intellectuals.

In this sense, I would argue that *Sandbed* should be placed in the domestic 'widespread and powerful' tradition of self-loathing in modern Chinese literature that 'satisfies a need to explain China's woeful modern history, while at the same time reaffirming a prevalent sense of national uniqueness', as Geremie Barmé observes, and, 'from the early 1990s onward, following the nation's increased economic growth, there has been a new twist in this tradition of self-loathing. […] Consumerism as the ultimate revolutionary action is seen by many as playing a redemptive role in national life, for it enables people to remake themselves not through some abstract national project but through the self-centred power of possession' (1995: 222 and 227).

In *Sandbed*, Zhuge initially seems to adapt to China's contemporary society of transnational consumer capitalism, but his worsening illness is almost immediately accompanied by a growing disillusionment. At first, Zhuge retreats from the outside world by creating a little male utopia at home where he peacefully lives with Xiaomin and Pei Zi: 'The Shanghai of February was cold, but our mood was only getting better; while Zhang Xiaomin did the shopping, washing and cleaning, Pei Zi did the cooking and the dishes' (189-90). Furthermore, Zhuge repeatedly reveals his increasing aversion towards China's consumer society, such as in the following witty depiction of their weekends:

> Let me also tell you about our weekend activities. These were generally decided by a democratic vote of the entire electorate of the three of us, but usually resulted in a two-to-one majority in favour of shopping expeditions, and since participation in the electoral process implies acceptance of the will of the majority, I was always obliged to go along. I always ended up strolling the streets until twelve at night, dead tired, but if you still hadn't actually bought anything, then it was crucial to conceal any hint of discontent, since after the slightest sign of frustration you would find yourself on the spot, and the shopping expedition, which was just about to end, would immediately change into a fanatic, marathon shopping spree that went on till dawn, with the cost of the exercise reverting to the dissatisfied party [...]. (190)

In the original, the sentence from 'I always ended up [...]' goes on for thirteen lines (see the passage starting with 'whenever we passed Häagen-Dazs [...]' at the very beginning of this chapter), summing up all kinds of products they would end up buying. The lengthy summation of foreign-brand consumption products evokes in the reader the same sense of tiredness Zhuge is feeling and reveals the absurdity of contemporary consumption society.

The one female character that does not follow the pattern of transforming from a seductress into a self-sacrificing admirer of Zhuge, but fully matches the classic *femme fatale* as a metaphor for the city of Shanghai, is Luo Xiao, Zhuge's fitness instructor, about whom the narrator remarks that 'just looking at her made me realise that this kind of physical condition is the most charming of all beauties, the very fountainhead of sex appeal' (152). After their first gym lesson, Luo Xiao flirtatiously asks Zhuge out for dinner and changes into the kind of outfit worn by a sexy Shanghai business women: 'She was wearing a high-collared tight-fitting sweater, a very smart, business-like skirt and red high-heeled shoes'. In the restaurant, Luo Xiao also shows her independence when she orders the dishes, instead of having them conventionally ordered by the man. Her choice reveals her sophisticated taste: 'king scallops, Australian lobster, a plate of grouper, taro roots, and a bottle of white wine to wash it down'. During their conversation, Luo Xiao and Zhuge discover they share an interest in classical music and philosophy, and Luo Xiao has even read some of Zhuge's academic books.

After dinner, Zhuge continues to submissively follow his seductress when she passes him the keys of her Buick car and orders him to drive them to her home – 'I like watching men drive' (159) – where they soon end up having sex, with Luo Xiao still being the one who seduces and controls: 'Luo Xiao had taken a condom, sheathed me with it, and was already straddling me. She had somehow changed the music to Rachmaninov's *Paganini Variations*, and after a moment of calm as the opening theme was presented simply, for the second time that day, she put me through my paces, this time with a short version of the Kama Sutra – not surprisingly, mostly the female-dominant positions' (161). But straight after they have sex, a post-coital tristesse overwhelms him: 'My heart was in a black wilderness, without a single guiding light to show the way'.

Zhuge's feeling of loss and emptiness after having 'conquered' his seductress strikingly reminds one of the disenchantment experienced by the protagonists in the works of the *New Perceptionists*: initially intrigued and mesmerised by the alluring modern city of Shanghai, embodied in the *femme fatale*, the male characters eventually fear her potential danger and either leave her or meet with an unfortunate end. In the case of Luo Xiao and Zhuge, Zhuge becomes increasingly reluctant to have sex in general and sex without love in particular, so when Luo Xiao tries to seduce him again in the novel, she fails. In this way, Zhuge's disgust with consumerist urban life seems to be mirrored in his sex life with the woman who represents this life the most. Zhuge tellingly describes his loss of desire as 'an empty ringing of his inner self' (163): the loss of self looms larger than the loss of desire, and the *femme fatale* loses out.

An Imagined Love Affair: Conclusions

Imagine CoCo and Zhuge inhabiting the same novel and falling in love. One day they go out for a drink; sitting in a quiet little corner of a pub in one of Shanghai's many bustling streets, they have an intimate chat. What would they talk about? If we merge lines spoken by CoCo in a dialogue with Tiantian, with (parts of) a letter from Zhuge to Pei Zi – both in their original order – their imaginary conversation might look like this:

CoCo:
> *I will h-a-t-e you.*

Zhuge:
> *I know you hate me, but the one who hates me most in this world is not you but I myself. [...] Now you hate me, but your hate can't last forever. When you find a new life, you won't hate me anymore. To be honest, I'm just an insignificant, passing visitor in your life. I'm the only one who can persist in my self-loathing; I'll have to live with that the rest of my life.*

CoCo:
> *I'm not going to bullshit you. In one word, you're degenerate.*

Zhuge:
> *You may hate me, but I know that your hate for me is finite. One day, you'll get bored of hating me, so I don't take your hatred too seriously. I can't take finite things too seriously, just as I can't take this finite life we lead too seriously. [...]*
> *Today when I was having lunch in the canteen, I told people that I was sick and that I had been having a stomachache for days. Then I told them about the dead body I had seen, how it had been lying in the middle of the road. That the police had put his leather jacket over his face, and that there was a pool of blood at his side. How his motorcycle stood at the side of the road, completely intact, while the crash had killed the man. You will probably ask*

'and then, what happened then?' There is no then. The conversation stopped here.

CoCo:

What are we talking about, for God's sake? Don't go on. Why do we have to talk about something so horrible here and now? Don't tell me about life and death, love and hate [the self and the essential self]. We're alive together, aren't we? If there is something about our life, get specific: I don't get the washing clean enough, I talk in my sleep, my novel isn't profound enough, it's utter rubbish – whatever. OK! I can change; I can try to do things perfectly. But for heaven's sake, don't say such horrible things...

Zhuge:

By now you should understand me, understand that when I say 'love does not exist', I don't mean that I don't want love, but rather that I am incapable of love. [...] People who can truly love are rare, but there are a few in this world: this person from Nazareth in ancient times and Albert Schweitzer, he wrote a book called Reverence for Life *that I would like you to read, but who else? Most of them can't even love themselves, how could they possibly love someone else? [...] Today I place my hopes in compassion, compassion for all the myriad things in the natural world. Compassion is a far nobler feeling than love. [...] Are you interested in the poet Haizi? How did Haizi say it? He said 'Elder Sister, tonight I am thinking only of you, I'm not thinking about humankind!' What an arrogant poet, he makes it his obligation to guard humanity, but he consciously relinquishes his duty to take a night off, thinking about his sister; how difficult is that?*

CoCo:

Whoever said that can drop dead! Don't read those books any more. You need to be among living beings. You need to do more physical work. My dad often says: 'work makes a person healthy'. You need sunlight and grass, and dreams of happiness and all the joy that goes with them.

(*Shanghai Baby*: 157-158; *Sandbed*: 57-61)

What we can hear in this dialogue are two positions, two attitudes to life in contemporary Shanghai. Zhuge's indulgence in self-pity and his fatalistic attitude – 'one can best just wait patiently, that which will come is bound to come, that which must go, will go' (65) – contrasts sharply with that of CoCo, whose pursuit of agency and self-determination helps her achieve her ultimate goal of becoming a famous writer.

Zhuge is more of an 'inner-motivated' character with a focus on 'eternal truths', which makes him feel incessantly misunderstood and disparaging about himself, people and the world. He seems to be in the clutches of a sort of world-weary cynicism, were it not for the morality he so applauds in Jesus and Albert Schweitzer. Although his belief that compassion is the major motivator of moral expression, Zhuge's compassion is mainly directed at humanity in general and at himself, but not at his intimates, as the reference to Haizi demonstrates. For all his self-loathing, Zhuge is rather obsessed with himself, and his moral consciousness seldom transforms itself into palpable, outward agency. As Zhuge explains himself to Pei Zi: 'I would rather take responsibility for the entire world, than having to take responsibility for one person' (58).

CoCo is precisely the other way around: an 'outer-motivated' character who always retains the initiative. While not reflecting as much on moral questions, CoCo does act morally when she is confronted with friends in need. For example, when Tiantian is away and CoCo is enjoying her time alone writing her novel and meeting her lover Mark, CoCo is not plagued by feelings of guilt for cheating; but, as soon as she hears Tiantian is in trouble, she travels to him to take him home and care for him. Remarkably, the women surrounding Zhuge show the same caring devotion, so in this respect *Sandbed* shares the same mixture of modern and traditional ethics and values that Sabina Knight identifies in *Shanghai Baby*: 'The novel reinforces both liberal and Confucian values as the characters reinvest in personal projects and intimate, particularistic relations in response to market transitions that compromise earlier expectations of collective solidarity' (2006: 243).

In short, where Zhuge could best be characterised as an outsider who observes his surroundings and reflects on reality, CoCo wants to experiment and, in her own words, 'suck dry the juice of life like a leech, including its secret happiness and hurt, spontaneous passion and eternal longing' (88). While Zhuge dwells on the absurdity of daily life in contemporary Shanghai – 'in this city people are either busy chopping large beams into wood chips or pasting wood chips into large beams' (161) – CoCo celebrates the chances it offers her and pragmatically uses the city as a source of inspiration for her novel.

For example, when CoCo retreats into her apartment, she does this to create another world by writing her novel, whereas Zhuge retreats 'to ponder humanity', reminding one of what Knight identifies in the works of 1980s avant-garde authors: 'In general, the greater the focus on interior monologue, subjective perception, and impressionism, the more disempowered the characters become. They reflect on the world and their relation to it but often conclude that they are too crippled by their recent experiences to act' (2006: 216). Unlike the characters in these avant-garde works, however, the younger Zhuge is not traumatised by the Cultural Revolution (1966-1976). Instead, his defeatism derives from his fatal disease that constantly reminds him of the temporality of life: 'This despair didn't come from outside, it came from inside. I know life has an end and death can always come. I can't do anything against it, I can't make it better or make it worse. I can only wait for it, let it arrive while I'm waiting, let it transform from a premonition into a reality, let it stealthily roam in the underworld until it violently storms over me' (241).

Ironically, it is not until the very end of the novel that Zhuge appears as a true self-determining agent when he decides to no longer wait for death, but to end his own life: 'There isn't any person in this world that can make a decision for you, you have to make all decisions by yourself and take responsibility for yourself. [...] Tell me, what could be more important than deciding one's own fate?' (241). It is Pei Zi, however, who has to perform the action for Zhuge by removing the compression bandage around his thigh that stops his artery from bleeding. In addition, Pei Zi decides, against the will of Zhuge, to slash her throat with a stiletto so she will die before him and does not have to witness Zhuge's death.

Hence, even at the final moment of Zhuge's life, he is powerlessly surrendered to a woman's initiative.

CoCo's story ends with a new beginning: after the successful publication of her novel she leaves for Germany on Halloween: 'I like Halloween, with its romantic fantasy, the way it uses the artifice of putting on a mask and pretending to be someone else to chase away the rotten smell of death' (255). As the city of Shanghai itself – driven by the slogan 'every year it looks new and every three years there is a tremendous change' – she is ready for yet another transformation of her self-image, yet another romantic fantasy. While CoCo's fear of death comes from fear of boredom (88), Zhuge fears death because it confronts him with the insignificance of the individual. In his quest for an 'authentic' self, Zhuge is unwilling to wear a mask and unable 'to chase away the rotten smell of death'. His story ends definitively, with his deepest fear: he dies.

In conclusion, Shanghai's embrace of consumerism has confronted writers with the dilemma of being trapped between commercial success and scholarly recognition; between an attempt to critique contemporary society, and dependence on that very society for their success. In addition, women writers seeking to attack male-dominated society – or at least conquer an equal social position – by expressing female sexual desire, risk turning *themselves* into a commodified object of male desire and/or the consumer's gaze. While the sensational bestsellers under discussion can arguably be described as 'star commodities of the spectacular society', to paraphrase Debord (1967), they simultaneously reveal the tensions imposed on the individual, and how the protagonists respond with a frantic search for self. In the final analysis, for Wei Hui's CoCo, this appears to be predominantly a quest for (female) identity – *Who am I?*, and for Ge Hongbing's Zhuge, an existential search – *Why am I?* Needless to say, both questions remain unanswered.

Notes

1. Unless otherwise indicated, all quotations come from Ge Hongbing 2003 and Wei Hui 2001 (translation by Bruce Humes).
2. Source: Zhu Hongjun 2003 and Shuyu Kong 2010: 137.
3. Online at http://ling-bai.blogspot.com/2009/05/you-abstracted-me-yes.html (accessed 19 July 2010).

References

Barlow, Tani. 'Buying In: Advertising and the Sexy Modern Girl Icon in Shanghai in the 1920s and 1930s.' In *The Modern Girl Around the World: Consumption, Modernity, and Globalization*, edited bij The Modern Girl around the World Research Group, 288-316. Durham: Duke University Press, 2008.

Barmé, Geremie. 'To Screw Foreigners Is Patriotic: China's Avant-Garde Nationalist.' *The China Journal*, no. 34 (1995): 209-34.

Baudrillard, Jean. *Selected Writings*. CA: Stanford University Press, 2001.

Bronfen, Elisabeth. 'Femme Fatale: Negotiations of Tragic Desire.' *New Literary History* 35, no. 1 (2004): 103-16.

Dai, Jinhua. *Cinema and Desire: Feminist Marxism and Cultural Politics in the Work of Dai Jinhua*. London: Verso Books, 2002.

De Certeau, Michel. *The Practice of Everyday Life, Volume 1*. Berkeley: University of California Press, 1988.

Debord, Guy. *The Society of the Spectacle*. Translated by Donald Nicholson-Smith. New York: Zone Books, 1994.

Des Forges, Alexander. *Mediasphere Shanghai: The Aesthetics of Cultural Production*. Honolulu, HI: University of Hawaii Press, 2007.

Dong, Madeleine Yue. 'Who Is Afraid of the Chinese Modern Girl?' In *The Modern Girl Around the World: Consumption, Modernity, and Globalization*, edited by The Modern Girl around The World Research Group, 194-219. Durham: Duke University Press, 2008.

Ge, Hongbing 葛红兵. Sandbed [沙床]. Wuhan: Changjiang Wenyi, 2003.

Jansson, André and Amanda Lagerkvist. 'The Future Gaze: City Panoramas as Politico-Emotive Geographies.' *Journal of Visual Culture* 8, no. 1 (2009): 25-53.

Knight, Sabina. *The Heart of Time: Moral Agency in Twentieth-Century Chinese Fiction*. Vol. 274: Harvard University Council on East Asian Studies, 2006.

Kong, Shuyu. 'Literary Celebrity in China: From Reformers to Rebels.' In *Celebrity in China*, edited by Louise Edwards & Elaine Jeffreys, 125-144. Hong Kong: Hong Kong University Press, 2010.

Kuoshu, Harry. 'Shanghai Baby, Chinese *Xiaozi*, and "Pirated" Lifestyles in the Age of Globalisation.' *Cocentric: Literary and Cultural Studies* 31, no. 2 (2005): 85-100.

Lee, Vivian. 'The City as Seductress: Shanghai and the Chinese Metropolitan in Contemporary Film and Fiction.' *Modern Chinese Literature and Culture* 17, no.2 (2005): 133-166.

Lu, Sheldon. 'Popular Culture and Body Politics: Beauty Writers in Contemporary China.' *Modern Language Quarterly* 69, no. 1 (2008): 167-85.

McDougall, Bonnie. *Fictional Authors, Imaginary Audiences: Modern Chinese Literature in the Twentieth Century*. Chinese University Press, 2003.

Rojas, Carlos. 'Authorial Afterlives and Apocrypha in 1990s Chinese Fiction.' In *Rethinking Chinese Popular Culture: Cannibalizations of the Canon*, edited by Carlos Rojas, and Eileen Cheng-yin Chow, 262-282. London, New York: Routledge, 2009.

Weber, Ian. 'Shanghai Baby: Negotiating Youth Self-Identity in Urban China.' *Social Identities* 8, no. 2 (2002): 347-68.

Wei Hui. *Shanghai Baby*. Translated by Bruce Humes. New York: Simon and Schuster, 2001.

Zhong, Xueping. 'Mr. Zhao On and Off the Screen: Male Desire and Its Discontent.' In *The Urban Generation: Chinese Cinema and Society at the turn of the Twenty-first Century*, edited by Zheng Zhen, 295-315. London: Duke UP, 2007.

Zhou Manzhen 周满珍. 'Some Straight Talk about Sandbed: An Interview with

Ge Hongbing' [关于《沙床》的一点直白话：葛红兵访谈], 2003. http://202.120.121.193/techang/gehongbing/fangtanlu11.htm (accessed 12 May 2011).

Zhou Weihui 周卫慧. *Shanghai Baby* [上海宝贝]. Chunfeng Literary Publishers, 1999.

Zhu Dake 朱大可. 'What is the Meaning of the Muzimei and Ge Hongbing Phenomena?' [木子美·葛红兵现象意味着什么？], 2003. www.cul-studies.com → 批评视域 → 批评第六期 (accessed 12 May 2011).

Zhu Hongjun 朱红军. '"I Can't Leave the Body Halfway": An Interview with Ge Hongbing' ["我不会离开身体半步"：葛红兵访谈], 2003. www.cul-studies.com → 所属栏目 → 批评第六期 (accessed 12 May 2011).

12. City Regeneration and Its Opposition

Ou Ning

The Life and Death of Cities

Everyone dies, but everyone believes that his/her city never perishes. For thousands of years, if they are not destroyed by wars, natural disasters or other irresistible impact, cities live forever in people's minds; by accumulating materials and inheriting spirit, they are historical carriers that extend production and the lives of human beings. But, in contradistinction to people's wishes, a city is also an organism that has a cycle of life and death, though it lasts longer, is more complicated, transcends humans span of short life and, therefore, is more than they could envision.

A city is not just a physical space (even physical space can be eroded by time) that is filled with streets and buildings. Rather, it is intertwined with generations of lives, with politics, economy, culture and history, all of which are tumultuous and gloomy. The lives and deaths of cities have never been easy to define and have always been controversial. People invented the profession of Urban Planning in the hope that it would give a city a thorough career planning and save it from decline, which would eventually extend its life forever – only to find that, unfortunately, it has often been referred to as a city terminator. Some reckon that developers invest in order to build a city, while historical protectionists argue that, with the profit-before-everything-else mentality, they have eliminated a city's collective memory and suffocated any vitality a city originally had. Some believe that architects construct cities, while others criticise them for indulging themselves in their own dreams, treating cities as tabula rasa, and changing the design whenever they feel like it without any regard to city users' life and death.

In 1961, Jane Jacobs published the famous *The Death and Life of Great American Cities*. Adopting the voice of an ordinary citizen, she strongly criticised the urban planning thinking represented by Ebenezer Howard's *Garden City*, Le Corbusier's *Radiant City*, and Daniel Burnham's *City Beautiful*. Reprimanded by Jacobs as pseudoscience, this kind of thinking was superficially tinged with a certain degree of idealism and was popular, for a while, in post-war America, before turning into the professional criteria and infallible principles of governmental planning officials, investment banks, developers and students. Under such a mindset, urban planning had ignored the practical need for various forms to co-exist and mingle in the city. Based on the need for different functions it had divided the city into different orderly areas, which were isolated from each other and were only connected by high-speed motorways. Large-scale green spaces, gardens, and shady avenues were constructed for visual effect, without considering humans' practical needs. Streets for walking in were nothing but a waste of space. There was a great aversion to slums. By vigorously developing the suburb to reduce population pressure on city centres, the poor, their land exchanged for plots elsewhere, were driven out, and different classes were separated into different neighbourhoods. Jane Jacobs viewed such planning as the sacking of cities, which caused the decline of city districts, resulting in the death of the city (1961: 4).

In his 1962 fictionalised article, City Destruction Corporation, Arata Isozaki described modernist cities influenced by Le Corbusier and CIAM as behemoths that strangled lives. For example, the traffic accidents they produced killed many people – death had become such a common sight that it greatly reduced the bloodletting cost of traditional assassins and dramatically increased the pressure on professional killers, seriously undermining their occupational dignity. Therefore, in order to get revenge, Killer S (Sin) decided to start City Destruction Corporation, which would destroy cities physically, functionally, and imaginatively. In the sequel of 2004, Rumor City, Isozaki argued that no corporations should ever bother to undertake such a mission, as cities had always been self-destructive. He took the 1995 Kobe earthquake, the Aum Shinrikyo sarin gas incident, and some suicidal urban planning in Tokyo as examples to illustrate that his predictions, made 40 years ago, had all been realised. The image of the death of the city had always haunted Isozaki. In 1968, in the 14th Milan Triennial, his work *Electric Labyrinth* pieced together scenes of the ruins of Hiroshima, Japanese ukiyo-e ravenous eaters, and designs of future buildings, revealing, picture after picture, a living hell. He satirised the unfounded optimism people had toward future cities, and declared 'the ruins are what our future cities will be like, and the future cities are ruins' (Arata 2004).

At the 2007 Shenzhen & Hong Kong Bi-city Biennale of Urbanism \ Architecture, chief curator Qingyun Ma proposed a topic for discussion, *City of Expiration and Regeneration*, which made another statement about the city's life and death. He argued that since the city has its cycle of youth, maturity, ageing, and even disappearance, urban planning and architectural design should abandon the pursuit of eternity. Instead, they should accept that this idea is overdue, as well as its loss of effectiveness, and allow mistakes as well as changes, realising the regeneration of cities in incessant adjustments. He argued that cities should learn from agriculture – farmers sowed and ploughed in certain seasons; their harvests, good or bad, never influenced their future plans, and they laboured and laboured, always hoping things would turn out better the following year. According to Ma, this was the essence of agriculture, and it represented the direction of future cities: 'Agricultural order represents the highest realm in rational life, and agricultural ideal is based on the omission of the being by the future'. Agricultural civilisation will one day be revived, and there will be Agricities in this world.[1] On 31 January 2008, in a symposium aimed at the Biennale, Rao Xiaojun warned people to be careful about mass utopian thinking: it required a very long process for cities to grow, as cities needed to settle, and, furthermore, they needed cultural preservation – you could not 'cut buildings like cutting wheat and start everything all over again'. The momentum Ma provided to revive cities was an unknown energy, something misty, and it was going to bring destruction to real cities.[2]

Is it survival or destruction? It is common understanding that cities grow, age and desperately need to be regenerated, and yet how they can be regenerated has always been controversial. In my opinion, we need to get beyond the concept of materialising cities. This is to treat cities as food that can go bad and stink, as rubber condoms that might dysfunction and cause accidents, and as hazardous walls eroded by wind and rain, without including in them any human beings, who live in them and are flesh and blood. It reflects the occupational disease of architects, who can see nothing but reinforced concrete, and who can think of nothing but sketches and fantasies. It also shows architects' pursuit of interests while practising their profession – if cities are rapidly overdue, the demand for architects to rebuild them will be a lot higher. As the declaration of overdue has to be made by the public power, Ma did not, at all, conceal his admiration for current Chinese public power: 'Only erasable urban planning is real planning. In western countries, the privatisation of land has completely eliminated such an ideal, and that's why there is no wisdom invested. But China can still do it! China has the perfect environment to regulate theories and renovate order, because the land is publicly owned!'[3]

Ma's agricultural dream did not emphasise agricultural settlement, which is one of many living methods humans can choose from, or serve as a friendly reminder of over-urbanisation; instead, it emulated the repeated usage of land in seasonal production. A city utopia constructed under such an idea could not possibly avoid the triggering of violence. Isozaki once concluded that the more utopias are constructed, the faster cities will perish. Le Corbusier's city utopia was once tempting, but if it became real, then it, in the collusion with power, would turn out to be a disaster for humans. Of the many different views, Jane Jacobs' is the most persuasive and penetrating. She used to roam the streets of different U.S. big cities, and, from a mother's viewpoint, think about the safety of streets, the degree of satisfaction people had with their lives, and the protection of different kinds of rights in city lives.

A city's number-one goal is to meet people's needs, and protect people's safety and rights. This is especially true when cities cannot adjust to new demands, are facing decline, and need to find new development spaces to regenerate themselves; at this point, they need to focus in particular on people – the city residents. Urban regeneration does not, as in Dubai, reclaim land from the sea, which satisfies architects and urban planners in terms of their worshipping of cities from zero and cities without context. It not only restructures current city physical space, but, in the process, also reorganises and re-allocates different social resources, which touches the intrinsic orders formed a very long time ago by different interest groups. When this happens, urban regeneration will certainly be accompanied by opposition, and will ultimately end up in complicated social changes and conflict. In dealing with such opposition, if public power is carefully employed, and if the interests of different classes are balanced and coordinated, allowing people to live in peace and work happily in the new city space while equally sharing different powers in the city, then eventually they can identify spiritually with the city and fulfil their duties as citizens; that is when the city can have a genuinely long-lasting life.

A Victory by the Common People?

China started its reform and open policy in 1978, and it has been going on for more than 30 years. During these 30-odd years, as national economic structures shift from agriculture, to industry, construction, real estate, services, and culture and then to science and technology, the urbanisation movement is becoming increasingly tense. According to a report by the Chinese National Statistics Bureaus, in China in 2006, the total number of cities reached 661, and the total number of city residents reached 577.06 million, the equivalent of 43.0% of the population. This raised the proportion of urbanised areas by 4.8%, compared with 2002. The report also indicated that in 2006, the total output value of Chinese cities of at least prefecture level (excluding municipal counties) reached 1322.72 billion Yuan, 1.1 times that of 2002 (642.92 billion Yuan), and its proportion of nationwide GDP increased from 53.4% in 2002 to 63.2% in 2006, a 9.8% increase. In 2006, the revenue of local government from Chinese cities of at least prefecture level reached 108.62 billion Yuan, 1.1 times that of 2002, accounting for 59.3% of nationwide local government revenue.[4]

The statistics show that urbanisation has become an important economic index in the national vocabulary, and it has been moving toward higher goals. The movement of urbanisation driven by economic strategy not only makes cities the most important productive space, but also draws more and more people to cities. A city has to keep upgrading and expanding itself to alleviate the pressure on development. It swallows the land in suburbs and in villages, and, in the name of urban regeneration, it regains the development space in older parts of the city. The former process incites farmers to launch group movements to safeguard their land, while the latter causes city residents to fight against the demolition and resettlement on their own.

In March 2007, the 'Most Stubborn Nail House in History' incident in Chongqing was one of numerous acts of opposition that occurred after China launched its urban regeneration movement. It happened not long after the Property Law was issued in China, and generated a visually infectious picture of the nail house, a house that stood alone like an an island amidst an area that was bulldozed away. This image circulated quickly via the Internet. This caused the outburst of opinion on the part of a public that, for a long time, had been unhappy about the violent demolition and resettlement, and which attracted a lot of attention from the media, at home and abroad. It started as strenuous opposition to developers and the government, moved on to negotiating, conciliating, and winning reasonable property compensation, and then finally became a landmark victory by the common people. The victims, Yang Wu, and his wife, Wu Ping, were considered heroes who struggled lawfully on their own to protect their private property.

They became models for numerous householders who, while seeing their homes demolished and being resettled, tried to safeguard their legal rights. And the comprehensive way the Chongqing city government handled the matter became a favourite topic of conversation.[5]

While everybody was talking about it, and while Internet citizen journalism was attacking it, the administrative order – demolition and resettlement incidents should never be exposed in the newspapers – was curiously enough rather relieved. It can be said that public opinion broke through the limits of Chinese government and traditional media. Moreover, after the Chongqing incident, many demolitions and resettlements in other cities were exposed and widely talked about. After the incident, official think-tanks and private academic organisations worked hard to digest its impact, trying to figure out its meaning for urban planning, for the construction of the rule of law, for individual rights, for media ecology, for communication strategy, and so on, intending to write it into history – a seemingly win-win situation in which everyone was happy.

But the image of the isolated island keeps lingering in my mind, as it strongly reveals China's unsociable city communities, without-any-support families, helpless individuals, and blocked political passages. If Yang and Wu had lived in a neighbourhood where residents actively interacted and communicated with each other, cared and supported much about each other, if a neighbourhood association or a non-governmental organisation (NGO) had represented and coordinated them, and if media had become involved earlier, opened up more ways for residents to express themselves and made dialogues more accessible, then the Chongqing Nailhouse incident might not have happened at all. Yang and Wu might not have been forced to become lone fighters, and the local government might not have had to, at the last moment and in a frantic rush, deal with this world-shocking crisis of trust that could have shaken the authority of the country's administration and justice.

In destroying communities, China's urban regeneration movement not only separates people who have been living in the same neighbourhood for years and puts them in different districts of the city without supporting measures, but also, in the process of demolition and resettlement, cuts off and destroys the normal spiritual bonds and family ethics among people. Developers and resettlement companies are all experts in negotiating and psychoanalysing. They apply professional strategies to block information from the households being demolished and resettled, and then destroy the households one by one in increasing order of difficulty. They even set one party against another – sowing dissent among couples and siblings and inciting them to fight each other, at the same time breaking through their mental defences – and eventually bringing down the cost of resettlement as much as possible. Now that the market economy and individualism have been prevalent in China for years, the collective consciousness and family cohesion among the Chinese are already weak, and they are totally broken up by such chaotic demolition and resettlement activities, putting people under enormous psychological pressure. Most Neighbourhood Offices, the organisations at the bottom of Chinese cities, are viewed by the households being resettled as antagonists when it comes to matters involving their interests. The offices have lost their credibility and function, and are no longer the lubricant of the neighbourhoods. What is worse is that people are living at a time of no faith. No great spiritual mentors can support them mentally. No authoritative opinion-leaders can show them how to get onto the right path, and help them understand their increasingly complicated and dangerous society. If people cannot be independent, spiritually and ideologically, they are even more powerless in the face of attacks and harms.

Besides, while it is stipulated in Chinese law that the land should be owned collectively in the countryside, which allows farmers to group together when their land interests are being violated, in the city, the nation owns the land, and people are on their own when it comes to fighting and protecting their private property. Another reason people seldom group together to safeguard their rights in urban regeneration is because to do so remains very sensitive in the current Chinese political environment, and people are highly aware of this. They do not want to be viewed as the ones organising political movements that target the national system and oppose the ruling party. With such a mental burden, even though different families and individuals share the same problems and interests, people dare not gather in groups, which makes them weak and passive when confronted by powerful developers and resettlement companies. In addition, the government still does not trust most NGOs. In dealing with conflict and opposition, when civilian volunteers cannot get involved in situations in which citizens need to safeguard their legal rights, there is no neutral third party to coordinate and conciliate; a waste of civilian resources that makes citizens even more helpless. Considering the fact that the only accomplishment here is the emergence of the most stubborn nail house in history, how can we ever call it the victory of the common people?

Since the SARS outbreak in 2003, the Chinese government has been heavily criticised for its inability to issue warnings about, control and investigate the social crisis. The government's treatment of urban regeneration, and the related processes of demolition and resettlement, is equally flawed. It has made the society feel as though it is walking on thin ice, as the government is slow to come to a solution in legislating, administrating and mediating urban regeneration. The Chinese bureaucratic system prefers to report what is pleasant and conceal what is not, and when there is an issue, it is swept under the carpet; major troubles are reduced to minor ones, and minor ones to nothing. They do not like things to come into the open and no one likes to take responsibility, while the messages they convey to their superiors are always inconsistent with the facts or are biased, making problems more and more serious till they finally burst out. At this point, when they would do everything possible to extinguish them, it is usually too late.

Of course, the attitude of Chinese citizens can be questioned. Some citizens increase the value of their housing investment at the last moment, treating the resettlement as an opportunity to gamble with the government and developers, in which they can ask for extra compensation. Such opportunists undoubtedly make the antagonism even more serious. Some citizens dare not say anything when their rights are violated, but step forward and ask to share the good results when others finally win them over under great pressure – such passive, selfish, and gaining-without-pain mentality only reflects their distorted souls. The government, in the process of guiding the regeneration of cities, should respect the wishes and interests of citizens living in them, help citizens to access civic education, open up more channels of public opinion, allow organisations to be legalised and invite them to participate in discussions and consultations, making all kinds of procedures transparent, while allowing the interests of the public, developers and citizens to be reasonably allocated within the framework of the law. A city full of vital power should provide rich soil for civic society to prosper, allow everyone to participate in a city's public affairs, and eventually help citizens exercise self-governance. In this respect, Chinese cities still have a long way to go.

On the Street that Resists Demolition

In November 2006, the Hong Kong government, in order to carry out the third phase of the reclamation project and the construction of urban motorways in Central District, decided to demolish the nearly 50-year-old Star Ferry Pier, as well as the bell tower on Edinburgh Square, which triggered a series of demonstrations and protests by Hong Kong residents. Though several young people broke into the construction site of the pier a few times – they even climbed into the bulldozers that were rumbling forward – they still could not stop the bell tower and the pier from being totally demolished. After the opposition failed, they immediately moved to the nearby Queen's Pier and started a new battlefield there. They changed from being spontaneous to establishing an organisation, Local Action. Afterwards, they started a long-term occupation of Queen's Pier, launched an even larger-scale protest, and, at a late stage, a sit-in and hunger strike. They had the support of different organisations, including the Hong Kong Institute of Architects. The movement, which had started with a simple petition to preserve historical buildings and collective memories, evolved into the declaration of and demand for the decolonisation of Hong Kong's identity, the establishment of Hong Kong's local subjectivity, participation in decision-making affecting the city's public space, and the democratisation of the process of urban planning. It elicited wide discussion in the media, got responses and at the same time gained support from different classes in Hong Kong, and became a deeply influential historical incident. The Star Ferry/Queen's Pier's Preservation Movement lasted for more than half a year, until 2 August 2007, when the Hong Kong government sent hundreds of police, firefighters, medical staff and engineering staff to enforce the clearing of the space and its demolition. Although Queen's Pier could not be spared in the end, the movement awakened Hong Kong residents' awareness of the need to protect history, and ignited people's passion to participate in public affairs in the city.

Unlike the individual opposition seen in Chinese mainland cities, the main goal of which was to safeguard private property, the Star Ferry/Queen's Pier's Preservation Movement was a social movement led by Hong Kong's new generation of intellectuals. The intellectuals here were not from the upper class with vested interests in Hong Kong society (the so-called elite class); rather, they were those who were good at thinking, and who, throughout the whole movement, were highly aware of their social responsibility and Hong Kong's history. In fact, they were students, Internet editors, independent reporters and freelancers in their twenties,[6] who did not think about any personal interests when they launched the movement, and who always held their appeal and set their target from the perspective of the general public. They were the representatives of the intellectuals who, having been born after the 1980s and emerged during the ten years after Hong Kong was returned to China, were totally different from the baby-boom generation. The latter, studying abroad in the 1960s and devoting themselves to Hong Kong's social movements in the 1970s, were either absorbed by the colonial administrative system and had turned into a cynical social elite, or became economic animals in a culture of mercantilism. Those born after the 1980s treated the return to China in 1997 as a watershed in ideological thinking. They refused to identify with the baby boomers' predisposition toward elites and the colonial system. Instead, they inclined themselves towards the history of Hong Kong's common people to find Hong Kong's identity, and tried to establish a local subjectivity in Hong Kong. That was why they treasured the Star Ferry/Queen's Pier so much, as since the 1960s, the Central Coastal Region, where the two piers were located, had been the public space in the city where common people protested, gathered and shared experiences, accumulating a lot of historical memories for Hong Kong residents.

But intellectuals, too, have their limits. Though they praised themselves as the spokespersons of the common people, the ordinary, profit-valuing Hong Kong people could probably better understand the desperate struggles of the nail house residents than the ambitious young people and their social movement, their grand historical exposition and identity theory. Speaking honestly, reading profoundly meaningful, highly-talented speeches and writings,[7] and demonstrating their strategies and skills throughout the movement, one would certainly be convinced by their broad and open ideological thinking as well as their excellent ability to handle their affairs. Despite the fact that they did not achieve the goal of preserving the piers, they did push the movement to a historical height they had expected. But, in most urban regenerations, preserving history is not usually a sufficient reason to halt the bulldozers; mostly, it is just the wishful thinking of intellectuals.

Take Beijing for example. In Beijing, people generally regard history as a burden (perhaps China's history is too long, and its roots too vigorous, whereas Hong Kong, which had always been a colony and had an unsettled identity, had a strong rootless feeling and was hungry for history), and nobody wants to live in small, fire-trapping alleys that are old, shabby and crowded, where everybody has to wait in line to use the public toilets. People compete to live in modern apartments, and, for them, bulldozers represent a brand new life. Only the intellectuals are extremely worried, hoping every brick and every tile in old alleys can be preserved. This is when the government and developers can easily control public opinion, treating intellectuals as physical protectionists who do not care about the improvement of people's lives. The reasoning about Hong Kong, in this respect, was the same. Patrick Ho Chi-ping, the Secretary for Home Affairs in Hong Kong, once said: 'The land in Hong Kong is very expensive, and there has to be a strong enough reason to preserve a piece of land'.[8] The collective memory of Star Ferry/Queen's Pier, obviously, was not strong enough.

It seems that a gap still exists between the advanced ideology of intellectuals and the understanding of the general public – including developers and officials. It is a gap of not only concepts, but also languages. Some said the level of the young people of Local Action was too high, and their thinking was too deep, making it difficult for the public to follow. Therefore, the strategy of Local Action, born after the failure of Star Ferry battle, was adjusted. In addition to decolonisation and local subjectivity, which kept on emphasising collective memories, it developed new demands – the right to participate in the city's public space and democratisation in the process of urban planning. They criticised the Hong Kong Town Planning Board, in planning the Central District, for only thinking about big banks, consortiums, and big corporations, and ignoring the interests of the grass roots, surrendering city public spaces originally belonging to all citizens to business development. They intentionally covered the fact that the People's Liberation Army (PLA) intended to build a pier for warships there, hurting the citizens in terms of their right to participate in the city's public space and to be informed about urban planning.[9]

Without a doubt, these views, compared with collective memories, could evoke stronger echoes among the general public, and they had come down from being intellectual, historical expositions at the high end to something lower that was strongly related to the public's interests, shortening the distance between the movement and the public, while lifting the movement from the level of culture to the level of politics. To avoid the possibility that only a few people would understand their elaboration, they specially published a book, *A Special Issue on Queen's Pier* by Local Action, in plain language and in the form of questions and answers. It included a simple sketch map drawn by architects, spreading the idea of the movement and the proposed alternative plans to Hong Kong residents (Chu and Chow 2007).

In short, the Star Ferry/Queen's Pier's Movement was not trying to maintain some measurable material interests; it could be regarded as an ideological movement directed toward urban regeneration and urban planning. What it opposed was the inequality in allocating city's land and space resources, as well as the unreasonableness of the allocation process; what it criticised was the tendency to put the interest of economy above everything else in the process of urban planning, sacrificing historical sites for commercial development and emphasising material interest without any regard to non-material needs (the city's historical memories and citizens' spiritual identity); what it asked for was the political right to share the city's public space and participate in the city's public affairs. It broke through the limit imposed by Hong Kong society, which has a strong mercantilist tradition, a depoliticised political system, and an enormous ability to absorb the powers of opposition,[10] spreading the concept that a city was not only a physical space, but a vivid form of life with diversified cultures and pluralistic spiritual needs. From this perspective, this movement had realised a conceptual revolution and accomplished something extraordinary.

Facing the Bulldozers

In Greater China, opposition movements have occurred in different cities in the process of urban regeneration. In the past 30-odd years, the economies of many Asian countries have developed rapidly. Hong Kong and Taiwan, one step ahead of China, became two of the Four Tigers of Asia. With their economies expanding, industries adjusted, and populations exploding, there has been an incessant demand for the reshuffling of city space, and opposition, inevitably, appears as part of this process. Taipei, in terms of democratic development, is a city that is more active than Hong Kong; and so, in as early as 1997, a movement called 'Opposing City Government Bulldozers' was born here. It was the first social movement directed at urban regeneration in Taiwan, which involved not only intellectuals and city residents, but also party forces. As the focus was the demolition of a slum that had developed with its own logic over time, which involved the actual survival right of residents in the neighbourhood, it provided a typical context for both urban regeneration and its opposition. For the intellectuals in the fields of architecture and urban planning who started and participated in the movement, the demolition plan was synonymous with the urban regeneration movement in the U.S., launched by the federal government in 1949 and which ran until 1972, and which was criticised heavily in intellectual circles (including the strong criticism from Jane Jacobs).[11] With their belief in social morality and civic society, these intellectuals were driven to devote all their efforts to the task. Therefore, it was not a spontaneous movement launched by city residents. From the beginning, it mobilised society on a large scale, and was continuously negotiating and operating on the level of politics. The movement could be regarded as a highly organised social movement with a mature language and style.

The site that set off the explosion is the current location of Taipei No. 14 and 15 parks, at the intersection of Linsen North Road and Nanjing East Road, a communal cemetery during Japanese occupation. After the Kuomintang (KMT) was defeated in 1949, soldiers and their families, retreating from Shandong and Jiangsu provinces via Hainan Island to Taipei, having neither residences nor jobs, voluntarily chose to earn their own livings and built simple shelters here. Later on, having absorbed residents from other areas in Taiwan, it developed into a community: Kang-le Li. In 1956, based on the urban planning drafted in Japanese occupation period, Taipei city government categorised it as a site on which to build a park, but, due to residential controversy and budget proposal reversals, the plan to build a park was never realised.

In 1994, the Graduate Institute of Building and Planning in National Taiwan University went deep into Kang-le Li, mobilised residents to participate in discussions, and proposed a design project, Fixing On the Spot and Rebuilding the Community, which won the first Award for City Residents Participating in City Design in Taipei. In 1995, Chen Shui-bian became Taipei's city mayor and maintained the plan to build a park, but he promised to build it before the demolition, and he also promised that the residents' compensation and resettlement would be properly handled.

In January 1997, Chen overturned the principles, and decided to start the demolition on 4 March. After Kang-le Li residents went to the city council to protest, which was of no avail, the Graduate Institute of Building and Planning in National Taiwan University, along with more than 100 celebrities in the intellectual field and NGOs, signed and launched the Opposing City Government Bulldozers movement.[12]

Before the demolition, the buildings in Kang-le Li were shabby houses constructed with bricks, wood, and plastic panels by residents themselves. About 3,000 people – 1,000-odd households – lived there. One-third of them were veterans, the handicapped, temporary workers, low-income households and poor families. In the eyes of the people who launched the movement, Kang-le Li was 'a neighbourhood that encompasses Taiwanese, Chinese mainlanders, and aboriginals, whose lives were closely linked', and it was also 'the last district with such unique quality in Taipei' (Huang 1997: np). For years, people here spent their time together every day, from morning until evening. Though the environment was not good, they took care of each other and helped each other pull through, and though they were poor and their plight wretched, their district was the one in Taipei that donated the most money in 1979, when the U.S. disconnected its diplomatic relationship with Taiwan and the movement, Donating Money to Purchase Planes and Serve the Country, was launched.[13]

However, in the eyes of Chen Shui-bian, Kang-le Li was comparable with hell:

> Considering Taipei's wealth, what we have here is the tumour of the city and the shame of its citizens. Thousand of people are, unimaginably, sleeping on graves, and right next to it is the five-star Grand Formosa Regent Taipei. It embarrasses me every time to think that it's such a slum that international super star Michael Jackson, living in the upper floor in the hotel, upon opening the window, would see in Taipei.[14]

Such arguments, identifying demolition targets as slums and regarding them as unsightly, are in fact commonly-heard excuses in resettlement. The argument is accompanied by the unconscious treating of the underprivileged people in Kang-le Li as garbage; his colleague, while negotiating with and confronting people launching the movement, once said firmly: 'Old folks eventually die even if they don't move'.[15]

These people, treated as useless, are the human waste Zygmunt Bauman wrote about in his book, *Wasted Lives: Modernity and its Outcasts*:

> The production of 'human waste', or more correctly wasted humans (the 'excessive' and 'redundant', that is the population of those who either could not or were not wished to be recognised or allowed to stay), is an inevitable outcome of modernisation, and an inseparable accompaniment of modernity. It is an inescapable side-effect of *order-building* (each order casts some parts of the extant population as 'out of place', 'unfit', or 'undesirable') and of *economic progress* (that cannot proceed without degrading and devaluing the previously effective modes of 'making a living' and therefore cannot but deprive their practitioners of their livelihood). (2004: 5)

When people go overboard for modernisation, lots of occupations become outdated, and lots of people become abandoned children. Modern administrative rulers hate slums because too much human waste has gathered there – slum-dwellers are not only unable to contribute to the government's tax revenues, but they also increase the cost of social welfare. To governments, slums are located right next to the most expensive city centre land, and their buildings are old and shabby, with a low volume ratio and no output whatsoever. Aside from serving, sometimes, as a target of being dirty, messy, and inferior and a place with high crime rate, where the police, from time to time, can make a sudden attack and launch a mop-up operation to reassure and appease taxpayers and increase their psychological reliance on the government, what else does a slum contribute? And so the following policies are formulated: drive away human waste at a low cost, clear the space, and sell it to developers to increase financial revenues; or, change the space into a park, win the good name of greening and beautifying the city and, at the same time, stimulate and increase the value of surrounding real estates.

In the case of Kang-le Li, it is indisputable that a dilapidated community was out of step with the times and needed to be regenerated. It is also true that plans had long ago been passed to build a park – a public space – which had to be carried out to maintain the authority of the administration, and which was in conformity with legal principles. This is not what the Opposing City Government Bulldozers movement opposed. What it opposed was how the quality of the underprivileged people's lives was being neglected, and the cruel removal of their right to live in the city by the Chen Shui-bian government, with a mindset that was shown to be nothing but tyrannical. As Chu-joe Hsia, the professor who launched the movement, said: 'A tyrannical government, in handling the park, is worse than a ferocious tiger'. When the park's design proposal was still in the primary stages – with the concrete details undecided – and before resolving the residents' compensation and settling them down in their new dwellings, they were forced to move within the limit of a few months, and their houses, where for many years they had rested and recuperated, were torn down by bulldozers. They became homeless and had to wander from place to place, despite what they had contributed to Taiwan and their historical memories – this was the true colour of Chen Shui-bian as a strongman. Even though party election interests were involved, and even though the then Central Minister without Portfolio Ma Ying-jiu, former Democratic Pogressive Party (DPP) leader Shi Ming-de, legislators Zhang Jun-hong and Lin Rui-tu, several KMT legislators, and New Party national assemblymen were there to show their support, no one could save Kang-le Li from being obliterated on 4 March 1997. The Opposing City Government Bulldozers movement's demand that the demolition be delayed was ignored. In the fire that suddenly broke out the day when the place was being torn down, people only heard the echo of a protest song: 'Cutting down the bridge of memories, whose hometown is Taipei? It's the sun of consortiums, and the graveyard of the poor!'[16]

Forgetting and Remembering

In fact, more than 20 years after World War II, America's experience in urban regeneration had proved that eliminating slums with bulldozers could not eradicate poverty in the city. After the elimination, people from the slums get together again in other spaces in the city and form new slums, and the incessant elimination and expelling further widen the gap between them and mainstream society, worsening their opposition and leading to unmanageable social conflict. After the mid-1960s, the discrimination policy in American regeneration projects caused large-scale riots and turmoil in big cities including New York, Los Angeles, San Francisco, Chicago, and Detroit. Each time, 30 to 40 people died, and hundreds of people were injured, with urban neighbourhoods badly damaged and up to tens of millions of dollars lost (Li 2004: 150-151).

This was an important reason for the U.S. to stop its regeneration movement. But, in Asia, the mindset of hating slums and eliminating them is still prevalent. Ten years ago, Kan-le Li in Taipei became the victim, and today, both the old business district of Da Zha Lan in Beijing, and the thousand-year-old Roman neighbourhood of Sulukule in Istanbul, can not escape such misfortune. In the Opposing City Government Bulldozers movement in Taipei, there were veterans committing suicide, and in Beijing and Istanbul, the protests against the demolitions and resettlements never stopped. People forget the pain after the scar is healed. Concealed by immediate interests, they never stop making mistakes, paying no attention to historical lessons. Forgetting is a major disease that humans share.

At the late stage of America's urban regeneration movement, during the late 1960s and early 1970s, artist Gordon Matta-Clark started his destruction activity in the city. At that time, in American cities, lots of houses had been abandoned, and their land and property rights had, at the same time, been collected. But as the government, developers, and different political forces were in conflict with each other, the budget could never be passed, the regeneration could never start, and the decline was getting worse and worse every day. Matta-Clark started to dismember these houses by stripping a wall, cutting away a door and a window, or drilling a geometrical shape, which not only showed the ruins inside the building, but also reminded people how fragile private properties and social structures were. His most famous project, *Splitting*, was finished in 1974 in Englewood, a city in New Jersey in the northeastern U.S.: cutting open a two-story empty house from the centre and separating it into two parts. Instead of saying that the artist had destroyed buildings, it would be better to say that he had invented a deeply-ingrained way of remembering the property rights of real estate groundlessly plundered in the urban regeneration movement. The clear rift on the house is mourning, and, even more, a symbol of class polarisation and social antagonism in U.S. cities. Matta-Clark died young (1943-1978), and most of his city destruction activities have been preserved in pictures, videos, words, and sketches, which, along with building pieces he cut from different places, are collected in American and European museums and galleries, passed on to later generations as artworks, countering people's forgetfulness.[17]

In England, as cities were largely destroyed during World War II, a large-scale regeneration movement was also launched after the war. The movement was different from that in the U.S. because the Community Architecture movement, which advocated citizen participation and protection of neighbourhoods, was well developed from the 1960s onwards. In addition, the consciousness of architects, the involvement of NGOs, and the adjustment of governmental policies were better coordinated. Prince Charles, with high-sounding assertions, has shown his support since the 1980s (his Prince's Foundation focuses solely on the construction of cities and communities). After the 1990s, with continuous development as goal, Compact City theory, which advocated mixing different functions, reducing energy consumption and combining community protection with urban regeneration, was developed. It can be said that the interests of citizens from different classes have always been respected.

In 1993, artist Rachel Whiteread was invited to create a work for a Victorian apartment building that was to be torn down. The building was at the intersection of Grove Road and Roman Road, in the East End of London. She poured concrete into the three-story tall building, and stripped the outer walls after the concrete had set. When the negative space of the building was exposed, it became a substance that could not be penetrated. The artist said that it was her sculpture, and named it *House*. Located in the East End of London, a special district infiltrated with historical memories of racial segregation and immigration dispute, the first graffiti sentence passers-by sprayed on the work was 'a house for all the white and all the black' (Massey 1998). No one was forgotten, and no one forgot history. This silent, heavy, and bulky public artwork is like a monument to civilian life that transcends racial discrepancies, which stimulates people's imagination regarding simple human values.

American and European cities, as economic entities that are mature or even saturated, either remain stagnant or are shrinking. They always like to portray the regional problems they confront as a global issue when they solve the problems. And as emerging economies, cities in Asia and other developing nations are still expanding with astonishing speed and scale; they are responsible for providing regional ways to tackle global problems. This is exactly the hypothesis Zygmunt Bauman proposed: 'Regional problems are solved globally, and global problems are solved regionally' 2004: 5). In order to admit a large amount of international capital, and operate in complicated economic systems, and move a large number of people, Asian cities are currently rushing and jumping forward, looking for spaces and rising to challenges.

To construct or to deconstruct? The question that Gordon Matta-Clark raised, in his work that was full of serious thinking and that was realistically urgent, is right under the eyes of administrative rulers. As Dan Graham said, the question is still unanswered, unsolved.[18] It is testing people's morality and wisdom. This article has investigated opposition movements that arose in the regeneration process in three different cities in Greater China; the issues the movements face are the same. The gain and loss of the opposing sides, in political and economic aspects, depend on whether humans have been left out, and whether every human's life is regarded worthy of protecting and remembering. The life and death of a city is strongly related to this.

Translated from the Chinese by Roan Shumei, in Columbia, Missouri.

Notes

Special thanks to Peng Yanhan, Chen Xia, Huang Jia-feng, and Li Xiu-jing for their assistance in gathering information.

1. Short Letters of Dialogue between Qingyun Ma and Liang Jingyu, *Contemporary Art and Investment*, no.2 2008, General Issue 14.
2. The record of the salon conversation on Shenzhen & Hong Kong Bi-city Biennale of Urbanism \ Architecture, http://news.sz.soufun.com/2008-02-01/1495211.html. Accessed 12 September 2010.
3. Short Letters of Dialogue between Qingyun Ma and Liang Jingyu, *Contemporary Art and Investment*, no.2 2008, General Issue 14.
4. 'Urbanisation in China is becoming increasingly tense, and the population in cities has reached 577 million.' China News Net: www.chinanews.com.cn/cj/hgjj/news/2007/09-27/1036849shtml. Accessed 12 September 2010.
5. For details on the Wu Ping and Yang Wu incident, see Zhang (2007).
6. See interviews on Chan King Fai, Chow Sze Chung, Chu Hoi Dick and Tang Siu Wah by Leong Man Tao, The Sun at 7 and 8 o'clock, Ming Pao, 5 August 2007.
7. For example, Chow (2007) and Chan (2007).
8. The Demolition of Central Star Ferry Pier Awakens Hong Kong People's Local Action, *Southern Metropolis Daily*, 9 June 2007.
9. I would like to express certain reservations about comments on the military pier; as every country and area has laws to protect its classified military information and rules about when to declassify it, the information about building military piers should be confidential, and should not become public to outsiders.
10. Sociologist Ambrose King Yeo Chi called Hong Kong's political system under British rule politics where the administration assimilates democratic politics in which every citizen participates, by way of opening up its administrative controlling system. See Qiang (2001).
11. In the 20-odd years after Congress passed the Housing Law, the U.S. federal government pushed forward 2,800 regeneration projects in 1,100 cities, federal appropriation reached 10 billion dollars, and engineering space 200,000 acres, with 80,000 acres transformed from slums. Later, as it was heavily criticised, in 1972 the U.S. Congress passed the Housing and Urban Development Act and ended the regeneration movement. But the movement did not truly end till Reagan became president in 1980. See Li (2004: 162).
12. See Huang (1997).
13. See Huang (1997).
14. United Daily News, November 12, 1996.
15. See Huang (1997).
16. The Graveyard of the Poor, adapted from Chen Shui-bian's campaign song *Taipei New Hometown* when Chen was running for Taipei city mayor, Lyrics by Huang Sun-quan and Peng Yang-kai. See Huang (1997).
17. See Discrens (2003).
18. 'To construct...or to deconstruct? This question, which Matta-Clarks work raised, is still unanswered, unresolved.' See Graham (2006: 96).

References

Arata Isozaki 矶崎新. *Unbuilt* [未建成/反建筑史]. Chinese version, translated by Hu Qian and Wang Yun. Beijing: Zhongguo Jianzhu Gongye Chubanshe, 2004.

Bauman, Zygmunt. *Wasted Lives: Modernity and its Outcasts*. Cambridge: Polity Press, 2004.

Chan, King Fai 陈景辉. 'Whose Hong Kong Story, What Kind of Hong Kong People' [谁的香港故事，什么样的香港人] *Ming Pao* [明报], 29 July 2007.

Chow Sze Chung 周思中. 'On the Street of Decolonization' [在解殖的街头]. *Today* [今天], special issue on Hong Kong, no.2 (2007).

Chu Hoi Dick and Chow Sze Chung. A Special Issue on Queen's Pier. Local Action, 2007.

Graham, Dan. 'Gordon Matta-Clark.' *Shrinking Cities* no. 2 (2006): 96.

Huang, Sun-quan 黄孙权. *We Live in Kangle: A documentary on Opposing City Government Bulldozers Movement* [我们家在康乐里——反对市府推土机运动文件], Taipei, 1997.

Jacobs, Jane. *The Death and Life of Great American Cities*. New York: Vintage Books, 1961.

Li, Yanling 李艳玲. *U.S. Urban Regeneration Movement and Inner City Transformation* [美国城市更新运动与内城改造]. Shanghai: Shanghai Daxue Chubanshe, 2004.

Massey, Doreen. 'Space-time and the Politics of Location.' *Architectural Design* no. 68 (1998): 3-4.

Qiang, Shigong 强世功. 'A Reflection on "The Administrative Absorption of Politics"' ["行政吸纳政治"的反思]. *Dushu* [读书] no. 9 (2007).

Zhang, Yue. 'The Investigation on the Inside Story of Chongqing Nail House Incident.' *Southern Weekend*, 5 April 2007.

13. Law, Embodiment, and the Case of 'Harbourcide'

John Nguyet Erni

Hong Kong's ever-worsening air pollution is now on everyone's lips, and the general talk, once again, is about a threat to economic livelihood. For policymakers, the threat reveals the conflict between economics (specifically, an economic engine fueled by the transportation sector and the multi-billion real estate industry) and public health interests (which too have direct bearing on the economy and on Hong Kong's overall strategic position in the region). For the environmentally minded, the threat is the high toll on our prime natural resource: the quality of air that we breathe in every day. As for the Hong Kong residents, air pollution is registered as a threatening problem at a much more visceral level, that of our senses: from the suffering of sore throat, itchy eyes, irritants to our noses, to the everyday experience of a dusty, choky way of urban living. Observers of Hong Kong's air pollution problem have been raising alarm since the early 1980s, and the recent escalation of public worries continues to demonstrate that a pollution-centred understanding of the environment still frames the problem of urban degeneration in Hong Kong. Though this pollution-centred way of thinking does tend to be overly technocratic, it is not unreasonable to have such a vision of urban decay. The price tag on our health bills, especially for respiratory and heart diseases, the negative impact on investment growth and sustainability, especially for foreign investors more accustomed to, and demanding of, a clean air environment, and the political toll on a governance all too clearly biased toward the transportation and real estate markets, are only some of the things that are directly affected by the persistently hazy-skied society.

But if this dusty, choking environment is a threat, it is not because air quality itself is the principle 'site' of urban corrosion. The real problem, as this paper argues, is that the air quality concern is but a signifying host to the environmentally destructive project of land creation in a laissez-faire urban economy that directly causes the acute accretion of pollutants in the city. To be specific, air pollution is only an indexical sign of an underlying material reality, which is the systematic destruction of the only major natural wind channel situated at the heart of the city, the Victoria Harbour. This paper builds on an examination of the politics surrounding the voracious reclamation of the Victoria Harbour in order to cast an alternative reading of Hong Kong's environmental decay, one which no longer calls on the predominance of the air pollution discourse, but rather on the visceral sensorium of a disintegrating Harbour. This alternative reading, it is hoped, would steer the critical question of environmental justice away from mathematical data, policy talk, and even environmental laws, to our sensory points, which, it will be argued, could help mobilise a different, more embodied, collective movement of resistance to halt further environmental destruction in Hong Kong.

Many forms of urban destruction – such as the dense construction of roadways, skyscrapers, the erection of jam-packed residential blocks, the emission of exhaust fumes – have been the sources of sensory assault. Why is the case of the Victoria Harbour so alarming? The answer lies not just in the jumbo scale of harbour reclamation in the history of the city, but also in its all-encompassing spread of what can be called a cultural crisis of the senses. The Victoria Harbour has been shrunk, re-contoured, and contaminated for so long it has warped a vista that, for better or for worse, has historically formed the crux of the city's domestic and international identity. In a telling change of such a vista, in recent years, the number and frequency of photographs and video images of a hazed-out, deep grey-toned harbour-scape has so significantly jumped in the popular press and on Youtube as to rival the more traditional postcard image of a pleasant-looking Harbour of a bygone era. No other space in the city has been so visible at the same time as it absorbs and reorganises all our other senses, recomposing not only our retinal economy, but also our visceral olfactory and auditory sensation of an urban crisis pressing up against our bodies. Put differently, the hazy visibility of the harbour shelters not only a stark history of warped urban development, it also shelters a sensory-based 'imaginary', which, as Wolfgang Iser (1993) defines from a phenomenological point of view, is a diffuse, indeterminate, and protean flow of impressions, images, feelings, and bodily sensations.

Again, let us be clear that the threat to the urban environment is not air pollution as such. This is bolstered by two practical realities. First, social understanding of the air pollution problem remains deeply contested as to whether the blame for pollution can be totally assigned to urban development *within* Hong Kong. An ongoing debate exists around the proportionality of blame to be placed within or outside Hong Kong, as government scientists have constantly argued that the most polluted air particles – called particulates – are blown to Hong Kong's shores from the factory-saturated unregulated zone of the Pearl River Delta (see HKUST & Civic Exchange 2007). Second, it is clear that air quality itself cannot be the only locus of 'purity' (real or imagined) tainted by urban development. Inevitably, pollution is, to use a scientific term, 'multimodal' (see Nagle 2009; Smith 1988). Therefore the only practical approach to looking at the crisis of urban decay is to consider multi-sensory encounters and social practices, and, at a more theoretical level, to consider the sensory imaginary of urban development projects. Further, although the multiple sensory pollutions mentioned here would not exist without government cooperation, the primary beneficiaries of urban development are corporations and the tycoon economy. They stand to profit most from the normalisation of an urban life where the destruction of the natural environment, along with the assault on the sensory environment, can be done swiftly, systematically, and without impunity. If corporations (specifically those in the transportation and real estate sectors) cannot be held to environmental standards and responsibilities – and the working reality of government urban planning boards and environmental departments does not consistently demand any of these – then ordinary citizens of the city will be at a loss to salvage any control over their urban futures.

We are only just beginning to understand how much our city is touched by the 'disappearance' of the harbour (again, the harbour being the only large-scale natural wind channel situated at the heart of a heavily congested urbanity). This kind of disappearance can rightfully be attributed to the impact of government deregulation and tycoons' profit-making extending back to the colonial era. But what about conservationist discourses? How should we fully understand the continued destruction of the harbour even after the enactment of a monumental piece of legislation in 1997, which to date remains the only legislation to regulate the harbour reclamation activities of the government? This piece of legislation is known as the Protection of the Harbour Ordinance, Cap. 531 (Harbour Bill), which was passed in the Legislative Council on 27 June 1997 as one of the last pieces of legislation enacted under the British colonial administration. How do we assess the usefulness and impact, if any, of the Harbour Bill? According to its doctrinal principle as a piece of environmental law, or its proven record to halt harbour reclamation through judges' decisions? What about the connection between this law and the sensory impact of harbour disappearance as a cultural crisis? To what extent can the Harbour Bill work toward a 'sensory justice' levelled not only on the ground of environmental protection, but also upon a sensory restoration of an 'embodied citizenship'? This essay offers a glimpse of the sensory relevance of the Harbour Bill, and by extension, of environmental laws (see Howes 2003; Urry 1999). It asks: how does the law sense? How does the Harbour Bill constitute the notion of the senses through its legal imagination of the Victoria Harbour, and of the practice and legal permissibility of reclamation projects? Put in another way, as a piece of environmental law, how does the Harbour Bill produce a 'sensory imaginary' of the harbour, the city, and the urban dwellers in it? And in actual adjudication situations, which sensory capacities do judges use and privilege? This essay centres on a reading of a major court case of judicial review in 2003, which concerned the legality of the government's final phases of harbour reclamation projects on the shorelines of Central and Wan Chai. The case was heard at the height of a public debate over the future fate of the Victoria Harbour due to (a) the legal importance of the Central and Wan Chai reclamation zones in testing, for the first time, the commanding strength of the Harbour Bill, and (b) the symbolic importance of the same shoreline areas as literally occupying the geographical centre of all urban imaginations of the Victoria Harbour. In short, this essay looks at the sensory jurisprudence enabled by the Harbour Bill, and contemplates briefly an alternative, more embodied, environmental legal apparatus that can better address, activate, and preserve the 'sensory imaginary' of the Harbour.

'Harbourcide'

Historically speaking, Hong Kong's Victoria Harbour, originally named the Hong

Kong Harbour, has been extraordinarily loyal both to the semantic meaning of 'harbouring' and to the political, military, and economic dynamics of a maritime Victorian city (see Yu 2009). The geographical location as well as the topographical features of the Harbour quite literally provides a 'shelter' to the city's urban development. If 'to harbour' is to shelter a thought or sensation, then one only needs to look at the physicality of the harbour environment to glean a sense of how it provides refuge to the very idea and performance of 'urban growth'. From a physical perspective, the Victoria Harbour area is both locationally and morphologically the centre of Hong Kong. It has sheltered not only maritime commerce and military operations that together gave rise to the city's reputation as offering a deep and safe body of water for passage and anchorage, but it has also been a natural refuge in the sense of being the only and remaining open space and wind channel formed in the shape of a bowl encircled by hill ridges and high-rise buildings. The 'bowl effect' has given rise to the harbour's nickname as 'the lung' in the body of Hong Kong. The growth of the city is therefore materially anchored in this topographical – and blatantly corporeal – imagination; the motifs of shipping, trading, wind-sheltering, open spatiality, and urban breathing are what underwrite the topoi or commonplace imagination of the city. If the Harbour has been a material and symbolic haven that nourishes urban growth, then its historical significance would surely be of an environmentalist persuasion. Put in another way, the function of the Harbour *depends on* the suppression of any imagination of urban transformations that would defile the morphological, ecological, and visual structure of the Harbour. If we proceed to think of this with a preservationist view of the Harbour, which many green advocates do so, then the link between the notions of preservation and 'urban suppression' provides an interesting perspective for thinking about the critical problem of land reclamation on the Harbour.

Preservation Versus Reclamation

Generally speaking, the ethics of preservation arises from a discourse that goes something like this: an environment has an intrinsic value, and this value-unto-itself produces a goal of allowing as little change as possible to the natural form of the environment. This broad goal is to be achieved through independence from the sources of power that threaten to deplete the environment, extending a moral imperative to form a sustainable community that affords a shelter to natural resources. This is, broadly speaking, a deontological view. Through this view, a 'suppressive' logic is produced that is antithetical to the liberal logic of development, since deontologically the worth of a natural environment is said to conform to the binding rule of preservation and thus resists derivative uses such as land reclamation. However, the very idea of reclamation suggests an opposite course of action aiming at *liberating* a certain way of life, a kind of community, or a type of development. Historically, land reclamation has been deeply led by a liberal economic logic couched precisely in terms of *a liberation of an economic life out of nature*. The creation of new land for use by human activities, the development of agriculture, the restoration of beaches after erosion from longshore drift, the construction of landfill as a solution for managing waste, and so on: these habitat changes have been the outcomes of a liberal transformation of the natural environment. Urban development is but an acute form of this liberal transformation, whereby the government's contention about land shortage in the city establishes a powerful basis for new reclamation and zoning exercises. The most ubiquitous form of water-for-land urban development takes a 'double depletion': from depletion of waterfront to make way for land, and from the depletion of land to create a built environment. That land reclamation and zoning practices are commercial in nature is patently obvious; but what needs to be thematised is that the primary transformation of nature into urbanity is one that constructs and adheres property interests to the physical environment. In this way, we see that the arc of urban development moves along points of interplay between a preservationist sense of 'duty' and a property-based notion of 'rights'. While this may strike us as self-evident, this understanding is in fact vital for thinking about the Victoria Harbour as a social and legal object.

The historical transformation of Victoria Harbour took place around crucial moments of Hong Kong's development. There was, first, the moment of a Victorian militarisation of the city, especially around the shorelines of the Harbour, in the second half of 1800s. Apart from building barracks, gun batteries, naval dockyards, and military hospitals at different points on Hong Kong Island on or close to the shoreline of the Harbour, the British commanders also utilised the biggest chunk of the Central business district – called the Victoria Cantonment at that time – for military ceremonies and parades. There was even a Battery Path that led up from Queen's Road Central to the Cathedral grounds. It was not until the 1960s that the parade ground in Central was released for commercial use. Historian Jason Wordie (1999) explains the linkage between this broad military build-up and the reclamation of the Harbour:

> The inevitable consequence of this land use by the military was the inability of the Central business district to expand towards the east, as the land was already occupied. Various attempts were made to get the military to move, without success. The western side of Hong Kong Island had been settled in the earliest colonial days, and land there was already fully utilised. Thus the only solution to this chronic shortage of space in the European business district was to move in the only direction possible northwards into Victoria Harbor.

As for the recreational use of the water, it has been a long-held fact that the Victoria Harbour used to be home to many different aquatic clubs and swimming contests. In the 1850s, Hong Kong's first sports club, the Victoria Recreation Club, held swimming and water polo competitions on the Harbour.

The second key moment of the city's development, needless to say, took place from the mid-1960s onward, when overpopulation, intense commercial developments, a land-selling model of generating government revenue, and the predilection of urban living and working spawned a strong policy focus on land reclamation in the Harbour. The Praya Reclamation Scheme from the 1860s to the early

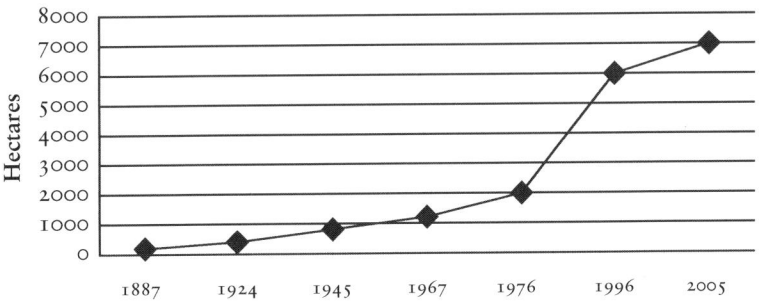

13.1. Reclamation of the Victoria Harbour over the years. Courtesy: Harbour Business Forum.

1900s,[1] which at the time was the largest reclamation project in the Central and Wan Chai areas, pales in comparison to the reclamation work done at the height of Hong Kong's industrialisation period. By 1997, at the end of the British colonial era, over 6,000 hectares (23 square miles) of the harbour had been reclaimed.

Towards the end of the colonial period, the government embarked on another large-scale programme to further reclaim the Harbour. The full scale of the intended reclamation presented to the Town Planning Board in December 1994 revealed the government's plan to reclaim a further 1,297 (4.5 square miles) of the Harbour (Chu 2002: 260). After the completion of the Central and Wan Chai Reclamation Feasibility Study in 1989, the then Land Development Policy Committee endorsed a five-phase reclamation process enacted around a three-cell shoreline formation (known as the Central-Tamar-Exhibition development zone).[2] But this three-cell shoreline development actually extends from Sheung Wan in the west to Causeway Bay in the east. The government reclamation plan, once again, directly reveals the powerful underlying interests of the transportation lobby, because much of the rationale for the reclamation rested in the need for land to provide several new and extended subway lines and new roads (such as the Central-Wan Chai bypass, the creation of Hong Kong station for the airport line, the creation of the future North Hong Kong island line and the Shatin to Central link, and so forth). Implicitly though, the new land would become fresh commercial space primed to the interests of the real estate lobby. To assuage public resentment toward the destruction of the Harbour, the government framed the reclamation as a case of solving the city's long-standing traffic congestion problem, poor waterfront utilisation, and the inconvenient traffic pattern in the city's subway system. Positioning itself as the problem-solver, the government envisaged the city's future with its visualisation of gleaming new roads without congestion, supple green waterfront parks and promenades, and figures of happy and relaxed residents and tourists enjoying the city's open space along the shores of Victoria Harbour. In this framing, however, what was made invisible is the *problem-generating* capacity of the reclamation work, namely the problem of new and more intense traffic congestion caused precisely by the new roadways, a definite escalation of the level and spread of pollution, and a higher density of high-rises to block the waterfront view. All of this will lead to further environmental degradation of the Harbour, which takes the form of water pollution, destruction of marine life, stronger waves and thus rougher sailing conditions for shipping vessels due to the narrowing waterways, and of course the increase in air pollutants trapped over and around the Harbour area.

The Toxification of the Harbour

Dredging is the primary action required of any land reclamation; the engineering of water-for-land necessarily involves a violent morphological transformation of the seabed from soft mud to hard concrete floor. The root meaning of dredging is 'to drag', meaning to pull or yank hard. In reclamation, the seabed is defiled and mud that has been sedimented with all kinds of toxic heavy metals is dug up. When activist groups such as Greenpeace requested mud samples from the barge on the reclamation site in 2003, the government and their contractor blocked the groups' entry and barred them from taking any mud samples away with them (Lee 2003). In 1992, the government's own Environmental Protection Department had already issued a report that found seven heavy metals in mud taken from Victoria Harbour, including mercury, copper, lead, cadmium, chromium, nickel and zinc. It found mud containing high levels of copper, lead, chromium and mercury, which if consumed can cause cancer, respiratory diseases and damaged blood cells in the brain and kidneys (Lee 2003). Greenpeace argued that those toxins were directly released into the sea along with industrial waste in the 1970s and 1980s. The 1992 report also found that the Central reclamation project alone would dredge 580,000 cubic metres of mud from the seabed. An environmental impact assessment conducted by the government had in fact classified over 63 per cent of that mud as 'class C', which was rated as the most seriously contaminated material, and the toxins would be swiftly carried away by the natural currents. 'Despite overwhelming evidence of the potentially harmful consequences of the reclamation, the government still insists that the ongoing reclamation work is reversible. The dredging company told us that they work 24 hours a day now', said Kevin May of Greenpeace in 2003 (see Lee 2003).

The dramatic decline in harbour water quality dates back to the 1970s, at the height of Hong Kong's industrialisation phase, which saw the rapid growth of factories – electroplating, bleaching and dyeing, and so forth – turning up around the Harbour. The factories discharged toxic industrial effluents directly into the Harbour with little or no treatment at all. With the implementation of new laws that required factories to treat their effluents before entering the Harbour, which incurred high running costs, many factories decided to relocate to the Mainland (thereby causing pollution in the Pearl River Delta) (see Hopkinson 2010). As pointed out by green groups, the toxins released over many years (such as heavy metals and organic chemicals) are still buried in the soft mud on the Harbour floor today.

Another cause of the Harbour deterioration has been the relentless increase in population and the sewage waste that it generates. The constant narrowing of the Harbour from reclamation has reduced the flushing action of tides, while more and more sewage is released into the water. The lack of oxygen and the high levels of bacteria and ammonia have destroyed marine life, while producing a strong stench. The high level of complaints by visitors about the bad smell at the old Kai Tak airport were among the reasons for relocating the airport away from the centre of the Harbour.[3]

Reclamation also takes its toll on wildlife and the ecosystem. As Lisa Hopkinson (2009) has pointed out:

> The loss of natural coastline caused by reclamation results in a loss of important habitat and shallow feeding areas for many inter-tidal creatures that live in shallow sandy bays or on rocky shorelines. The hard straight unnatural seawalls that have been constructed along much of the harbor waterfront supports little wildlife [...] Dangerous toxins [from dredging] can build up in the food chain, and eventually contaminate locally caught fish.

Two other problems also arise from excessive reclamation. Environmental groups have warned that as the dredged mud is barged off and dumped in an area near Chek Lap Kok airport, it threatens an area heavily used by pink dolphins and migratory whales and near to a marine park. Additionally, since the reclamation itself requires clean, coarse sand, often dredged from different, more pristine parts of the ocean bed, it is performed at the cost of coral and other bottom-dwelling organisms.

The term 'harbourcide' is used here to refer to the historical destruction of the Harbour through the morphological reduction of the Harbour into a channel, the toxification of water, the decimation of marine life, the intensification of water currents and thus destabilisation of the passageway for shipping vessels. These scientific facts aside, harbourcide also points to polysensory defilement in multiple forms, including visual pollution, stench caused by toxic sludge and foul-smelling landfills, irritation of the eyes caused by air pollutants, persistent noise created by dredging machines, and as a result, the permanent end of unmediated human contact with the water, since swimming in the Harbour – a favourite pastime of a bygone era – has become unthinkable.[4] Sensory violence is an important part of the understanding of harbourcide. It is also, as will be argued later, a locus for a legal rethinking that would embrace a principle of 'embodiment' in order to reimagine a viable future for the Harbour.

Time's 2005 article, 'How to Lose a Harbor', graphically detailed the societal, cultural, and economic losses that resulted from years of unregulated reclamation of the Harbour (Estulin 2005). The article remains one of the few international exposés of this local problem. Yet it managed to reach many organisations outside Hong Kong, raising serious awareness and calling for tougher measures to regulate, if not halt, future reclamations. Long before *Time*'s report raised international awareness, however, Hong Kong lawmakers had already struggled to enact an important law to limit the destruction caused by reclamation work. What were the specific regulations stated in the Protection of Harbour Ordinance (Harbour Bill), which became law in 1997? What legal principles and environmental legal ethics were behind the Ordinance? When this law was mobilised, how did the court envision and construct the Harbour, the harm done to it, and the remedies sanctioned? To what sensory capacities did the court appeal to in its rulings? How can the Harbour Bill be strengthened via a theory and politics of the senses? These are some of the questions discussed in the next section.

Sensing the Law, Embodying the Environment

Like other critical legal theorists and analysts, I take the law as a crucial site of cultural struggle in this study (see also Erni 2009; Erni 2012). One of the aims of this study is to exert a cultural and political reading of environmental law. In the case of the Victoria Harbour, decades of destruction by reclamation projects had finally reached a point of crisis in the early 1990s that warranted urgent legal intervention. To date, the enactment of the Harbour Bill remains the only powerful weapon against unregulated and excessive reclamations. In fact, enabled directly by the Harbour Bill, a series of judicial reviews in 2003 and 2004 did significantly slow down the government's reclamation plans. The power exercised by law, it is insisted in this study, must be understood as a matter of conjunctural struggle, whereby the constituting power of law enters into an intricate negotiation with the site upon which it is supposed to constitute its own power. It bears reminding that, for instance, with Foucault, the power of law is never conceived of as a total or totalising sphere (Foucault's famous phrase about cutting off the king's head), but as a network implying an intricate interweaving of many micro-events of power and counter-power. As Rosemary Coombe reminds us, 'If law is central to hegemonic processes, it is also a key resource in counterhegemonic struggles' (1998: 35).

The enactment of the Harbour Bill grew out of civil society actions in the community. The public, along with professional institutions, some community leaders, political parties, fishermen, and green groups, had supported a series of high-profiled protests and campaigns spearheaded by the Society for Protection of the Harbour (SPH, established in 1995). As the former Legislative Councillor Christine Loh presented the Harbour bill to the Legislative Council in 1996, she was met with strong opposition from the government, but strong support from the public. A 1997 survey conducted by the SPH and the Social Sciences Research Centre of the University of Hong Kong found a 92.6% favorable rate from the public to support the passing the Harbour Bill (Chu 2002: 262). Only a few days before the historic Handover, on 27 June 1997, the Harbour Bill was passed into law, re-creating the Harbour as a cohesive legal object for the first time. The major substance of the bill lays in Section 3, which states:

> Section 3. Presumption against reclamation in the Harbor
> 1. The Harbor is to be protected and preserved as a special public asset and a natural heritage of Hong Kong people, and for that purpose there shall be a presumption against reclamation in the harbor.
> 2. All public officers and public bodies shall have regard to the principle stated in subsection 1 for guidance in the exercise of any powers vested in them.

Winston Chu, the former Chairperson of and currently advisor to the SPH, states that in drafting the Harbour Bill, lawmakers stressed that:

> [...] there was no precedent anywhere else in the world. Despite conscientious research, no similar legislation could be found. Accordingly, the entire legal concept of the Harbor Ordinance has to be invented and original expressions, such as designating the harbor as a 'special public asset' and a 'natural heritage of Hong Kong people', had to be coined. (2002: 263)

However, despite a lack of absolute corresponding precedents, by that time, the discourse of sustainable development was already in vogue, not least since the historic enactment of the 1992 Rio Declaration on Environment and Development. If the Harbour Bill is considered a discursive extension to the Rio doctrine, then it is worth remembering that 'the pursuit of purely "environmental" values is not what the concept of sustainable development is intended to serve. Yet, if integration may not be a panacea, it remains the most likely means to secure a balanced view of environmental needs within competing priorities' (Birnie and Boyle 2002: 87). In the parlance of environmental laws, 'integration' means that environmental protection constitutes an integral part of social and economic development; the two cannot be considered in isolation. Todd Aagaard, a scholar in environmental law, elaborates:

> Narrowing the definition of environmental law to include only laws that focus primarily on protecting the environment or that reflect an environmentalist ethic [...] ignores a crucially important feature of environmental law: the inherent and pervasive trade-offs in environmental decision making. As a result of these trade-offs, environmental protection is almost never the only or overriding purpose of a law that applies to the environment. Indeed, environmental law is better understood as a field in which the goal of environmental protection sits in a position of constant tension with countervailing interests and values. Environmental laws always reflect a balance of objectives, and envisioning environmental law as exclusively or primarily devoted to environmental protection would counterproductively obscure the essential question of how to balance among competing goals and interests that include, but are not limited to, environmental protection. (2010: 263)

Integrationism – and its underlying principle of the balancing of interests between environmentalist and developmentalist goals – permeates the Rio Declaration and many subsequent international and domestic legal instruments. The Harbour Bill is no exception. The integrationist principle can be found in the phrase 'presumption against reclamation' in subsection 1.

This presumption requirement in the Harbour Bill was written as a powerful deterrent to any public officers or public bodies who proposed reclamation projects. The threshold for overcoming this presumption, as we shall see shortly, was set rather high. Nonetheless, as a legal principle, it is understood that this is not an absolute presumption in the form of a hard substantive rule, but more like a 'rebuttable' presumption. Winston Chu explains: 'it was never the intention [of the Harbor Bill] to stop reclamation altogether. To meet the needs of proper urban development, for example the provision of essential infrastructure facilities, some reclamation must be tolerated and allowed' (263). In this way, the Harbour Bill was crafted in such a way as to allow a conquerable presumption, making reclamation an immanent possibility. In what follows, I shall focus on the 2003 judgment of the Court of First Instance dealing with a judicial review case lodged against the government by the SPH in the latter's attempt to halt reclamation work on the Harbour, and attempt to read from it the assortment of discursive constructions around the question of immanence. Special attention will be paid to the use and consideration of the sensory constructions embedded in the Harbour Bill.

The Protection of Harbour Ordinance in Action

In April 2003, after several phases of the Central and Wan Chai reclamation projects had already been accomplished and irreversible damage had been done to the Harbour, the SPH lodged a judicial review procedure, which essentially took the government to court to halt its permission of reclamation work. Two grounds were put forward as the basis of the application for judicial review, namely that the government made 'an error in law' (non-compliance with the purposive construction of the law) and that the decisions in the proposed reclamation were 'irrational' (either unnecessary or out of proportion, or both). These were grounds aimed at challenging the fact that the government had not successfully overcome the statutory presumption against reclamation.

From the initial phase of public consultation on the reclamation proposal, through the process of making amendments to it, to the stage of court hearings, different parties of the case collaborated on the interpretation of the Harbour Bill with a strongly visual language. Not surprisingly, the construction of the phrase 'special public asset and natural heritage' turned on the visual significance of the Harbour view as the prime special object needing protection from reclamation. This was partly a result of references made to the 1972 Convention for the Protection of the World Cultural and Natural Heritage, Article 2 of which defined 'natural heritage' to include, *inter alia*, 'natural sites [...] of outstanding universal value from the point of view of science, conservation or natural beauty'. Aesthetic value, itself a reductive interpretation of an environment's value, was further reduced to visual beauty. Another source that influenced the parties to rely so heavily on visual beauty in their arguments was the Town Planning Board's expressive missions, which stated, among other things, 'our goals for the Harbor are [...] to enhance the scenic views of the Harbor and maintain visual access to the harbor-front [...] to enhance the Harbor as a unique attraction for our people and tourists [...] to create a quality harbor-front through encouraging innovative building design'. When attention was skewed to the visual qualities of the Harbour, it was not hard for the phrase 'special public asset' in the Harbour Bill to be radically limited to an ocularcentric precept. With this as our basis, we may now examine the court arguments more closely.

In ascertaining the SPH's statement claiming that the government had committed 'errors in law' and that their decisions were 'irrational', the judge in the Court of First Instance centred her arguments on two legal technical grounds. First, to prove whether any errors have been made in law, judge Chu called forth a reading of the plain words of the Harbour Bill through what was known as a 'purposive construction' approach. By this, she meant to take components of the Harbour Bill, particularly the key phrases, and subjected them to legal benchmarking with authoritative jurisprudence found in other courts around the world. For instance, in referencing *South Lakeland DC v. Secretary of State for the Environment* (1992), the judge concluded that the purpose of preserving or enhancing the environment had to be afforded a high priority, whereby the object of that preservation or enhancement was referred to as 'the character or appearance of conservation areas' (*SPH v. TPB* 2003: 53). Second, the judge applied the 'mischief rule', which was a device in legal reasoning that construed past violations as a legitimate and appropriate ground for considering the likelihood of violation in the present. In this, judge Chu stated:

> It cannot be doubted that the Harbor Bill was enacted against a background of resorting to reclamation for the provision of land for housing, economic and social purposes. The enactment was preceded by a motion condemning excessive reclamation of the Harbor [...] It is thus fair to say that the mischief that the Ordinance and section 3 set out to remedy is excessive and unnecessary reclamation of the Harbor. (*SPH v. TPB* 2003: 57)

The judge further stated that:

> [i]t is pointed out there were a number of instances in the past where the reclamation was proposed to meet community needs, but after land was reclaimed, it was rezoned for development or commercial use. In the present case, even before the draft Outline Zoning Plan was finalised, proposals to rezone some of the reclaimed land have already been approved.[5] (58)

Through the purposive construction approach and the mischief rule technique, the judge cleared the ground for stating the specific thresholds that the government would have to overcome before the statutory presumption against reclamation could be rebutted.

Here, the entire case rested on three legal tests. First, there was the 'compelling, overriding and present need test', which accorded protection and preservation an absolute priority, unless clear, cogent, persuasive, and objective evidence suggested that reclamation would satisfy a greater public need, something that was 'truly exceptional, so urgent and compelling that it ought to override the public need to protect and preserve the Harbor' (45). It should be noted that the bar on the understanding of 'public needs' was set unusually high, implying the importance of collective needs to protect and defend the Harbour on social, communal, and even sensory-experiential grounds. The second test was the 'no alternative test', making unavoidability a bar that any reclamation plan would need to overcome. The third test was the 'minimum impairment test', which stated that the scale of the reclamation proposed should be restricted to what was strictly necessary. The second and third tests are essentially tests based on liberal principles. Here the Harbour and its fate were subjected to a balancing of competing interests on the basis of necessity and proportionality. Rather than the absolutism of the first test, these two parameters sought to minimise damage (rather than to maximise protection). Throughout we see not only how the judge displayed strong preservationist ethics, but also how the entire proceeding utilised only one type of evidence in argumentation: visual evidence in the forms of maps, graphs, photographs, display boards, and so on. The shaping power of visuality, despite helping the SPH to successfully squash the government's proposed reclamation plan, condensed the Harbour into a simple and one-dimensional object. The preservation was essentially a preservation of a view. What was a juridical victory could in fact be a symbolic loss, because the outcome of the case, I argue, did halt the reclamation but weakened the Harbour Bill itself. Why is this so?

Out of this court case, the Harbour to be embraced by the public in law became a visual spectre, whose preservation meant that other dimensions of the harm done to the Harbour failed to be legally recognised by the Harbour Bill. As a case that sets the precedent in Harbour protection, this ruling, it can be said, wrote into the Harbour's future a singular and radically restrictive vision. In writing the Harbour as a visually valuable thing, the meanings around the provision of preserving the 'special public asset' and 'natural heritage' are therefore partial and limited. In any future potential case, the weakening of the Harbour Bill would be most obvious when the case presents a reclamation proposal that manages to keep the beauty of the Harbour but degrades its water quality, toxifies life forms, human or otherwise, and creates a malodorous environment. The fact that these forms of harm did not get recognised in an ocularcentric ruling is sufficient for us to raise serious doubt about the effectiveness of the Harbour Bill in future hearings.

Conclusion

In the legal landscape, environmental law is an infant domain of law. Notwithstanding the increasing mobilisation of neoliberal political pressure to discredit the scientific validity of environmental work, the social imaginary around the natural environment today remains relatively unstable. It ebbs and flows along with the state of technoscience and the economy, among other things. In the common law tradition, environmental laws stand at a unique crossroad between a tort law approach that privileges a view of environmental problems as market failures and thus builds legal relations of damage control with and into markets, and what has been called a deontological preservationist legal approach seeking to step outside of the liberal framework to embrace the value of nature qua nature.

In the case of the struggle to save the Victoria Harbour, it remains to be analysed as to how a new legal imaginary can be constructed, one that is no longer ocularcentric, but one that embodies a robust sensory imaginary. Perhaps a conceptual condition and two legal apparatuses can be considered. The conceptual move involves theorising the natural environment as a pervasively interconnected and radically constructivist materiality. As Donna Haraway argued a long time ago: 'We must find another relationship to nature besides reification and possession' (1992: 295). An approach adherent to Haraway's critical artifactualism would reposition nature as both fact and fiction. Yet while Haraway privileges nature's artifactualism as something made in technoscientific practices, there is ample opportunity for thinking of this artifactualism as something additionally made through the acute sensory capacities. Making nature a matter of strategic sensory production is not so much a question of denaturing as a particular production of nature. It allows for an embodied reconstruction of nature as a 'sensorium', a supple materiality of complex web of sensations: sight, scent, sound, touch, balance, kinesthesia, and so forth. The production of nature-as-sensorium would entail doing away with the Cartesian dualism that plagues the legal imagination, for this dualism suggests why law has rarely questioned its own senses, that is, its own sources of knowledge, the way it senses particular circumstances, the manner in which it mobilises the senses in decisions, and so forth. Since law associates itself purely with reason, the marginalisation of the sensations produces partial and distorted legal operations (see Bently 1996).

But how does this critical artifactualism translate into an alternative legal practice? I suggest that legal cross-fertilisation is inevitable. A borrowing of legal precepts and tools from outside the domain of doctrinal environmental law may present a new opening, particularly for rethinking the Harbour as a legal terrain of struggle. What I have in mind are two different legal apparatuses: public nuisance laws and patency laws. Briefly, public nuisance law conceptualises the harm principle in law as centring upon public nuisance that threatens the welfare of a social body. There is room for this legal approach to include sensory nuisance as statutory harm. Patency law, on the other hand, requires specification of what is known as 'preferred embodiments', which are the codified extensions of a property protected by the patent. Both of these legal apparatuses, it could be argued, are extensions of the common law approach that provide a liberally-orientated possibility of making legal claims on a protected property. Some of the questions that these legal methods can help to pose for the Harbour protection case include: how would an approach that includes sensory nuisance as statutory harm reorient the Harbour Bill and its privileging of sight as the locus of protection? Who are the collective subjects claiming nuisance? How do we refigure the 'actors' in the construction of the sensory categories of nature and culture, bearing in mind, as Haraway does, that they include the organic and the inorganic, the human and non-human?[6] Should the Harbour be conceived, crudely, as 'patented property', and how can its water, marine life, seabed, and shorelines be thought of as preferred embodiments that augment the very notions of 'special public asset' and 'natural heritage' already codified in the Harbour Bill? These and other related questions, I hope, will open an alternative gateway to a different jurisprudence. Further legal research on the cross-fertilisation of laws would be needed, and it should be performed alongside a cultural interpretive approach with the aim of preserving and revitalising the multi-sensory beauty of the Victoria Harbour.

Notes

1. See 'Praya Reclamation Scheme,' Wikipedia: http://en.wikipedia.org/wiki/Praya_Reclamation_Scheme, accessed 20 July 2011.
2. See 'Central and Wan Chai Reclamation,' Civil Engineering and Development Department, HKSAR, http://www.cedd.gov.hk/eng/about/achievements/regional/regi_central.htm, accessed 20 July 2011.
3. Since 2004, the Hong Kong government has passed tough laws to control sewage release and treatment.
4. In September 2010, the Amateur Swimming Association of Hong Kong proposed to revise the cross-Harbour swimming contest, which was halted in 1979 due to high level of bacteria found in the water. See: www.skyscrapercity.com/archive/index.php/t-1208389.html, accessed 20 July 2011. The cross-harbour swimming contest was eventually held on an experimental basis in 2011 and 2012. The number of registered entrants increased from 1,000 to 1,800.
5. Major examples of the danger of re-zoning of reclaimed land include: (a) West Kowloon Reclamation (340 hectares): the once promised public park, being the main justification for a large reclamation has been re-zoned for commercial and cultural development; (b) Central Reclamation Phase I (20 hectares): the former Central Bus Terminal and Yaumati Ferry Concourse have been re-zoned for commercial development and the bus terminal and ferry concourse will be moved to the new Central Reclamation Phase III; (c) North Point: a large public playground on the reclaimed waterfront zoned as Open Space on the Draft North Point Outline Zoning Plan No. S/H8/15 was re-zoned in October 2002 for development of government offices.
6. Haraway sheds important light here: 'The actors are not all us. If the world exists for us as nature, this designates a kind of relationship, an achievement among many actors, not all of them human, not all of them organic, not all of them technological. In its scientific embodiments as well as in other forms nature is made, but not entirely by humans; it is a co-construction among humans and non-humans...The commonplace nature I seek, a public culture, has many houses with many inhabitants which/who can refigure the earth. Perhaps those other actors/actants, the ones who are not human, are our to pick gods [local gods specific to places], organic and inorganic' (1992: 231).

References

Bently, Lionel and Leo.Flynn, eds. 'Introduction.' In *Law and the Senses: Sensational Jurisprudence,* 1-17. London: Pluto Press, 1996.

Birnie, Patricia and Alan Boyle. 'The structure of international environmental law I: Rights and obligations of states.' In *International Law and the Environment,* second edition. 79-177. New York: Oxford University Press, 2002.

Chu, Winston Ka-sun. 'Legal control of harbor reclamation.' *Hong Kong Law Journal* 32, no. 2 (2002): 259-269.

Coombe, Rosemary J. 'Contingent Articulations: A Critical Cultural Studies of Law.' *Law in the Domains of Culture* 21, (1998).

Erni, John N. 'New Sovereignties and Neoliberal Ethics: Remapping the Human Rights Imaginary.' *Cultural Studies* 23, no.3 (2009): 417-436.

—. (2012). 'Who Needs Human Rights: Cultural Studies and Public Institutions.' In *Instituting Cultural Studies,* edited by Meaghan Morris and Mette Hjort, Hong Kong: Hong Kong University Press, 175-190.

Estulin, Chaim. 'How to Lose a Harbor.' *Time,* 25 April 2005. http://www.time.com/time/magazine/article/0,9171,1053690,00.html, accessed 20 July 2011.

Haldar, Plyel. 'Acoustic Justice.' In *Law and the Senses: Sensational Jurisprudence*, edited by Lionel Bently and Leo Flynn, 123-136. London & Chicago: Pluto Press, 1996.

Haraway, Donna. 'The Promises of Monsters: A Regenerative Politics of Unappropriate/d Others.' In *Cultural Studies*, edited by Lawrence Grossberg, Cary Nelson and Paula Treichler, 295-337. New York & London: Routledge, 1992.

HKUST and Civic Exchange. Relative Significance of Local vs Regional Sources: Hong Kong's Air Pollution. www.civic-exchange.org/eng/upload/files/200703_HKAirPollutionPres.pdf, accessed 10 May 2010.

Hopkinson, Lisa. 'The Environmental Impact of Harbor Reclamation.' www.friendsoftheharbour.org/articles_4_en.php?lang=eng, accessed 10 May 2010.

Howes, David. *Sensual Relations: Engaging the Senses in Culture and Social Theory*. Ann Arbor: The University of Michigan Press, 2003.

Iser, Wolfgang. *The Fictive and the Imaginary: Charting Literary Anthropology*. Johns Hopkins University Press, 1993.

Lee, Matthew. 'Mud in Eye for Activists.' *The Standard*, 30 October 2003. http://www.thestandard.com.hk/news_detail.asp?pp_cat=&art_id=30628&sid=&con_type=1&d_str=20031030&sear_year=2003, accessed 20 July 2011.

Loh, Christine. 'An Overriding Public Need,' *South China Morning Post*, 4 January 2007.

Nagle, John Copeland. 'The Idea of Pollution.' *UC Davis Law Review* 43 (2009): 1-78.

Smith, Kirk. 'Air pollution.' *Environment* 30, no. 10 (1988): 16-35. Court of First Instance. *Society for Protection of the Harbor Ltd. V. Town Planning Board* (2003), HKCU, 793.

Urry, John. 'Sensing the City.' In *The Tourist City*, 71-86. New Haven & London: Yale University Press, 1999.

Wordie, Jason. 'Land-Grabbing Titans who Changed Hong Kong's Profit for Good.' *The Standard*, 18 April 1999. http://www.thestandard.com.hk/news_detail.asp?pp_cat=&art_id=27127&sid=&con_type=1&d_str=19990418&sear_year=1999, accessed 10 May 2010.

Yu, Richard. 'Why We say the Victoria Harbour is an Irreplaceable and Irrecoverable Special Asset as well as a Natural Heritage of the Hong Kong People?' www.friendsoftheharbour.org/articles_3_en.php, accessed 10 May 2010.

Contributors

Ackbar Abbas (University of California, USA)
Professor of comparative literature at the University of California, Ackbar Abbas is a leading scholar and is widely published in the field of Asian urban studies and comparative literature. His research interests include globalisation, Hong Kong and Chinese culture, architecture, cinema, postcolonialism, and critical theory. His book on the disappearance of Hong Kong (1997, University of Minnesota Press) received wide critical acclaim. Other works include *Internationalizing Cultural Studies* (co-edited with John Erni, 2005), *Chen Danqing: Painting After Tiananmen* (1995), and *The Provocation of Jean Baudrillard* (1990). Abbas currently serves as a Contributing Editor to *Public Culture*.

Chua Beng Huat (National University of Singapore)
A leading scholar in the field of Asian cultural studies, he is co-founder of the *Journal for Inter-Asia Cultural Studies* (Routledge) and has published widely in urban planning and public housing, comparative politics in Southeast Asia, and emerging consumerism across Asia. His publications include: *Communitarian Ideology and Democracy in Singapore* (London and New York: Routledge, 1995) and *Political Legitimacy and Housing: Stakeholding in Singapore* (London and New York: Routledge, 1997). He has also edited *Consumption in Asia: Lifestyles and Identities* (London and New York: Routledge, 2000), and published *Life is Not Complete without Shopping* (Singapore: Singapore University Press, 2003).

Gregory Bracken (Delft University of Technology, the Netherlands)
In 2009, Gregory Bracken defended his PhD thesis entitled *Thinking Shanghai: A Foucauldian Interrogation of the Postsocialist Metropolis*. He has lived and worked in Asia since 1993 and has written the series of 'Walking Tour' guidebooks to cities in the region. His current research at the Delft School of Design is on the postcolonial global cities of East Asia, a topic he also researches in his capacity as research fellow at the International Institute of Asian Studies at Leiden University (www.iias.nl). Bracken is also a writer of crime fiction.

Yomi Braester (University of Washington, USA)
Professor of comparative literature and cinema studies, Yomi Braester has written extensively on urban changes and their representations in the fields of

popular culture and art. He has published numerous articles and authored two monographs (*Witness Against History: Literature, Film and Public Discourse in twentieth-Century China*, Stanford University Press 2003, and *Painting the City Red: Chinese Cinema and the Urban Contract*, Duke University Press 2010), and co-edited *Cinema at the City's Edge: Film and Urban Networks in East Asia*, Hong Kong University Press 2010.

Jeroen de Kloet (University of Amsterdam, the Netherlands)
Jeroen de Kloet is Professor of Globalisation Studies at the University of Amsterdam and director of the Amsterdam Centre for Globalisation Studies (ACGS). He is also affiliated as Senior Research Fellow to the Amsterdam School for Cultural Analysis (ASCA). He has published widely on Chinese popular culture, youth and cultural globalisation, and is editor of the *Journal of Chinese Cinemas*. He co-edited the volume *Cosmopatriots: On Distant Belonging and Close Encounters* (Rodopi 2007) and in 2010 published his monograph *China with a Cut: Globalisation, Urban Youth and Popular Music* (Amsterdam UP). Together with Yiu Fai Chow, he authored *Sonic Multiplicitie: Hong Kong Pop and the Global Circulation of Sound and Image* (Intellect 2013).

Jeroen Groenewegen-Lau (Beijing, China)
Jeroen Groenewegen-Lau defended his PhD dissertation (cum laude) entitled *The Performance of Identity in Chinese Popular Music* at Leiden University in 2011, supported by a grant of the Hulsewé-Wazniewski Foundation. He has published in journals such as *China Aktuell*, *The Journal of Inter-Asia Cultural Studies* and *Norient*. In Beijing he is involved in the music industry conference Sound of the Xity (2012, 2013).

Margaret Hillenbrand (University of Oxford, UK)
Margaret Hillenbrand is Lecturer in Modern Chinese Literature at the University of Oxford. She is the author of *Literature, Modernity, and the Practice of Resistance: Japanese and Taiwanese Fiction, 1960-1990* (2007), the editor of special issues of *Postcolonial Studies* (2010) and *The Journal of Chinese Cinemas* (2012), and the co-author of *Documenting China: A Reader in Seminal Twentieth-Century Texts* (2011). She has articles published or forthcoming in journals such as *Screen*, *MELUS*, *Postcolonial Studies*, *Journal of Asian Studies*, *Cinema Journal*, *Journal of Japanese Studies*, *positions: east asia cultures critique*, and elsewhere.

Stefan Landsberger (University of Amsterdam and Leiden University, the Netherlands)
Stefan Landsberger holds the Olfert Dapper chair of contemporary Chinese culture at the University of Amsterdam and has published extensively on political propaganda in China. Among his books are *Chinese Posters: The IISH-Landsberger Collections*, published by Prestel (2009) and *Chinese Propaganda Posters: From Revolution to Modernization*, published by Pepin Press (1995). His articles include 'Contextualising (Propaganda) Posters,' in Christian Henriot & Wen-hsin Yeh, eds., *Visualising China, 1845-1965 – Moving and Still Images in*

Historical Narratives, 2013; and 'Designing Propaganda: The Business of Politics,' in Zhang Hongxing & Lauren Parker, eds., *China Design Now*, 2008. He maintains the website

John Nguyet Erni (Lingnan University, Hong Kong)
John Nguyet Erni is Professor and Chair of the Department of Cultural Studies, Lingnan University, Hong Kong. He has published widely on critical public health, Chinese consumption of transnational culture, queer media, and youth popular consumption in Hong Kong and Asia. His books include *Understanding South Asian Minorities in Hong Kong: A Critical Multicultural Approach* (with Lisa Leung, HKUP, 2013), *Cultural Studies of Rights: Critical Articulations* (Routledge, 2011), *Internationalizing Cultural Studies: An Anthology* (with Ackbar Abbas, Blackwell, 2005), *Asian Media Studies: The Politics of Subjectivities* (with Siew Keng Chua, Blackwell, 2005), and *Unstable Frontiers: Technomedicine and the Cultural Politics of 'Curing' AIDS* (Minnesota, 1994). Currently, he is completing a book project on the legal modernity of rights.

Ou Ning (Beijing, China)
Ou Ning is a curator, critic, filmmaker, artist and blogger. As an activist, he founded *U-thèque*, an independent film and video organisation; as an editor and graphic designer, he is known for his seminal book *New Sound of Beijing*; as a curator, he initiated the biennale exhibition *Get It Louder* (2005, 2007, 2010, 2012); as an artist, he is known for the urban research projects such as *San Yuan Li*, commissioned by the 50th Biennale di Venezia (2003), and *Da Zha Lan*, commissioned by the Kulturstiftung des Bundes. He is a frequent contributor to various magazines, books and exhibitions. In 2009, he was appointed the chief curator of the 2009 Shenzhen & Hong Kong Bi-city Biennale of Urbanism and Architecture (09SZHKB). In 2011, he curated *The Solutions: Design and Social Engineering* for the 2011 Chengdu Biennale and launched a new literary magazine, *Chutzpah* (*Tian Nan* in Chinese). He is based in Beijing, and is the director of the Shao Foundation.

Gladys Pak Lei Chong (University of Amsterdam, the Netherlands)
Gladys Pak Lei Chong is lecturer at Amsterdam University College and postdoctoral fellow at the International Institute of Asian Studies (IIAS). She graduated from the University of Hong Kong with B.A. in Comparative Literatures and English and from the University of Amsterdam with MA in Sociology. She has recently received her PhD from the Department of Media Studies of the University of Amsterdam. Her doctoral research is an interdisciplinary study, in which she examines the processes of subjectification and the interplay between the technologies of domination and the technologies of the self. She has published on subjects related to Chinese governmentalities, place-making, and Olympic security. Her research interests lie in the area of power-relations, state legitimacy and maintenance, processes of subjectification, the politics of identity, youth culture, discourses analysis, and the media. She is affiliated to the Amsterdam School for Cultural Analysis (ASCA).

Lena Scheen (New York University Shanghai)
Lena Scheen is assistant professor faculty fellow at NYU Shanghai. Her research focuses on the social and cultural implications of urbanisation and globalisation in China. In 2012, she defended her PhD dissertation on *Shanghai: Literary Imaginings of a City in Transformation*. Her publications include: 'Sensual, But No Clue of Politics: Shanghai's Longtang Houses,' in Gregory Bracken (ed.), A*spects of Urbanization in Asia: Shanghai, Hong Kong, Guangzhou*, University of Amsterdam Press (2012): 117-135, and Lena Scheen (ed.), *Hartenvrouw* [Queen of Hearts; short stories by Su Tong], De Geus (2012).

Robin Visser (University of North Carolina, USA)
Associate Professor of Asian Studies, Robin Visser analyzes Chinese urban design, art, cinema and literature. Her book, *Cities Surround The Countryside: Urban Aesthetics in Postsocialist China*, was published by Duke UP in 2010. Her numerous articles include: 'Satellite Towns and Virtual Urbanism: A Case Study of Beijing and Dujiangyan' (forthcoming in *Ghost Protocol: Development and Displacement in Global China*, Duke University Press), 'Diagnosing Beijing 2020: Mapping the Ungovernable City' (2008), 'Spaces of Disappearance: 1990s Beijing Art, Film, and Fiction in Dialogue with Urbanization' (2008), and (in Chinese), 'The Imagined City: Urban Planning and Aesthetic Criticism in Contemporary China,' in Sun Xiaozhong, ed., *Methodology and Case Studies: Collected Lectures on Cultural Studies*, 2008. She serves on the Editorial Board of the *Journal of Urban Cultural Studies*.

Index

1
14th Milan Triennial   212
15   36
2007 Shenzhen & Hong Kong Bi-city Biennale of Urbanism \ Architecture   212
2008 Beijing Olympics   138, 144, 146
20th Century Fox   160
24 City   68
798 Art Zone   17, 77-79, 81-83, 87-89, 94

A
A Better Tomorrow   24
A Magical Tour of Shanghai   69
A Map of Our Own   107, 115
Aagaard, Todd   236
Abbas, Ackbar   17, 21, 121, 129, 136-140, 142, 145-147, 149-151, 158-159, 166, 180
Abbing, Hans   85
Abu-Ghraib prison   93
Acharya, Shrawan K   136
Acquisitive society   21
Action Theatre   34
Activist   18, 53, 233
Agency   13, 18, 45, 46, 49, 53-55, 113, 115, 193, 198, 200, 206
Ai, Weiwei   77, 146
Akutagawa, Ryûnosuke   178
Alienation   11-12, 34-35, 98, 109, 115
America   35, 198, 211, 223-224

American capitalist jungle   198
American imperialism   121
Amsterdam   32, 151
An Anthology of Chinese Electronic Music 1992-2008   100
Anachronism   159
Anderson, Benedict   138, 142
Andreu, Paul   64
Angkor Wat   184
Anglo-centrism   16
Antagonism   22, 28, 215-216, 223
Anti-ideology   17, 44
Antihuman   44
Appadurai, Arjun   13, 16, 175
Appiah, Kwame Anthony   146
Arata, Isozaki   212-213
Architecture   *See also* Chinese, Koolhaas, *and* Spectacle
   Architect   63-64, 66-67, 71, 165, 211, 213
   Architectural icons   16
   Architectural simulation   61, 64
   Herzog and Meuron   13, 16
   Star architects   13, 16, 17
   Wood and Zapata   165
Area Studies   15-16
Art
   Aesthetics   27, 31, 37, 39, 45-46, 48-49, 51, 62, 70, 79, 84, 93, 99, 108, 157, 172, 175-176, 180, 184
   Art language   176
   Art zone   17, 78-79, 86
   Avant-garde   72, 98, 117, 196, 207

Conceptual art   114
Critique   11, 17, 19, 98
Objet d'art   46
Sound art   17, 97-117
Art Basel   54
Art World   106
Artifactualism   240
Asia Television Limited (ATV)   151
Aum, Shinrikyo   212
Aura   86, 89, 180
Australia   32, 191
Authenticity   50-51, 82, 91, 113, 141, 146, 171, 180, 208
Authoritarianism   12, 16, 21, 30-31, 45, 77, 91

B

Bai, Ling   197-198
Bakhtin, Mikhail   91
Bal, Mieke and David Vanderburgh   144
Bal, Mieke   91
Baltimore   33
Bangladesh   29, 40
Bank of China   70, 91, 128
Bank of Chinese Contemporary Art (BOCCA)   85
Banks, Christopher   161-162
Bardenstein, Carol B.   138-139
Barlow, Tani   196
Barmé, Geremie   203
Baudrillard, Jean   48, 50, 142, 198, 201
Bauman, Zygmunt   221, 224
Beijing   11-13, 17-19, 22, 54, 62-64, 67-68, 77-81, 86, 100-104, 106, 108, 112-113, 121-122, 125, 127, 131-132, 135-151, 176, 218, 223, 225, 244-246
   Olympics   11, 13, 18, 22-23, 45, 62, 67-68, 78, 81, 105, 108, 122, 125, 129, 131, 132, 135-136, 138, 140, 144-150
   Olympic City   135, 138, 144, 147-149
   The Bird's Nest Where A Dream Begin   147

Beijing Art Fair   85
Beijing Boom Tower (BBT)   65-66
Beijing Foreign Cultural Exchanges Association   135, 138
Beijing Grand Theatre   72
Beijing Investment Guide   138, 148
Beijing is Coming   11-12
Beijing Municipal Planning Commission (BMPC)   146
Beijing Official Guide   138, 142
Beijing Organising Committee for the Olympic Games (BOCOG)   146
Beijing Planning Exhibition Hall   138, 140
Beijing Subway   149
Beijing Tourism Administration   138
Beijiung Municipal Burea of Commerce   151
Bell, Clive   103
Benjamin, Walter   89
Bently, Lionel   240
Bergère, Marie-Claire   124
Berlin   158
Berman, Marshall   167
Big Movie   68
Bildungsroman   47
Bird's Nest   *See* Olympic Stadium
Birnie, Patricia and Alan Boyle   236
Böck, Ingrid   67
Borer, Michael Ian   56
Bourdieu, Pierre   85
Boyer, M. Christine   160
Boym, Svetlana   171
Bracken, Gregory   18
Braester, Yomi   13, 17, 45, 57, 66
British Council   102-104, 108, 110
Bronfen, Elisabeth   196, 198
Brothers   43, 46-49, 52, 57
Broudehoux, Anne-Marie   45, 136
Brownell, Susan   140
Buck-Morss, Susan   46, 55, 83, 93
Buffet, Peter   81
Buffet, Warren   81
Bunnell, Tim G.   139
Burnham, Daniel   211

C

Cai, Ruohong 123
  Callahan, William A. 140
Cambell, John Edward and Matt Carlson 56, 58
Cannes Festival 35
  Un Certain Regard 35
Cang, Lang 43-44, 51
Cao, Fei 12, 17, 46, 53-54, 57, 71-72, 79, 84, 90-93, 115
Cao, Xueqin 48-49
Caochangdi art village 77, 79
Cape no.7 176
Capitalism 14, 18, 21, 29, 34, 39, 43-45, 55, 82-83, 85, 90, 94, 157, 165-166, 193, 198, 200
  Cognitive capitalism 46
  Global Capitalism 11, 31, 34, 44, 57, 80, 82-83, 87, 167
  Transnational consumer capitalism 194, 203
  Western Capitalism 81
Cartesian 45, 47
  Cartesian dualism 240
  Cartesian epistemology 44-45
CCTV Tower 13, 53, 61-64, 70, 86, 91, 131, 147
Central Axis 144-145, 147
Central-Tamar-Exhibition 232
Chan, Alan 176
Chan, Heng Chee 30
Chan, King Fai 224
Chang and Eng 34
Chang, Eileen / Zhang, Ailing 159, 163
Chang, T.C. 136, 138-139, 142, 144
Chang, T.C. and Shirlena Huang 136, 139
Charney, Igal 146
Chen, Joan 106
Chen, Kaige 176
Chen, Liyun 78
Chen, Shaoxiong 85
Chen, Shui-bian 220-222
Chengdu 68, 104, 193, 197
Chengdu Biennale 245

Cheung, Mabel 101
Chiao, Peggy 183
Chicago 223
China Construction Design International (CCDI) 146
CHINA NOW 112
China Pavilion 132
China Sound Map 115
China Tracy 53, 71-72, 90, 115
Chinese
  Architecture 17, 21
  Art 17, 81-85, 123, 146
  Chineseness 13, 16, 80-83, 142, 147, 149, 174
  Cinema 17-18, 22-23
  City in Art 12-13
  Civil War 123
  Communist government 168
  Communist Party (CCP) 12, 121-123, 128, 130
  Contemporary city 14
  Courtyard house 162
  Femininity 90
  Popular culture 12, 99
  Public power 213
  Sex worker 35
  Soundscape 97-99, 102, 104-106, 109-110, 112, 115-117
  Urban sound ecology 103
  Urbanism 47, 64, 110
Chinese Arts Centre 112-113
Chinglish 194
Chong, Gladys Pak Lei 18, 129, 131, 147, 149
Chongqing 102-103, 176, 214-215
Chow, Rey 78, 81-82, 85, 179
Chow, Sze Chung 224
Chu, Hoi Dick 232
Chu, Hoi Dick and Chow Sze Chung 219
Chu, Winston 236-238
Chua, Beng Huat 17, 30
Chua, Beng Huat and Wei Wei Yeo 36
CIAM 212

City
  Asian   11, 27, 224
  Chinese   12-14, 19, 21, 53, 73, 77, 112, 124, 132, 151, 194, 214, 215, 217
  Consumerist city   67, 205
  Imagination   12-15, 52, 112, 129, 149, 168, 182, 224, 228, 229-230
  Instant city   63, 73
  Southeast Asian   27
  Utopian   17, 53, 57, 61-73
City   70-72
City Beautiful   211
  City Destruction Corporation   212
City of Expiration and Regeneration   212
City Pictorial   109
Clarke, David   13
Close, Askew et al.   140
Colonialism
  British colonialism   32
  Collonial past   137
  Colonial   13, 27, 161, 165, 168, 172, 195-196, 218
  Decolonisation   217, 219
  Neo-colonialism   115
  Post-colonial   136, 138, 150, 166, 177
  Quasi-colonial past   159
Communism   14, 24, 31, 79-83, 87, 90, 123, 125, 167, 168
Community Architecture movement   224
Compact City theory   224
Consumerism   18, 33-34, 39, 56, 90, 192, 203, 208
Content exhibition   63-64
Coombe, Rosemary   235
Cosmopolitan   12, 14, 80, 91, 109, 146, 150, 159, 165, 192, 195-196, 199
Crasneanscki, Stephan   106
Crazy Racer   68
Creative China   79

Creative industry   78, 81-84, 91
Crilley, Darrel   146
Cui, Jian   92
Cultural map   23
Cultural Palace of the Nationalities   125
Cultural Revolution   24, 47, 81, 83, 87, 126-127, 158, 165, 176, 207
Cultural Studies   15-16, 18
Cultural theory   16
Cunningham, Maura Elizabeth   122
Cusack, Peter   103, 110
Cyberspace   46-47, 56-57, 72

D

Da Zha Lan Project   105, 107, 113, 115, 223
Dai, Jinhua   171, 174, 187, 196
Dal Lago, Francesca   101
Dalian   104
Davis, Jeffrey   136
Dawn Market   105
De Certeau, Michel   199
De Kloet, Jeroen, Gladys Chong and Wei Liu   131, 135, 147
De Kloet, Jeroen   17, 45, 55, 57, 82
De Meuron, Pierre   146
Dean, Jodi   45
Debord, Guy   11, 14, 17, 18, 21, 43-46, 51, 56, 58, 97-99, 101, 106, 108-110, 115-117, 147, 193, 208
  Comments on the Society of the Spectacle   21, 45, 58
  Society of the Spectacle   13-14, 18, 21, 43, 97, 108, 116, 147, 193
  Theory of Dérive   99, 103, 106, 109, 112-115
Declaration of Tree Village   101
Deleuze, Gilles and Felix Guattari   15, 92
Deleuze, Gilles   83, 92
Delirious New York   62
Demimonde   27, 29
Democracy   30, 45, 55, 93, 204
Deng, Xiaoping   128-129

Depoliticisation 31, 121, 126, 128
Derleth, James and Daniel R. Koldyk 130
Des Forges, Alexander 196
Donald, Stephanie Hemelryk 16
Dong, Liming 140
Dong, Madeleine 196
    Dongcheng district 130-131
Droitcour, Brain 54
Du, Fu 48
Duara, Prasenjit 174
Ducasse, Isodore 116
Duoyichu 142
Dynamic City Foundation (DCF) 64-66
Dynamic Density 65
Poésies 116

E

Earthbound China 174
East Asia 18, 171-175, 177, 179, 186
East Asian Studies 172, 175-176
Economic globalization 16
Economy 22, 27-30, 34, 36, 39, 52, 83-84, 93, 98, 113, 130, 137, 227-228
Ecstasy 199, 201
Edinburgh Square, Hong Kong 217
Edo 176
Eisenman, Peter 63
Ekachai, Uekrongtham 34
Electric Labyrinth 212
Eno, Brian 103
Environmentalism 109, 112
Erni, John Nguyet 18, 235
Esplanade 27
Essays in Idleness 181
Estulin, Chaim 234
Ethnicity 28, 82
Ethnographic studies 38
Eurocentrism 16
EveryCities 126
Everyday life 14, 32, 46, 86, 88, 93, 104-105, 163, 166, 227

F

F1 Grand Prix 27
Fabian, Johannes 16
Fairs, Marcus 62
Fang, Ke and Yan Zhang 136
Farrar, Margaret 180
Fei, Xiaotong 174
Femme fatale 191, 193-205
Feng shui 162
Fengjie 23-24
Fetishism 47, 49, 63, 69, 86, 197
Feudal 13
Fin-de-siècle 171
Fixing On the Spot and Rebuilding the Community 220
Flagstaff House 137, 139
Florida, Richard 77
FM3's Buddha Machine 110
Forbidden City 12, 79, 91, 127, 131, 140, 144-145, 147-148
Forsaken Alley 66
Foucault, Michel 32, 148, 235
    Heterotopia 32
Four Tigers of Asia 220
Frampton, Kenneth and Silvia Kolbowski 67
Freud, Sigmund 137
Fullerton Hotel 27
Fung, Anthony 81, 139
Future 19, 135, 140-151

G

Gandalsonas, Mario 158
Gang-of-Four 127
Gao, Ping 83
Gay 35
Gaze 38, 47, 72, 160-161, 196-198, 200, 208
Ge, Hongbing 191-194, 203, 208
Gender 18, 29, 32, 52, 90, 146, 193-205, 208
    Phallus worship 198-199
Get by in Beijing 138
Get it Louder 104, 108, 112-113
Geylang District 17, 28, 32-35, 37-39

Gilley, Bruce 129
Gilman-Opalsky, Richard 43
Global city 158, 165, 167
Global cultural salon 23
Globalisation 16, 93, 115, 166
Going Home (Or Not) 105
Gold, John Robert and Stephen Victor Ward 136
Gonghe Road 202
Google 93
   Graafland, Arie 166
Graham, Dan 224
Gramsci, Antonio 31, 44
Great Hall of the People 72, 125, 127, 132
Great Leap Forward movement 122, 125-126, 147, 165
Great Wall 128
Groenewegen-Lau, Jeroen 16, 101, 107-108
Grossberg, Lawrence 15, 172
Gruffudd, Pyrs 136
Guanghe Theatre 141-142
Guangzhou 102, 104, 111-112
Guattari, Félix 15, 92
   Haptic Machine 15

H

Hainan Island 220
Han, Xu 102
Hangzhou 104
Hansen, Mark 45, 54, 71-72
Hao, Zaijin 171
Haraway, Donna 240-241
Harbin 113, 115
Harbor Ordinance 236
Harbour Bill 229, 234
Harbourcide 19, 227, 229, 234
Harmonious society 16, 53, 130
Harvey, David 165
Hawke, Ethan 158
He, Xincheng 64
Hedonism 194
Hegemony 31, 39, 44, 46, 49, 52, 85, 108, 121, 235
Heidegger, Martin 177

Heimat 175
Hell's Kitchen 33
Hemmings, Sarah 161
Hero 22
Herzog, Jacques 146
Hewison, Robert 144, 165
Hillenbrand, Margaret 18
Hiroshima 212
History 22-25, 30-32, 48-49, 61, 66, 91, 112, 128, 137-142, 144, 157-159, 173, 203, 211, 215, 218
HKUST & Civic Exchange 228
Ho, Patrick Chi-ping 218
Ho, Wing Chung 129
Holm, David L. 123
Home Show 104, 110
Homeless Literature 175
Homme fatale 202
Hong Kong 13, 18-19, 70, 91, 105-106, 111, 128-129, 136-140, 150, 157, 159, 166, 172, 176, 178, 184-186, 217-220, 227-236
   Cinema 11-12, 24, 101
   Government 105
   Institute of Architects 217
   Town Planning Board 219, 237
   Visual Arts Center 111
   Walled City (Kowloon) 166
Hong Kong Connection 135
Hongkong and Shanghai Banking Corporation 168
Honjo Ryôgoku 178
Hopkinson, Lisa 233-234
Hornsby, Adrian 64
Hotel of Overseas Chinese 125
Hotel of the Nationalities 125
Hou, Hanru 90, 92
Hou, Hsiao-hsien 183
Houhai 142
House 224
Howard, Ebenezer 211
Howes, David 229
Hsia, Chu-joe 222
Hu, Fang 53
Hu, Jintao 129-130, 132
Hu, Jiujiu 82

Hua, Guofeng   127-128
Huang, Chengjiang   127
Huang, Jia-feng   221
Huang, Michelle Tsung-yi   165-166
Huang, Rui   77, 90
Huangpu River   126, 150, 180, 198, 199
Hubbard, Phil and Teela Sanders   32
Hudsucker, Rudolph   101
Humanism   24, 38-39, 109, 194
Hundred Flowers Campaign   165
Hung, Chang-tai   125
Huyssen, Andreas   144, 186

I

1-24   112
I • Mirror   71, 115-116
Iberia Centre for Contemporary Art   83, 90
Iconography   49-50, 53, 81, 124, 129, 131, 196
Idealism   211
Idema, Wilt   49
Ideology   39, 43-45, 52, 66, 87, 98, 108, 173, 77, 193, 215, 218-219
In a Quiet Night   173
In the Mood for Love   180, 184-185
Inaugural Virgin Beauty Contest   50
Individual *See also* subject   18, 36, 39, 57, 61, 101, 107, 110-111, 116, 164, 174, 193, 203, 208, 215-216
Inequality   16, 97
Information Office of Beijing Municipal Government   138
Instant City   63, 66
Integrationism   236-237
International Art and Culture Foundation   84
International Monetary Fund   44
Internationalism   131
Internet   17, 56, 79, 85, 115-116, 130, 214-215, 218
Intimacy   11-12
Iser, Wolfgang   228
Ishida, Eiichirô   173

Ishiguro, Kazuo   157, 161-162, 164
Istanbul Biennale   53

J

Jacobs, Jane   211-213, 220
   The Death and Life of Great American Cities   211
Jameson, Fredric   62, 171, 176
   Genuine historicity   176
Jansson, André and Amanda Lagerkvist   200
Japanese occupation   159, 161-162, 164, 220
Jarvis, Robert   103
Jay, Martin   14, 89
Jeanneau, Laurent   107
Jia, Zhangke   17, 22-23, 25, 67-68
Jiang, Jun   53
Jiang, Qing   127
Jiang, Zemin   129-130
Jiangsu Art Publishing House   178
Jiangsu province   220
Jin Mao Tower   70
Jing, Wang   177
Joan of Arc   50

K

Keane, Michael   77, 81
Kelly, Joan Marie   33-34, 37-38
Khoo, Eric   36, 38
Kill the Skycraper   62
Killer S (Sin)   212
King, Anthony D. and Abidin Kusno   140, 142
Kispert, Matthias   113
Knight, Sabina   207
Kobayashi, Hideo   175-176, 187
Koolhaas, Rem   13, 21, 53, 61-66, 70, 72-73, 91
   Office for Metropolitan Architecture (OMA)   62-64, 66
   Generic City   13, 62-63
Kracauer, Siegfried   22
Kuomintang (KMT)   176, 220, 222
Kuoshu, Harry   192
Kwan, Stanley   176

Kwanyin 101, 110
Kwun Tong 105

L

Labour 13, 31, 39, 44, 46
Lady Meng Jiang 50
Lai, Gina and Rance Pui Leung Lee 136
Land Development Policy Committee 232
Landay, Lori 55
Landsberger, Stefan 18, 130-131
Langlois, Ganaele 55
Language 14, 17, 44, 77-78, 83, 93, 98, 194, 219
    Visual language 172, 186
Lash, Scott and Celia Lury 46, 49, 93
Latour, Bruno 13
    Actor-Network Theory 13
Law 18, 31-32, 215-217, 227, 229, 234-235, 238-239
    Environmental Law 236
    Property Law 214
Lazzarato, Maurizio 57
Le Corbusier 211-213
    Radiant City 211
Lee, Ang 12, 157, 159
Lee, Bono 11-12
Lee, Haiyan 174
Lee, Lillian 176
Lee, Matthew 233
Lee, Vivian 194-195
Lefebvre, Henri 57
Leung, Kubert 106
Li, Bai 48-49, 173
Li, Gong 106
Li, Guangtou 43, 51
Li, Kang-le 220-222, 223
Li, Mubai 123
Li, Qiang 103
Li, Ruihuan 125
Li, Wenjun 78
Li, Xiu-jing 224
Li, Yanling 223
Li, Zhenhua 101

Liberalism 30, 36, 39, 207
    Neoliberalism 16, 17, 44, 67, 73, 239
Liberation Monument 102
Liebow, Elliot 38
Lin, Biao 126
Lin, Hong 43, 47, 50-52
Lin, Rui-tu 222
Lin, Yilin 83
Linden Dollar 54
Linden Lab 53, 56
Lindner, Christoph 15
Liu, Tianyun 104
Lo, Edwin 112-113
Local Action 217, 219
Locality 15-16, 80
Lockwood, Christopher 199
Loh, Christine 235
Lorong 28-29
Louis Vuitton Soundwalk 106-107, 115
Lowenthal, David 175
Lu, Ban 125
Lu, Chen 104
Lu, Hanchao 171
Lu, Sheldon 200
Lu, Xun 174
Luo, Peilin 80
Luo, Xiao 192, 204-205
Luo, Ye 12
Lust, Caution (Ang Lee) 12, 157, 159
Lyotard, Jean-François 51

M

Ma, Ke 123
Ma, Qingyun 212-213
Ma, Ying-jiu 222
Mak, Anson / AMK 105
Manovich, Lev 61
Mao Zedong 11, 12, 22, 47, 81, 91, 123, 125-127, 140, 174
    Maoism 45, 49
    Maoist era 13, 140, 168, 173, 175
Map of Beijing 138

Maravillas, Francis 82
Maridet, Cedric 111
Mars, Neville and Adrian Hornsby 65
Mars, Neville 64-66, 72
Marvin, Carolyn 136
Marx, Karl 98
   Marxism 174
   Marxist 44, 46, 98, 108
Massey, Doreen 140, 224
Matta-Clark, Gordon 223-224
Mattern, Shannon 62
Matthews, Kaffe 103-104
May Fourth era 174
May, Kevin 233
McCarthy, Caroline 56
McDougall, Bonnie 203
McQueen, Alexander 37
McWorld 193
Mediation 46, 48
Mee Pok Man 36
Mei, Langfang 142
Meishi Street 105, 150
Memory 12, 18, 23, 136, 138-139, 144-147, 149, 166, 171-172, 174-175, 177-182, 185-187
   collective memory 211, 219
Meys, Olivier 105
Mian Mian 193
Michael, Sullivan 182
Michaels, Anne 179
Middle class 34, 37, 39
Migrancy 16, 28, 35, 53, 84, 198
   Migrant workers 131-132, 146, 150
Miike, Takashi 18, 180, 182-187
Military Museum 125
Mini Midi festival 101, 107
Ministry of Information 31
Mission: Impossible III (J.J. Abrams) 157-158
Mitchell, W.J.T. 69
Modern girl 195-196
Modernity 11, 16, 113, 126, 128-132, 148, 150, 171-172, 174, 177, 180-181, 183-184, 186-187, 194, 196, 212

Modernist aesthetics 49, 51, 62, 128
Modernisation 221-222
Modernist Chinese fiction 196
Postmodernity 47-49, 51, 62, 171
Modernity at Large 175
Moholy-Nagy, László 72
Moonlight 160
Moscow White House 124
Moving Soundscape 104, 112, 115
Mu, Shiying 196, 200
Murakami, Haruki 176, 179
Murray, Stuart 52
Museum of Agriculture 125
Museum of Chinese History 125
Museum of Contemporary Art (MoCA) 68, 70-71
Musical culture 17

N

Nagle, John Copeland 228
Nail house 214-216, 218
Nakaba, Riichi 182-184
Nanyang Technological University 33
Narcissism 191, 199, 202-203
Nation Builders 36, 38
Nation-state 16, 77-78, 80-82, 93
National Art Gallery 125
National Grand Theatre 91
National Opera House 64
National Stadium 144
National Taiwan University 221
National Theatre 147
Nationalism 129
Nationhood 14, 23, 29, 122
Natural heritage 235-237, 240
Neighbourhood Offices 215
New Beijing 138, 144, 147, 149
New Perceptionists 196, 205
Ng, Hui Hsien 29, 33, 39
Ng, Petrus 129
Ni, Haifeng 85-86
Noble, Jonathan 197
Nora, Pierre 142

INDEX

Nostalgia 18, 24, 47-48, 50, 78, 80-81, 83, 94, 106, 109, 116, 140-142, 157-158, 160-162, 165-168, 171-187
    Armchair Nostalgia 175-176
    Shanghai Nostalgia 188
    Taiwan Nostalgia 171

O

O'Rourke, Dennis 32
Occularcentrism 14, 18, 86, 89
Okuno, Takeo 178
Olds, Kris 151
Olympics
    Main Press Centre (MPC) 145
    Olympic Forest Park 145
    Olympic Green 18, 138, 144-147, 150
    Olympic Stadium / Bird's Nest 13, 16, 53, 70-71, 91, 131-133, 144-147, 150, 247
    Olympic Village 67, 145
    Water Cube 70, 131, 145-147
On the Japanese Landscape 173
One Child Policy 167
One Hundred Shanghai Beauties 195
Ong, Ryan 140
Open Door police 128
Opposing City Government Bulldozers 220-223
Orientalism 173
Originary Landscapes in Literature 178
Other, the 149, 202
Ou, Ning 18, 82, 104-105, 112, 150
Outline Zoning Plan 238
Ouyang, Jianghe 77, 84
Ozu Yasujirô 183

P

Pace Gallery New York 89
Pang, Laikwan 81
Pathos 32, 37-38
Patterson, Carol 64
Peace Hotel 199

Pearl River Delta 13, 228, 233
Pei, I.M. 128
Peleggi, Maurizio 139, 141-142, 144
People's Action Party (PAP) 30-32, 36
People's Heroes monument 125
People's Liberation Army (PLA) 23, 219
People's Park 70
People's Republic of China (PRC) 16, 61, 63, 97, 100, 102, 106, 121-125, 129, 131
People's Square 127
Pi, Li 85
Pipan 'critically' 83
Place and the Literary Arts 174
Pleasure Factory 33-35, 37-38
Popular culture 12-14, 16, 19, 81, 99, 157, 195, 244
Post-cinematic medium 71
Post-human 46, 79, 84, 92-93
Post-socialist 47, 66, 81
Praya Reclamation Scheme 231
Production of place 16
Proletariat 38, 108, 117, 126
Propaganda 18, 66, 121-132, 136
Prostitution 28, 32, 43, 51, 166
PTW Architects 146

Q

Qianmen 18, 138-144, 149-150
Qiu, Zhijie 101
Queen's Pier See Star Ferry

R

Rabbit Travelogue 112
Rachmaninov's Paganini Variations 204
Rancière, Jacques 11, 19
Rao, Xiaojun 212
Reciprocal Fetishism 85
Red Guards 87, 126-127
Red light district 17, 32, 34, 39
Red tourism 175
Reinvent Your City 108-109, 115, 118

Ren, Xuefei 146
Rentegration 109-110
Representation 12, 18, 22, 35-38, 44-49, 51-52, 56-57, 61, 63, 70-73, 78-79, 83-84, 86-87, 91, 93-94, 97, 99, 113, 115, 122-123, 126, 128-129, 136-142, 147-148, 159, 163, 165, 173, 176, 182, 195-197, 200-205
Reproduction 16, 89, 114, 175, 200
Revolution 97, 116, 123-124
Reynolds, Bryan 49
Rio Declaration 236
RMB City 12, 17, 43, 45-47, 52-54, 57, 61, 71-73, 79, 84, 90-94
Robertson, Jennifer 173
Rock Music 100-103, 104
Rojas, Carlos 194, 197, 203
Rowe, Peter G. 165
Rumor City 212

S

Sandbed 191-194, 201-203, 207
SARS 122, 216
Sassen, Saskia 53
Saunding Beijing Festival 100
Scale model 17, 30, 34, 57, 61-73
Scanner (Robin Rimbaud) 103
Schafer, R. Murray 109-110
Scheen, Lena 18, 157, 187
Scheeren, Ole 62, 64
Schnapp, Jeffrey 54
Scott, A.O. 38
Second Life 46, 53-56, 71, 90, 93, 115-116
Secretary for Home Affairs 218
See, Martyn 36
Self 113, 202-203
Sense 14-15, 22, 45-46, 70, 81, 86, 89, 94, 99, 102, 111-112, 117, 147, 171, 173, 177-178, 180, 198
Sensory imaginary 228, 229, 240
Sensory violence 234
Sex 29, 38, 159, 162, 192-193, 204-205
    Desire 208

Heterosexuality 35
Promiscuity 43, 93, 194
Sexist 52
Sex trade 32-33, 35, 37, 39
Sexuality 32, 46, 55, 200-201
Sexual union 50
Sex work 35, 39
Shanghai 12-13, 16, 18, 21, 67, 91, 102, 104, 106, 112-114, 121-122, 125-127, 129, 132, 136-138, 140, 151, 157-168, 176, 178, 180, 191-193, 195-196, 199-201, 203-204, 206, 208
    Art 12, 18, 123
    Bund 126, 129, 160, 167-168, 180, 185, 199
    French Concession 165
    Longtang 157, 163-164
    Miss Shanghai 194, 198
    Pudong 13, 21, 129, 158, 160, 168, 180, 199
    Oriental Pearl TV Tower 70-71, 91, 129, 198-199
    Shanghai Circus World 201
    Shanghai World Expo 14, 18, 68, 90-91, 108, 122, 125, 131-132, 151-152
    Treaty Port era 194
    Xintiandi district 157, 158, 165-169
Shanghai Baby 46, 191-194, 197-198, 200-202, 207
Shanghai Reflection 158
Shanghai Triad (Zhang Yimou) 159-160
Shanghai World Financial Centre 70
Shao, Dazhen 123
Shen, Congwen 173
Shenzen & Hong Kong Bi-cty Bienale 212
Shenzhen 13, 16, 21, 104, 128
Shi, Lu 123
Shi, Ming-de 222
Shiga, Shigetaka 173
Shimazaki, Tôson 173
Shophouses 28-30

Shu, Haolun 188
Shu, Qi 106
Shue, Vivienne 148
Sign 44, 50, 73
    Signified 47, 109
    Signifier 44, 47-48, 51, 91-92, 109
    Thingified 46, 93
Simmel, Georg 172-173
    Uninterrupted habitations 172
Singapore Film Commission 35
Situationist 14, 44, 99, 116
    Stratigy of détournement 17, 44, 46-47, 51, 57, 99, 104, 107, 111, 116
Sloterdijk, Peter 111
Slowness 18, 21, 62
Smith, Kirk 228
Social atomization 99, 109-110
Socialism 22, 24-25, 90, 126, 132
    Post socialism 47, 66-67, 81
    Post-real-socialism 39
    Posthumous socialism 22
    Socialist Realism 123-124
Society for Protection of the Harbour (SPH) 235-239
Soho Shangdu 109
Sonic Bicycle Ride 103
Sonic tourism 112, 115
Sonic_Bed Shanghai 104
Sound and the City 103-104, 106, 108, 110
Sounding Beijing 100
Soundscape China 107
Space
    Cultural 136, 138
    Erratic 23
    Factory 81, 83
    Freedom 17, 31, 39, 77-78, 82, 105, 164
    Global 180
    Humanized 177-178, 180
    Immaterial 22
    Public 217-219, 222
    Sexualised 193
    Virtual 22, 46, 53, 56, 68, 70-71, 73, 90-92, 115

Special Administrative Region 128
Special Economic Zones 128
Spectacle
    Anti-spectacular 22, 98
    Antitopia 17, 67
    Appear 21, 79, 94, 121, 136, 138, 147, 150
    Architecture 13, 61-63, 65-66, 68, 73, 122, 136, 146, 157-158, 220
    City-as-spectacle 14
    Cityscape 13, 14, 18, 46, 53, 62, 68, 79, 85, 90, 122, 199
    Concept 13-14, 17
    Desire 14, 24, 31, 39, 43-44, 48, 50-52, 56, 63, 77, 196, 199, 201
    Disappear 21, 24, 77-79, 86, 98, 136, 137, 139, 142, 144, 149-151, 212, 229
    Disruption 17
    Dystopian 17, 66, 72, 92
    First of May Parades 121
    Global capital 78, 94
    Global capitalism 11, 14, 31, 34, 44, 57, 80, 82-83, 87, 167
    Image 14, 16, 25, 43, 45, 48, 52-53, 55-56, 61, 65-66, 68, 71, 73-74, 79, 86, 92-93, 99, 111, 124, 147, 149, 160, 165, 178, 195-197, 199-202, 214-215, 228
    Integrated spectacle 17, 21, 43-47
    Non-spectacular 17
    Performance 22-23, 39, 49, 115, 200
    Reappear 77-78, 136, 148-151, 196
    Smell 14
    Sound 14, 17, 18, 97-98, 102, 104, 107, 113, 115-116, 118
    Spectacularisation 33
    Speed 17, 21-22, 24, 53, 65, 147, 180, 196
    Sport 33

The founding of the nation   121
Visual   14, 16, 33-34, 36-37, 44-46, 52, 62, 66, 68, 70-71, 73, 79, 84, 86-87, 98, 101, 107, 123, 185, 187, 230, 237, 239
Splitting   223
Star Ferry / Queen's Pier   18, 217-219
   A Special Issue on Queens Pier   219
   Star Ferry/Queens Piers Preservation Movement   217
Stein, Gertrude   179
Still Life   22-25
Straits Times   34
Subject   56, 172, 196
   Subjectivity   44, 49, 53, 86, 217-219
Sublime   51, 57
Summer Palace   79
Sun, Jiaming and Xiangming Chen   129
Sun, Jianchu   84-85
Suzhou River   12, 158
Symbolic order   51
Symbolic power   86

T
Takahashi, Yoshitaka   178
Tan, Royston   36
Tang, David   176
Television Cultural Centre (TVCC)   62
Temple of Heaven   88, 131, 144
Ten Great Buildings project   66, 122, 125, 127, 131-132
Teo, Stephen   185
Thank You, Mr Moto (Norman Foster)   160, 168
The Chinese Dream   64
The City of Eternity   138
The first novel by a Stud Writer   193
The Glass Factory   77, 79, 83-84, 86-87
The Golden Cangue   163
The Good People of the Three Gorges   24
The Good Woman of Bangkok   32
The Long March Gallery   81
The Mass Ornament   22
The Matrix   69
The Painter of Shanghai   161
The Song of Everlasting Sorrow   157, 162
The Spaces International   109
The West   16
The World   67, 74
Theme-park   67-68, 78, 81, 86, 89, 142
Three Gorges Dam   24
Tiananmen
   Tiananmen Gate building   128
   Tiananmen massacre   129
   Tiananmen Square   12, 23, 79-80, 88, 91, 105, 121, 125, 127, 139, 140, 144, 147-148
Time   18, 78-79, 85, 91, 94, 115, 147, 181
Time Magazine   36
Tingzijian   163
Today's Beijing   138, 144, 147-148
Tokyo People   178
Toop, David   103
Topoi   121, 230
Town Planning Board   232
Truax, Barry   109
Tsai, Ming-Liang   12
Tuning the World   109
   Turkle, Sherry   5
TVB   105

U
Uli Sigg   54
Union   31
Universalism   16
Urban   64, 65, 78, 87, 91, 94, 102, 105, 109, 125, 128-130, 136, 145, 148, 150, 158-159, 164, 167, 175-177, 211, 219-220, 223-224, 227-228, 230-231
   Hyper-urbanity   13-14, 62, 73
   Regeneration   211, 213, 215-217, 219-220, 223-224

Sound ecology   117
Space   44, 52, 84, 99, 111, 121
Suppression   230
Transformation   11, 18, 43, 62-64, 73, 97, 105, 109, 117, 136, 138, 148, 150-151, 230-231, 233
   Urban anthropology   38
   Urban frenzy   21
   Urban Redevelopment Authority   30
   Urbanisation   15, 18-19, 90, 121, 124, 129-130, 132, 157, 214
   Urbanism   47, 73, 110
Urban China   53
Urban Planning Exhibition Centre   69-70
Urban Studies   15-16
Urry, John   175, 229
Utopia   17, 53, 57, 61-73, 80, 87, 90-92, 127, 177, 203, 212-213
   Antitopian   17, 67, 73

V

Vendel, Saskia   65
Victoria Cantonment   231
Victoria Harbour   227-233, 235, 239-240
Virginity   35, 43, 49-51, 62, 202
Virtopia   71, 73
Virtual Reality (VR)   53, 68, 70, 72
Visser, Robin   17, 43, 53, 72, 86, 136, 193
Vitamin Creative Space   53
Voyeurism   29, 33-35, 38-39, 43, 46, 51-52, 105

W

Wang, Anyi   157, 162-164, 176
Wang, Changcun   115
Wang, Chia-chih   159
Wang, Guangyi   81
Wang, Yiyan   177
Wang, Youshen   86
Warhol, Andy   81

Washing Beijing   86
Wasserstrom, Jeffrey N.   132
Wasted Lives: Modernity and its Outcasts   221
Waterland Kwanyin   101
Weber, Ian   194
Weber, Maximilian   82
Wei, Hui   191-194, 197-198, 208
Wei, Te-sheng   176
Wen, Jiabao   132
Western imperialism   126, 147
When We Were Orphans (Kazuo Ishiguro)   157, 161-162
Whiteread, Rachel   224
Why Are Artists Poor?   85
Williams, Raymond   187
Wong, Aline and Stephen H.K. Yeh   30
Wong, Kar-wai   18, 180, 182, 184-187
Wordie, Jason   231
World Soundscape Project   109
Wu, Fulong   129, 136
Wu, Hung   125, 140
Wu, Ping   214-215
Wu, Youru   195
Wu, Yu'an   102

X

Xie, Zhiguang   123
Xu, Feng   130
   Xu, Guoqu   140

Y

Yan, Jun   101-102, 104-105, 107, 112-115
Yan, Jun & Hitlike   112
Yanagita, Kunio   173
Yaneva, Albena   63, 64, 67
Yang, Wu and Ping Wu   214-215
Yang, Xiaobin   51
Yang, Zhenyong   85
Yangtze River   23
Yellow culture   32
Yeo, George   28, 32
Yi-fu Tuan   177

Yin, Yi   106-108, 112, 116
Yong Ø He   109
Yoshida, Kenkô   181
Yoshimi, Shunya   177
Your Favourite London Sounds   110
YouTube   36, 54, 93, 228
Yu, Albert   106
Yu, Hua   17, 43, 46-52, 57
Yu, Richard   230
Yuanmingyuan art village   77

Z
Zhang, Anding   116
   Little Sound   115
   Zafka   73, 102, 108-109, 115-116
   Zafka Ziemia   116
Zhang, Jun-hong   222
Zhang, Tianxiao   70
Zhang, Wei   173
Zhang, Xiaomin   201-203
Zhang, Yimou   17, 22-23, 25, 68, 159-161, 176
Zhang, Yuqing   121
Zhang, Zhen   135, 147
Zhao, Jingrong   185
Zhao, Yuezhi   81
Zhong, Dianfei   123
Zhong, Kangjun   70-72
Zhong, Xueping   202
Zhongnanhai   78
Zhou, Manzhen   193
Zhou, Wandering   50
Zhou, Zuang   158
Zhou, Zuoren   174-175
Zhu, Jianfei alfabet   125
Žižek, Slavoj   51
Zukin, Sharon   136, 166

13W60313/ T6/ 9789089644459